Mail Order Moonlighting

by Cecil C. Hoge, Sr.

Ten Speed Press

TEN SPEED PRESS
P.O. Box 7123
Berkeley, California 94707

You may order single copies prepaid directly from the publisher. Paperback $7.95 + $1.00 for postage and handling. Clothbound $14.95 + $1.50 for postage and handling. (California residents add 6% state sales tax; Bay Area residents add 6½%.)

Library of Congress Catalog Number: 78-61866
ISBN: 0-913668-95-8 cloth
ISBN: 0-913668-94-X paper

Cover Design by Brenton Beck

10   9   8   7   6

Printed in the United States of America

My Thanks
to

My dear wife, Fritzi and fine son, Cecil whose efforts subsidized my writing efforts.

Adele Pollack whose flying fingers and gentle smile launched this book in manuscript.

Lynn Sanders and Elizabeth Obolensky who struggled so hard to preserve within this book . . . the English language.

Contents

Preface

My Mail Order Moonlighting Method helps those starting in mail order to make money at it.

My method is simple and fundamental. It eliminates much of one of the greatest threats to any starting business . . . overhead. It reduces other risks as well.

Mail order moonlighting is the way many big and sound mail order businesses have started. Many of these have gone on to employ large staffs with big plants and latest technology. Many now have gone beyond mail order to manufacture and distribute products in conventional ways through normal channels. Those owners who have never forgotten the lessons of their moonlighting start have rarely later failed.

In acquisition work for others and ourselves I have looked at financial statements of many, many small businesses . . . and analyzed their beginnings as well. The sound businesses usually started soundly from the beginning. Again and again I discovered that those who started part time . . . from home . . . on a moonlighting basis . . . were even years later far sounder than many others which I investigated.

Some huge money makers in the mail order business have started this way. For years I earned a living elsewhere and moonlighted in our family business while my wife worked full time at it. That's when our family business built the base of its present capital.

Mail order is suited to more people with more background than most activities. My method is safe, entirely practical and based on the methods of sound, conservative and successful mail order people.

My method is no panacea . . . just as mail order is not for everyone. My method can help you analyze whether you are suited to mail order at all . . . whether you can go it alone . . . or best *combine* your strength with others . . . for a real chance . . . and if so, how to select the right partner . . . and negotiate the right deal.

I have helped others get started in mail order . . . and some I've helped have made a great deal of money. It is my hope that Mail Order Moonlighting Method can help far more people than I could personally.

I tell it as it is in the real mail order world . . . with its difficulties as well as opportunities. I try to advise you as if you were in my office . . . and keep working with you as if you were in business with me.

Most of my alumni after their success have kept in touch with me. And if you succeed with my method, do me a favor. Just drop me a line and tell me about it.

Your example may then help others as I hope I help you.
Best of luck.

Cecil C. Hoge, Sr.
Oldfield, New York

BOOK I
Welcome to Mail Order

...the real mail order world

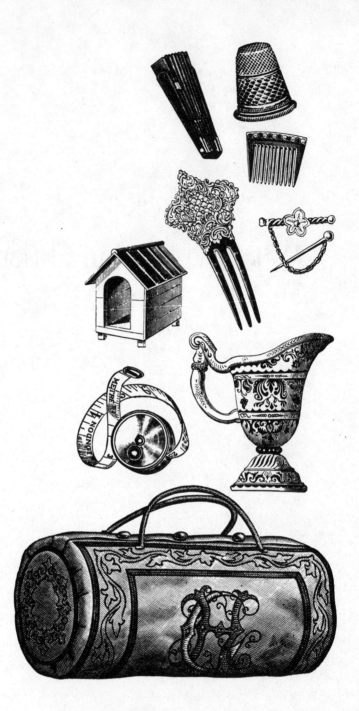

Chapter 1

Roller Coaster

Thrills . . . frustrations . . . fun . . . dangers
. . . satisfactions of mail order

Your tingling spine as you check the mail each day never fails to excite . . . thrill . . . or *frustrate* you.

When you start my mail order moonlighting method at home, in spare time, you will probably open each envelope yourself.

Later, however huge your business may become, and however busy your mail room, you will always be impatiently waiting for the mail count to reveal fate's latest cast of the mail order dice. In either case, mail order is fascinating, if sometimes unnerving. And once in your blood, it's a business hard to leave. The mail order roller coaster can start off as the real one does . . . slowly.

As tests are successful, it can pick up speed just as at the amusement park. But this roller coaster can *race upwards* faster and faster . . . to express train speed as ad after projected ad pays out profitably . . . until you're seemingly jet propelled.

You can get *hooked* on the intoxicating thrill of it. A successful campaign can rocket ahead so fast and so high that its upward racing progress can seem *perpetual* . . . often just as it is about to slow. Then, it can pick up speed again, this time racing *downward* at sickening speed. It can twist, curve, turn...up, down, all around. Your future can seem wildly, erratically different from day to day. Always, the mail

3

order count regulates its speed.

One day the mail can come in unexpectedly heavy and fat. . .fairly bursting with nice checks for you. Another day you may see a thin, rubber-banded *sliver* of mail. When you least expect it, good counts from a test ad of a new item can make you feel like a millionaire. And when you are really counting on a certain new test ad to succeed, the mail can be so bad that you may want to give up mail order for good.

Yet, there is an art and science to making money in mail order that can reduce risk and greatly level out the roller coaster effect. Mail order can be more predictable. It is possible to get into mail order more safely. It is possible to maintain a steadier and more continuous upward grade. Our family business has been able to do so for quite a few years. My "Mail Order Moonlighting" method is my effort to help you do so...from the beginning.

Mail order has been good for my family and our business and way of life and can be for you. I have made money in mail order and lost money. I've been fortunate to have had some great mail order talents pass through my portals first in the advertising agency of Huber Hoge and Sons (handling top mail order clients) and then also in the mail order business itself.

Some of our alumni are quite rich today as business owners. Some are highly paid advertising executives. Some are the men in big mail order divisions of largest companies. And some have found rewarding riches of a different kind. They own and operate smaller enterprises or activities they've nurtured with loving care and that now provide them with not just a living but a way of life. They've used their mail order know-how to change and balance their life style. They live where they want and divide their time between working and other interests, as they will.

Let me help you risk less and make more in mail order and direct response. Let me pass on to you lessons I have learned in a business lifetime.

Mail order is suited to more people . . . in more fields . . . of more varied background than most activities. It's an extra leg for the career table of an executive, business beginner or professional man or woman. Mail order is an ideal man and wife business. It's perfect for a woman to own and operate and even raise a family at the same time. It's a perfect way to help launch a business in stores, through catalogues or in specialized fields and it's open to anyone.

Mail order has wide scope and many benefits. Mail order can be

4

operated anywhere . . . in the most pleasant climate and the most attractive surroundings. I know of one quite profitable mail order business operated in the U.S. from Nice, France, for years. Mail order can be combined with world travel, a favorite hobby or retirement.

Mail order is often a *cash* business, important in today's world when cash is King. It's a way to *borrow* money and finance trade business. It's a way to move slow inventory at a profit. Mail order can build up income and draw peripheral trade customers.

Years ago, mail order know-how began to give us many extras. Gradually, we learned how to *capitalize* on mail order to get benefits we had never fully realized existed.

We used mail order advertising to get a hearing from retail stores. We used the success stories of our products to persuade mail order catalogues to stock our goods.

We learned to modify our mail order ads and convert them to department store cooperative ads. We learned to apply them to an electronic counter action display, to a billing insert, and to a take-one folder at a counter. We learned to use quick mail order cash to finance long term dating orders from wholesalers. We learned to use mail order to launch and distribute store businesses that could survive long after the mail order faded away. And it can give you extras, too.

Mail order know-how has helped us in our businesses . . . selling through stores, in our packaging, in our trade catalogues, and in any consumer advertising we do. We apply it to mailings to the trade and each business letter we write. And there's scarcely a retailer, service company, wholesaler or manufacturer of any size which cannot apply the principles of mail order and direct response in various ways to get far more benefit from dollars spent. And whatever business you go into, you can too.

Mail order know-how is surprisingly applicable to operating any business, because mail order is like any other business.

Its main characteristic is that it is *measured* by each day's mail. Mistakes are almost *instantly* revealed. It's harder to brush errors under the carpet . . . or to pass the buck. It disciplines you to meet problems *head on and act quickly* on them.

And the same strategies and principles convert to almost any field, any method of selling, and any product. If you can succeed in mail order, it becomes an exceptional business course to succeed in almost any kind of business.

Mail order is so huge that you can be in it any number of ways.

You may wish to build a specialized catalogue in any of many fields, or a more general one. You may wish to sell only on TV, entirely to doctors, or only to schools . . . all by mail.

You may wish to use mail order methods *but* avoid all mail order risk. We did so for four years. We turned over the mail order sales of all our items, with our ads and artwork, to a firm that did a total sales volume of over one hundred times ours. I wrote new ads myself. We took the short end of the stick, but none of the risk, and prospered.

Whatever field of mail order you care to concentrate on, I want you to succeed; not to fail. I cover as many areas as I can. I can do so because the research for this book is all my mail order life. I've put the essence of all I've learned into it.

In my life in mail order, I've helped some who had never before been in business at all and others, already extremely successful in business but unfamiliar with mail order. Some of you I am writing to, have a great deal of business experience. Some have none. Some are in between. I hope that however experienced or inexperienced you may be you will find good value in my course. If anything in this book is so simple and familiar (or so advanced) that you have no need of it . . . just skip through that part.

Had someone told me in advance what I so painfully later learned, I would have saved much grief. I want to warn you, in time, of mail order dangers. I tell it as it is. I want you to stay away from mail order if after getting the facts you feel that it is not for you. Because mail order can be a great business, I hope that you decide to stay in it, develop a "feel" for it, and succeed in it.

That's why this book walks a tight rope between caution and encouragement. Let's start with the dangers of mail order. . . and then, what it takes to surmount them.

Chapter 2

Great Expectations

. . . misconceptions. . . slaughter of the mail order innocents. . .
and survival in the real world.

For all too many, mail order can lose money faster and more certainly than most businesses.

All that's needed is to pay too much for too standard an article without advantage over competitors. . . then, just sell it for too little. . . advertise it to the wrong potential users and pay too much for the advertising for each thousand people reached. Now, just say and show too little or too much or too inadequately in your advertising. Simply advertise in the wrong place, the wrong season, too early or too late or just commit for too much inventory, too much advertising, too much overhead or too much personal draw from the business.

As in any business, there are countless ways to lose money in mail order and most losses occur because newcomers to mail order simply assume it's more *automatic to make* money than is possible. Unfortunately, many people starting off are foolish in mail order. And a fool and his money are soon parted. . . superfast in mail order.

Don't get discouraged too fast. There's plenty of money to be made in mail order. Hang on in and I'm going to make a real effort in my course to help you make your share safely. But if any friend asked me my advice about going into mail order and I did not point out these dangers and misconceptions, I would not be a friend. I'd like to warn you and then try to help you in my course to overcome such problems.

Many products will not sell profitably via mail order. Potentially profitable mail order products, even with ample margin and perfectly made, will fail with ineffective advertising. And developing successful advertising, even with the aid of the greatest experts in the field, still involves great trial and error. I have never ceased to wonder how regularly test ads I expect to succeed, fail. And I am not alone.

To survive in mail order, every advertisement in any form of advertising must produce a *minimum quota* of dollars of sales. This is the *break even* figure. Now, if your advertisement produces 60 percent, 70 percent, 80 percent or even 90 percent of your *minimum quota*, you will lose money. A losing advertisement loses more money each time it runs. Yet, I have proudly created mail order advertisements that produced 5 percent to 10 percent of the minimum quota. We made money by keeping such test costs small and making so much more on successful offers run very widely as to do well overall. But the mail order newcomer with no reason to be in mail order may never find a successful item.

Yet, if you are an able salesman or sales manager, you might get your product into retail distribution store by store. . . and make money with each sale to each store.

But in mail order, *every* advertisement has its *minimum quota*. And in projection, you really need to roll seven almost every time or you'll be wiped out.

The truth is that making money in mail order is not automatic. For if it were so simple as some newcomers expect. . . *and always worked*. . . we'd all be billionaires. The real mail order world is hard and tough. Yet, many make fortunes in it. And many, many more find safe niches in it to build income and create capital.

The first thing to remember is that there are no simplistic solutions . . . contrary to get-rich-quick ads.

It's hard to make money and even to survive in any business today. To survive in mail order, some sort of special advantage can help. Those who do survive and prosper often find some special "edge" over others. . . made possible by their special situation.

Big mail order advertisers get bargain rates and prime positions in publications or broadcast time. That becomes their "edge." An advertising agency, which goes into mail order on its own as an entrepreneur, may consider its fifteen percent agency commission on advertising it buys as its edge. A sales representative of a publication or broadcast station may go into mail order as an entrepreneur and consider *his* commission on advertising in his media as an "edge". Sometimes, one organization, both advertising agency and sales representative, will go into mail order as an entrepreneur and consider its two commissions on advertising as a *double edge*.

A magazine publisher or a broadcaster may sell his own mail order items in his media. His advertising in his own media costs him less than the higher rate which he charges outsiders. This is his "edge"

Our "edge" is that we use mail order to launch store distribution products. We consistently make money on mail order alone, but our real benefit is that our extensive mail order advertising creates demand and trade acceptance for a store distribution success.

Don't feel that *you* can't compete. As a moonlighter, you start off with the special advantage of almost no overhead. Just realize the importance of gaining your own special additional advantage. As you continue with this course, and afterwards, keep looking for that extra "edge". And you will find it.

Let's examine in a little more detail how others succeed in mail order.

Chapter 3

A Quick Zoom Close-Up

. . . of mail order's biggest success. . .
and what it can teach us in making our own

Let's take a quick look at the operation of a firm which year after year, decade after decade, *always* makes a profit in mail order. Let's see what makes the biggest mail order operator of all time *tick*. . . in the real mail order world. Let's take a stroll through the pages of the Sears Roebuck catalogue.

Here, *every* article *is* sold by mail order. And the items seem to be just about *anything* people might ever dream of buying. And Sears has *specialized* catalogue after catalogue, which gives infinitely *more choice* of endlessly more items.

And Sears sells each item without any great excitement. There's no mystery to it. Sears shows it attractively and describes it factually. So, what *is* the great complication and mystery of selling *anything* mail order? If Sears can do it, why can't we do it? Because you and I, and even General Mills or General Foods, *cannot* do in mail order *what Sears can do*. To go into mail order as Sears does it is about as easy as going into computers as IBM does it, and even General Electric gave up their computer operation after competing against IBM.

Sears is *unique in mail order*. . . and in retailing. The Sears catalogue is a market place; it took just about a *hundred years* to create. Next to the bible, the Sears catalogue is the #1 most popular book in the world. The Sears catalogue is *only* available to people who *prove* they are Sears customers by *buying* from Sears a *minimum* determined by Sears. Sears is *trusted;* Sears is *believed...*as you and I cannot *hope* to be for *any product* we initially sell by or through mail order.

Sears is bigger than many countries in total gross product produced. Behind every Sears mail order product, is the giant buying power of its store operation. Sears has been considered, over the years, the *best run* retail operation in the world. Sears has an *army* of buying talent, all over the world. In any consumer distributor business that you and I succeed in, Sears will probably be our biggest customer. Sears owns its own factories for item after item. Sears can produce its catalogue at lower cost per thousand copies; pull more dollars of sales from each square inch of catalogue space for each thousand catalogues; pick up more related sales from each customer and sell more, later, to that customer. Sears can *buy* most items Sears is seriously interested in (or make them itself) at lower cost.

Let's turn the pages. In item after item, Sears simply offers more value than you or I could ever hope to. Furthermore, in most items Sears makes itself, few companies could possibly afford to *set up* any competitive manufacturing operations without investment so great most of us could not conceive of it. Even giant companies could find it unjustified for the potential profit.

Well, if so, who are we to try to sell *anything* by mail order at all?

Let's see how Sears started. . . without any catalogue. . . any money. . . any mail order know-how. . . any of the advantages Sears now has. . . and without *some* advantages you and I now have.

Mr. Roebuck started first, selling *one item only. . . watches,* and only one basic kind of watch with very little choice of styles and sizes. Mr. Sears took over and sold one additional item after another, until he spread or, it is said, rather sprawled his operation all over Chicago. . . in lofts and cellars and small offices. . . and initially *without* a catalogue. Mr. Sears, like some mail order men today, was said to be a bit of a mail order buccaneer. Not all his items would pass the laboratory tests Sears now requires. Not all of his first advertising copy (and it was often longer then) would now clear through the Sears internal censhorship for factual truth and accuracy. Mr. Sears ran ad after ad in the same issue of individual magazines; sometimes up to thirty or forty of them. The catalogue seemed to come into being as an overgrown cluster of package enclosures, which in turn started one by one.

And it was only when Sears was taken over by a pants salesman, that it began to take its present form. Before that, the pants salesman could never understand what Mr. Sears was doing with all those pairs of pants he sold him. With no store to buy all those pairs of pants, more than he sold anyone else, he had to find out where those pairs of pants went. And the more the pants salesman found out, the more fascinated he became about mail order, (just as you and I become today), and the more shocked he became about the day to day operation of Mr. Sears' business. When the pants salesman took over, he *organized* as it never had been before, until all the fun went out of it for Mr. Sears. But without Mr. Sears, Mr. Roebuck would have possibly been another single item mail order man, with the business fading out with the item. Without the pants salesman, Mr. Rosenwald, Mr. Sears might have had more fun, but never built a *lasting* business. Mr. Rosenwald was the orderly *builder* who made possible all that you see in the Sears catalogue today.

Let's see how *we* can become a winner in mail order, even if we're not Sears Roebuck. Mr. Sears and Mr. Roebuck started *without most* of the mail order *advantages* that you and I have today. Thanks to Sears Roebuck and others, more and more people, overwhelmingly more than in their time, are *willing* to buy mail order, *willing* to send you and me *bigger* sums of money, because they feel *safer* buying mail order from *anyone* than in those early days. There are many, many *ways* of selling mail order that never existed then, and many, many *helps and allies* for mail order people that never existed then, either.

Today, there are innumerable mail order niches, nooks and crannies where new mail order operations can survive and prosper, do undreamed of volume and make proportionate profits. . . all *without* head-on competition with Sears or any other giant. But it requires selectivity, judgement and a "feel" for mail order.

Chapter 4

The Key Ingredient

. . to mail order survival and success.
With it you can get rich.
Without it chances are slim.

Mail order is a feel your way. . . stop. . . start. . . test. . . project method for people with a "feel" for it to get rich surprisingly fast. Mail order loses money for far more people than it ever makes money for, simply because they don't have a "feel" for *any* business, but get tempted into mail order as an *easy* business. . . often by shrewd entrepreneurs or biased advisors who get rich luring the ignorant and unbusiness-like into activities they are often unsuited for.

Mail order is a rare opportunity for those with a "feel" for it and not at all simple for anyone else. I call it mail order "fingerspitzen". In German this means the tips of your fingers; it refers to a special sensitivity. For the man or woman with a "feel" for mail order, it's a goldmine. . . the secret of mail order success. That "feel" is the basic know-how of correct mail order principles. It's a sound sense of correct mail order strategy. It's quite vital in today's mail order.

I have seen profitable ways of doing business, faithfully followed almost as a religion, suddenly become unprofitable business heresy. Techniques and tactics that had worked like clock work, began to fail almost automatically. Profitable practices of yesterday can become business suicide of today or tomorrow. That "feel" tells you how to use and benefit from latest mail order tactics and techniques. It guides you to drop those suddenly obsolete.

13

Today's swirling mail order world is fast moving. The tactics and techniques are complex and constantly changing. The principles and basic strategies are extremely simple and do not change. The latest tactics and techniques are great, but more painfully acquired, and only practical to use. . . if you have the mail order "feel" to do so safely. Without a firm understanding of correct principles and sound basic strategies, trying to use latest tactics and techniques is like trying to steer a latest model ship without a rudder.

With middle and large size companies, the greatest limiting factor in their entrance into and growth in mail order is the know-how, experience and mail order "feel" of those they select to manage their mail order operations. For these companies, *mail order disasters are overwhelmingly due to the shortage of executives with the background, skills and ways of thinking necessary.*

If you can master mail order and get a "feel" for it, *you have* developed a highly marketable asset. Here's one moonlighting activity that can make you substantially more valuable to your present employer (even with no present plans for mail order) when the moment of decision comes for that new mail order division.

And if you develop a "feel" for mail order, you may become the catalyst that suggests and gets your employer into mail order and direct response. Mail order know-how may get you a raise or a better job.

Let's discuss your suitability for mail order and the practicality of your going into business on your own.

Chapter 5

You and Mail Order

Psychology needed. . .
and hidden mail order assets you may have. . .

In any business, each day is a threat; every transaction, a possible time bomb; and every agreement, a possible misunderstanding. Because mail order moves fast, failure to *see* and *act* on what is wrong can quickly get you out of business.

Analyze yourself. If too cheerful, and if you can't suspect anything and don't like detail, stay out of mail order or team up with a trustworthy negative type. . . and make a fortune together.

How are you at buying and selling. . . *anything*? Some people seem born with the trading instinct, perhaps inherited for hundreds or even thousands of years.

Others feel helpless in any transaction. To buy cheap and sell dear is the first step to maximize profit. Sheltered first at home, then at school and college, and later in a corporate cocoon, for many, it's emotionally disturbing, distasteful, and psychologically almost impossible to be ever vigilant on costs, overhead, commitments and risks.

If money vigilance is not suited to you, you're not suited to business operation. . . by yourself. Even so, you could still make good money in mail order. You may have some assets perfect for mail order and be able to get a partner to buttress any weaknesses.

If you are creative, with ideas for products and advertising, you

15

can still make a fortune in mail order. But you can only do so with the right associations. You can be the creative partner with a money sense partner by your side. . . perhaps your own spouse. You can be the creative star employee of a money sense owner with an income based partially on the results of your own creativity.

Whatever your background, even if unbusinesslike, there may be ways to cash in on it. In a little field like manufacturing fishing lures, dentists who like to fish have designed better lures and retired on them. These lures have usually been made out of metal. Realize that every dentist has the makings of a metal sculptor. They simply sculptured lures in metal. A supplier of foam rubber upholstery to French automobile factories liked to fish and came up with a rubber minnow. An employee of a Detroit plastics factory came up with hard plastic lures. Each used his background.

I've seen artists create jewelry sold by mail; music teachers create home piano courses; doctors come up with medical items to sell to hospitals; beauticians with cosmetics and so forth. Housewives often do best of all because the items they create are usually those used in the home and therefore are most universal.

Countless people have perfect situations for mail order and are *not taking advantage of them,* simply because they've never been told the facts regarding just how to go about getting into it.

You *may* already have a unique "feel" for mail order. Your present background, company or job, your interests or hobby may have given you just the set up you need to benefit. Your skills, your needs, and the way you like to work can determine the correct answer to the item you select to sell, how you handle your advertising, and your entire mail order operation.

Whatever you do for a living may give you an advantage that can be helpful in mail order.

Certain activities give a good deal of off-time: being a member of an airline crew, a school teacher with summer off, anyone with less than average pressure most of the time, fireman or post office worker. Occasionally, a company may wish to cut certain executive jobs to several days weekly. Any of these situations may give you a particular advantage in operating a moonlighting mail order business.

Some activities give you the knowledge of a product need or exposure to *new* intriguing products. If you're a lawyer, accountant, bookkeeper, credit manager, you may have the ability to watch costs and risks better. If you're a buyer, a technician, engineer or chemist you may know how to find, create, or improve a mail order product better

16

with better continuing quality control.

Use your background, experience, hobby or interest. Do what you're good at and like. Team up with others to *compensate* for any areas you feel weak in. There are many forms of profitable mail order marriages.

The right association may overcome your lack of experience. In our case, we may create an item, pay a royalty to someone else who creates it, buy it from a U.S. supplier, import it, go into a temporary joint venture (or permanent partnership) with someone who controls it, hire a specialized expert to run it, or work for a client as the advertising agency for it. In each case we make a profit putting *our* know-how to work on it.

If you are in financial difficulties, read this carefully.

"To him that hath it shall be given and from him that hath not shall be taken away that little which he seemeth to have."

In any business, desperate people usually lose money. Mail order as a straw to grab at is usually a loser. The man or woman out of a job who takes last savings out of the bank and gambles it in mail order. . . usually loses it. Those in financial trouble who resort to mail order usually lose still more.

Desperation warps judgement. In mail order, it usually means selling the wrong thing at the wrong price in the wrong place with the wrong margin. Desperation causes out of season rush testing of advertising, usually too early or too late to pull. Desperation means rush. Rush always involves much more cost of advertising production. Desperation accepts a worse advertising position, often at too high a price for the advertising.

When you're broke is the time to get a *money partner*. . . get someone *else* to take the risk. . . and then operate as if you're rich. A newcomer to mail order, who is not desperate and who capitalizes on past experience or know-how, whether in business, profession, hobby or interest, *does* have a *better chance*. Money makes money and starting any business with ample money is desirable.

Being financially independent of a business, makes the decision for that business far sounder in most cases. But what do we do if we're out of work. . . can't get a job. . . have used up our savings. . . are pursued by creditors. . . and desperately need to get back on our feet?

Of course, you must first get a job, even part time. This may be difficult or even impossible. But in my experience, most unemployment problems are aggravated by ego. There is a fear of loss of status. . . a hesitation to go back a rung. . . a holding out for equivalent importance

17

of job and money benefits. Often, such poker playing pays off. But I grew up in the depression when unemployment was high and employment often could be gained only at far lower wages than the lost job. I believe that when you're down, you are not out, that water seeks its own level, that you must take some employment, however disagreeable. Then, you can only get started in mail order by using hours off the job.

You must first gamble your time to find the right mail order product. . . or with someone who has one. Being broke does *not* keep you from *seeing* the right mail order item. It may not prevent you from getting a sole rights contract. Only you know fully your financial condition. Others may have more confidence in you than you realize, even if they realize your financial limitations.

You may be able to sign an option contract on a protected patented product that is unobtainable elsewhere. You may then be able to turn the rights over to a strongly financed, big volume mail order company.

As long as you're willing to risk your time and ability, instead of money, you'll find ways of making money without risk in mail order. Being broke does not prevent you from gaining mail order skills. You will find a way to cash in on them. If you take *no* risk of any kind and can in some way live independently of your mail order activities, you will gradually build up mail order capital. Later, we'll discuss simply *selling* your product to mail order firms.

A newcomer in your business or profession would make mistakes through lack of knowledge and experience, mistakes that you with your expertise would not make.

People knowing nothing of mail order can do the same and compound the problem by selling an article that they know nothing about. Frequently, the same people could easily capitalize on their background and greatly improve their chances of success. They could actually use hidden mail order assets which they don't realize they have.

We pay royalties to fishermen, who know *nothing* of business and care only to fish twelve months a year, if possible!

But these are *expert* fishermen who have often successfully started in a small way to sell fish lures profitably. . . *mail order*. . . before selling out to us. Their sole advantage was their unique ability to create, perfect and quality control a superb fish lure superior to others...and their intimate knowledge of those who could benefit from using it. . . and how to appeal to them.

I've seen airline pilots, firemen, dentists, teachers, lithographers *each* succeed in this way with fish lures *because* they were *master*

18

fishermen. . . and knew their subject. . . and their market.

The same is true of housewives with a flair for home sewing, creative stitchery or other hobbies. Again and again, I've seen them succeed in mail order with no previous knowledge of it.

Because each developed a superior product filling a real need. . . quality controlled its making. . . started making and shipping from her home. . . and was frugal all the way. These hobby items needed the explanation and demonstration of mail order. Often, the mail order *led* to store distribution.

I know one housewife, who, as a cub scout den mother, developed simple craft item instructions using leftover material around the house, often from packing of groceries, etc.

The kids were delighted and their mothers too, because it was fun, simple and almost costless. The same housewife began to sell mail order the same kind of kits and instruction in a little magazine for mothers and children. First with her husband and now also with her son, she has built a more than million dollar a year business.

Are you an executive? In my lifetime, executives have become less independent and more dependent on their companies and bosses. Today executives feel less secure. The perils of the economy may affect your job. You may be asked (virtually ordered) to move to a location your spouse doesn't like. Your company may be acquired and personnel duplication (perhaps you) eliminated. Becoming an executive moonlighter, *before* such problems occur, can have benefits for you.

The largest corporations can be perfect launching pads for home businesses on the side. Often, time off is substantial, vacations long and pressure low for some jobs. Take your time to get started. Find or develop one item at a time. Stick to a field your business background or hobby interest gives you some expertise in. Team up with one or more partners if each background strengthens and supplements the other and you work well together. Your first successful mail order test can give you a greater personal strength and confidence than in years. How would you like to start a business with your spouse? A husband and wife mail order business can be quite a marital thrill.

Husbands and wives seem to complement each other in business as naturally as in home life. A woman naturally seems more cautious, more careful, more thorough, often shrewder in buying and watching payroll and day to day expense. A husband is freed by his wife to do what he is best at. . . planning. . . negotiating. . . closing deals. . . making sales. . . creating increased business. But activity can split any way.

19

Sometimes, the wife is designer and creator of the products and the man the business manager. Often both husband and wife can start by *each* moonlighting from their respective jobs. Then, after some success one can work *half* time, often the one with the lower salaried job. Then that one can go into the business full time and later, the other can do the same.

At one period long ago, when business was very bad, I made money *outside* the business and came to our business one day every five or six weeks. My wife ran the business entirely in between and we did very well.

If you're a working mother, even a small home mail order business can give you income and keep you with your children and maybe give you a chunk of capital as well. One woman built a ten million dollar business, starting that way.

A mail order business is not recommended just to get out from under emotional strain. Only go into it if, after taking this course, you feel suited to it. Investigate it. Start cautiously. If you find some initial success, proceed further. . . alone or with others.

Are you retired? Many people succeed in mail order after retirement.

One company, started in mail order by a retired executive, hires only retired people. The staff ranges in age from 67 to 94. It does over $2,000,000 yearly.

Some psychologists believe retirement shortens lives. Many a man or woman feels a void after retirement, and longs for some business activity to participate in. And those who are retired have a wealth of experience to draw on.

If you're retired and smart, you can find a form of mail order to cash in on that experience. Take your time. Proceed at your own pace. Work as few hours a day as you're up to. You can work in the morning. . . take lunch and a nap. . . and work in the afternoon. You can match your experience with a younger, physically stronger partner and use your brains and his brawn. You can keep the entire enterprise as *small* as you desire or let it grow to whatever size you prefer.

Caution! Mail order *can* strip you clean. If retired, gamble in mail order what you can afford to lose. Don't risk a small retirement income.

Attention, young people! When you start work, you've got all the common sense that you'll ever get. All that's added is experience. In our business, we've seen some mighty young people make a lot of mail order money fast. I've had a partner in his early twenties make sixty thousand dollars. I've seen clients in their twenties make hundreds of thousands of dollars. My belief is that a man or woman can come straight from college, own his or her own mail order business and make a fortune in the first few years. I've seen it done without college, straight from high school with only two or three working years first.

The biggest danger for young people is *judgement*. I've seen them make money in their own mail order business superfast and then ruin themselves financially for life. My advice is don't wait if you feel confident. . . but be *cautious* and *discipline yourself*.

Young people *trust others without investigation*. Young people are optimistic. . . and can't believe potential disasters can occur. Young people find it more difficult to force themselves to thoroughly carry through.

You're *strong*. These are your *prolific* working years. You're enthusiastic. You're at your most creative period. Business can be more fun for you. Go to it! You can succeed in mail order with no experience. . . and *stay* successful. . . if you can be super cautious and super suspect of all eventualities.

You can even get started without a penny. If you're young, even if you're unemployed but live at home, any temporary distasteful job from washing dishes to supermarket clerking can actually finance your tiny first tests and get you on your way.

Today, there are disagreeable jobs that most people on unemployment don't care to take. My suggestion is take *anything*, even the most menial job, but *preserve* free time. Work *four* days at something you don't like. Work every spare minute at something you like. If mail order is your cup of tea, *do it*.

Get *others* to take *all* risks. . . or work so hard you put aside $100. Hundreds and possibly thousands of mail order businesses have started with tests of $100 or less. Many have started with a classified ad. Don't be afraid to team up with others and own a *minority* of a joint venture. Just don't mortgage *all* of yourself with a lifetime partnership. We'll discuss this later.

Good luck and good hunting!

What are your chances in mail order if you have no idea how to apply past experience, no idea of a better product or service and no contact with anyone who has?

The majority of those considering mail order are in this predicament. Most fail. . . and I believe often needlessly. I believe that many by going about it correctly could still develop a "feel" for mail order and still succeed in it.

In our own employ, I have seen beginners, completely unfamiliar

21

with mail order, hired to be a messenger clerk or typist develop that "feel". Most had no suitable past experience and before being hired had no idea of a better mail order product or service and no contact with anyone who had. Yet, some achieved lifetime success in mail order.

And many successful in mail order started out equally unfamiliar with it. Simple *exposure* to mail order and its opportunities, *encouragement* that success in it *was* possible, and some guidance seemed most important in my helping others to succeed in mail order.

This course is an effort to give anyone in a similar situation a similar chance. And willingness to *be exposed* to mail order potentials and pitfalls is the first necessary step. Otherwise, chances in mail order become those of a lottery ticket.

Just taking it easy. . . taking your time. . . and saturating yourself in mail order background may plant the seed of that "feel" for mail order that can make success sure.

But the safest formula for individuals has been to take a product you create and perfect yourself in a field you intimately know. Be sure it's unique and needed. Know your costs. Have ample margin. Keep your present job. Start moonlighting. Draw nothing from the business. Then, let the profits accumulate. But, whatever your situation, don't rush in or give up. . . too fast. The more familiar you get with mail order, the safer and *easier* you will find it.

I believe that most of you *can* develop a "feel" for mail order. . . and that my method plus your own future experience in mail order can give you that "feel". . . *if* you give both my method and mail order a *real chance*. Let's discuss what that means and whether you are willing to do it.

22

Chapter 6

Making a Hobby
of Making Money

What it takes and what it gives

Success will come fastest to those who apply to mail order the advantages they possess. . . develop a "feel" for it. . . and work at it.

Most people like making money and gladly work harder for more money. The border between work and fun is in your own mind. Most people work harder at a hobby and call it fun. My "Mail Order Moonlighting" method makes a hobby of making money. Give it the same interest as you would to any hobby that you want to become really good at. Give it the same time and emphasis that you would to become a good cook, fisherman, dressmaker, athlete or winner at anything. . . avoid emotional hang-ups, go at it simply, and with any aptitude for it you should succeed. Mail order is suitable to more people than many hobbies and interests.

But with my "Moonlighting Mail Order" method, there's a big difference. You find out if you're unsuited to it faster than in most activities. You don't have to work as long to master mail order as many other activities. Instead of becoming a slave to it, it becomes easier with time. If you start making money, you can make more of it with less effort in the future. Mail order takes very few years of above average effort to enjoy long years of below average strain. It's really the laziest way to live in the long run.

This is a hobby that brings greater security for you, your wife and children. Often, this hobby can be mixed with another hobby. You may invent or improve ways to garden, cook, play tennis or whatever activity you know best, sell it mail order and *combine* two hobbies for a favorite superhobby.

In any sport or hobby, as you put more time and effort into it, you get better. As you research your subject, observe those more expert than you, get the experience of others up against the same problems, read what experts advise. . . you improve still more. It's the same in mail order moonlighting. You don't have to develop a manual dexterity. Tedious practicing is not required in this hobby. What is needed is study of what others do, analysis of your own past actions and judgement decisions regarding your future actions. The more effort you put in, the more you take out. . . in cash.

Initially, you may feel quite ill suited for mail order, yet find later that you do have an innate feeling for it. A horseman has to work hard from early years to feel "part of the horse". . . a surfer to feel "part of the wave". . . and mail order takes time and effort to become just as natural for you.

To train yourself for mail order means training yourself to be frugal, to work, to avoid unneeded expenditures and to watch pennies to accumulate dollars. You must drive yourself to be a self starter, *create* sales and not wait for them. You must sacrifice now for future benefits. It's the old Puritan ethic. . . sorry about that. But often it's fun. . . the fun work ethic.

If you do train yourself this way, making money is absurdly simple. We have to know enough to stay out of the business rain and cut risks when things are bad. We have to go when the goin's good and go all out. We've got to keep things simple and not over complicate them.

If this hobby makes work fun, it can't be all bad. If having fun tempts you to work more, you may work a lot less later. If what I describe is more effort than you care for, you may prefer to forget it. It becomes too dangerous a lottery.

24

Chapter 7

Making It In Mail Order

Sizing up your chances
. . . IQ, emotional stability and work needed. . .
overcoming fears

For most, making it in mail order comes down to willingness to work sufficiently and overcoming fears of dangers. I propose to make the work fun and take out some of the fear and use the rest to make mail order safer.

The overwhelming majority of people with enough I.Q. to read this simple book have the I.Q. necessary to operate a business as simple as mail order can be. They also have enough emotional stability.

I assure you that you can have a lot of fun in mail order with my method. You don't lose money on needless overhead. I advise you on ways of starting with little or no other risks.

My "Mail Order Moonlighting" method is simple. It's safer. It makes a hobby of making money. You don't have to rush and can take your time. If you have almost no overhead, keep losses below savings from your job and develop any "feel" for mail order, success should be almost inevitable.

I am going to try to give you that "feel". But I can only help you if you follow my method.

First, you apply your know-how or contacts to find or create a better mail order item. Next, you develop a more effective way to present it yourself or with others. Now, you develop an edge in some

25

way over others in the mail order business. You may have this edge or associate with those that do. It may be a lower advertising rate, a specific, very responsive list to mail to, the ability to get placement of packaging enclosures, a creative skill, a product buying advantage. But in some way, you want a better chance than average. Then, you apply extreme frugality in every phase of operations.

Remember that most tests fail. If you go into mail order with one item and a one time test, your chances are small. The more tests you run, done professionally, the greater chance you will have that one test will work.

A mail order "test" is a mail order ad run to prove something. It can be run in any form of advertising.

The first test is to determine whether you should proceed further with the product. It is simply the best ad you can create. Running ads in more places is called "projecting".

There are many kinds of tests to determine if a change of presentation increases orders or inquiries. Counting the mail gives the answer. We'll discuss it all in more detail later.

If one test is successful and if professionally projected with national advertising, profits should wipe out test losses and give you a net profit overall. Some successful items have short lives. Others give income for years. Once you get your first "hit" item, you can far more easily get the next and so on.

Once success starts to snowball, mail order is such fascinating fun that even the laziest of us enjoy the extra work that makes still more money. And some fear or lack of courage, properly used in mail order, can help *insure* success by avoiding mis-steps. . . in time. Incidentally, you may get that big "hit" the first test you make. It does happen. You're probably better off if you don't.

Each successful test has the thrill and excitement of a winning lottery ticket. . . but we often learn more and make more money in the end from tests that fail. Each unsuccessful test helps prepare you for later success. No lesson sinks home quite the same as your own personal post mortem of the test that has just failed.

Lessons learned from unsuccessful tests are so vital that sometimes initial success from an early-in-the-game test can greatly lessen chances of later, bigger success. Whenever there's a downward economic trend, I rejoice at starting work in 1934. The coming collapse has the cozy "gemütlich" feeling of old times "deja vu." All that I learned in those days of 25% unemployment can now become my secret weapon.

And adversity in tests can help you too.

26

Mail order, like any other business, loses money when incorrectly operated. Its virtue is that you usually see immediately the losses that occur. With any "feel" for mail order, mistakes are glaringly apparent. Often, you can quickly stop wrong moves. It, therefore, becomes easier than in other businesses to overcome weaknesses, to learn and improve, to catch an error before it's too late. And it becomes safer too.

If you're willing to go ahead, knowing the odds against you and the effort and discipline required, let's get started.

From here on in my method takes up the basic factors that determine mail order success or failure divided into: what you sell, how you sell, and how you operate your day to day business.

First, we'll discuss what you sell. . . selecting the product. Let's get into finding that mail order item that just may make us rich.

BOOK II
The Expanding Universe

*. . . the many worlds of today's
product selection. . .
new wider scope of
what you can now sell profitably*

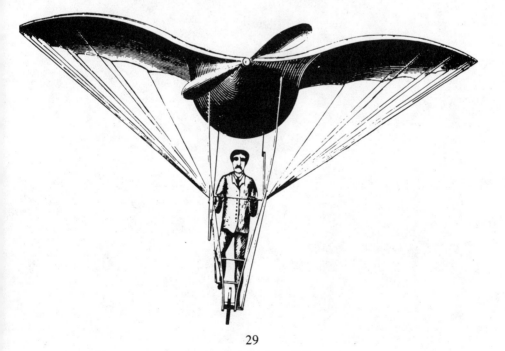

Chapter 1

The First Mail Order Misunderstanding

. . . what to sell. . . pay for it. . . and charge for it
. . . what you can't profitably, legally or practically sell

More money is lost in mail order from poor product selection than in any other way. But the flair and "feel" for right product selection makes fortunes for mail order men and women.

The advertisements in magazines luring little people into mail order often mislead them on the ease of finding mail order items. They are the greedy leading the blind.

The impression is that everywhere articles exist. . . easy to sell by mail order, easily available from wholesalers, and with ample margin to sell at a fat profit after all costs.

The truth is sadly different. *Most* items are quite *ill suited* to mail order. Even if an item is a fine mail order item, purchasing it through a wholesaler rarely leaves adequate margin to pay for mail order advertising. . . and show a profit.

Even most manufacturers find that most of their own products are *not* suited to sell via mail order themselves, even with the *full* gross profit they enjoy. And the occasional successful mail order product a manufacturer or importer may find for himself out of his line usually yields only modest profits when the manufacturer-mail order man has his *entire* profit to work with.

If the manufacturer makes a profit and sells to you as a mail order

31

man, usually you can't make a profit. And if the manufacturer sells to a wholesaler and makes a profit, and the wholesaler sells to you and makes a profit, then mail order chances for you grow even dimmer.

As in other fields, some mail order is based on substantially lower margins.

The more staple the article, usually the less suited it is to mail order, *except* at a bargain price. This can only be possible when advertising costs are very low as in a package insert in a mail order shipment. Or again, it may be possible if the merchandise is bought at an unusual bargain, as in a distress odd lot.

Some mail order businesses perpetually seek and rely on such distress merchandise. But this, in reality, can only be achieved irregularly by happenchance, and a regular flow of merchandise at known costs can be rarely achieved.

You may find a specific list of customer names so responsive, so above average in its response per thousand, that you can afford to pay more for an article particularly related to the list such as a sewing article for a sewing list.

And of course, in both selling through the trade and via mail order there is considerable variation in needed margins by products and situations. You can buy from a manufacturer or even a wholesaler and make a mail order profit in specific situations.

If you develop a catalogue with a variety of items, you will normally have a substantially lower selling cost than for a specific mail order item sold through most forms of advertising. You can then afford to buy smaller amounts of a variety of items from manufacturers or even wholesalers.

What can you sell by mail order? Lots and lots and lots!

Below are items sold over the years by mail order direct response methods for Huber Hoge and Sons' clients (including ourselves). In considering selling such items yourself, please realize that special factors which caused any success of these items might not hold in your case.

Each item was a special *kind* of seed, knife, comb, toy or whatever, with unique advantages over others. Margins were right. Cost was low enough and selling price high enough to provide enough gross profit to give hope of returning profit after advertising. Advertising presentation was painfully accomplished and above average. Buying the advertising was carefully negotiated. Timing was right. Another caution: what worked in one *form* of advertising often failed in another.

So, don't rush in where mail order angels fear to tread. . . until we've spent a little more time together. Incidentally, this only represents 38 years of one advertising agency's experience and one mail order man's business lifetime. The experience of other mail order authorities will indicate far more possible items, fields and areas ideal for mail order direct response methods.

But our list may give you some ideas of mail order items you'd like to consider. Here's our list!

pianos
sheets
fish lures
seeds
combs
glassware
dish cloths
kitchen knives
perfume
TV sets
night driving
  glasses
refrigeration
trays
travel books
live turtles
auto accessories
paint brush
  cleaner
language
  records
razor blades
cigarette making
  machine
bed spreads
auto insurance
roasters
IQ tests
men's socks
wind up cars
wallets
creamers
steak knives
water heaters
electric razors
toasters
car oil additives
telephone
  appliances
slip covers

pillow cases
cowboy suits
globes
bibles
children's
  records
car washers
reducing tablets
hosiery
juice
  extractors
health books
pens
piano courses
curlers
buttons
life jackets
classic records
steam irons
beauty courses
jewelry
pools
book clubs
patterns
train sets
beach
  mattresses
saws
record clubs
magnolias
pipes
men's shirts
pencil
  sharpeners
tools
recipes
additives
rug making
  kits
art courses

cutlery
roses
pencils
indoor plants
toys
thread
real estate
silver polish
fryers
mixing bowls
defrosters
paint sprayers
cosmetics
drills
mops
name stamps
T-shirts
fertilizer
broilers
homework
  courses
plastic kitchen
  gadgets
ironing sets
sun visors
plastic dishes
power saws
seats
plastic banks
canoes
games
will forms
coverlets
bulbs
rafts
staplers
TV antenna
land
aprons
lamps

33

food mixers
sewing machines
memory courses
towels
dinghies
adding machines
clothes
apartment
 rentals
fuel oil
 additives
auto seat
 covers
food covers
harmonicas
garment bags
art prints
mechanical
 knitters
magic sets
shampoos
hair vacs
home dry
 cleaners
Christmas trees
dress forms
language aids
gladioli
lawn sprinklers
boats

kitchen slicers
vacuum cleaners
paint rollers
electric paint
 peelers
drug products
knife holders
correspondence
 courses
dolls
graters
corn poppers
magazine
 subscriptions
vitamins
wool remnants
tonics
electric
 heaters
law books
TV repair
 manuals
toy zithers
rolling pins
art materials
jiffy whippers
cigarette
 lighters
history books

Christmas gifts
accident
 insurance
adult education
tulips
blouses
paint brushes
awnings
insecticide
inspirational
 books
watches
life insurance
rat killer
flatware
scarves
vegetable
 preparers
fishing clubs
model airplanes
cooky presses
wafer molds
pet care
coffee makers
club plans
vegetable
 steamers
grass growth
 retardant

The above is mainly in the broad consumer field.

It doesn't touch the technical field, office field, industrial field and innumerable special hobbies and interests.

In the book field alone, I once calculated that we have sold for our clients over 300 kinds of how-to instruction books. Opportunities to find the right products and services, perhaps in your present business, are everywhere. But sure *losers* are even *more* prevalent.

How do you find the right mail order items? You *look* for them or stumble over them. They sometimes walk right in the door.

I have looked at over ten thousand different items over a lifetime. I've investigated seriously several thousand.

For clients and ourselves, we've tested over a thousand items. Let's discuss what can often make the difference between losers. . . and winners. . . and particularly what may be the right item or items for *you*.

In considering the sale of anything by mail, there are certain mundane but vital factors.

First, does it *do* what it purports to do? You are legally responsible that it does. Have you personally used it? Have you tested in the simplest way what it does vs. what you have been told it does?

Is it dangerous to use? Can it be misused by a child or whomever? Can it harm or hurt anyone by *overuse*? You are responsible. Your ignorance is no legal or moral excuse.

Is it *any good*? Is it made well? Do the parts *fit*? If shipped disassembled can anyone ever put it together? Is it made yet or are you just setting up to make it? If so, how do you know you can ever make it right? Can you get more of it? Can you get more parts for it? How much does it cost vs. its replacement cost to you? Will you go broke assembling, painting or decorating it?

Is it *practical* to sell it by mail? Is it even shippable via post office or UPS? Does it weigh too much in relation to its price? Is it too bulky? Are its dimensions too odd? Is its package *printed* in a way unacceptable to the post office? Is it too perishable to ship or too fragile? Is it dangerous or even *illegal* to ship?

All this is primary but it happens! So let's see how we can avoid it.

35

Chapter 2

How To Be A
Mail Order Detective

Snooping. . . shopping. . . listening. . . advertising
. . . answering ads. . . analyzing trends. . . developing your own

Finding the item is the first chore in going into mail order.

And finding a new item will be all important to you for the rest of your mail order life. Of course, the fastest, easiest and safest way to get a new item is to "steal" one. We don't, but others do it regularly.

The first step is to *study* mail order advertising. We do it to spot new trends and techniques. Every publication that carries mail order ads becomes your text book. Next, open your mail, particularly your 3rd class mail—junk mail (advertising you may usually throw away) and particularly your office advertising mail. Now, file every direct mail piece carefully away.

Watch the movies on TV where most mail order commercials run. Tune in when you drive. . . from radio station to radio station.

Start answering mail order inquiry ads. As the literature comes in, file it away. Start *buying* by mail yourself.

Go through trade and technical magazines. In each, you'll find mail order items for that trade. Go through Popular Science, Popular Mechanics, Mechanix Illustrated and Science and Mechanics. See what they feature editorially and what is advertised mail order. Do the same with the credit card magazines and direct response post card publications you run across.

The more you study and analyze, the more you'll form opinions as to the type of mail order item you prefer yourself. Start attending trade shows. . . and roam from booth to booth. Go to the Premium Show in New York or Chicago. Try the Stationery Show, the Gift Show, the Hardware Show, Housewares Show, Business Shows, the Boutique Show. There's even a Mail Order Show. . . whatever shows are most convenient to you.

At every show there are some provocative items exhibited by underfinanced companies that are hoping to find a promoter angel. If you're financed to do volume and want to go after it, you have a chance to negotiate a take over of *all* distribution rights. You can start with a mail order test. . . project in mail order and right on into distribution. Question such exhibitors closely. They may already have had a successful mail order test and need only help to project it. Each conversation you have gives you more of a "feel" for mail order.

Every retail store is a "new item trade show" for you.

Particularly study off-beat, intriguing, small specialty stores. . . the ones with flair, style and character. The bigger the city, the more specialized stores can survive, but stores with personality are popping up everywhere.

Look for craft stores, fashion boutiques, hobby stores, off beat stores like African import stores, the Kite Store in New York, art print and book stores, college campus stores of all kinds, lapidaries and gift shops. Many times, the owner is also the designer and creator of some of the most intriguing items. Here again sometimes the owner would like to do mail order but lacks finances or feels insecure. Often, it's possible to acquire mail order or complete distribution rights on a royalty basis or on a joint venture basis.

The next step is to look for imports. Study "Made in Europe" and equivalent publications advertising products made in different parts of the world and available. You're even told when items are available on a sole rights basis. If you can afford it. . . travel. Go to the great fairs in Hanover, Frankfurt, Milan and other parts of the world. You're now a step ahead, looking at some items *before* they've been exported to the U.S. at all. Besides, you'll enjoy it.

Often a new item comes from a friend of a friend. If people know you're in mail order, and believe you're honest and competent, they'll recommend you to people they know who have new items.

It's hard to launch a new product. Small entrepreneurs trying to get traditional distribution are more and more frozen out. Small enterprises are always running out of money, often with a quite desirable product.

37

We try to keep arms length from past losses and mistakes, but to take over rights of intriguing items either on a royalty basis or a 60-40 basis ownership.

If the old corporation owns inventory, we offer to pay for it at cost as needed and approved by us as acceptable. If the old corporation invested substantially in tooling, we offer to pay an extra 3 percent or so tooling royalty on our sales until their original layout of cash is returned. Of course, we do so only after we verify the reasonableness of the costs. In this way, we can help bail out money tied up but never really risk any money other than on new tests.

Once you succeed with one item, tell your suppliers, your friends, your acquaintances that you're looking for another item. As soon as you succeed with one item, they'll be far more likely to recomend you to the owner of another. It will become easier and easier. Don't grasp at straws. Don't be in a hurry or feel that you must get a new item by a certain date.

Consider remnant books. Go to a remnant book wholesaler or the equivalent. Browse through the remnant shelves. Find a how-to book that appeals to you. You can buy it at a bargain. . . and advertise it at full retail price. It will usually sell, or not sell, based more on your presentation than on price. Often, you can arrange, if your tests are successful, to reprint the book on a royalty basis. . . and even to sell back some of the edition if you can't sell it all. . . or to joint venture the edition.

Best of all, develop your own item yourself or with some creative person who seems to have something better in the works. Take your time. Develop it gradually. But be proud of it. Often the slower pace of developing and perfecting your item is far safer and often less liable to be copied.

Analyzing the mail order items you see can teach you a lot.

Particularly, watch the items that run in the publication more than once. Let us assume, as we hope, that you do not choose to "duplicate" the other fellow's apparently successful item. But you can cash in on the *trend* it indicates without hurting him at all. If it is a "nostalgia item" that's repeating, running the same ad in the same publication or even the same ad in many publications, then consider finding or creating another "nostalgia" item. If it's an energy saving item, consider a quite different kind of energy saving item and so forth.

Study mail order catalogues, particularly the specialized ones. Notice the items that are featured in largest space and most prominent position. . . in successive catalogues. Learn from them in the same way. Read editorial pages of shelter magazines like House & Garden, Better Homes and Gardens, American Home. . . not just the shopping column pages but main editorial pages. Look for their interesting items.

One old time legend says a man in London once sold the sun for a shilling. He had found a shilling in the road, and for the rest of his life, walked the streets of London, head bent down looking for another shilling. . . and never saw the sun again.

Answering ads for items and businesses can work out the same way. Many are called and few are chosen. We have bought businesses located through such classified ads. My brother heads a $6,000,000 business he acquired, after locating it in just this way. We have acquired items this way as well.

But it requires great patience and an ability to screen out quickly proposals impractical for you. Many of those advertising are dreamers. Some are liars. Most are failures. The big majority can be time wasters. Just reading the ads, day after day, takes time. We try to answer such ads with the briefest of letters, sum up our background and give our Dun & Bradstreet rating. We try to screen the proposal on the telephone. We only have a personal meeting with someone who has the rare proposal that seems to make enough sense to justify it. In the meeting we try, within ten to twenty minutes, to screen out those who slip in quite different terms and variations to their proposal as stated by telephone. If the individuals seem honorable and competent, their business or product desirable, and if their reports of test results of sales are encouraging, we try to get an option agreement to make our own tests. Generally, our tests do *not* verify theirs. Often, the product turns out to be manufacturable only at far higher costs. Sometimes, their mold (if they have one) turns out to be defective. Occasionally, the product cannot be made at all. But it all comes out in the wash.

As for advertising for items ourselves, it can be even more frustrating. Often, we are deluged by answers. Many of them seem intriguing, although we can screen out many more as obviously unsuited to us. When we advertise, no matter what limitations we put in, we often get inquiries from all kinds of people with all kinds of products. The percentage of dreamers is still higher. Just the cost of telephoning inquiries all over the country is far greater than running the ad. And answering by mail only prolongs the agony. But we have occasionally found items this way.

Run and answer ads. Be jaundiced. Expect to work long and hard to find that one good item we all need.

Chapter 3

Each To His Own

*Personal judgements. . . items we like
and don't like. . . where our best items come from
. . . suiting the item to you*

There are items that our policy will not permit us to sell. . . items that make big mail order money. . . but not for us. Because gradually, over the years, we've made certain basic policy decisions on new items. We will not sell an erotic item. . . contraceptive or even sex information; the effect of which, on younger people, we are not sure. When I think of such items, I always think of my children, nieces, nephews, children of friends and what it may do to their future life.

I can't look at any weapon or possibility of a product being used as a weapon without visualizing a possible crime committed with it. When I see guns, I think of President Kennedy killed with a mail order gun. When I see hunting knives, I think of teen age gang warfare with mail order knives. Items like these are the safest items to sell, but perhaps the most dangerous to buy. . . and we don't touch them.

Most other dangerous items are harder to spot. We don't sell internal medicine or remedies. In some kinds of items, we erred in our youth and have, thereafter, stayed away from them like the plague.

You will quickly develop your own "do's" and "don'ts" regarding selecting items.

We avoid hand crafted items because we like to do a volume business. But if you have a "feel" for crafted items and love to travel,

40

you can travel all over the world as a business expense seeking out fascinating crafted items. Do you like original Mexican hand woven hammocks, ponchos from Peru, hand crafted African jewelry, hand made crafted items from Mainland China, or shell necklaces from India? They can be a joy to buy and at the height of their appeal highly profitable to sell. They are not for us, but could be for you.

We avoid ancient artifacts like old Roman coins. We're not archeologists. We assume that many items of this sort sold by mail are frauds. We don't want to take a chance by going into them. But if archeology is your hobby, here's your chance to pursue it as a business expense and make money from it as a hobby.

We usually avoid fashion items because we're not fashion designers. We do not have a professional fashion merchandise buying background. But perhaps you have a flair for spotting fashion trends in clothes, accessories or jewelry. If so, mail order is often a perfect way to turn your private fashion hunches into big profit.

Some of my friends (and alumni) have been among the most successful entrepreneurs of records via mail order TV. They have no previous background in the record business. But for years we have sold "Worlds' Greatest Books", excerpts of fifty famous best sellers and popular classics, for a publishing client! Applied to records, this has been successful in many forms. They simply used know-how gained in the book mail order field to sell many millions of dollars worth of records.

You may have either a perfect professional background or a flair for selecting the mix of songs that sell best in bargain combinations. And you may have just the right professional contacts. Or you may have a flair for an off beat record success like the sound of birds, insects, thunder, and the running water of natural springs . . . which, incidentally, sold well.

Once we helped launch a piano course with a piano teacher of many years. He had also been an arranger to a famous band leader for years. His background helped make his course a success. With a famous pianist, a performer of delightful light musical comedy music we helped develop another piano course. We sold over 287,000 of them, first for a top publisher, and later for ourselves.

The piano is less popular now. But you may be a teacher of . . . or devoted student of . . . or professional performer of . . . the coming new instrument. It may become more popular than the guitar is today. And you may have just the teaching method that can be sold in big volume mail order.

41

To me, publishing in all its varied forms is particularly fascinating.

Whether we work as advertising agency . . . are in partnership . . . or sole owner is far less important than just working on the creating and selling of books or courses, newsletters or publications, cassettes or videotape. It's all publishing to me.

Years ago we used to create special network radio shows on hobbies and interests. On each show the commercial was for a book. For just one field, sewing, on just one network, we created and produced programs amounting to over one million words a year on sewing. We created such programs in field after field. We did the same on each TV network and most top TV stations. This has been a field suited to me. From the age of seven, I have been a voracious reader. For over twenty years, our advertising agency work for large publishers kept teaching us our trade. Our adult education subsidiary succeeds because of this background. The hobby products we sell came about from our knowledge of how to sell hobby books and publications. For clients we've sold just about every kind of how-to book and fiction magazine or book club. It's simply our cup of tea.

And it may be *yours*. You may be a teacher of any subject or hobby . . . a coach or star performer in any sport . . . a writer in any such field . . . or a devoted hobbyist or amateur sportsman. You may have made a hobby of devising a better way to do anything . . . from helping your children in homework, your wife in the kitchen, your husband in his work to whatever. And you may be able to express it perfectly in a better instruction form than yet available. It may be for a brand new interest just becoming popular, whether it be hot air ballooning or paddle tennis. If you can't, you may know someone who can, for whom you'd be the most perfect editor or business partner.

If so, do-it-yourself instruction may be your field.

Many items *we* avoid may be just right for other mail order firms.

We avoid ties, shirts, socks and shoes that are staple. But the Haband Company has built their big and successful mail order business on just these items. Old clients of ours have, too. We avoid such items because the margin is usually tight. Also, most efficient retailers everywhere offer the widest possible selection. But Haband has built a loyal customer list happy with similar purchases from them, who respond well to just these items. And once you succeed in selling any item, you quickly develop buying power that improves margins.

We usually avoid "gag" items like Beethoven sweatshirts or funny bumper stickers. To us, they're too unpredictable. But others thrive on them . . . bring out one after the other . . . and pay out on a satisfactory percentage of them. And you may have a flair for this type of item. If so, be cautious on inventory. Any such hit item might drop dead at any time.

We avoid one-time items like an item tied to a candidate in a presidential election. We confine tests to items that can sell year after year. But others make money with one time items.

A number of years ago, the leading single mail order advertising agency expert in the country was approached by an ambitious young man seeking advice. The young man wanted to sell a tape recorder for $99.95. The expert told him to save his money and forget it, an item that expensive could not be sold for cash. The young man thanked him politely and then tested an ad which succeeded in the New York Times. With more ads, he quickly sold $300,000 worth of tape recorders. Sometimes, experts must live and learn.

We sell items in a variety of price ranges. For an all-cash offer, we prefer five to twenty dollars. We occasionally sell items for under five dollars. Very rarely, we sell items for as low as one or two dollars. Each year, the average sales price goes higher, even in the lowest price ranges.

We also sell items for up to one hundred dollars - and more. We get checks for up to two hundred and fifty dollars every day for single and multiple orders for such products. We also offer to sell via the four major credit cards. We do so because more people prefer to buy more expensive items in this way and because we can take orders by telephone.

The mail order item we like best is one that has just succeeded, but not yet projected, and that we can still acquire.

But this is very rare. We like items that are fresh and ingenious but related to items that have had great past success. We like revivals that some cultural change suddenly makes ripe for a comeback.

We like universal appeal items, but not yet broadly distributed. We like bigger ticket items of the *widest possible* appeal. I once analyzed the biggest purchases which the average family buys. It starts with land and a house, then a car, and nowadays, a camper or boat, then appliances of every sort, then clothes and food. Other items can be major purchases. The New York Times costs over $180 a year to have delivered. And $150 or more spent on a hobby or sport you're interested in is just the beginning.

We like many hobby items. We believe do-it-yourself has been a bit overdone. We avoid any item that has too great investment for our bank account or in relation to future sales. We avoid religious items selling to members of a religion (from a matter of personal taste). We avoid very limited potential items, although many mail order people make a living safely and happily, lifelong, from just one of them. We'd rather have a chance at broader sales. One of the first questions my wife asks about any new item is, "How many colors and sizes does it have?" And we avoid the item if too many are required. We're trying to cut down and not add to inventory.

We avoid shopping for bargains which we can advertise at a special reduced price, but others thrive on them. Odd lot purchases of distress merchandise usually mean real and major reductions. We don't like them, because it's hard to get more. It's difficult to project in volume.

If you're small, you can do some things that you can't do later. In the book publishing field, there is always a supply of "remnants" (leftovers) of editions — often of how-to books ideal for mail order. You can buy low at a distress price. You can often sell high and sometimes at full or higher retail price. The same is often true in other fields.

We only like such bargains when — as is sometimes possible — you can obtain the plates, dies or molds, on a royalty or cash basis and develop a proprietary product.

Sometimes, a sweeping technological change can greatly lower manufacturing costs and make possible dramatic savings as in digital watches. We're usually afraid of such situations, because competition can wipe us out overnight with still lower reductions. But sometimes, rare and perfect situations come about.

Before long playing records, a certain mail order language course, using the old 78 records, required half a dozen records. It sold for $29.95. With long playing records, one old client of ours began to sell the identical course on one record at $9.95. He built a big, successful business. Not only was the saving overwhelmingly dramatic, but the reason why, the technological improvement of long playing records, was instantly accepted as believable.

Our best mail order products have come either from research or association in something else!

Later, I'll go into more detail on research. But it's impossible to research anything without stimulating some ideas for something associated or quite unrelated. At least, this is so for my grasshopper mind. And most contacts for items we sell came about from introductions for quite different purposes.

Researching the background, to help sell a how-to book, will come up with a fascinating do-it-yourself product in that field. Often, the author will discuss in the book ideas for improved products for that interest. In publishing, any subject briefly described in any fairly encyclopedic coverage may seem worthy of a book itself. Researching any new product can sometimes uncover a needed accessory which can be a business in itself, such as an electric pump of proper pressure for inflatable furniture.

We've been importing and selling pocket adding machines because a representative for a cosmetic business we operated brought around his uncle. We've been selling dress forms for home sewers for twenty-three years because a young Dutch importer, from whom we bought four million bulbs, met a movie starlet who had invented a dress form and introduced her to us. We're in the inflatable boat business because a young Frenchman, who first approached us with a pair of glasses to better see fish underwater, became our good friend and partner later.

As you research first your own background and contacts, and then start actively researching possible mail order projects and selling your first items, one thing will lead to another.

Try to base the selection of the item you choose or develop on your special background and know-how. It gives you a big advantage. Use that special engineering, sales or creative experience. The more you do this, the sounder your mail order business will be.

Chapter 4

Surprise Hits

*The unexpected...fun gag items...ugly ducklings
...trend items...revivals...future item portents*

This is the story of the fun gag that started a $100,000,000 business. Once upon a time, there was an ambitious young man who longed to get rich in mail order.

His first job was writing the mail order shopping column of a national magazine. All sorts of mail order items came across his desk. His job was to select from the intriguing items and describe them in his column. He noticed that amusing, fun, gag items often did well and came up with one of his own.

He announced it to the world in a one inch ad in Esquire magazine. The first ad made him over $3,000, and he ran it in many more magazines.

I personally would not have selected this item or any type of fun gag item. Success would have seemed too wildly improbable. But this man (since then my good friend and personal client) has an uncanny knack for selecting the right mail order item at the right time. And that, combined with many other talents and incredibly hard work, has catapulted him to almost unbelievable mail order success ... living in palaces, surrounded by luxury, finally culminating in the selling out of a business of over $100,000,000 yearly ... a business he acquired with mail order profits and made a success of, with mail order direct re-

46

sponse methods.

I mention it because he developed a "feel" for mail order success in directions I personally do not have. And each mail order man develops his own "feel" and touch, often uniquely personal.

And let us hope you will too.

Here's the story of a mail order ugly duckling. Some years ago one of the world's largest publishers gave up on selling an inexpensive art course. Sales had been running about $75 a month *at retail*. The publisher turned over the rights and the plates for $250 to the artist author.

The creative head of Huber Hoge and Sons, our family owned advertising agency, met the author in Doylstown, Pa., where the author had an art instruction class. It turned out that the artist-author had since had some success on a TV test, demonstrating the course and shipping it himself. It further turned out that the publisher was a client of ours.

We asked the publisher to take back the publishing rights and let us take a try at selling the course. We felt we knew the way to project widely the success the artist-author had on his own test.

The publisher and author signed a new contract. The publisher was Doubleday. The author was Jon Gnagy. We sold one out of every fourteen TV set owners in the U.S. a Jon Gnagy course. Arthur Brown, the art materials firm, launched a Jon Gnagy art materials line and became our client. The Jon Gnagy art materials business became a public company on its own with store distribution nationwide for its products.

TV presentation and Jon Gnagy's performing talent made the difference between a product gathering dust on a counter and undreamed of mail order and direct response store distribution success.

Moral: You may find mail order success from a store distribution or even present mail order failure...with proper mail order "feel" and know-how.

How would you like to ride a mail order success on a national wave? Cashing in on a trend is the way to make money in any business ...and certainly, in mail order.

Timing is all important...to sell an item or service at the very peak or just before that peak of it's being desired. Many trends seem apparent only years later. Then, you may realize that you made money in a certain item because you got into it when the trend was ripe. But your objective should be to spot one in time.

Every enormously, popular activity creates an entire train of associated accessory opportunities. The enormous rush to the suburbs of

47

city dwellers created a hunger for products and services to beautify and improve their new houses. Mail order helped fill the gap with plants, fertilizers, painting applicators, decorative items and an ever increasing number of home improvement products.

The former population explosion of the age group that moved through nursery school to college and into jobs like army ants created an entire array of mail order opportunities from remedial home work courses to aids to getting a better job. The trend towards far greater leisure time has produced opportunities for every type of hobby, sport and special interest equipment and instruction. Within weeks of the Arab oil boycott, entrepreneurs were selling new mail order items. These ranged from new kinds of fireplaces, to get more heat from less wood, to energy saving kits for office and home.

And with every new lurching swing of popular activity, there will be huge new mail order opportunities, often *reviving* mail order items long in moth balls. So, keep your eye on the next trend and cash in on it in mail order. Some mail order items seem eternal, others transitory and some cyclic. Consider revivals.

A former creative head of Huber Hoge and Sons was a student of mail order and advertising in all its aspects. He located an advertisement run successfully before 1900 for a book on how to make money in real estate. It was short, simple and effective. A Huber Hoge and Sons client currently published a book on how to make money in real estate. Our creative director transposed a word or two out of the old ad to bring it up to date and applicable, and ran it for our client. The old ad sold the new book quite successfully, apparently pulling as well as it had before 1900.

On the other hand, for another publisher client we re-ran one of the great mail order ads of all time (in another form of advertising) ... the "which fork should I use for chicken salad" ad of the 1920's ... for the same Lillian Eichler Book of Etiquette brought up to date. The old magic died. In fact, no ad we came up with pulled by mail order for any etiquette books we tried. People were no longer socially insecure in this way.

The recession made some depression mail order items revive successfully, particularly economic survival books of various kinds. Cable TV revived some of the mail order items of the early TV, which in turn revived long dormant demonstration items of all kinds. We used to drive to Atlantic City, pick up demonstrators and drive them back to film studios or TV stations. The same demonstration that worked in Atlantic City usually worked on TV.

48

This is the story of a portent of a quarter billion dollars of mail order sales from outer space...many years before it happened. A number of years ago, in a few months time our family-owned company, Harrison-Hoge Industries, Inc., sold over one million dollars of pocket adding machines.

The machine was the ADDIATOR made in West Germany, a superb, meticulously made, but extremely simple, stylus-into-slots machine. You simply pulled down the stylus to get the solution in the answer window.

What opened my eyes was it's absolutely universal appeal. We could run a page in Time or in Woman's Day, run on radio or TV...daytime or night...equally successfully. We obviously sold housewives, students, salesmen, shop keepers, whatever. I realized that it indicated a hunger for an adding machine far away from offices. I felt that someday an electric office model would be low enough priced to get this market.

This was the market that was ready and waiting when the first chip calculator (a by-product of the space industry) was advertised in small ads in the Wall Street Journal, the New York Times and magazines. The ads as they got bigger, had an uncanny resemblance to our ADDIATOR ads of years before, but asking for only about twenty five times as much for the product.

The rest is history. The mail order introduction of chip calculators burst like a comet on the distribution scene, outmoded every previous method of selling calculators, created an undreamed of giant industry...leading to huge markets overseas and even an improved U.S. balance of payments. It happened so fast that few people got in on it. I didn't.

So, let's keep our eyes open for the next mail order bonanza.

Chapter 5

Item Decisions

Right items for the medium...luxury vs necessities...
personalized...demonstration...seasonal...Christmas items

Each medium of advertising creates its own associated offers. TV, radio, The Wall Street Journal, credit card magazines have each had powerful mail order side effects. And so does every important medium of advertising.

Years ago, Top Hit bargain combinations in batches of 16, 24, and so forth, current hits first began to succeed on "Top 40" radio stations and then to boom on "dance party" teen TV shows. Old movies proved the perfect vehicle for *old time* nostalgia record hit combinations.

The Wall Street Journal's incredible mass circulation of business men made every type of business aid and executive luxury sold to business men suddenly capable of surprising mail order success. The credit card magazines — "Signature", "Carte Blanche" and "Travel and Leisure" — opened up still higher ticket merchandise of the same type. Jewelry selling for $100 to $200 ... executive training courses ... lavish wallets ... language records and innumerable other executive items, particularly those that could be charged to business and used personally became suddenly far simpler to sell.

At our suggestion, a client of ours once bought fifteen minutes on network radio before and after the Metropolitan Opera. Week after week, we played records of next week's opera and advertised and sold

50

tens of thousands of "Stories of the Great Operas", edited by Milton Cross who regularly announced the Metropolitan Opera programs.

We call them "related offers" because, in a sense, the entire medium becomes a vehicle for the offer, greatly multiplying the effectiveness of the advertising and making the purchase of the advertising often an extreme mail order bargain. And with every new media success, there's new opportunity for you to tie in with mail order items.

Let's consider luxury items vs. necessities. Your choice will be largely determined by your operation and by the general economic situation at the time.

In the late depression, when I started out, a dollar taken from a wallet for a purchase could give the owner a traumatic shock. He or she might resent being sold. Only some overwhelming benefit could justify the awful wrench of parting with that dollar. We had to concentrate on necessities in those days.

I knew one publisher who specialized in taking "blotting paper" editions, sets of lots of volumes of thick paper pages and small numbers of pages, and compressing them with the same number of words into bulging fat, giant, one volume editions at a bargain price. He did well in the worst of the depression ... and badly when business conditions improved ... and the market for "blotting paper" editions revived.

For quite a few years, the trend has been to luxuries. I know a wine and liquor importer, who has become rich since the depression with a simple formula. He sells only the most expensive wine, champagne, or liquor. If a liquor store or restaurant lists a competitive brand at a higher price, he doesn't want to sell them anymore. He has found his market of successful, prosperous executives and coupon clipping retired people and widows who are insecure about wine and liquor selection. They can afford the best. They are happy to solve their selection problem by choosing the most expensive wine or liquor on the list.

In mail order, even the lowest cost items have usually been far from necessities. Mass circulation of above average income like the Wall Street Journal made higher price luxuries more easily saleable. The credit card revolution made it far easier still. But each time economic conditions look bad, I get out my list of depression mail order hits. Luxury items may continue. Some mail order firms may have an affinity for selling them. Yet, I feel that for some years the public will again be far more selective, less content with battery powered swizzle sticks and such, and more determined to get real value and benefit from articles they buy by mail.

Fads and fun items are the most speculative of items. They tend to

51

lose their appeal as suddenly as they originally gained it. They may become even more speculative if unemployment continues high and incomes continue to buy less than formerly. The future trends will probably be more and more to *value* as far as luxuries are concerned and with more emphasis on basic necessities.

Personalized products are often ideal by mail order but many fail via mail order.

While some retailers offer personalization of some items, most retailers do not. Most personalized items are not generally available via stores. Yet, the vast majority of personalized items *can be* handled via mail order. Often, someone who has purchased a personalized product likes the idea of personalization, and will gladly buy more personalized items from the same mail order company.

Many manufacturers have items ideal for personalization. Many retailers are set up for personalization. Yet, many of them have never *explored* mail order operations based on their present capabilities. Some businesses are entirely based on personalization, and far more suited to mail order than to store distribution. Coats of arms, birth signs, place mats, greeting cards, pens and pencils, clothes markers, name plates, book matches, mail boxes, address number signs, the numbers and kinds of personalized items are endless.

We have sold TV tube tester instructions individualized for the TV set you own. We know of birthday records with the name of your child played on the record. The computer hath wrought many personalized wonders from I.Q. tests to individualized story books with the name of your child all through the book. The percentage of personalized products that sell well via mail order is higher than other items. But the percentage of nightmares in fulfillment is higher, too. We have dropped some personalized offers as impractical *for us* to fulfill. Often, a percentage of orders *cannot* be fulfilled.

When personalization was based on stocking a variety of alternatives, we often found no way to automate the picking of items. Often, labor cost was also out of line. Frequently, too much space and too much inventory was required and some inventory loss was hard to avoid.

Go into an intriguing personalized product. . . if your "test" advertising succeeds, if you've made some sort of time studies of labor time of fulfillment, and still feel you can make money.

The typical mail order item is a demonstration item. It's an item that, seen by itself, does not convey what it can do. And packaging and ordinary display alone rarely does the job. It's a product that can do something better or has an entirely new use, but that has got to be seen *in action* to be appreciated and believed.

Without display, it often gathers dust in a retail store. But with a demonstrator, it becomes a lead item. To project *personal* demonstration *in stores nationwide* is more complex than we have up to now been capable of. But sometimes, the identical demonstration can simply be shortened, streamlined, filmed for TV and run with a mail order offer in huge and profitable volume on stations nationwide.

Sometimes, a successful demonstration can be converted into a newspaper or magazine ad. It often can be successfully done with step by step picture sequences in direct mail brochures. Sometimes, we've successfully demonstrated with an automated electrical display.

Demonstration items can be in any field. They're frequent in housewares, hardware, toys, games, hobbies, sports, and in industrial, technical and business office products and for accessories for almost anything from cars to appliances. Demonstration items run up against resistance from many of the giant retailers. Such retailers can only handle so many demonstration items. Life is simpler for many in the organizations without them. But demonstration items are the most sought after items and best opportunities for mail order people.

Seasonal items are sometimes neglected somewhat by retailers and can be a mail order opportunity.

They also can be more *dangerous* in mail order than more year round products. They require advance planning far ahead of the season. They usually require more gamble in inventory than year round products. If you test a seasonal new product and get a hit, it's often too late to get adequate supply for all you can sell that season. Therefore, it's tempting to stock up ahead of season, perhaps before your product is adequately tested. We make money with seasonal products, but find the testing and projecting frustrating.

Testing and projecting a non-seasonal item is considerably safer. There's less likelihood and less of a problem in "carrying over" unsold inventory. Go into seasonal items, but with extra caution.

Christmas items can make big profits, but can be dangerous.

Some Christmas items are hard to sell the rest of the year. Carrying them over can tie up money. If people buy a Christmas item, they want to get it in ample time to mail it themselves and have it delivered before Christmas. If advertised in December, it will arrive too late and cause angry, disappointed customers. The big holiday advertising issues are in November, either delivered to subscribers or on the newsstands.

I have known a mail order man to take as many as ten pages of

53

Christmas items at a maximum discount price in the peak gift issue of November in the one magazine he found best. Sometimes, he and his art and production man worked *all night* to prepare it. But selling cost was usually lower and profit per dollar higher for that one issue than otherwise during the year, so the effort was usually well worth it.

Often, a new item which must be explained and demonstrated is best pioneered at other times of the year. It is not yet a *demand* Christmas item. As we advertise more in our normal season, the desire for the product grows. The concept of giving it for Christmas becomes acceptable. Finally, the Christmas season can become its peak selling period.

A new item that has swept the country for the previous year or so becomes the best Christmas item of all, as, for instance, the electronic mini calculator did. Many successful mail order items can become Christmas items. Many sell poorly at Christmas.

Many successful Christmas items in stores lose money in mail order. Children's Christmas items such as toys and games and children's hobbies are bought in stores in the worst of times when the scrimping is more in adult presents. Jewelry, both for men and women, will sell far better at Christmas than otherwise. But we have been in the toy manufacturing business and found it difficult to sell most of the toys we made as mail order items. We've been in the costume jewelry manufacturing business and found most of the jewelry items difficult to sell mail order at Christmas or any other time. The items were not suited to mail order.

If you advertise a toy or game "footballed" before Christmas in the discount stores, and sold very widely at substantially lower prices than you advertise mail order, you will probably lose money with your mail order ad. You're best off with an item not sold in stores.

We rarely sell games. The old favorites are sold widely and discounted. New games are difficult to predict, "fad" items that may or may not catch on. Often, they're hard to explain as to purpose or rules. But some games seem so instantly simple and clear and yet different and unique that they may be ideal for a gift.

Executive gifts, luxury gifts and hobby gifts are often ideal. A Christmas item that is low in price, as well as strong in appeal, has maximum chance. New toys, instantly desirable when demonstrated, are perfect to sell before Christmas on TV. This was more so before the giant toy companies advertised heavily on TV. We have sold huge volumes of toys by TV before Christmas.

We avoid Christmas items for mail order that cost less than several dollars and those that cost much more than fifteen dollars. We avoid them if they seem hard to explain or demonstrate. We avoid items that might break in shipping. In jewelry, we also prefer items from $3 to $20. We seek an item that has already succeeded as a Christmas item, yet is not at all widely available.

Every year Christmas items are tested successfully-too late to project that year. It may be in a fall issue of a home magazine like House & Garden or in just one mail order catalogue. It may be in just one store catalogue like F.A.O. Schwarz or as a cooperative ad for just one specialized store like Brentano's. It may be advertised on just a few TV stations.

The test results can be invaluable information. If it's your item, keep it quiet. Your chances of a killing during next Christmas time are largely based on your secrecy during the long months in between. If you find someone that has had such success, and you can acquire the item on a sensible basis, do so. Every year, there are tiny entrepreneurs who, with their last dollars, find some Christmas success.

Such items have to be re-tested the following year before projecting. Conditions can change radically in the meantime. It may have been seen and copied at a far lower price or copied and radically improved . . . making your item obsolete. You may have been lied to about results. I'll discuss this more in our section on testing.

Chapter 6

Finding Items to Sell Items

*Keeping eyes and ears open for items as giveaways,
self liquidators and partial self liquidators*

When you find your first item, you may want to look for a giveaway, another item to give with the item that you will sell. The right giveaway can increase tremendously your item's chances of success.

The perfect giveaway, for us is an item we have just *heavily* advertised mail order and that is *related* to the items we are selling. It is *low enough in cost* so as not to significantly reduce the gross profit margin of the item we are selling. It is light enough and compact enough, preferably *flat*, to slip into the item package without significantly added postage. It will please and not disappoint. The ideal giveaway, of any type, should lend itself to demonstration. A giveaway that carries a trusted, famous brand name can extend its prestige to the product being sold. It should be instantly desirable when illustrated and require very few words of explanation. Its use should be clear and apparent. All this is not always feasible. Most items are impractical giveaways—and the wrong item can *decrease* your sales.

It can *cheapen* your advertising and lower the readers' opinion of your product. Its advantages may not be sufficiently clear. It can take precious advertising space or time away from your product that will lose more orders than it adds. A merchandise giveaway, packed with a book

56

can require a higher postage rate than the far cheaper book rate postage, and cost more in added postage than the giveaway costs itself. It can break itself, or break your product in the mail, or harm it in some other way, as for example a chemical staining your product. It can cost too much, and require more extra orders than it secures.

To find the right one and avoid the wrong one, you have to be a giveaway detective, just as you need be an item detective. You can be both at the same time. Fortunately, giveaways with just some of these desired qualifications are sometime extremely successful.

We try to combine two successful items related to each other. Sometimes, a giveaway fits a product ideally and greatly increases sales. We have sold water soluble fertilizer and plants with great success, mailing advertising of one to the just secured mail order customers of the other. When we took a successful offer of three different color roses growing on one plant and gave it free with water soluble fertilizer, we had a hit.

All over the world, sewing machine companies have given away our Perfect Fit ADJUST-O-MATIC Dress form with their sewing machine. The dress form, by making custom fit dress making possible, increases the benefits of the sewing machine. It also adds a substantial value known gift. By running a great deal of advertising for years, we have established price value as well as desirability of the form.

We often succeed with a giveaway with just some of our preferred qualifications. An unrelated item, for instance, is often great. When new automated equipment first brought ball point pens down to a small fraction of their former price, successful bargain offers, often twenty pens, 40 refills, etc., began to be made. We had recently sold close to $1,000,000 of ADDIATORS mail order, but results had just dropped badly to below the break even point. By combining a pretested offer of ball point refills with another pretested offer of ball point pens, and offering both free with an ADDIATOR, we got a new hit that did almost another $1,000,000 at good profit.

An excellent giveaway is frequently an instruction book or booklet in a related field, which can make or save many times the product's cost. Sometimes, an accessory giveaway can increase the use value of your product. Sometimes, a remnant item, preferably related, has previously sold at a substantial price and is a perfect bargain giveaway.

Instead of a giveaway, you may look for a self liquidator; an extra item that you offer at cost including mailing. You give a bigger bargain in return for the customer purchasing your item. The saving you offer is often far more dramatic than the value of a pure giveaway. When first

57

introduced, self liquidator prices were low. For years, the average self liquidator price asked, has constantly risen. Products offering self liquidators have broadened from staples to luxuries and items in between.

But now, inflation limits the choice of giveaways and self liquidators. As it has become more difficult to give dramatic savings in either, partial liquidators have come in, making it possible to go into more desirable items.

In mail order, self liquidators are widely used and very effective. Selecting a self liquidator, or partial self liquidator, has the same requirements as selecting a giveaway, but you can spend more per item. It's easier to select a mail order hit or one that's just begun to drop off, at its original higher price.

Each is only effective if it produces enough extra sales to justify itself. In each case, ability to slip it in the package containing the item can greatly lessen, or even almost eliminate, extra shipping cost and enable you to give more value to the purchaser.

Between giveaways, self liquidators and partial self liquidators, you have a wide spectrum to consider. While you look for items, keep your eyes and ears open for all these as well.

Chapter 7

Item Conclusions

Item morals. . . doing what you want. . . keeping things simple
. . . keeping up the .perpetual search

Should you copy or originate items? Some say it's as American as
apple pie to "knock-off", "copy" or "steal" an item.

Certainly, it's safer to go into an item someone else has originated
than testing something brand new yourself. We do not like others to
copy us and vigorously sue them if our product is patented, as it usually
is. We do not copy others for this reason. But it's a matter of choice and
personal belief. Of course, many products are so generic that the item
you might be considering copying can hardly be original.

There *are* drawbacks to copying. You may be "stealing" a failure.
You may be copying something that has scraped the cream and you will
get the skimmed milk. In any case, you're at best sharing the business
. . . and as the Johnny-come-lately. Generally, those who believe in
copying will copy *frequently*. They will happily accept a smaller share
of other people's successes time after time and virtually eliminate
testing loss. Those who mainly originate, may hit a far bigger jackpot
and become entrenched first for a far more permanent business, particularly important if they go on to trade distribution. So, take your choice.

A mail order business can be what *you* want it to be—far more than
any other business:

You can *select* the item or items which you care to sell—and later

59

shift into any other item or items almost at will. Mail order men who make big money, most safely, usually choose to make the simpler of two choices.

Large and bulky products require 10,000 square feet to do several hundred thousands of dollars of sales. Small, light and compact items can do several million dollars from the same 10,000 square feet.

Some items require getting inquiries and closing the sale by direct mail. Others can be closed in a one step sale. Some items are complex to make. Others are extremely easy.

My wife, and associate, asks, "Is it smelly? Is it noisy? Is it dirty?" in regard to making anything. A "yes" answer gets a "no" vote. We try to select the simpler, easier, more pleasant products that require least financing in relation to sales. And you can keep things simple, too.

The search for new mail order items never ends.

Every business and every item has a birth, life and death. But a business can have an indefinite number of item lives. Business growth is based on adding successive life span curves of new products to old. Therefore, a successful business has at all times more new growth rising curves (or a bigger single one) than the declining curves of dying products.

In mail order the birth, life and death of an item is often telescoped. Usually, the greater the intensity of the mail order campaign, the more different forms of advertising used; the bigger the advertisements, the more frequently run—the more competition is attracted and the shorter is the overall product life. That's why the more successful a mail order man is, the more keenly that he feels the necessity of having another hit in the oven, preferably several, to replace his present hit or hits as it or they inevitably, and ultimately, decline.

Every mail order man or woman gradually forms his or her own criteria as to the kind of mail order item sought after, feeling an affinity for some kinds of items, being repelled by others. The acceptable item is rare. The items rejected, almost by reflex action, are a multitude. The right item decision becomes the "sixth sense" of the mail order operator. And you will get this "feel" for mail order items too.

Next, we'll take up selling the product.

BOOK III

Mail Order Persuasion

*Developing skills in creating . . .
testing . . . buying . . . getting full value
from publication, broadcast and
direct mail advertising*

Chapter 1

The Catapult

Understanding. . . respecting. . . harnessing
advertising's power to propel you where you want to go

Advertising, effectively used, has again and again catapulted tiny mail order firms to big success.

Your success, and survival, in mail order will be greatly determined by your ability to get more effective advertising and more value from each advertising dollar, from others or yourself. In mail order, it's usually the only way to grow.

Clemenceau said war was too important to leave to the generals. And in mail order, you may feel advertising is too important to leave solely to outside advertising specialists. Many successful mail order operators feel that to leave advertising entirely to others while risking your money is playing blind man's bluff. Whether you wish to get more value from your advertising agency or become your own advertising agency, it's important to develop your own mail order advertising skills.

No advertising agency or free lance writer can be perpetually available for every creative task remotely connected with advertising. This is particularly so for a mail order moonlighter. Besides, it's a rare thrill to make people do what you want. . . by your own proposal, your words, or your demonstration.

An actor gets applause for his ego bath. A salesman feels a surging sense of personal power each time he makes that sale. But to see the actual mail of hundreds, thousands, and in time, tens of thousands or even hundreds of thousands of people who never intended to perform the action *you* caused them to take—can be a supremely rewarding power thrill.

It's a great satisfaction to be able to check thoroughly into each advertising buy before you risk your money.

Any operator of a mail order business *can* develop a "feel" for making each advertising message more effective and each advertising purchase safer. The first step is to understand the *power* of mail order advertising and the tremendous variations in effectiveness of the dollars and effort that you put into it. Yet, few do.

A salesman of a nationally advertised product realizes that the advertising is an effective help to him, but often wonders *how* effective it is, and is apt to credit product success largely to personal sales ability.

A production man may consider advertising effective, yet feel that it cannot be measured and that the real secret of sales is simply to make the product better and more efficiently. . . at lower cost. And, if unfamiliar with business or advertising, you may wonder whether advertising works at all.

My observation is that advertising is underappreciated by most small *non mail order* businesses. . . is less effectively used by them. . . and less value than possible is obtained by them for each advertising dollar spent. The cost per thousand readers of mass publications used by large advertisers is often a fraction of the cost per thousand readers of small publications used by small advertisers. Few, very small advertisers are knowledgeable in the media selection open to them and are influenced by salesmen often for the *wrong* publication for them. Even medium size advertisers rarely get the use of top advertising creative talent—and if they do, rarely get the attention and time required. Large advertisers have a near monopoly of top advertising talent employed by large advertising agencies.

Some small town radio stations are often overshadowed by big audience stations of nearby metropolitan areas. If so, they compete for a tiny share of the overall radio audience and are sometimes overpriced. Printing costs for small advertisers are often several times per thousand those for large runs used by large advertisers. A surprising percentage of advertising and promotion dollars of smaller advertisers go into kinds of advertising the largest advertisers feel they cannot afford, from ads in banquet programs to advertising novelties. Much of the advertising of smaller non-mail order advertisers is wasted, largely because it cannot

66

be measured and because the operators of smaller businesses have often, never been told some of the advertising facts of life that are commonplace to the largest advertisers.

Many, who go into mail order, expect mail order advertising to produce profitable results almost automatically. I have seen many small (and some big) mail order firms fail to get off the ground, simply because of poor use of advertising. They did not have enough knowledge of, or respect for, the potential power of each advertising dollar spent. They did not harness that power fully enough.

Often, it's simply a matter of quick and careless creating and buying of advertising. This can be true of some advertising agencies as well as of mail order firms. If a copywriter or art director has been trained to please, to ''sell'' creative work whether good or bad, to work too fast, to create too carelessly, it's hard to become a mail order perfectionist.

Advertising buys can be *sold* to the client, rather than scientifically bought for the client—justified instead of analyzed.

There are superb mail order advertising agencies and consultants. My method emphasizes the enormous contribution of these talented professionals. You may well find an able advertising associate or small agency. The reality is that, as a mail order moonlighter, you may not get such top talent interested in handling your advertising. We'll discuss it later. But, there's no reason not to be able to master mail order advertising yourself. The ad either works or it doesn't. Effective copy writers and art directors are those, who create profitable ads. Effective buyers of advertising are those, who consistently project a successful test into a bigger and more successful schedule. The results tell all. Much of the act of creating or buying advertising that makes money is the thoroughness of the effort put in. In my course, I'll try to give you the basic understanding and ''feel'' for it.

If you're in mail order, whatever your previous background may be, mastering mail order advertising can mean a great deal to you.

If you're a top advertising professional, just *improving* your creative skills can jump your income. If you're a businessman who must rely on employees, consultants or advertising agencies, acquiring your own skills can help you get far more out of your creative people, avoid mail order losses from weak advertising, and perhaps get the satisfaction of a mail order *hit* created entirely by yourself. If you are a younger executive or just starting your business career, by developing creative skills, you're gaining a highly marketable asset.

If you're a salesman, a skill in advertising copy enables you to translate your salesmanship into print or broadcast media, a far easier step than starting from scratch. And if you're an inventor or creator of the product, you're able to take all that know-how cooped up inside of you and convert it into money making advertising ability.

I was born into advertising. My father started an advertising agency, Huber Hoge, Inc., in 1920. As my brothers and I grew up, we lived advertising. . . ate it and drank it. . . and slept and woke up talking it.

Today, over five decades after my father founded Huber Hoge, Inc., of our little group of companies, we're proudest of Huber Hoge and Sons Advertising, Inc. We keep it small and we are choosy about clients.

My father, Huber Hoge, was an old timer in advertising. For years, he had been with one of the several blue chip advertising agencies of the day and had worked with some of the largest companies and highest quality products.

I remember as a child going to the Advertising Club in New York at 35th Street and Park Avenue, where he was a founder. As I grew up, I sensed from others that he was a dean of the advertising field. And later, being part of Huber Hoge and Sons was a family thrill.

At first, my older brother, John, and then I, became fascinated with mail order. As we gathered expertise at Huber Hoge and Sons, we became fortunate enough to work with the finest blue chip mail order advertisers.

We became specialists in broadcast advertising for direct response, first in radio and then TV. Later, we went heavily into magazine, newspapers and direct mail advertising for mail order.

I took no courses in advertising. Mine was on-the-job training, as yours may be too. First, I learned to analyze, select and negotiate advertising buys. Then, I learned to create advertising.

At first, I was a catalyst bringing together talented people, urging them on with encouragement, teasing them with incentives. Then, I provided them with research—more and more of it. Gradually, my experts taught me. Step by step, I began to write myself. . . first in one form of advertising, then in another. . . first, for simplest advertising and finally, most complex.

As my mail order copy stars taught me more and more, I trained younger writers with the know-how passed on to me. And as each of them developed, each taught me more. Still, today, as we develop new talent, I learn from them.

Much as we had learned working as an advertising agency for

others, our thinking about mail order advertising began to change when we began to test our own products and apply our mail order know-how to making money on our own items.

We began to spend our own money. . . make our own profits. . . and take our own losses. And quickly, we *really* began to understand advertising for direct response to a fuller potential than we ever had before.

We built the business we wanted. . . created the way of life we desired. . . and obtained it from mail order know-how.

Chapter 2

The Beginnings of Inspiration

Creating a product or company name. . . logotype
. . . instructions. . . a classified ad. . . a shopping column edit

What is it? Who are these people selling it? That's the reaction of those reading your ad.

The right name for your company can increase the number of orders you receive every time you advertise. The wrong name can decrease these orders. And the right or wrong name of your product can do the same. Yet, mail order names are sometimes selected carelessly. Mail order company names are sometimes selected with little thought. Often, the product sold seems inappropriate to the seller's name.

A name familiar for groceries may be inappropriate for sewing items. That's what General Foods thought when they started their mail order subsidiary selling fabrics to home sewers. They created a new name, FABRIZAAR. And what a name. . . a fabric bazaar. Aided by its logotype, the rich four color advertising laid out with an overflowing cornucopia effect of color fabrics instantly conveys the feeling of the widest choice of an unending variety of luxurious quality fabrics. . . an image of a bargain bazaar as well. . . and all before you read a word of the copy. And each time you just glance at the latest FABRIZAAR double page or rich "solo" mailing, the feeling is reinforced.

A logotype is an artist's rendition of your company or product name, hand lettered or in special type, often combining the name with a symbol.

If the product name is in no way indicative of the product field, it takes extra words and valuable space in your advertising just to make clear what you are selling and to identify your product name and company name with it. If you ever plan to launch your product into store distribution, this identification becomes overwhelmingly important. It's the only way for you to get the business and not a competitor.

So, let's discuss selecting names for your company, division or product. The right name can come to you in the night.

Anyone can think of it, from your five year old daughter to Grandpa. You may stumble on it by sheer accident. Any friend or passerby may give it to you. Users of the product under its old name may become so fond of it they give it a pet name—that is perfect. But we think it can best come from working on the advertising. The research alone can come up with endless name possibilities. We usually start creating advertising before we finalize the name selection. During this period, we give the product a working name for use in preliminary copy. Then out of all our research notes and all our drafts of working copy, we pick possible names.

Now we list all the names from every source that seem at all worth considering. Sometimes, we have several writers working on the project, each with his own list. Everyone in our office and factory is demonstrated the product and asked to submit a name. Sometimes, we get a blend of two names, each originally on a different list.

We own a dress form for home sewers whose name we selected this way. On one list was the name Perfect Fit. On another list, the name Adjust-O-Matic. We chose the name Perfect-Fit ADJUST-O-MATIC. And that is the way our logotype for this product name appears today.

Sometimes, the right name comes to you quickly. Sometimes, it takes a little agonizing over. . . for days and weeks. Sometimes, you later come up with so clearly superior a name, that it becomes worth changing.

When you select a company name, it better be good, because you hope to live with it a long time. And it better be appropriate for activities your business will conduct later, as well as those it conducts now.

Decades ago, companies were often content to make one product line and their company name indicated their product line. But then, gradually things would happen. General Electric bought the Hot Point Stove Company. . . making Hot Point Electric stoves. Years later, the

71

new hot item of the Hot Point division of General Electric was a refrigerator. General Electric had to spend millions of dollars to persuade people that a company famous for hot things was good at making cold things. One of our trade customers for inflatable boats is Soporific, a name chosen when the owners anticipated that their sole business would be waterbeds. Now, their big business is bicycles and that will probably change as the bicycle boom tapers off.

General Electric felt Hot Point was a trusted name and that since both products were electrical, it would be better to use the hot name for cold things. Soporific felt that their name was trusted too and kept it for bicycles or whatever. I would prefer to avoid inappropriate image associations.

Your company name (as our parent company name) may have no special connotation for a specific type of product. It may be based on your location. Ours was. Or it may be based on your family name. Ours is, partially. But the reason for name selection may change.

From the standpoint of order and simplicity, it only seems logical to have one umbrella name for all activities. But, the variety of products we sell is sufficiently odd so that it seems inappropriate to advertise wildly different products under the same company name. So, gradually over the years, we tend to create divisions with names appropriate to one product line.

My advice is to try to think ahead of the possible future contingencies that may occur before you finalize your product name. I would recommend a product name that clearly indicates what you sell, and if possible, even indicates competitive superiorities. I would recommend that you not select your company name on geographical location or your family name. If you keep getting partners, you may end up sounding like a law firm.

Later, we'll discuss procedures for clearing the name.

A logotype is an artist's rendition of your company or product name, handlettered or in a special type, often combining the name with a symbol.

A trademark is a U.S. registered name and logotype. The first creative step for your copywriter or writers (or yourself) is to come up with the name you want to live with. The first creative step for your art director (or artist) is to come up with the perfect logotype for your product and company. It is the clothes your company and product name wear. Your logotype will largely determine the effect your business card, stationery, billhead, packaging, and name of product or company in any form of advertising or even trade show booth, will create. A major company will spend thousands of dollars simply to develop the perfect logotype.

We can't. We're too small with too many products. And possibly, you can't either. But we can try our very utmost to get the most effective logotype our widow's mite will buy. Today is a time of innovative and imaginative company names. . . from the smallest retail shop. . . and tiniest mail order firm. Their very names and logotypes call forth images of uniqueness, flair and style, and enhanced desirability. In mail order, it simply means more orders from every ad, even acceptance of a higher price as reasonable.

So, suffer a little as you change that name and as you pay the art bill for your logotype. And even then, don't hesitate to change the name and logotype later if your changing situation warrants it.

After selecting a name for product and company, your next job may be to write "idiot proof" instructions.

Most mail order items are shipped disassembled. Many are do-it-yourself kits. And customers who can't put your item together will return it to you, particularly if it's not cheap. . . and sometimes not pay you at all if you sell on credit. Instructions that are simplest and easiest to follow are often the hardest to write.

Inventors are in love with their product, find it ridiculously easy to put together for anyone and feel it requires scarcely any instruction at all. Scientists have their own language incomprehensible to us mortals. Salesmen are optimistically vague in instructions they write. Translated instructions are ideal material for TV comics. And writing instructions, if you've never done it before, is enough to drive you out of the business.

It takes a cool head and a disciplined mind to attack the problem. It requires guinea pigs you're not related to and don't know, who've never used the product before, to read your instructions, look at your instruction diagrams and pictures, and actually put the thing together.

If you go about writing directions in a thorough, organized way it will be done correctly and save time, work and money in the end. You cut returns, eliminate correspondence with confused customers and save the work of having to re-write a careless first attempt.

Let's assume that you have your product and find that you can ship it knocked down with a saving in labor and in postage, but that you have no instructions for the user to put it together. Let's get started.

Find someone who has never seen the product, but who is a logical potential user. Get the product inventor, owner or other, proper person (perhaps yourself), to demonstrate to him or her how to put the product together. . . from opening the package to final assembly. . . and how to use it.

Bring a tape recorder to the demonstration. Have someone use a camera to take one picture after another of each phase of the demonstration. Include close ups of important hand and arm movements, an exploded picture of all parts side by side on a table or on the floor, closeups of picking up of parts and connecting one part to another step by step to completion, and with any product use pictures.

Make sure that the specific name of each component part is given by the demonstrator. Check that the demonstration is clear to the prospective user. Tape the demonstration and the user's questions and demonstrator's answers. Ask the user to open another package, assemble and use it, with the demonstrator watching. If the user makes errors, have the demonstrator explain and correct them. Tape this as well. Take more pictures.

Transcribe the tapes on the typewriter. Step-by-step, write and type a description of each visual action as seen in the demonstration, but not heard on the tape. Arrange the pictures into a sequence of steps in the order as demonstrated. Pick the best picture to demonstrate each step.

Paste a big sheet of paper down on a big drawing board. Place each selected picture in proper sequence in a column on the far right of the sheet. Start with the exploded parts picture and end with a picture of the completed article. Scissor out appropriate demonstration words taken off the tape. Paste them down to the left of each matching picture. Start with the naming of each component part opposite the exploded parts picture. Give yourself ample room on the sheet for pictures and description of each step. Scissor out the appropriate descriptive words of the visual demonstration and paste them opposite the matching picture and underneath the demonstration words. Use several pages if necessary.

Read and re-read. Begin to edit into instruction form. Try different breakdowns into step sequence. Reduce the number of pictures. Select the best to illustrate each step. In editing, make each step crystal clear as to what you are asking the user to do. Specify the use of left or right hand, thumb, index or whatever finger. Give each instruction in exact detail. Make sure that the name used for each component is as simple and self-explanatory as possible. If not, rename it—hopefully improving it. Always, refer to any one part with the same name and not an alternate name. Keep all words simple. Try to write to about a sixth grade level. Keep re-editing. Cut or expand copy as needed for each step. Sharpen. . . simplify. . . and clarify, until satisfied. Excerpt words and phrases that can be used as captions underneath or with arrows to important parts of pictures.

If you now feel that instructions and pictures are completely understandable to anyone who has never seen the product before, photocopy six sets. Find six logical prospective users, each of whom have never seen the product. Give each a package of your product with your instructions inside the package. Ask each to assemble and use the product. Watch each attempt to do so. If misunderstandings of instructions occur, get help from your demonstrator. Re-edit and try out your instructions on more virgin users.

If the directions are proven, photo-offset enough copies for your first test. Don't worry about lack of professional finish. Do worry about clarity. Clear instructions reduce returns. More professionally finished package inserts pull more re-orders, but can come later. Your problem initially is understanding—not prestige.

Once your ad is successful, you can consider more professional photographs, drawings, diagrams, typography and higher grade paper. Only spend money to upgrade the effect as more volume justifies. You are very unlikely to have extra refund requests from photo-offset typewritten instructions with simple photographs, except for quite luxurious products. If so, you may consider working with your art director from the start, but your initial costs will be far higher. I recommend waiting in either case, until the ad pays out.

Only big volume of shipments justifies the added investment. If so, consider with your art director whether drawings will be superior to photographs and whether one or more diagrams can help clarify. Your art director can sketch out appropriate diagrams and equivalent drawings for each picture and undoubtedly greatly improve the styling with his layout. Each added professional touch improves and costs more money. Your situation will determine your decision. You can compromise and upgrade as you reprint, a little at a time.

And even after your labor (it's happened to us after seven executives successively refined and improved one set of instructions) you'll be told that you've got a great product, if anybody could be told how to use it. But, patience. Instructions can and must be written and illustrated in a simple, understandable way.

How would you like to write a simple, classified ad? Just reading classified ads can be quite an education. And writing classified ads and testing them can be a cheap and sound introduction to effective advertising.

Each classified ad that may only cost a few dollars, by either succeeding or failing, is *teaching* and at pretty low cost. Even in national magazines, the cost of one classified ad is very low. It takes a longer than average ad, in a two million circulation magazine like Outdoor Life, to cost $60 to $70. And one such ad has often started a profitable business that has lasted for a lifetime.

Look at your Sunday newspaper. Read help wanted and situation wanted ads. Read real estate ads for sale and rental of apartments, offices, factories, houses, land. Note that in these classifications there's a market place. Buyers are *seeking* sellers and vice versa. *Attention-getting* devices are less important than how desirable and believable the ad makes the real estate. In times of few apartment vacancies, just the fact that *any* apartment is available that has anywhere near the qualifications you seek is *news*. In such times, the ads tend to be tiny, often the minimum of two lines, or whatever required. Because one ad, in one paper, one day, will usually rent the apartment, *frugality* is important. Why take three lines to rent an apartment, when two lines would do just as well?

Perhaps, only ten to twelve words are allowed. The phone number is usually counted as two words. This leaves 10 or 8 words. The answer, in such cases, is abbreviation. The apartment seekers have to work at it; soon they can guess, fairly accurately, what the ad is trying to say. The copy need only be factual and understandable. Clarity is important.

Now, let's assume that you own a house, but have just been given a new job in another part of the country. Mortgages are hard to get and expensive. Real estate taxes are going up in your area. Houses are not moving. You must sell, or at least rent your home *quickly* or you'll be saddled with the *double* expense of *two* homes.

The right ad may get you a handsome profit. The wrong ad, or even just an average one, may cause a capital loss. You've dressed up your home in its Sunday best, touched it up with a little painting, cleaned it top to bottom and manicured the grounds with a little raking, weeding and planting. It looks better than it has in years.

Research the *advantages* of your house and grounds. Recognize its *disadvantages* to help you in realistic pricing. Brokers will tell you what equivalent houses, with equivalent acreage and grounds, in equivalent areas, are now actually getting. Pick the broker who, more than any other in your area, is identified with sale or rent of the nicest properties of your type. Run an ad under his or her name, advertising your property. The broker's suggested copy may be better, but *write* yours first. *You* have most at stake. Study the broker's ads for other desirable properties. Ask which one pulled most inquiries serious enough to

76

produce a sale, *despite* the market.

This ad can be your model.

Follow its style Substitute your property's strong points for the strong points advertised. Note the adjectives. Come up with your own which honestly describes the best features of your home. As you write, you'll think of more points. Your ad will become longer. Keep writing. Let it grow. Let your headline grow out of your most effective selling point. Compare your headline to that of your model. Try alternative headlines.

If your price is a bargain, feature it. If not, make them read your ad, and hopefully, become interested. Give the price near the end. If above market, but worth it, say why. Leaving the price out will draw many more inquiries, and probably most will be unable to pay your price. If time is urgent, it's best to include price.

Study the way your model ad is organized and spaced, how long each sentence and each paragraph is. Note the amount of white space in margins, above and below the ad copy ad between paragraphs. Set up yours accordingly. End with the name of the broker and his address and phone number.

Start to cut your copy; not paragraphs or sentences, but single words. Consider abbreviations, but *carefully*. As you cut, if you think of more good selling points, put them in. As you cut; copy, phrases and sentences can become jerky and harder to read. Revise words, so the ad reads smoothly. It's work, but it's worth it. Now, read the ad from beginning to end. Is it confusing? Are some points in the wrong order? Do some adjectives seem too flowery or even inappropriate?

Change the order, correct, delete or add adjectives. Keep working on it. Remember, every word must *work*. Cut out the *lazy* words. Put in warm words in place of cold ones, live words in place of dead ones. Put the love you have for each part of the house, and each advantage, into the ad. Think of its special advantages for a special situation. . . as a doctor's house. . . for a family with very young children. . . for one that loves gardening. . . or swimming or whatever. Try to bring out advantages so vividly, that your house becomes appetizing, even in a dead market. Show it to your wife, husband, best friend, someone who's practical and realistic. Find out if you've left something important out, made inaccurate statements, oversold or undersold your property in some way. The advice may be good or bad. Make up your own mind and act accordingly. Now look at your real estate broker's ad. Your broker's ad may be better because real estate is the broker's business. But your ad may be better, because you know your house better, have more at stake, and have put more time and work into the ad. Very likely, each will have some strong points. If so, now take stronger points and better adjectives from your broker's ad and revise your own accordingly—or if your broker's ad is better, vice versa.

Rewrite the ad in the first person, as if you were the broker and had just discovered an unusual value was on the market and were reporting it to your clientele looking for a house. The effect can be *news*. . . of something of more than average desirability and highly recommended by someone who is an authority. Now, cut your revised ad one more time. If you're happy with it, run it—and good luck. If it doesn't pull, you better consider reducing your price.

This is not a course on real estate. You may be better off selling without a broker. I have suggested running under the broker's name to get the added recommendation power into the ad.

Why put so much time and effort into such a simple task as writing a tiny classified ad? What I am asking you to do will take you a matter of hours for a day or two. It costs you not one cent more to do it. It can make you thousands of dollars. Do you know of a faster, easier way to make so much?

Writing another kind of clasified ad is a similar problem.

If you need to hire someone when jobs are short and the job you offer is desired, it's the same as renting a scarce apartment. Your ad can be short. You can abbreviate freely. If the labor market is tight and your job is harder to fill, work harder on the copy. It can be a little longer.

Assume that you own a school which trains beginners to work with a mini-computer, file and work with micro-film, work with a computerized typewriter or master another new automated office skill. Your ad is listed under "instruction." A subheading states the kind of courses you teach.

You can't increase the number of people reading the section. They are only some of those reading the paper. You're getting people looking for instruction. Readers are unfamiliar with your field and may be considering instruction in another field. They may never even read your ad unless attracted to it. You must explain the opportunities which your course opens up, as well as what it is.

You have to find out the present employer market for graduates with these skills. . . if employers expect to need such employees soon. . . what employers pay or expect to pay for such skills. . . and whether they prefer to train present employees or hire already trained employees.

Your research may come from employees, manufacturers of the

new equipment, employment agencies, those newly employed in such fields or your own experience.

Keep your eyes and ears open for necessary facts. There may be news on any of the very fields which you are teaching in your Sunday paper, on TV, in the latest issue of the leading trade magazine in the field, on radio, in the Wall Street Journal or whatever.

You should only be in business if your research has shown a real need at attractive pay for those you train. Be sure that your facts are accurate before you use them in copy. If so, you need to tell this story in your ad. Sell the results of taking your course as well as the course. It's news to most people. Be the reporter gathering the facts and the editor selecting the most important to feature.

You're selling the hope of earning more. . . of being a desired employee. . . of bypassing far more senior employees. . . of being relied on, perhaps, by a boss who doesn't fully understand the new equipment himself. You may be selling the chance of a higher status job. . . of a more glamorous job. . . of working more with the boss. . . of joining an exciting company and meeting more interesting people. . . of traveling to exotic places.

You rarely need some unusual attention getting device. You attract by dramatizing in your headline and subhead the news of exciting opportunities in the field. Follow with one or more lines specifying the new kinds of jobs open at what pay. Capsule your description of your instruction. Ask for action featuring phone, address and name. Model your ad after a successful ad for other kinds of courses. Keep editing, modifying and improving, until convinced you've got your story across. Work and rework every word of your ad, as suggested for selling a house.

I'm asking you to work this hard on such a little ad because it can launch your business. You're competing with other education ads. I want yours to be the best and *you* to win. You want to have the *best* school and the *best* ad. If it works, you can run it more times, in more papers, perhaps for some time. . . with no more effort. Good luck!

The sheer number of tiny and unusual businesses, and their variety, whose products are sold through small classified ads, never ceases to amaze me.

Just looking through the classified sections of Grit, National Enquirer, The Village Voice or any underground paper is an eye opener. Sometimes, the classified ad asks for money, usually only several dollars. More often, it asks for an inquiry to which literature or a specialized catalogue is mailed. Often, the specific items are extremely specialized, such as live night crawler worms offered in the classified columns of the outdoor magazines.

In Grit, some of the same classified ads have run continuously and presumably successfully for decades. In each magazine carrying a substantial mail order classified section, the variety of unusual businesses and items creates readership. People read the section because they are intrigued by the unexpected. Each little ad is a different news dispatch. Few of them can attract attention as effectively with any device as they can with the very uniqueness of the item and the business. The art of attracting attention is based on capsuling the uniqueness in the headline and provocatively describing it in the opening line or so.

These sections are marketplaces of the unusual. Trying to make an ordinary product or service appear unusual will rarely work. Your job as a writer is to be a reporter of the unusual. Your first task is to find it. The first step in writing a provocative classified ad is often to start a provocative mail order business. The more specialized the magazine is, the more specialized is its mail order classified marketplace. The shortest ads usually pull inquiries. The ones that ask for actual orders are only a little longer. The longest running ads are often the shortest. The shortest ads get about the same readership as longer ones.

Capsule your story. Make it as short as possible. Keep your headline to one, two or three provocative words. Often simply capitalizing the first word or so is the headline. Boil down your name and address to a one or two word name, town, state initials and zip code. Between headline and address, use the least number of words, perhaps seven to twelve, to tell your story. Pick them carefully and edit them painfully. Model your ad after the other longest running ads. Try it and good luck.

Your next aggravating job may be to write a publicity release for one of your items to send in to shopping columns of magazines.

At your library, look through the shopping columns of House Beautiful, House and Garden, Mademoiselle, Glamour, Woman's Day or whichever magazines you wish to send your release to. Read carefully each editorial write-up of each magazine you look at. Shopping column editors are human. The easier you make it for them, the better your chances. Write your release to the exact size of the average write-up.

Most shopping columns have nine lines. Each line should be no more than forty characters. A capital letter is counted as a character and a half. A space between words is counted as a character. Write one on your own product. If you already have a longer ad, painstaking cutting will usually produce a better write-up than starting from scratch. Don't take a section or paragraphs from a longer ad. Take the headline, main subhead, small subheads, key words in the copy story and close and put them in proper sequence with proper connecting words. It's probably still long. Cut and rework until satisfied.

If you have no longer ad, model your write-up after an actual shopping column edit. Research your product enough to fill in equivalent facts. Work on colorful words. Make your opening words, in caps, provocative. More than a word or two in caps will eat up characters. Creating a write-up is great training to write mail order copy for an actual ad.

Rewrite it until you feel it's perfect. It costs you only time to labor over the writing and each improvement may bring more orders. Now, study the photographs or pictures used with each write up. You can even take your own picture of your product, if you can't afford a commercial photographer. Or try to talk the most superb, amateur photographer friend you have into taking it as a favor. When you get it developed, get an artist friend to retouch it and crop it. Your object is to make that picture jump right off the page and, like a magnet, draw eyes to your write up.

How effectively you write and illustrate your shopping column write-up may help it become accepted and greatly determine how many orders it pulls.

If you start without money, a free write-up can create your first capital without risk. If you buy a test ad and get a free write-up, how effectively you create it can determine whether you make a profit or loss from your ad risk. And it's perfect training for writing a display ad for a shopping column section.

But before we discuss writing any display ads, let's go into the research that can make any display ad, broadcast commercial or direct mail piece far easier to write, and more effective.

Chapter 3

90% Perspiration

Research. . . asking. . . reading. . . digging. . . pulling nails. . .
the extra question that created a million dollar business

"Did you ever see a robin step up behind another robin. . . and kick its legs from underneath it?"

This opening line of a radio commercial helped the commercial sell thousands of Audubon bird books. This line was not in the Audubon bird book. One of our greatest young copywriters (long since one of our most prolific alumni) found it while doing research on birds in the public library. The Audubon bird book was, of course, primarily a bird recognition book. But presumably, a reader of the book, who became a bird watcher, might well see any such phenomena.

If you are buying a product simply for a catalogue, or some special mail order sales purpose in limited volume, a great deal of such research is not necessary. But if you plan to create and build a business on the product, if you're out to create a "solo" piece in direct mail or a page ad or a TV commercial or program, then it is worth it. If you have an exclusive, are a sole rights importer, or make or plan to make it yourself, this research is even more necessary. It may avoid or win a future law suit. It may cause you to go into the product far more cautiously—or drop it entirely. It may uncover a possibly dangerous association. It may correct a label error, or revise wholly inadequate instructions.

82

We like to think that while other companies may have greater resources, far bigger staffs and many advantages over us, we will always be determined to *dig* a little deeper than others in researching any product, service or field. Because, all it takes is time and work. And we know that no copy can do a product justice until adequate research is done. Respect for any product *demands* research. I'm not talking about elaborate research by huge agencies and top research companies. For our small business, we cannot afford the cost of such research. But we can go to the library. We can phone for days or weeks to get research answers.

I've often taken over a hundred pages of notes, to help write *one ad*. When I'm finished, I feel like blotting paper, but writing for me has been a difficult acquired art that I actually learned from my own top writers. I learned research from them also. I have long, secretly felt it was my only strength I could count on over other writers. I could *outwork* them in research...and you can too.

It not only pays off in far better copy, but the best ideas I've gotten have come from research on something else. Research has many by-product advantages. It gives us *new* products, entirely fresh approaches to products we were not researching for, and forever unexpected insights that have helped build our business.

If you never wrote a word of advertising in your life, research may open the door. If you've written copy for years, with little or no research, the first research you really work at can open your eyes to what it can do for your copy. Sometimes, you will find all the research material you need already done. Sometimes, you will get it very quickly from one of several sources. It may not be at all as time consuming or as tedious as what I'm about to describe. But let's discuss how we go about it.

The first source of research on a product is the man you got the product from. Perhaps you bought a company that made it. Perhaps you took over a product from a manufacturer and are having it made elsewhere or making it yourself. Perhaps you are importing it. Perhaps you're taking it over from an inventor who has been making it in his garage. In each case, there should be a good deal of information just waiting for you. And it could be invaluable in the preparation of any mail order advertising.

Some people who make a product are quite inarticulate about it and give you very little information. Others give you *misinformation*, inaccurate, vague or deliberately misleading, or even untrue information. Many times, at a European or American trade show, I've talked to the owners of an item and have been told that the item is patented, unique and unlike any other. . . only to walk down the next aisle and see *a duplicate* competitive item. But there are many product owners who *can* give you *exactly* what you need. An inventor who has struggled for years to develop a product usually has a considerable story to tell about it. A salesman, particularly a salesman demonstrator, or salesman instructor, may have gradually created or perfected a very detailed presentation on the product.

Often, those who have information have no idea which of it can be useful to you. Getting necessary information from those who know can be like pulling nails. It starts with determining what you're trying to find out.

Research is too important for skimming through. Research *before* you take over an item can quickly warn you of drawbacks or competition that simply make it undesirable for you to take it on. Without *thorough* research, there's little chance of effective mail order advertising.

We usually make up a detailed questionnaire before we talk to anyone. Question by question, we take notes of the answers. Many answers seem to lead to nothing, but suddenly a breakthrough clue may come up. Often, years after you have a product, research can pull out new facts you never were aware of and open the door to a completely fresh and entirely different advertising approach.

We start by asking what reason is there for the product to exist at all? What are its competitors? In what way or ways is it any better than competitive products? Is it *faster. . . cheaper. . . longer lasting. . . lighter. . . stronger?* What is it made of? How does this compare with competitors? Why does it use each material it consists of? Is there anything unique, or patented, or exclusive about each material? What about component parts? How does each differ from the equivalent part in a competitive product? If the product is unique and has no competition, how was the same function performed before?

And how much faster is the function performed with the new product than before? Does it save trouble over the old way? If so, how? Is it safer? Is it easier? Does it require any *skill* to use? If so, how long does it take an average person to use it? Is it easier to use than the competition? What is the history of the product? What was the reason to invent it? Was there a problem that bothered or upset the inventor and caused him to develop it? What is the history of the field? Which is the biggest competitor? What is the history of this company?

What do users say about the product? How do they compare it with others? Can they save money using it? Can they use it in any way to *make* money? Is it a convenience? Is it decorative? Is it fun to use? Is using it good therapy for worries or problems? Is it practical for children? Is it safe for them? Is it easy to put together? How long does it take to do so? Has it won any awards? How long does it *last* before wearing out? How does this compare with competitors? How many colors and sizes does it have in comparison with competition? Is it adjustable, and if so, more or less than competition?

What testimonials exist for the product? What publicity is there on it? Are there any shopping column write ups, any major stories, and if so, are photo copies available? Has it been featured on TV or radio shows, and if so, are there tapes available? Is it patented? If so, can we have a photo copy of the patent? Or do they object to our writing Washington or abroad for a photo copy?

What documentation is there for any product claims? Have time study tests been made comparing the product in use with competition? Has any university, hospital or government authority tested it? If so, are the results available? Were there any unusual obstacles in inventing, developing or perfecting the product? If so, how were they overcome?

Once, while doing this sort of research for a fish lure, I pieced together an interesting story from the exporter and inventor.

The inventor was a science teacher, a skin diver, and an avid fisherman. He would go under the surface near an area fishermen were casting in. He would observe, underwater, exactly what happened to each lure and natural bait underwater and how fish reacted to it. Then, he would come out of the water and make research notes. From his research, he determined that minnows were the most effective in getting strikes once the fish came near. In lengthy letters in French to me, he told how he sculptured a rubber minnow out of a piece of an old tire and gave me much detail on its effectiveness. We have sold over two million of these lures and told the story countless times in mail order advertising. We have long since purchased the world rights and now manufacture it here.

More research provided the way to get store distribution. The previous importer, whose business we later purchased, had failed with this particular lure before we succeeded with it. But often, a failure has within it the seeds of success, if dogged research can dig it out. I asked the previous importer whether the firm had ever successfully sold the lure by mail. The answer was no. Had it been successfully sold by a catalogue customer? The answer was still no. Had a retailer ever run an ad successfully for it? Another no. I went on and on with still more

85

no's. Finally, I asked whether an unusual display had ever been used successfully. The answer was yes. A store had put in a transparent tank (powered by an electric motor) with the lure pulled through the water demonstrating its action. The store sold over 150 lures in a week. And then what happened? Nothing! The former importer took back the display. Did you ever use it again? No! Where was the display now? In their cellar. Could we borrow it? Why, of course!

Within two weeks, we took space in a public outdoor show and did over $1800 in a week with the original display, which had cost $150. Within months, we were duplicating the expensive glass tank and motor with a plastic tank and simple motor for $25 and doing business in key retailers. Within a year, we were making a much smaller, even simpler tank and motor, assembling it ourselves, by the thousands, and selling lures all over America as though there were no tomorrow.

Yet, it all came from asking that one last extra research question.

Research, effectively done, can help us assist our advertising agency, freelance copywriter or ourselves, to write far more effective advertising. Research can be the majority of the creative work. It can vastly speed the entire process of *learning* how to write effective advertising. Selecting research facts. . . assembling them, classifying them, rearranging them, and editing them ... goes a long way to getting ads to write themselves.

Naturally, we seek and collect every piece of previous advertising, every booklet, every transcribed radio or TV commercial, every sales letter, all instructions. . . anything we can get.

If we're dealing with an importer, we try to get all material in English, but ask for photo copies of any other advertising or publicity in the original language. We get on the phone, or visit personally, and talk to distributors, wholesalers, dealers and salesmen and ask each question on our questionnaire. Often, answers contradict one another. And if so, we dig until we come to our own conclusions as to just what the correct answer is. The best research of this kind is talking to the actual consumer-user.

An actual user, who likes the product, may have used it in ways never even contemplated by the inventor and found that it's perfect for the purpose. Just why a user likes a product can provide selling points the copywriter might never think of.

Call each trade paper in the field the product is in. You can do it discreetly, not even mentioning your own product. Get the name of each competitor and any information on each the trade paper can pass along. Get copies of past articles on the field and previous companies in it. If a giant company does a big business in the field, check Fortune, Forbes, Business Week and the Wall Street Journal. Find out if major stories have appeared on the product, field or any product or company in it, and get a photo copy of the stories. Go to trade shows and retailers. Get a copy of every piece of advertising and promotional literature and all instructions for assembly and use of any competitive product.

My father studied industries this way, one at a time. He built an ever growing file on each individual major competitor, kept it up and added to it for years, until finally he knew more about individual products than many executives in the company making them. He got advertising accounts by *knowing the product* far more thoroughly than most of his most inspired competitors.

Make a list of libraries that may have material that can help you. The trade association should have a good one and perhaps, one or more of the trade papers. A big city public main library and its more specialized business or industrial branch will head your list. If a hobby or sport, magazines on the subject should be followed up. Check if each has a library that may have something on the subject. The public library periodical department may have many years of every copy of virtually all such publications. If you feel unsure of yourself in library research, just explain your problem to the librarian and get suggestions on how to look up books on your subject. Before starting, check the *general* reference works usually out on the shelves.

Start with the Encyclopedia Britannica. The latest edition is divided into the Macromedia, longer articles on subjects of great interest, and Micromedia, short summary articles on other items. Each article lists sources. A Macromedia extensive article on jewelry will quote many sources on the History of Jewelry, Jewelry in Mythology, Jewelry Making, etc. The articles are well written and can be photocopied for you by the library. The sources quoted are the best. Look for *specialized* encyclopedias closer to your subject. Big libraries have many of them. And one of them is almost certain to provide more information and more sources for you.

The libraries will keep you busy for a while.

Now, begin work on your notes. If you're like me, you'll now have a lot of them, disconnected, repetitive and duplicating. The notes are therefore rather useless until you arrange them in order. I usually get a number of yellow legal size pads. I take about six or so pads to rearrange my notes. Each pad I give a heading to. On one I mark at the top of the first page ''Product Premise''. Another I mark ''Development

Story". Another I mark "Ease and Speed'. Another I mark "Other Specific Product Advantages." One I mark "General Advantages"; another "Miscellaneous" and so forth.

Now, I get the same number of manila folders. With scissors, I cut each page of my original notes into clippings logical for each of these headings. There should be no clippings left on each page after distributing. I clip together all clippings on one subject and put them into a manila folder. I copy all my notes from each of my folders on to one pad. I still have disconnected notes, but under the proper heading. I rewrite my notes on each pad atempting to give the revise a logical beginning, middle and end. The first effort is an improvement, but still quite disconnected. I see obvious duplications and red pencil them out. Each time I revise the pad of notes, it has more lucidity and continuity. I develop my original phrases into sentences. It's hard, tedious, headache work. But as I work, I'm becoming saturated with the subject.

Originally, I set up this method of research to aid my copywriters. They were expensive when on my payroll regularly. Free lancers were of little use because they had no time to learn our product or business. But given enough effective research, a top writer became a bargain and a free lancer far more practical to use. Having difficulty getting others to research so intensively, I started doing it myself. Effective research can be 80 percent to 90 percent of the time, effort and capability of creating great mail order advertising.

I would summarize my research in a lengthy memorandum of ten to twenty pages. This meant combining my product premise notes, which gave the main justification for the product, with the development story, the advantages and any documentation and testimonials.

To aid my writers, I tried to do this in an orderly way with first things first. I tried to keep the memorandum from rambling too much and kept cutting and simplifying it. Then, I made a discovery.

It was not a big step to write entire ads myself. *I* began to master the writing of mail order direct mail, magazine and newspaper advertising as I never had before. I had always written complete radio and TV commercials and programs, but now found that my research greatly improved this ability as well.

You can do the same. Simply research your product as I have described and take your notes. This may seem tedious, but it's surprising how much easier it makes everything else.

Should a mail order moonlighter run his first advertising in direct mail, on radio, in newspapers, on TV or in magazines?

Most mail order moonlighters start in magazine or newspapers.

What you begin with will depend on your product and situation. You will be able to see more for yourself as we take up the characteristics, advantages and disadvantages of different kinds of advertising.

Whatever form of advertising you start with, you can try other forms later as well. Sometimes, if you fail in one form, you will still succeed in advertising in another. Let's examine some different approaches in advertising and some differences between mail order and other advertising. Then, we'll take up creating each leading form of advertising.

Chapter 4

Emotion in Persuasion

Why they buy. . . psychology in salesmanship
. . . different environments for mail order advertising

What *persuades* people?

What causes sweeping popularity of anything? What causes mail orders to pour in for the wildly desired item of the moment?

We don't know. Far from having power over people, the mail order man's only chance is to find out what people really want at the moment. . . give it to them. . . and stay away from all else.

Whatever persuades a percentage of people to do something when an advertising test is run, usually persuades roughly the same percentage of people to do it when the same advertising is exposed to other similar groups. This will happen surprisingly regularly—in different areas, even in different countries. It will happen for a period of time and then stop as inexplicably as it started.

The mail order man can no more force his prospective customers to buy, than King Canute could command the waves. The mail order man can only observe the tide and go with it. Mail order persuasion can only take place when conditions are right.

We have learned a little about what makes it a bit easier to persuade. Let's go into it. As you glance through the next few pages, don't get too concerned if it seems at all complex. The background will be useful to you in applying the quite simple mail order copywriting method we will then take up.

Often, emotion makes people buy. They then seek a logical excuse for buying, for spouse and self. Advertising gives a one-two punch. . . emotion to cause desire. . . and rationalization to provide the excuse.

We think we act logically, and try to, but our actions are often caused by instincts and compulsions we are unaware of. Elections are won, and soap sold, by appeals to emotion. Let's consider emotion as used in selling. But when we use it, let's be fair. There is a line that integrity dare not cross.

Sex in advertising helps sell anything. In advertising, sex pulls, but can corrupt your children. Use it with care. Love is still sex, but less raw. Everyone wants affection and warmth. Arthur Murray sold dancing as a key to popularity with enormous success.

We all want to survive, but some of us are more worried about it than others. Appeal to survival sells super locks, insurance, atomic shelters, a year's supply of frozen food, anti-ideologies, the manly art of self defense, guns, automatic switch-on lights when you're not home and Adolph Hitler. Appeal to the survival drive can sell relatively harmlessly or be emotional dynamite. Handle with care.

The sweetest music ever heard is the sound of your own name. Anyone unappreciated suffers inside. We all need praise, a pat on the back and a build up. "With these pieces of ribbon I'll build an empire," said Napoleon (according to legend) as he founded the Legion of Honor. Entire industries are based on building other people's ego. Every salesman knows that ego building helps sales. And much advertising gets in on the good work too.

Power! People want it. The need for power has helped catapult the automobile industry to its present size. Every driver is a knight in armor. Big cars give a heady sense of power. The word POWER sells when used from POWER STEERING to POWER LEARNING. The most humble member of any aggressor nation feels a shared sense of aggressive power—another form of dirty emotional pool. If you appeal to the drive for power, take it easy.

Appeals to retain youth and health, gain longevity and immortality are part of the urge to survive. People never stop seeking some new way to stay young, look younger, get and keep health and live longer. In this irreligious age, they seek a religion. . .new or old. . . that promises immortality. Cosmetics, tonics, inspirational books and endless products offer help. Before you do, remember that these are the greatest fields of quackery.

Rationalizing emotional appeals in advertising has gone a bit far.

Men are offered feminizing cosmetics under wild animal names in commercials delivered by famous athletes, so that a man can feel masculine as he goes feminine. Women are offered prepared warm-up drop-in-the-pan food with one or two tiny steps still left for the house-wife so that a woman can still feel creative in the kitchen. People want to feel that longed for luxuries are necessities, catering to themselves is sacrificing for others, and the new easier way is pioneering the old hard way. They often respond to advertising accordingly. Anyone who sells and advertises can corrupt or improve readers, listeners or viewers making them a little worse or even a little better. Be kind to them.

A cow is calm and placid and not very creative.

As we rise above our animal origins, we become a bit more neurotic and more subject to psychological manipulation. Fear. . . anxiety. . . suspicion. . . envy. . . greed. . . desire. . . keep working on us. We seek escape, flight, to run away. We desperately need companionship, stability, roots, our safer yesterday and the nostalgia of old remembered times. We long for the familiar and become frightened of the new. We're troubled by too much change, too fast. We don't want to be left out. We want reassurance that all's right with our world. No wonder advertising, like Pavlov's bell, seems to be able to make the consumer dog froth at the mouth, hungrily expecting the food he longs for. But, as explained, this is only partially so.

Psychologists say that very little veneer covers primitive reactions in man or woman today. Each product, service and institution can become a symbol, sending a message to our subconscious antenna. . . attracting us or driving us away, appealing to some inner urge, and flashing "stop" or "go" to instincts and emotions or long buried fears or desires.

Fortunately, mail order advertising is not just a push button human reaction machine constantly working on emotions, as does advertising for some nationally store distributed products.

Mail order advertising is simpler, more straight forward and less devious than much non-mail order advertising I have seen or heard.

For one reason, there is usually a good deal of news in a mail order ad. It is announcing something, telling a story of change and improve-ment. Often, the mail order ad is for a new product with new advantages performing a unique new function. Mail order products that are dupli-cates of widely distributed and advertised trade products often do not succeed. Those mail order products that do succeed, often have product differences that are more real and less trivial than many distribution products.

Mobil Oil and Texaco are quite similar, as are endless numbers of advertised trade distributed products. Coca Cola is great, but hardly news. To tell the Coca Cola product story in depth would drive away readers, listeners and viewers. Going for the psychological soft underbelly is particularly tempting for the product that no longer has news value.

There can be plenty of psychology in mail order advertising. But the main thrust is usually news, fundamental and factual, about the product itself, along with persuasive demonstration and instruction. A lot of the effectiveness of a mail order ad is your proposal. . . your guarantee. . . your request and incentive for immediate action. . . and above all, your credibility.

One of the earliest books on advertising divided all products into three stages: the pioneering; the competitive; and the retentive.

This is still true of mail order products, as well as those sold in any other way. The advertising for the mail order pioneer is most similar to the pioneer distribution product. Mail order can be the best way to pioneer a product for later store distribution success. The mail order competitive product varies more from its store distribution brother, and the mail order product in the retentive stage varies most of all.

The pioneer product is a *different* product, whose very use and satisfactions are unknown to most people. Yogurt, wet suits, photo copy machines, and any new dance, game or hobby started in the pioneer stage. Advertising tells the entire story of the desirability of the *activity*, as well as the product itself. Advertising a competitive stage product is usually a race to feature specific advantages in latest models that make them more desirable before competitors catch up, or even surpass these advantages.

Cars and sewing machines; cameras and TV sets; boats and golf carts; and most products advertised, are largely or partially in the competitive stage. The demonstrator type of selling is often ideal for both pioneer and competitive products. Mail order is often the ideal way to win a competitive stage race before competitors are even in wide national distribution. The retentive stage is Coca Cola, where the biggest news is the big bottle. A book club is in the retentive stage, but stays competitive with its latest offer and giveaway. Advertising of the club's operation is short, but on giveaway, and offers it is as long as ever.

Where most mail order advertising parts company with advertising of most products distributed in other ways, is in continuity.

Intensively distributed products are usually advertised *far more*

93

continuously, with higher intensity than even major mail order "hits" in full projection. The single item mail order advertiser soon learns that the first ad pulls best, the second substantially less, the third far off that and so forth. Usually, only a new giveaway, new offer or entirely new copy approach revives the pattern. A dramatic price reduction usually picks up results, but dies soon after. Only a rare concept, like a book club, is capable of *continuous* full page advertising, really a series of individual ads for specific giveaways and offers, each with a typical mail order life pattern. While the life span of distribution products is far shorter now that intensity of promotion is increased, a *campaign* of ads or commercials even built around a single theme can still rotate different advantages. The reader, listener or viewer is expected to absorb a little here and a little there, with a constant drip, drip, drip of water effect. It's ideal for products with simple, or nominal advantages.

But mail order is perpetually in the pioneering and competitive stages. It's far more necessary to tell the entire story each time. For a small mail order advertiser (like ourselves), each time each ad or commercial is run, more readers, listeners or viewers are *unfamiliar* with our product than are *familiar* with it. If we were to tell a little of our story each time, it would be in the hope that prospective buyers would take notes each time and assemble the entire story themselves. Before then, they would never know enough about the product to make a buying decision.

Yet, often a mail order product *is* news. Often, the giveaway *is* news. And usually, a mail order ad or commercial has its best chance of success simply by reporting the full news story.

For a number of decades, advertising has been called "salesmanship in print."

But what kind of salesmanship should be used? My father taught that advertising broke down into two main types: the "Fuller Brush Man approach" and the "Dugan Baker approach". The Fuller Brush man was, at that time, a one time call approach and hard sell from the foot in the door to the lengthy canned sales talk. He was always in the pioneering stage. The Dugan Baker man was a driver-salesman who sold bread and other items on a weekly visit to customers. He had to have a friendly face, a cheerful greeting, some news of a new product, a special price on one of his items and he could not wear out his welcome. He built a repeat business. He was in the competitive and retentive stages. Later, I discovered subdivisions of these.

The pitchman draws his people in as an entertainer. He amuses, puzzles or intrigues the onlooker. His opening line often leaves no hint

94

of what he's leading into. He gradually secures nodding agreement from bystanders to some of what he is saying, perhaps with a knock pitch that they do not know is related to his future "sell". Then, he comes to the "turn" into the heart of his selling message, the point when his audience will drift away or stay and perhaps, buy. Gradually, he builds up credibility. He demonstrates the proof of what he's saying with the product. He can still lose more of his audience than he can sell. He picks up speed. He offers the incentive to stay and buy now, not later. He establishes a rhythm of excitement—a shortage psychology. He causes those on the outside of the group to feel that they may be *too late to get theirs*. They push in.

Take out the brashness, cheapness, and misrepresentation, and there's still a lot to learn for anyone creating an advertisement.

I've admired a certain jewelry designer in action. The way he dresses, his accent, his entire approach is as much a setting for each piece of his jewelry as the red velvet he removes with such care when he unveils his latest work. Simply by unwrapping the package, picking up the lowest priced piece of costume jewelry, holding it with reverence as though it were infinitely precious and extraordinarily delicate, he adds untold desirability. For luxury merchandise of every description, his equivalent can be found. This, too, can be translated into advertising.

As home appliances and business and industrial equipment were invented and improved, the salesman trained to demonstrate came into his own. He looks assured, simply approaching his product. He often can adapt to a wide variety of products. He can pick up a new kind of fishing reel or electric mini-calculator, put it through its tricks like a circus dog, and never be awkward.

Without effective demonstration and salesmanship, the cash register might never have gotten off the ground. The troops of IBM might never have started their march to world domination and product after product might have died aborning. Demonstration salesmanship can be translated into any form of advertising.

The instructor-salesman is a teacher-missionary. He or she is spreading the word. . . enthusing. . . teaching. . . making it easy, fun and fast to learn how to get in on it.

The home sewing industry was created by home sewing teachers. Entire magazines are based on instruction in specific hobby fields. On public TV, Julia Child made French cooking so easy and such fun with her wonderful accompanying chatter of instruction, that innumerable viewers bought her books. Every new game that sweeps the country is sped on its way by instructor-missionary men.

Jon Gnagy, for whose art course and products we were advertising agency, looked on TV as though he had stepped from the Paris left bank. But he *talked* as he was, a mid western-farm boy, in the most reassuring friendly and folksy manner possible. He instructed as he sketched—at an easy pace, with not the slightest rush. He demonstrated as he taught—starting with triangles, squares, circles and cubes, sketched out so roughly it was obvious any ten year old child (or adult) could do the same. Erasing line segments, he would turn them into houses, seascapes, fruit or whatever. At each step, each viewer felt he or she could easily do the same. At the end of the shows, when Jon Gnagy put a frame around the finished drawing, each viewer was sure he or she could do as well.

Salesmanship takes many forms. Consider the used-car salesman, direct descendant of the age-old horse trader. Observe those apostles of health who warn of the dangers of all we normally eat and drink and offer us relief at a price. A salesman can be a father figure, a fashion reporter, an irrepressible clown, an underdog, a sex symbol, a folksy countryman or any combination thereof. A salesman can be a psychologist, a strategist or a great tactician. And salesmanship in advertising can be just as varied. Each different environment creates a different atmosphere, which greatly affects selling any product. Walk through the Gallery in Milan. . . along Fifth Avenue, New York. . . up North Michigan Avenue in Chicago. . . on Wilshire Boulevard in Los Angeles. . . or almost anywhere in Paris.

You become part of a pageant in the well dressed crowds, the succession of stunning display windows, the heady atmosphere of fashion and wealth. Everything is affecting you. You are being prepared to pay more for anything that you're shopping for than you originally and innocently anticipated.

The same salesmanship takes place in any expensive and popular night club. The lighting, the constant to and fro movement of people, waiters, bus boys and cigarette girls, the drink-up music, the dancing bodies, all blend, confuse and prepare you for a higher and higher bill which you become more and more tolerant of. A luxury ad in a luxury publication can have a similar effect.

Each type of publication, broadcast program, catalogue or retail store offers its own selling environment and tries to create its own atmosphere. One of today's top department store merchants says an exciting sale should be like a party, the store like a theater. Let's consider how its selling environment affects a department store ad and different selling environments for mail order ads.

96

A department store show window *displays* goods in a setting. A few words and a price are the only copy. A department store ad for merchandise is much the same. The familiar art style and layout, the famous logotype of its name, and the surrounding merchandise it also advertises provides the setting. Its ad is a show window in print.

Often, that brief graceful message will sell out all stock of an item in the store and force reorders. It has for us. But, when we ran the exact words and picture in our mail order ad for the same product in another newspaper, it has often failed miserably.

It's always a surprise to our beginning creative people. They always start with the firm belief that advertising should be short and brief; long wordy ads can only insult the intelligence. They see many short and simple advertisements, some for mail order, that seem to succeed. If others can succeed with brief copy, why can't we, they ask. The answer is we can, if we can *duplicate* the original conditions—all of them. To duplicate the department store ad condition, we must find a marketplace similar to the one the store has created and that has taken some of them a hundred years to do so.

Department stores pay substantially less than national advertisers for the same size ads. Department stores and other retailers usually have *franchise* advertising positions. The same store often has the same page number day after day, week after week, month in, month out, over long years. As they build up their advertising schedule to run more pages per day, their ads run again and again in the old familiar positions. This creates the marketplace that people love to turn to. Each store has a solid core of loyalists buying the paper for no reason other than to *shop*. Surveys show department store ads get as much or more readership from women, as most front page stories. These women are *looking* for the store ad, seeking something offered by that store to select. It's often part of their life, something to do, their truest pleasure. Often, these women are not looking in the same paper for *my* mail order ad or *yours*.

The training of department store customers to, *telephone* their orders in, took decades to accomplish. The building of huge numbers of charge account customers, who now find it so easy to telephone their order in, took decades too. These department store customers are nowhere near equally ready to telephone their order to you or me. It's their *habit* to order from the department store's brief description and illustration of an item. It's their *habit* to *resist* buying the same way from an unfamiliar mail order advertiser. And remember, the manufacturers and importers have already done much to make that simple, easy sale possible. National advertising is creating retail demand.

Only a minority of all the products in a department store are advertised individually by the store. The rest are sold as a result of the constant traffic of customers coming into the store, usually attracted by the advertising for specific items. The effectiveness of the store's advertising is based on an interplay of the national advertising of the manufacturer, editorial stories in the newspapers, features in the magazines, current popular trends, interviews or stories on TV or radio, tie-ins with famous personalities or a combination of these factors.

It may involve offering an item that's hard to get elsewhere, a major price break, a new competitive item with a lower price, or obvious extra product advantage.

Go-Get-It national advertising drives buyers to stores. Retailer We-Have-It advertising pulls them in. The national advertising has to do the major convincing; the dealer advertising simply tells where it's available and for how much.

But mail order advertising usually combines both functions. It often has to introduce both an unknown product and an unknown company to a far more Doubting Thomas reader, viewer or listener. It usually takes more convincing.

To convince, we must provide reasons to buy our product. To find those convincing reasons, we must uncover every research fact that could possibly influence a buying decision in our favor.

The nearest equivalent in mail order to a department store advertising marketplace is created by a publication, broadcaster, catalogue or co-op mailing. Few are as old, established or have as many advantages as a department store marketplace. But often, such a mail order marketplace has been successfully established for many years and decades. Often, special advertising rates in it are substantially lower than outside the mail order marketplace section in the same medium. There are limited numbers of such market places, but more are being established all the time.

An ad in such a marketplace is far more comparable to a department store ad than one run elsewhere. It needs more sell and explanation than the department store ad, but far less than a mail order ad *outside* such a marketplace. It is the simplest, easiest mail order ad to write, takes the least time to write and gives brief copy its best chance. Writing it is just a small step beyond making up a shopping column write-up. If you've done your research as suggested, it's easier yet.

Many small and successful mail order firms only run small ads in mail order marketplaces. It limits the sizes of the business, but escapes much of the headaches of creating larger ads.

The classified section of a newspaper is such a market place. Habits are deeply engrained to look in this section to find a job or an employee; or sell a house, car or appliance. The shortest ad may produce an avalanche of inquiries. But run the same ad in another newspaper, not carrying such a section, and you may not get a single call.

The Sunday classified display section of newspapers for antiques, travel, real estate, boats, or whatever, is sometimes such a market place where small ads and brief copy pulls. But many papers have only a smattering of such ads and no such effective market place. The same ad run with them simply dies.

Home and garden magazines have built up remarkable mail order shopping market places often with two or three hundred ads in an issue. Mail order offers of records and tapes have run so frequently for years on the same TV stations (usually in the same movie programs) that TV has created a mail order market place for records.

Recently, co-op mailings with many circulars for different products in the same envelope have become such market places. Packages of loose return postcards with advertising for a different product on each, or the same principle with postcards bound into a direct response publication have begun to create new mail order market places in many fields. In each case, the habit of mail order shopping is being built up and brief copy often works.

Readers of advertising in a mail order market place are mail order shoppers. They may be "window shoppers" casually looking. They may be looking for a specific item or advertiser. But wherever attention is caught, each will read an ad more carefully. Many buy regularly by mail order. If so, they are predisposed to buy by mail order in the future if they find an item desirable enough.

Many trade, technical, hobby and special interest publications, or co-op mailings in such fields provide mail order market places for appropriate specialized products and services.

In any mail order market place, your advertisement competes for interest with other mail order advertisements. Yet, every other advertisement helps yours by contributing to the creation of a market place. Note the editorial shopping column write ups, each with an individual picture on the same pages. Your ad is also competing with each of these. Yet, these help even more by contributing editorial credibility to the mail order market place.

Of the many mail order ads in such a market place, some fail, some break even, and some only succeed because of other benefits to the

99

advertiser that you may not receive. Often, a catalogue house is willing to break even or even lose money on such small ads, simply to get new names to mail to regularly in the future. Some firms feel that the ad helps their store sales as well. Some may have far lower advertising cost because of a frequency or big volume contract. Judged only on sales of the item offered, and based on the advertising rate you will pay, *most* may be failing. This means that you need the most unique product that you can find and the best ad that you can create. If your ad is to succeed, it should be seen, and believed, more so than the other ads and write-ups on the page. Year after year, people start out as you are doing and *pay out*. You can, too, if your ad, as well as product, is *better* than most others.

In your newspaper, certain stories seem new and intriguing. Others seem stale and boring. Your first glance forms this opinion.

A quick glance at a shopping column write up and picture and at the headline and picture of the smallest ad on the shopping column pages does the same. Each editorial shopping column write-up is news. Each shopping column picture is a news picture. And so is each ad and its illustration.

Some shopping column write-ups and ads hardly get your attention. Their story seems to be merely a rehash about some product that's been around for years. The most dramatic attention getting device does not help. Some shopping column write-ups and ads are genuine fresh news of an entirely new product or real product improvement. And some are really exciting news.

If your ad is news of something better, the reader is *looking* for it. If your message seems reasonably believable, the reader is predisposed to buy. If your product itself is not interesting news to enough people reading your ad, it will probably fail.

If your ad is in a standard size newspaper like the New York Times, and not in a mail order marketplace, it looks small and forlorn against its readership competition of news stories, department store ads and other type ads. Readership studies show that national ads average a readership far below that of the department store ads and news stories. And you are one of the smaller and least known of these general national advertisers. Usually, your product is not known, your company is not known and the reader is not considering a mail order purchase. Nobody is looking for you. And often, mail order results from such ads are next to nothng.

On a tabloid page, your ad is nowhere near as lost. But in bulging, fat, big city tabloids your ad seems to drown in a sea of department store ads and little news. On a magazine page, your ad is less lost, but is usually relegated to a position far back where overall magazine readership is lower.

Occasionally, the position of your small ad is surprisingly good, at the very top of the page on the right hand side, next to the carryover of a high interest number one news story, right on top of a high readership department store ad, or next to a *related* magazine article in the field of your product.

But this is a lottery ticket usually beyond your control. Results are often poor and erratic.

For most of the products we have worked on, outside of the mail order market place, the smaller the ad we have run, the more speculative have been our results.

Very small ads have usually proven profitable in very special circumstances. Normally, it has been because something about the ad has *grabbed* the attention of the hurried, wandering eye of the reader usually because of the *offer* or *product itself*. Few people are not drawn to a bargain, anywhere, any time. A tiny ad for a big bargain even with a modest headline draws readership like a magnet.

The warts remedy style product with an ad using the one word, WARTS as a headline, can appeal to the urgent need of a small minority and with a small whisper of an ad, draw as though with a shout. But few mail order products are feasible for such ads. Most need more explanation than a small ad can give.

It's hard to achieve *belief* with a few words and an unknown name and address. The most provocative attention getting headlines may attain abnormally high readership, yet solve neither of these problems. Generally, smallest space mail order inquiry ads have a better chance than smallest space mail order complete sale ads.

Sometimes, small ads have worked outside the mail order market places when combined with a catalogue offer. In such cases, the small ads have rotated items and gradually familiarized readers with the name. Sometimes, an extra position rate has been paid in newspapers to get a forward position and keep it week after week for different items.

There are major differences in creating a small mail order ad *outside* vs. inside a mail order market place. The ad must fight far harder for attention. It must struggle more to convert a glance into readership. It must convince, despite a more casual interest. It must persuade a person far less inclined to act to do so. This is often, too big a job for a small ad.

Often, the small ad that works in the mail order market place will fail miserably in the harsher environment outside. Its product claims must have quite self evident advantages. Its offer must be particularly risk free to the Doubting Thomases. If so, it still must *leap off the page and pop right at you* to gain necessary readership. This means the headline and illustration has a far more difficult job to do. Outside the mail order market place, bigger ads usually have a higher *percentage* of success and are more *stable* in projection.

They also produce far more volume and hopefully, overall profit. The volume of new names builds lists far faster. The volume of shipments provides a vehicle for related product inserts. The result is more income from mailing your own list, renting your own list and package inserts. Bigger ads are time consuming to write, but per dollar of profit potential, they are the easiest and fastest way to make money in mail order space advertising.

From one inch to half column to one-third, one half, two-thirds to full page we have found the full page *safer* for broad- appeal products. It's a more adequate test of the pulling power of such products. But many successful mail order businesses have started with a small mail order ad. Even if an inadequate test, it may be the only one that you can afford. But if your ad for a broad appeal item shows *life* in a small ad, it's usually deserving of testing in larger space.

The bigger the ad you write, the more you avail yourself of all the research you have done. With larger space you can tell more and more of the *full* story of your product. You can demonstrate better in fuller form its uses and advantages. From research on, a great deal of copywriting is in *choice* of what to say. In bigger ads the choice is easier, because you can select *more*.

Usually, I start by writing a full page ad and then smaller ads. The simplest way to learn how to make more effective smaller ads is to learn how to create bigger ads. We find that we create far better smaller ads *after* we have completed a successful *full page* ad for the same item. Sometimes, with each reduction to a smaller size the cutting and editing required make each word left work harder.

Therefore, let's discuss creating a full page ad and then work backwards to smaller ads. But before we can create and complete any ad, we must construct the offer we wish to make.

Chapter 5

Increasing and Speeding
Mail Order Desire

*Offer components. . . price. . . terms. . . giveaways. . . add-on
. . . cash-up. . . credit cards. . . telephone. . . guarantee*

Claude Hopkins, author of "Scientific Advertising" used to say that the right offer should be so attractive that only a lunatic would say "no".

If you want to persuade anyone to do anything, it's best to think out every possible inducement. You want to make it as attractive as possible to do what you request, and to the fullest extent. Before you say a word, you need to plan out your proposal and make it hard to resist. And it is the same in creating a mail order ad.

You have your product and have done your research. Before you write a word, you need to construct your offer to your prospective mail order customer. You are constantly torn between making your proposal more attractive (and possibly less profitable to you) or making it more profitable to you (and possibly less attractive). But you must decide. Until you do so, you cannot complete your ad. And how you decide, may greatly affect how you create it.

The offer that you make in your first test ad is simply the one you "feel" has the best chance of success and is still safe to make. This opening offer may be varied in future tests. Much of the money made in mail order comes from a later test of a variation from the original offer. Never stop trying to make your offer *more* tempting, while still safe.

What *should* you charge for what you are selling?

Too high a price may kill orders. Too low a price may lose money. The *right* price may be the difference between mail order success and failure. One thing is sure. The Good Lord did not figure out the price of anything sold. A human being did and the price can be *wrong or right*.

The psychology of price constantly surprises me. In the depression low price was all important and may be again. But the right price varies by product as well as by the economic condition.

In every price range, some items seem more trustworthy at a somewhat higher price and more dubious at a lower price. Other items, particularly bought by housewives, seem to them to be outrageously overpriced if higher than some arbitrary figure in their minds. Some items are "blind items" which a prospective buyer has difficulty in identifying as to what price is reasonable. But determining the right price to sell your product can be quite important to your mail order success.

Has the price of your product recently been reduced? Or could you reduce it and still sell it profitably?

An offer is often made more attractive by a price reduction. The more real it is and seems, the more it should be so. Often, it can extend the life of a product for years. Sometimes, it can even bring a dead product back to life.

The worse the economic condition is, the more vital a price reduction appeal is. In the best of times, price reductions are less effective. For some products we have never reduced the price. For others we have waited years to do so. And for others we have been able to give reductions early in the game. Decide for yourself before you write an ad whether to sell the product at regular or a reduced price and if so, for how great a reduction.

The terms on which you sell your product are a component part of your offer.

Usually, the more favorable terms you give the more orders you will get. Selling for cash often takes the most convincing. Selling C.O.D. usually takes less and gets orders from those who don't have cash handy when they order. The words "Send no money. . . just pay the postman" may have first made big scale mail order possible.

More recently, selling via credit card often charged by telephone has revolutionized mail order. For the first time, it has made possible selling far higher priced items, up to hundreds of dollars and more. Those who have the capital and organization to sell on credit charged directly to their company usually do even better. And those who are strongly enough financed, and well enough organized to sell on time payments charged directly, often do best of all.

From a persuasion standpoint, you want to offer the most favorable terms. From a practical standpoint, you must be safe and keep things simple enough to be able to control what you do. As a moonlighter, you will probably start selling for all cash. Many successful mail order people never sell in any other way. Next, you may consider C.O.D. or you may skip it as too much paper work and trouble. You may, sooner than you expect, start selling via credit cards. You may never bill any mail order customer directly—or if you decide to do so, you may only bill on a thirty day basis and never sell on time payments.

You will probably first make a sensible compromise between the most liberal terms that might get the most orders and the most cautious terms. You will have to consider which terms are easiest logistically for you to handle.

A very important part of your offer can be stating that you will accept telephone orders. These can be C.O.D., via credit card or charged direct. But most important is the use of the telephone in taking credit card orders.

Credit cards, WATS lines and computerized credit checking of individual phone orders by the credit card companies have been a mail order powerhouse combination for higher ticket items.

The net effect is, that the same cost advertising sells a higher cost item than formerly possible, gets more orders than formerly possible, and gets the orders faster than formerly possible. You ship faster than formerly possible, with a happier customer. You can finance your advertising easier than formerly possible. And small mail order companies can grow far bigger, far faster than formerly possible. Your willingness to accept telephone orders can sharply increase total orders. We usually feature the telephone in our offers and advertising.

Another component part of our offer can be a giveaway, an extra gift item to add value.

The right giveaway, alone, can be the difference between profit and loss, in the very first test of an item. If an item pays off initially *without* a giveaway and results from the ad later drop below the break-even point, sometimes the right giveaway can make the ad profitable again and give it an entirely *new* lease on life.

Sometimes, a surprising switch in the offer of a giveaway can create an unexpected bonanza of increased business. One of our alumni ran a test, selling harmonicas with instructions as a giveaway. Results were unprofitable, and he almost decided to give up the project. Instead, he converted the instructions into a more detailed *harmonica instruction course*, sold the course, and gave away the harmonica. The advertising on the air, and in print, was overwhelmingly devoted to the ease, simplicity and speed of learning how to play the harmonica. The new offer was a great success and he sold hundreds of thousands of harmonica courses.

A self liquidator, an extra item offered for its actual cost including mailing, or a partial self liquidator, offered for part of its cost including mailing, may be preferable. Either may offer a greater bargain. Whether a giveaway, self liquidator or partial liquidator, the effect is that the total cost of merchandise and shipping is a higher percentage of the money you take in, and percentage of gross profit is smaller. It may produce enough extra orders to be worthwhile.

In our family business, we often test an offer without a giveaway, self liquidator or partial liquidator. Sometimes, we add one later. Offering one can often greatly increase orders. Some mail order people scarcely make a mail order offer without one. I feel that each case should be judged individually and hope that your completion of this course will help give you the "feel" to do so.

Another component part of your offer can be an add-on. This is a request for an extra and usually related purchase. An add-on can be simply offering two or more of the same items, usually at a saving, or a set of several items at a saving otherwise individually offered at full price in the advertising. It can be a larger package. An add-on can be a deluxe edition of a book or deluxe version of an item. It can be a closely related and easily explained item, as a fishing rod with a fishing reel.

An add-on is included in an offer not to make it more attractive, but to make it more profitable. For us, an add-on of two of the items for a saving, a set for a saving, a larger size or deluxe model at modest extra cost, almost always pulls quite well; usually 20 percent to 40 percent more and occasionally even more. We often run our first ad without an add-on and test later whether it's more advantageous to use one.

Another component part of your offer may be a cash-up. A cash-up is an incentive offered to send in full payment now, as an alternative to buying on credit on one payment, or on extended time payments. It is not used to get more orders, but simply to bring in more cash.

The incentive can be a specific giveaway, only given for full cash payment. If there is already a giveaway for prompt action, a cash-up can be an additional giveaway for full cash payment. Often, it is simply an offer by the seller to prepay shipping costs to the buyer, but only for full cash payment. Sometimes, it's an actual reduction in price for full cash payment. Simply making the full cash option the first option, and the credit option the alternative, can make full cash payment more the expected choice, and can increase the cash payment percentage.

A cash-up usually pulls a smaller percentage when used for higher priced items than for lower priced items. It usually pulls a bigger percentage against a choice of several credit cards only than against a choice of billing direct vs. several credit cards. This is because most people realize that if they purchase through credit cards, and pay after twenty five days from the date of purchase, that they will start paying interest.

We often do not use a cash-up to start but do so later after testing.

A most important component of your offer is your guarantee. But for the mail order firm that is not yet famous, and is offering one or more items in one advertisement, direct mail piece, or broadcast commercial, it is particularly important. Each prospective purchaser fears the possibility of being disappointed or even being taken advantage of. Each worries as to whether the mail order ad claims are true. Most people still prefer not to buy mail order. For each customer who buys, other readers of your advertising will determine to wait until a trusted retailer carries the product.

Only by removing all risk on the part of your prospective customer can you overcome the reluctance to deal with a stranger, and buy an unknown product. Either your product works or it doesn't. Either it is a value for the price or it isn't. Either your advertising claims are accurate or overly exaggerated. Mail order products are returned if they disappoint. Satisfied customers keep their purchases. If your product is shoddy or overpriced, you should drop it. If your advertising is untruthful, you should correct it. And if not, usually you have nothing to fear from the strongest guarantee for lower priced products.

When mail order began, the very idea of sending money to an unknown person seemed to most to be too great a risk to consider. It was assumed that no product would ever come. Today, infinitely more people will send money, in larger and larger amounts per item, to an unknown mail order firm. As trust is built up, occasionally, surprising confidence will be shown. I have known of a customer sending a letter asking a mail order firm to select certain items at their discretion, giving authority to ship, and even enclosing a signed blank check. But more people are still afraid. And removing that fear is largely the job of the guarantee. In our business, we endeavor to make a clear, unequivocal guarantee and act on it promptly, and without question.

We always offer a free trial. This is standard in mail order and expected by the customer, and by any governmental agency or consumer group to whom a dissatisfied customer might appeal. Any publication or broadcast station you advertise with expects that you will give a dissatisfied customer, buying from the advertisement, complete satisfaction! The post office and the Better Business Bureau expect it. The result is that for all practical purposes, you *must* give replacement merchandise, or if not desired, a refund to any customer requesting it.

In lower priced items of good quality and value honestly represented in advertising, and sold for cash, the percentage of returns will usually be minimal, no matter how hard you emphasize the guarantee. It is obvious that if sales go up 20 percent then that a percentage of returns up to 10 percent *would be profitable. Yet, it is usually under 3 percent*, and often a fraction of 1 percent.

For such items, we have found that the length of the trial period makes no significant difference. Whether the trial period offered is five days, a week, ten days, thirty days or six months, returns are about the same percentage. The inertia of the average person is all on your side. Who wants to take the trouble to put something in a box, wrap it up, address it, get to the post office, buy stamps and mail it just to get back a very small amount of money? Yet, we find that a longer trial period in the offer *increases* orders!

One component part of your offer is any limitation on the length of time that the offer is available or on supply of the item. If your offer expires on a certain date, it becomes an added reason for acting before that date. If your product or price is not available through retail stores or anywhere but through you, that is a reason for action. If there's a limit to the quantity of the items that you have in inventory and you cannot get more at anywhere near the price, this is also a reason for action. Even if you simply don't know when, if ever, you can repeat the offer in this publication; this is a reason for the prospective buyer to buy now. Get the facts, tell the truth and include any such legitimate limitation in your offer.

It's surprising how much easier your entire job of creating an ad becomes once you determine exactly the offer you wish to make. But price, terms, giveaway, guarantee and any other offer components must be decided *before* you write your ad. Throughout my course, we will further discuss the advantages and disadvantages of specific offer components and how to obtain the greatest advantage from each.

In your first tiny classified and display ads, you will only excerpt from your research a few essential words and you will simplify your offer to suit the number of words available. In your largest ads, you will find that your main news story is surprisingly pre-planned and organized by your research. Even creating the elements of your ad will be greatly based on the component parts of your offer.

Each step greatly helps the next. Let's start creating ads.

Chapter 6

The Elements

*. . . of bigger ads. . . headline complex. . . boxes. . . captions
lead story. . . presenting offer components. . . coupon*

If we could say in one sentence how a product would benefit the user, that would be enough except for two reasons. Many do not believe advertising they see or hear. And of those who do believe and plan to buy or inquire, only a minority do. Otherwise, only the price and name and address of the seller would have to be added. Long copy, most pictures, demonstrations, testimonials, documentation of claims, are simply to get believability and action. A short message about an unknown product, by an unknown seller, can usually not achieve this. When a mail order ad fails for a good product with apparently effective copy, it may not be believed. The reader may have been afraid to buy it by mail and didn't trust or believe the mail order seller.

A recent survey of college students revealed that 94 percent did not believe TV commercials they watched. Readers, listeners and viewers take all advertising with a grain of salt. They believe less of the advertising, accepting some points, and rejecting others. Yet, people regretfully disbelieve. To attain believability in a skeptical age, the first step is to tell the truth, the letter and the spirit, in what you say, your qualifications and the average person's understanding of them. One legally safe, weasel-worded paragraph that does not conform to the spirit of truth can make your entire advertising lose belief. Extreme claims are like hyperdermic needle injected drugs plunged deeper and deeper to attain the same effect. More extreme claims by more advertisers cause more disbelief. Legitimate claims can be over dramatized.

The purpose of a mail order ad, in any form, is usually to cause the reader, viewer or listener to order or inquire. Mail order persuasion means to cause action at once. Yet, research shows that three times as many people who read, view or listen to a mail order ad, mailing or commercial, intend to buy or inquire than actually do. Tests prove that the more inducement you give in your advertising, the better chance you usually have of getting action on your proposal. The right incentive and repeated reminder to act now can cause more people, who intend to buy, to do so.

Attaining believability and causing immediate action takes more words but not overlong selling copy. You want to get across certain selling points, first things first, in the order of importance. The only purpose of each selling point and word is to get the desired belief and action. There's a limit to the importance of any product. Its story may fascinate you, bore anyone else and drive away otherwise interested readers. Everyone knows the salesman who makes the sale in the first two minutes and loses it in the next ten—not knowing when to stop. Such overselling can be like trying to kill flies with sledge hammers.

Some odd and unusual research fact about your product may not be important news to readers. You are not writing an essay, but primary news to readers. There's no room for the majority of your research. Your job is selection of the most important news facts. Shorter and simpler, more believable ads, with more pictures and less words usually win out against overcrowded black masses of overselling words. But such shorter, simpler ads can best be written after mastering the creation of longer ones. Let's analyze what goes into these longer ads. If it seems complex, don't worry. I'm going to give you an easier way to create complex ads. Then, we'll go into creating simpler ones.

Once, a competitor hired a fairly expensive copywriter. For weeks, the writer was given just one job, to read and re-read each ad which our advertising agency, Huber and Hoge and Sons, had recently written. Only then was the writer given a copy assignment.

After research, the first step to writing successful mail order ads *is* to study successful mail order ads selling similar products in a similar price range. Collect page mail order ads, run widely and frequently, for broad appeal products in mass media where the product and company name is new to most readers. This requires a good deal of convincing and long copy. Let's observe one such full page ad.

111

Draw a semi-circle from the middle of the headline through the main and subsidiary subheads, further through the main copy blocks down into the coupon. This is the main readership path. Note carefully how these ads are constructed to avoid losing readership of the impatient, while providing answers for the most picayune objections of slow moving, cautious doubters.

The most necessary, vital facts are in the headline, the main subhead; subordinate subheads, and subheads that interrupt copy. For a prospective buyer who doesn't want to read long ads and can make up his or her mind fast, the readership path becomes a speedway to the coupon. Some buy just this way, scarcely reading the detailed copy in the ad. Others, who want a fuller story, can follow the same readership path and read the full main copy story, but skip the supporting evidence. Many buy this way. The interested, but still dubious, can read thoroughly in detail every scintilla of evidence before making their decision. Notice how frequently the copy asks for action right through the ad.

Notice certain similarities in most page mail order ads. The headline is rarely pure attention getting. It is normally a sweeping product claim. Sometimes, it is both. The main subhead usually follows up with subsidiary claims or immediately starts citing proof. Usually, there is a prominent box up on top citing documentation of claims. Often, the main picture is upper right. Normally, the coupon is bottom right. The main copy block usually starts upper left under the main and subsidiary subheads. Often, there is more detailed proof in a box at lower left. Sometimes, for book ads, it is a detailed catalogue of contents.

The type size can vary considerably. Even in a crowded ad, the opening lines of the main copy can be in bigger, more readable type. Sometimes, it can drop in size after several paragraphs and toward the close, drop in size again. Pictures, subordinate to the main picture, can often be graduated down to quite small size. Captions can be in type so small that in the main body copy it would discourage reading. In boxes citing evidence that prove claims, copy can be smaller than the main copy story. Reading these portions of the ad is optional. This is the extra evidence for Doubting Thomases. A catalogue of claims may contain just one so urgently interesting to a specific reader that it clinches the sale. It's worth including more claims or contents, but in small type.

How do you start creating a big ad?

For the simplest or most complex ad, your first problem is to get anyone to even notice your advertising; then to read it; and finally to order or inquire. Many creative people start with an idea for a picture and headline; then the main subhead; then the lead to the copy story; main copy block and supporting elements. Sometimes, the picture idea stimulates the headline. Sometimes, the headline idea calls up the picture concept. I start with research and build from it a main story concept. Then, I come up with subhead ideas from the copy and last of all the ideas for headline, picture and main subheads. You will find, by trial and error, the method best for you.

Headlines, subhead, pictures and even copy story of an ad are often only parts of its effectiveness. Much of the strength, and sometimes the clincher, can come from supporting evidence carefully prepared and strategically placed throughout your ad. A full page mail order ad is often a complex combination of painstakingly put together elements, each designed to do a specific persuasion job.

Copy starts and ends with your offer. You want them to buy something or write in for information. The more you wish them to do, the more convincing is usually needed. A sale takes more convincing than an inquiry, a request for cash payment usually takes more than just to charge, and a request for a higher cash or charge payment usually takes still more.

An inquiry can usually be secured with briefest copy. A qualified inquiry usually requires more copy, not so much to presell, as to discourage curiosity seekers. More copy will often prepare inquiries and pre-sell them sufficiently to cause a higher percentage of closing, either by follow-up literature or by salesmen.

Writing a big ad is a big job.

It becomes much simpler when subdivided into little jobs. Each ad section is a little job, we call an element. We build an ad element by element.

Let's discuss the elements of which many full page ads are constructed. Some will simply present component parts of your offer. Just clarifying your offer helps write each such element. Some component parts will be repeated and emphasized in different elements of your ad.

Most copywriters consider the most important ad element to be the headline complex: headline, main subheads and overline (if any).

Many times mail order defeat in a test has been turned to victory by a change in headline. Books could be written solely on the art of creating headlines. Newspapers have been propelled to huge circulations by the skill of their headline writers. The best copy in the world can't work if it isn't read and often it is the headline that turns glancing into reading or gets any glance at all.

Some copywriters devote as much time and effort to creating the headline complex as they do for all other parts of the ad combined. Some never start to write the rest of the ad until they write the main headline complex. I occasionally start with a working headline complex and then write the remainder of the ad. But usually, I come up with a better headline complex later.

Often, a headline complex has a headline and a smaller line above called an overline. Sometimes, a headline has no overline. Often, it has one or more smaller lines underneath called the main subhead. Sometimes, there's no main subhead or overline. A headline can be one word or a number of lines. It can use an accompanying picture to prove or dramatize what it is saying. It can be subordinate to and introduce the main picture.

Sometimes, a headline is used entirely to arouse curiosity, sometimes just to signal a special group, and sometimes to make just one vital overall claim. Sometimes, the headline will be small in relation to the size of the ad. Other times, it will dominate an ad with thirty percent or more of the total space of an ad. Some mail order men find that the more dominant the headline is, the greater are chances of success.

Often, in a big mail order ad, overline, headline and main subhead capsule the entire story of the ad, give the main promise, fan out to subsidiary benefits, feature claim documentation and sometimes signal to kinds of users who can benefit. But there are many headline approaches.

Cub reporters are taught that "Dog Bites Man" is not a major headline, but "Man Bites Dog" is. Our headline, "Frog Murders Bass" aroused curiosity, signalled bass fishermen, promised what each wanted to do, and sold one hundred and twenty-three thousand kicking frog fish lures for us.

To sell a dress form for home sewers, we combined its most powerful appeal, custom fit, with its guarantee. The headline "Custom Fit Guaranteed. . . or no cost" sold over two hundred and ten thousand dress forms for us. Such combinations of claim and offer are often done. People love a winner. . . and a bargain. "America's Most Popular Inflatable Canoe—At A New Bargain Price" sold our Pyrawa canoes for us by the thousands.

A winning headline can come from endless research, one phrase in a testimonial letter or from constant reworking and editing of body copy. Often, it's worth working for.

Sometimes, a "signal box" will be another element. It will list and call the attention of special groups to whom the ad is directed.

Often, an element in an ad is a box featuring product claims. If under six strong product claims, such a box is often put up towards the top, sometimes next to the "signal box" and both become almost a part of the main headline complex. If there are many encyclopedic product claims, often a bigger box is used and placed further down in the ad, sometimes at lower left. This becomes a "contents box" for book publishers.

The biggest element in your ad is usually your main copy story. Often, you find the basis for it in your premise and product development research notes. It's often a summary of key points from your other ad elements. The job of its opening words is to pull the reader down further into the story. Often, this is done with a summary of your headline complex.

Step-by-step, your main copy story must get across your main selling points, always tempting the reader on to read more. Its interest should smoothly and continuously pick up. From the opening words, each sentence and paragraph, one by one, should be building rhythm and pace.

Think of yourself as part lawyer, part salesman, part reporter and part editor. As a lawyer, you draw from your research more and more evidence until you build an irresistible case for your client, your product. As a salesman, you draw on this evidence to build a sales story to demonstrate your product in use, tempt with end benefits, surprise with competitive comparison and come up with *an offer no sane person would logically refuse.* As a reporter, you tell a crisp, dramatic news story of product development and benefit. As an editor and rewrite man, you follow the old newspaper adage. You tell what you're going to tell (in headline and main subhead). . . then you tell 'em (in the main body copy). . . then you tell 'em what you told 'em (in the close).

Usually, you break up your news story with subheads. Each is a miniature headline of what is to follow. We try to keep subheads to several words each and one line each. But some subheads of several lines are very effective.

Words should be simple and sentences and paragraphs short. We try to precede and follow a subhead with an even shorter paragraph, sometimes only one sentence long. White space above and below each subhead, margin on either side, and these short paragraphs before and after can create an open and easier reading look.

The main copy story usually mentions price and terms only if an advantage. It rarely mentions an add-on or cash-up. In such cases, a box or the coupon can do the job. The main story usually repeats and emphasizes any advantageous offer component, any giveaway or variation, any time or product supply limitation, and any desirable guarantee.

So far, we've discussed copy only as though the picture was an afterthought. Yet, the picture or pictures often govern the entire ad as any art director will tell you. From your very first look at your product, your mind is open and alert to any intriguing picture ideas. Pictures in your ads become picture elements. It may simply be a striking way to make your product look stunningly beautiful. It may be an exciting picture proof shot, dramatically proving an otherwise hard to believe claim. It may be a step by step demonstration picture sequence. It may be an exploded shot showing all component parts. It may be two before and after shots. It may be a photograph, line drawing or wash illustration with shading and contrast.

Each step of your research brings up picture ideas. As you write and rewrite copy, you come up with more picture ideas. Some are practical. Some are not. Your patent may have pictures of the product in use and of the results of using it. A salesman's presentation will often have intriguing picture ideas. Engineers' drawings and blueprints sometimes give more. For fertilizer, we've used time lapse photography sequences of treated vs. untreated identical plants. For dance instruction, we've used high speed, stroboscopic stop motion shots showing the dance step in action in sequence pictures.

Make several lists of your picture ideas. Classify them under A, B and C. The "A" list should be the most practical, most immediately available, least expensive as well as effective. The "B" and "C" lists may seem more speculative as to whether they will work. They may require more time than preferable. They may be more expensive than you'd like. We'll consider them all when it comes time to make your layout and put your ad together.

You've worked hard to create a persuasive offer. Let's discuss how best to present in your advertising the component parts of that offer. Some component parts go into ad elements. Some become ad elements. Some do both jobs. Let's start by presenting most advantageously the price component of your offer. If it's a bargain, document it by price comparison with competitive products. If it's a price reduction, compare the new with the former price. If your price is higher than competition, try to justify it with greater savings from use, lower costs of use, longer years of use or however the facts prove.

If price is not an advantage, you will not mention price until the coupon and there will be no price copy element. If your offer has real price advantages, state them in a clear and orderly manner. The stronger

116

your price story is the more you can emphasize and dramatize its facts. It becomes a copy block, perhaps several paragraphs. Your job is to construct each element as tightly as possible, with no unnecessary word, each in the right order, and each right for the job.

When the reader becomes interested in price and glances at this small piece of evidence, the spotlight is suddenly on it. You want it to be a little gem. It's the same with each element throughout your ad.

The terms may become another element. If you sell for all cash or C.O.D., you will probably only say so in the coupon. If you sell via credit cards, you may wish to emphasize it. If you offer cash or credit cards (or cash or direct billings), you may prefer not to emphasize either form of charge billing. If you sell a luxury product, you may feel that emphasis on credit will cheapen the ad. In any of these cases, you may still prefer no terms element. Advertising credit for higher price items often sells items far less saleable for cash only. More advertising emphasis of available credit, often gets more orders.

When advertising offers to charge via credit cards and to take orders by telephone, orders can climb further. Your phone number in the ad will get calls. If you say that you will take phone orders collect, you get more. If you feature the 800 toll free number to the customer, you get a lot more. The customer is sometimes embarrassed by and does not want the trouble of the collect call. He prefers dialing 800 plus your number.

If you use a WATS 800 number, emphasize that in your advertising. Your advertising should make clear that the customer pays nothing for the call and can order by telephone merely by giving his or her credit card number. On a large ticket item which we have in ample stock, we can usually ship in twenty-four hours. If you can, say so. This alone can increase orders. If you use a twenty-four hour, seven day a week phone answering service, state prominently in your ad that you can accept orders on a twenty-four hour basis.

Whatever you do say about terms must be crystal clear. Misunderstood terms can reduce orders. Contradictory terms can sharply reduce orders. Either can lose you money.

Featuring a giveaway, self liquidator or partial liquidator in your ad is another element.

If you sell anything, you know how important any special offer is as a conversational door opening or to close your sale. In your mail order ad, it's news. It attracts attention more than most attention attracting devices. Present it dramatically in conformance with the character, style and taste of your business. Do so in as exciting or as

117

discreet a manner as that of your product.

An old publishing client of ours kept coming up with low cost related premiums which were extraordinarily effective when shown in advertising. For a thick one volume encyclopedia at a bargain price, the giveaway was the two dimensional "flat globe" clearly illustrated in color as it actually was, a brightly colored map on circular thick cardboard with one hemisphere on each side. It dominated the ad.

Their best pulling giveaway ad offered their "Anatomical Manne-quin" set with their "Modern Home Physician". The mannequins were of a man and woman, each with several layers of foldouts. Mannequins with each layer were shown in full color at the top of the ad. The outside layer of each was a discreetly nude body. The next layer showed the muscular and nervous system. The next showed the circulatory system and all important organs. The last layer was the skeletal system.

Sometimes, the giveaway presentation can add to the impact of product copy. For an elaborate set of kitchenware, an additional set of four or five pieces of far less expensive but related items can add to the image of an overflowing cornucopia of product value. Inexpensive plastic ware can be an added gift, for instance, with an elaborate set of china. The same principle can apply to a tool set, sewing kit, fishing tackle combination, etc.

An effective giveaway is usually emphasized. Sometimes, its copy and illustration is the most important segment of your ad. Often, it can be in a prominent box, in the headline, pictured dominating the ad and repeated in the body copy, the close and in the coupon.

Warning! To use the word FREE in your advertising concerning your giveaway, you must state an offer to buyers of your product to keep the giveaway, even if returning the product. You must state this clearly and prominently close to the word "FREE". You can check your BBB or the FTC for latest FTC rulings on this.

Another ad element is the guarantee. The more convincing it takes to get an order, the more important a guarantee can become. For less known or unknown products, it's even more important.

A guarantee paragraph can increase orders, a guarantee display box or certificate, even more so. Spelling it out, emphasizing and repeating it can turn more readers into buyers. Its effective use can start in your headline, subhead or overline, be in a prominent box on top, go through the opening, build in the body copy, peak in the closing paragraphs and culminate in the coupon. Often, the guarantee box or certificate is directly above or next to the coupon.

Some mail order people worry whether too great a guarantee and return privilege emphasis will increase returns. We find that far more is gained in emphasizing the guarantee of lower priced items than is lost in extra returns. It can cause a problem for only a shoddy product. For more expensive items, too strong a guarantee emphasis can attract the something-for-nothing set. For direct time payments, overselling the guarantee can sell people who really cannot afford the product.

We are more cautious in guarantee emphasis for bigger ticket items. We are more so for sales via credit cards than for cash. For sales via direct billing, we are still more quiet. If on direct time payment, we give least emphasis. For luxury and fashion items, we handle the guarantee more discreetly. The more prestigious your approach is, the lower key will be the style of your guarantee, but it will still be important. The emphasis will vary with the tone of your business and style of your product.

However strong or discreet the handling of your guarantee is, make it simple and clear to the average person. State its limitations and length of trial period.

Another ad element may be a group of testimonials by users praising your product. A good product gets testimonial letters. It's often possible to get a legal release with permission to quote them. Their words and phrases will often be better, more colorful and more believable advertising than you could ever write. You'll often get new copy points, and sometimes new uses for your product.

A user may compare favorably and specifically your product with others. He or she may say how much more it saved or made money in a real situation, how much faster it did the job, how much more it produced, how much longer its use life was, how much more trouble free, exactly how it was more convenient, more practical or more versatile. Warning! An enthusiastic user can write in a testimonial that your product can do things that your product cannot do. To use such quotes is fraud, as it would be to make the same claim elsewhere in your copy. It then becomes subject to prosecution by the post office fraud department and by the FTC among other government agencies. Use judgement in using quotes.

Testimonial letters can be goldmines of true claims. But sometimes a testimonial letter rambles. Irrelevant words, sentences and paragraphs straggle in between wonderful quotes. Usually, space limits the use of testimonials. Using too much of one lengthy letter can keep you from using other highly desireable ones. More individual testimonials covering more situations can be more convincing.

Carefully extracting most favorable and to-the-point quotes leaves

119

room to use other quotes and make the overall effect more powerful. Careful selection can feature different advantages. We often take a longer quote from the most coherent, favorable letter with very short excepts from quite a few others. We use the full name for a larger quote and initials for short ones. Often, we'll then quote a half dozen one or two word quotes, preceding them with "other users report".

Testimonials pull orders in a paragraph, more in a copy block, and more with a series of pictures. Pictures of users photographed with or using the product are most effective. Testimonials can be so powerful as to cause the entire ad, from headline and main illustration through the main copy story, to be built around them.

Testimonials from name personalities can be particularly important. Paid testimonials from sport and entertainment personalities are under criticism by government agencies. But in some form, celebrity testimonials will continue. Personalities are people. They eat, sleep and use products.

I know a man who started a modest business with one product which was bought by the most famous broadcast personality of the time for his own use. This personality liked it, gave a strong testimonial with full permission to use it—for no payment—and then invested $250,000 in the business—which prospered.

A big name personality in show business or sports can fear becoming obsolete and dream of a related business that he can play a part in and retire to. If he likes your product, you may be able to make him a partner or give him a royalty to advertise your product. If so, surely he can say he likes and uses your product.

Personalities are known to people who don't know your product or you. If the personality recommends your product, and asks that the reader try your product, perhaps even giving your offer guarantee, usually more orders come in the mail. And the more that the recommendation of the personality is featured in your ad, the more the results can improve.

Let's hope that you get associated with the right personality and present his testimonial to maximum advantage in your ad. Again, it can be a paragraph, a box, or the personality can write and sign your entire ad.

Another element may be any documentation you may have of your product claims. A form of this is association with other firms stronger than yourself. The old story of Rothschild, who when asked for a loan said, "I won't give you any money, but I will let you walk with me across the floor of the Exchange" is still true. The visible association with Rothschild was enough to get credit and backing. If your product uses a component or material with a famous trade name or made by a famous company, feature it in your advertising. Such a component or material may play an important part in the effectiveness of your product. Tests made by the famous company laboratories may be able to prove this dramatically. Your own research may uncover it. Or you may be able to suggest and arrange such tests, and get permission to feature the results in your advertising, preferably showing the logotype of their brand name.

Your product's use by prestige companies may be important if you can simply get permission to use their names. A big name company may tell you why it uses your product and how it finds your product superior and do so with a testimonial letter along with permission to quote it. If you do so in an ad, you attain far more credibility. Your product may have been used and competitively tested by the U. S. Government, the Armed Forces, a university, hospital or institution, by any organization famous, unbiased and in a position to know the merits and defects of any product it uses or tests. If so, and if you can get permission to quote their reaction to, or tests of your product, this helps gain credibility.

Perhaps you can demonstrate what your product can do for such an organization and get permission to publicize results. Perhaps a famous publication has tested your product and published an article with pictures about such tests. Perhaps you can interest an appropriate publication in researchig your product and in doing a story on its merits. In any case, quotes (with permission) from an article on your product vastly increases believability of your advertising.

Your inventor may have been associated with great institutions, government or giant companies. If so, featuring this in your advertising helps achieve trust in him and thus in your product.

An add-on is usually not brought up until the prospective purchaser is at the point of ordering. Sometimes, it's only mentioned in the coupon, sometimes also in a small box next to the coupon, and sometimes it's emphasized more. A cash-up is rarely featured in an ad or mentioned until the coupon.

Don't forget yourself and the concept of your business. People like to deal with people. Small people like small business. If you can establish a personality, flavor and atmosphere by your name, concept and what your are trying to do, you will get more orders. And getting across that concept also becomes an element in your ad.

The final element in your ad is your coupon. A coupon is your only contract between the buyer and you. It is also easier for the buyer to use than to write an order without it. A coupon should be simple, clear and large enough for easy filling in. A cramped coupon can discourage orders.

Most mail order people feel a coupon in a full page ad should be in the lower outside corner, and strongly favor a right hand page with a right hand coupon. But we have had success with coupons on top of the ad or even in the ''gutter'', the inside bottom of the page. The coupon size and location, considered mandatory, varies among mail order people.

A coupon cannot be confusing. It can more easily contain alternative options than mailing instructions without a coupon. A coupon is more essential for a sale than an inquiry, although also favored for inquiry advertising.

For lower price items, it has been more and more customary to add postage charges, plus an internal handling fee for mail order shipping for each order, cash or credit. A simple added phrase in a coupon can explain this. In recent years, it has been mandatory to collect any sales tax due from residents of the State from which you ship or to pay the sales tax and absorb it.

A coupon should lead off with the guarantee. It usually emphasizes the privilege of reserving the item for inspection and trial with final buying decision to be made only after trial. The concept of the cash payment is often treated as a deposit, which only becomes a purchase if you do not return the item before the trial period ends.

A company name inappropriate to the product sometimes pulls less orders than one more appropriate. An address like Fifth Avenue in New York often pulls more orders than a box number. Any address in a cosmopolitan city (for fashion, jewelry,etc.) often pulls more than an address in a small village. A more appropriate area (Vermont for maple syrup) will often pull more for any product.

We'll discuss later the correct keying of coupons so that you can know the response to each of your ads and how to test different kinds of coupon offers.

If you're like me, when you first complete each of your elements, each will need editing. Now, comes the time to turn confusion into clarity. Writing and cutting, putting more in and trimming more down, this is the first step in editing.

My first sentences are long and wandering. But overlong sentences can be divided into two, three or more. My first paragraphs are also too long. But each paragraph can be subdivided as well. My first product news facts come out of sequence. The disorder of my mind comes tumbling out in the disorder of my wording. I murder grammar and crucify the King's English. I'm foggy about commas and confused about proper sentence construction. But somehow, it all gets straightened out by simply redoing it, by writing it and reading it and rewriting what doesn't seem to come across. I keep changing the order of sentences and even paragraphs. I lengthen a sentence that doesn't seem clear and cut every word I can.

In copy (and later in layout), something works or it doesn't. Trial and error, writing first one way and then another, often indicates what works and what doesn't. I cut my sentences down and down. I make my paragraphs shorter and shorter. Between interrupting subheads, I try to open with a one sentence paragraph. I try to close with almost as short a paragraph. I try to keep paragraphs to three, four or five sentences. When I'm finished cutting and capsuling, I read and re-read the final version. Often, I find sentences turned to gibberish by *overcutting*. Now, I must put back some of what I took out. It's a slow back and forth process.

It costs no more rent and causes no more overhead for me to work and rework each ad until it becomes the best effort I am capable of. And one such ad properly written can often pay rent and overhead for some time to come. Now, let's look at several specific kinds of big ads. To introduce a new product in a new field, the ad must explain the entire field as well as the product. The reader doesn't understand what it is or does. Your ad must show the need, create desire and close the sale. It may require the instructor type of selling. Sometimes, there's romance, tradition and nostalgia to be dramatized by pictures and words. The product may have exciting new use applications to show and describe. Instruction picture sequences may be able to make using it seem easy and quick. The component parts may need to be pictured.

The headline and subheads may be able to capsule the new popularity, the ease and speed, and the many applications of your project. The contents boxes may be able to catalogue "use" projects. The copy may tell of the development of the product and the use benefits it makes possible. It may close with savings the product makes possible and the no-risk examination privilege. Quotes from leading magazines and newspapers or famous personalities may document the new wave of interest. Testimonials may tell how easy and quick the product is to work with, how much fun the projects are and how much each finished project can give you in satisfaction and savings.

A format quite natural to the introduction of a new product is an editorial ad.

For years, the Reader's Digest ran occasional stories on new miracle products in which the development of the product over obstacles was presented dramatically. Often, the magazine sections of the Sunday papers will run a story on the leaping popularity of a new hobby or even on new developments in a particular field. Often, a national magazine will run such a story. Occasionally, we've had our own products mentioned in such stories. The growing popularity of any field of activity is news, as is the development of any product (particularly over difficulties) which does something of popular interest better, faster or easier. The public wants to read such stories or publications would not run them. An advertisement modeled after such a story has a good chance of added readership and added credibility. Both are increased by adhering, as closely as possible, to the editorial format of the publication in which the ad appears. Even when the word advertisement is printed at the top (as required by some publications), results are often increased by this format.

The development of the electronic chip calculator had everything to make it news. Today's scientist is our romanticised culture hero. The field of microelectronics is all that Buck Rogers, decades ago, prophesised. The background of a product, first developed as part of the space program, is fascinating. As variation after variation of the chip calculator was developed, *each* was an exciting news story.

One mail order firm catapulted to big success running nothing but editorial style ads on different, new, specialized chip calculators. At such a time with such a basic product, the hunger of the public for more and more information on any product variation seems insatiable. For decades, the automobile industry had such an aura about it. Every new car was an exciting news story. Each new model of a car was news. Just unveiling it was news.

There was a time when one of today's most everyday products, the ball point pen, was dramatic news. Today, a full page editorial ad on a ball point pen would have all the appeal of a story on the safety pin. Make sure your product is exciting news before you try an editorial ad.

Some kinds of mail order products are best sold with ads quite unlike distribution product ads and other kinds with ads far more similar to them. The more of a luxury a product is, the less difference there is between mail order advertising and advertising of the same product in retail stores. The more style and fashion oriented the product is, the more this is so.

A hard sell would make it undesirable. An encyclopedic list of advantages would bore. Style and atmosphere make it wanted, despite its price. The feeling of the advertising conveyed by art, layout and typography can be more important than the words, whether the product is sold mail order or via stores.

A technical or industrial product filling a specific need requires clarity and technical accuracy of description. Usually, emotional appeals are out of place and may hinder rather than help sales. What the product is and does can be important news to the audience reached. The difference between the advertising mail order and the *introductory* advertising of the same industrial or technical product distributed elsewhere is often not great.

Often, the entire ad can be built around one overwhelmingly important element. Sometimes, the entire ad is constructed to indicate a tremendous bargain. If a single item, one big, beautiful, dramatic picture will sometimes dominate the ad. The product will be glorified and shown to maximum advantage. The low price for the expensive looking product will probably be right in the headline. The opening copy will start off with the price story. The copy story and boxes will cite proof *why it is possible*. The close will be an appeal to see and judge the value for yourself *at no risk*.

If it is a set of items at a bargain, the picture can be a cornocopia shot with the items arranged so profusely it can seem scarcely possible that *so many* items could be available for the price. Then, next to the coupon can be the shot of the *extra giveaway,* another set of less expensive items but still further emphasizing the overall generosity of the offer. The main copy story will start off with the summary of what you get, often repeating in only slightly expanded form...the headline and subheads. The copy will move into each item included, citing in detail the virtues of each. The cumulative effect of listing the items and uses and advantages of each builds constantly. The cataloging box lists each with still more descriptive detail. The prospective buyer can read a little or a lot, fill out the coupon at once or brood over it for weeks.

Price reduction ads pull. Rarely does a retailer's advertisement for any item at full price pull anywhere near as well as a price reduction ad. In mail order, a special limited time reduced price offer often has a similar effect. A publisher offering a new book mail order at a pre-publication price dramatically lower for ordering before publication date, has traditionally done well.

More dramatic price reductions pull better. A price reduction ad pulls best when the product has been heavily advertised at the older, higher price already presented as a bargain.

For each who bought at the old price there have been others

tempted, but feeling they could not afford the product at the time. Now, the price reduction opens the door to selling this already, almost sold market. Many millions may have seen the product advertised. They have never read the ad through or even seriously considered buying. Drawn by the price reduction, many *will now* read the ad.

The price reduction goes right into the headline. *The reason why* goes in the subhead. A prominent box on the upper right may show the old price X'd out with the new low price and the saving in big bold type underneath. The copy opens with the price reduction, goes on to the reason why, and closes with the value made possible by the reduction, all at no risk.

Some product claim copy has to go to make room for the price reduction copy. As in any cutting, it's necessary to fight for every word. It usually proves possible to streamline the entire ad, speed it up, make the copy better than ever and include the price reduction story. Price reduction in a new ad is often best used in the close and in a box near the coupon. It's an extra argument to buy now, but effective only after the reader becomes almost sold by the copy.

A price reduction ad for a "blind item" which the purchaser can't easily tell the value of is far less effective than for an item which has an established price. Some mail order firms consistently run one campaign to introduce an item at full price and then run a follow-up at a dramatically lower price. Some publishers run a title, like a damp towel, through a succession of price reduction ringers, each at a lower price level.

As you collect more ads, you will notice different kinds we have not taken up due to lack of space. We will later discuss the creating of smaller ads. Right now, we want to decide how to *finish* an ad based on what we have learned to date. The process of completing a big ad is like putting together a puzzle or a prefab house with sections you've already constructed.

The greatest difficulty in creating initial big space ads consists of decisions. How much in space and words should you devote to each element? Which of countless approaches should you use? How big should picture and headlines be? How do you fit it together? And how much will fit in at all?

Here's the way some of my greatest copywriters have disposed of these problems and how you can, too.

126

Chapter 7

Putting It All Together

. . . "easiest, simplest, fastest, way"
to start writing complete mail
order ads...however complex

Once, one of our star copywriters brought in his latest masterpiece. As soon as the ad was read in the office, the praise began. It was at once considered the best ad that he had ever written. I started to read it. I saw at once *why* it was such a great ad and looked over at my star. He looked back and began to smile.

His ad was an overwhelmingly successful paraphrase, great because it was modeled after one of the greatest ads of all time. His product was for Lythrum, a plant just propagated in a Canadian Government horticultural test station. His ad was modeled after the great classic Canada Dry Ginger Ale ad, written by James Mathes a number of decades before.

The Canada Dry ad started with the line, "Down from Canada came tales of a sparkling new beverage". The Lythrum ad started with the lines, "Down from Canada came tales of a new horticultural discovery". Line for line and word for word, the appropriate copy for the Lythrum story was substituted for the great Canada Dry copy. The rhythm, the pace, the poetry feeling was kept intact. Our writer had written the ad originally as a lark for the sheer fun of it. But it sold Lythrum with great success.

Paraphrasing is the quickest way to write ads. It teaches beginning

127

writers faster than any other way. Paraphrasing can be of ads for products in fields remote from yours, in no way affected by your paraphrase of their success.

Once, on the desk of another star copywriter of ours, I saw a radio commercial pattern available for *any* item. It was taken from one of his most successful radio mail order commercials. But the *specific* descriptive words for the product were taken out and replaced with blanks. All that was necessary was to put in equivalent descriptive words applicable to the product and voila! There was a new mail order radio commercial and a pretty good one.

This writer later became a competitor and developed a talent for paraphrasing that was uncanny. Our writers would take several months to create a brand new, successful ad for a new product. Our alumnus could paraphrase it in one day for a totally different product. When our writers would get upset and complain, I would advise them to master the technique of paraphrasing their own ads themselves. No one was hurt by such paraphrasing. I am not amused when a competitor copies our product and our ad. I am not at all disturbed by paraphrasing our ad for a product in a quite different field.

I could only smile when I saw how ingeniously our alumnus paraphrased our automobile oil additive ad into his orchid ad or his fertilizer soil conditioner ad "Turns hard baked clay into soft loamy soil" into his cosmetic ad "Turns dry baked out skin into soft, youthful complexion."

What will science think of next?

Let's do what they did. Let's select one full page ad from the file of ads collected and paraphrase it element by element, paragraph by paragraph, sentence by sentence, and word by word. Let's use a layout plan for the ad modeled exactly on the sample ad. Let's adapt our ad to the successful model ad in every way. For your first full page ad, it is particularly helpful to be guided by a model ad.

And you will find many of them. Clip them, classify them, file them and study them. Observe differences and similarities. Some are crowded with type. Some have far more pictures. A few are predominantly one or more big pictures and shorter than average copy. From your collection of full page ads, pick one as your model.

The model ad can be on a completely unrelated product, but should be related in style and purpose. Take a luxury product ad as model for your luxury product ad, a price reduction ad, a product introduction ad, an industrial, technical or whatever ad is most similar to yours in what it is trying to do. Take a *successful* mail order ad that runs widely and repeats its insertions. Use your research notes.

The first thing you'll realize is that no matter how big your ad, you'll never be able to use all the research material you've gathered. Usually, you still must select, no matter how much you boil down and streamline your product story. Just starting on your paraphrasing gives you ideas for more research that results in still more material.

Select a working headline to start. As you work and re-work your full page ad, you'll develop more and more headline candidates for later consideration. Select a working subhead and subsidiary subheads. From your research, begin to make a list of subhead possibilities to interrupt the main copy story.

Count the words in the main copy story of your model ad. You'll quickly discover that the number of words allowed for the main copy story is not nearly as many as you might have expected. Before you start paraphrasing the main copy story, look over the other component parts of your model ad. Any enlargement in your ad of your *equivalent* element will *reduce* available copy elsewhere.

Look at your working headline. If it takes two lines instead of one in your model, you will have to reduce the ad elsewhere. Try to reduce your working headline to approximately the same number of characters per line and number of lines, as in your model ad. Perhaps you can *save* characters in the headline versus your model, even reduce from two lines to one.

Look at the picture or pictures in your model ad. Does your product for some reason *require* more or bigger pictures? Do you have the picture possibilities to use effectively *as much* space? If so, the rest of the ad will have to be adjusted accordingly. Look over each caption. Can you paraphrase your captions to the approximate number of type characters as those of the model ad?

Look at the boxes in the model ad with testimonials or other documentation and with cataloguing of contents or listing of product claims. Do you have equivalent testimonials, documentation and contents or claims? If not, how will your paraphrase vary from the model? Look at the guarantee box, if any, and the coupon. If you paraphrase either, modify it to your offer. It can be done quickly and will either fit in the same size guarantee box and coupon as your model, require larger space or occasionally *less* space.

Assume that your other elements, outside of the main copy story, can be paraphrased in about the same overall space as in your model. If your coupon is a bit larger or smaller, adjust the number of words allowable for your main copy story accordingly.

129

Now, just paraphrase the main copy story, word for word throughout.

Keep the same number of subheads as your model with approximately the same number of words in each subhead, the same amount of white space above and below, the same margins on either side.

You want your ad to have the same rhythm and pace as your model. This means that each sentence must have about the same number of words and each word must have about the same number of characters. If you substitute a longer word for a shorter word, delete an extra small word and balance out the syllables. This keeps the rhythm.

Build sentence by sentence, paragraph by paragraph. The more you have saturated yourself with your research notes, the faster the right substitute words come to mind. Keep editing, sharpening, smoothing. Read your ad to yourself for rhythm and pace. If you make one sentence or paragraph longer than your model, make the next shorter.

Re-read what you have written yourself. Does it have the rhythm and feel of your model? If so, the rest will follow. If you're mentally fatigued and blocked, go back to reworking your research notes. Go at your own pace. The right words will start coming. Thomas Mann wrote a page a day, but a perfect page. If in doubt, write alternate words, sentences, paragraphs.

The opinion of others may be helpful, but most will not understand what your ad *should* be, why you follow that style and write to that length. You, yourself, must be the judge. Does each word, sentence and paragraph leave you more anxious to read the next? Do they build interest, desire and belief? Does the rhythm and pace have an excitement and electricity? Are the news facts *news* or *stale*? How does *your* story compare with similar *actual editorial news stories?* Would your ad cause *you* to keep reading, *and buy* if you had no association with the ad or product? After you've completed only your first *third* of the main copy story you will know the answer. If it "works", keep going, however slow your progress, and your entire copy story will "work" as well.

If the first third doesn't "work", keep rewriting it until it does. Once you've written the main copy story, completing the rest of your ad becomes a certainty. Think of each other element as a separate ad, which you want to write equally perfectly, however long it takes. It may come far, more quickly than you expect, and completely to your satisfaction. Reread your research notes. What *important* points are not covered in your main story? How can you best work *each* in?

Take it easy. Do an easy element first. Write your *guarantee box*

130

or section. Here, the equivalent guarantee section of your model is most easily paraphrased. What in *your* offer of a return privilege *varies* from that of your model? What about servicing, the length of your free examination period, your policy on factory defects and all other points of your guarantees? Adjust accordingly.

Does your ad have a documentation of claims box? Look again at your research notes for equivalent documentation. If the U.S. Government uses the product in your model ad, who uses yours? If a celebrity recommends the product in your model ad, what star personality recommends yours? If General Motors supplies the key component in the product of your model ad, what giant corporation supplies the key component in *your* product?

The more you've done your research homework, the faster your paraphrased ad writes itself. Primarily, what you need to do is to *select* the most appropriate news facts for the blanks in your paraphrasing. The actual words and phrases that have most color and excitement will come straight from your research notes. You're putting together a jigsaw puzzle. And you can take plenty of time to do it, because it can make your fortune.

Now, let's get to the box cataloguing contents or listing product claims. Here again, your research has done almost all the work for you. You need only list contents or claims on a long priority list. One extra item can get extra sales. You want to include all you can. But priority goes to the most important and not all can get in. In this box, you may vary more from your model. You want to keep total words in the box to the same approximate number. But perhaps you can make each listing tighter and briefer, use three words instead of five or two in place of three. You may be able to get in *more* listings than your model. Or you may *need* more words for each listing and not be able to fit in as *many* listings. Adjust accordingly.

Does your model ad have a demonstration picture proof box? Your research should come up with the right equivalent. Does your model ad have testimonials? If your research hasn't uncovered any, interview users and ask for product opinions. Where favorable, get testimonials and signed releases. What about the other picture elements in your model ad? Does your research give you picture idea equivalents, either photographs or drawings of any kind? Now, take a further look through your entire notes. Are there any important points you still haven't covered anywhere in your ad? Can one or more of them be worked into picture captions? However tiny the type of the captions, each may get more readership than the average line of your main copy story.

Now, put your entire ad together. Read it. Compare it from beginning to end with your model. Sleep on it. Modify it or let it stand and prepare to meet your art director.

Before you do, make a "copywriter's layout" of your own. Many copywriters (perhaps most) will make a "copywriter's layout" as soon as they come up with first headline and picture ideas. We have used the layout of the model ad. Now, we need to make our own layout showing each adaptation we have made.

Now, you must make what may be your most important creative decision, your choice of picture or pictures. Study the layout of your model ad. Select from your "A" list the picture or pictures that seem to do the most equivalent job.

Get a ruler. Measure your model ad. Rule out a space 50 percent larger, but in the same proportions, on a 14" x 17" pad of layout tissue paper. You can get it from any art store. Measure the exact height and width of the headline of your model ad. Do the same for the subheads, then for the illustration, next for each paragraph of body copy and coupon. Measure the space between paragraphs, above and below subheads and margins on each side of headline, subheads, illustrations and body copy. Now, rule out the equivalent space but make it 50 percent wider and 50 percent deeper for each section within the layout space you've ruled out. It will be easier to work with this space 50 percent larger than your model ad. It can be reduced back later.

Roughly sketch in, however crudely, your indication of the picture or pictures to be used. If this is too difficult or time consuming, simply write in the space you've ruled out for the picture what the picture or pictures will be.

Now, letter by letter, pencil in your headline. You've already ruled out the bottom line and top line of each letter. It's simple to pencil out the letter fully from bottom line to top line. Use upper or lower case letters exactly as your model ad does. Carefully write in your substitute wording, line by line, throughout.

For each line of copy in your main news story, make a double line. Indicate the number of lines of actual copy and any indenting at beginning and close of each paragraph with these double lines. If you have paraphrased a paragraph pretty exactly as to numbers of words and characters, the paragraph length and structure should be the same as your model. If you have lengthened one paragraph and shortened another, roughly indicate so by the number, length and indentation of the double lines you show for each paragraph.

Keep proportionately the same white space between paragraphs and also between columns of copy. Pencil in your new subheads in place of those of your model. Allow the same proportionate margin above and below.

Rule out in proportion each box which you have adapted from your model. If your paraphrased copy is shorter or longer for any box, reduce or enlarge your ruled out box in proportion. Pencil in your new box headline and subheads. Rule out double lines to indicate copy.

Do the same with your coupon. Indicate double lines of proportionate length for your subheads. In brief, indicate in proportion the equivalent of each element in your model ad *but* reduced or enlarged in proportion to your copy adaptation.

Execution of any ad *can* be far from the great expectations of your copy and ''copywriter's layout.'' Fighting to insure that the final effect equals or surpasses your expectations is an unending battle.

Before we discuss that battle in detail, let's get back to creating smaller ads. Doing so will help prepare you to learn simplest, fastest, easiest and most economical ways of finishing ads as they actually appear in print. The first step is to build a big collection of every size of smaller mail order ad from an inch up.

Compare the ads that come from mail order market places with those that run outside such sections. Notice that specialized products, run in *related* specialized publications, often use briefer copy.

Let's consider writing a small ad for another item. If for a specific mail order shopping section, study ads in it closest in size to the ad you are about to write. Study carefully a number of issues. Note the ads that *repeat* most frequently.

Study how many words each uses in its headline, how much white space above and below it and in the adjoining margins. Study the picture or pictures each uses, their location, and their space allowance in relation to copy. Notice the body copy. Count the total words of copy in each ad. Count the words in each line of copy, the words in the average sentence, the number of sentences in the paragraph. Note where parts of sentences are used and where abbreviations are used. Notice the size of the type in headline, subhead, and paragraphs. How many words are in each subhead? Select a model ad to paraphrase. After creating a page ad, it will seem far easier.

Now, paraphrase the model ad. Make your headline the same number of words. Substitute for any subhead your own subhead of the same number of words. Count the number of characters of headline and subhead. Keep your substitute headline and subhead each within several characters of the original, as well as cutting to the same number of words each.

Does it have one or more pictures? Plan to use an equivalent picture or pictures in the same spot or spots. Paragraph by paragraph, line by line, and word by word, count the characters and substitute your own paraphrased words. Include equivalents for any boxes or captions.

You may have to simplify your offer for a small ad. The offer in your model ad may differ from the kind of offer you are making. If so, look for another same size model ad *just for the offer wording*. When you find it, paraphrase your offer to it as close to word for word as you can. Use this copy block instead of paraphrasing the offer copy block of your original model ad. Notice if the model ad has a coupon. A one third of a page or larger ad is seldom without it. Smaller ads sometimes have one and sometimes don't. Smallest ads down to an inch seldom do.

If your model ad has a coupon, paraphrase the coupon wording to your product or to that of the alternate model ad just mentioned, using your price and terms. If there is no coupon, paraphrase the appropriate mail-in instruction as close to word for word as possible. If necessary, paraphrase a more appropriate alternate coupon. Be sure to remember to include any shipping and handling charge and tax in your state that you do not wish to absorb. Be sure your ad states your address correctly with a proper mailing key. We'll give keying instructions later. The entire job is far less complex and far simpler than creating your full page ad.

Research writes your ad to a surprising degree. Actual writing starts with *selecting* from the wealth of news items uncovered by your research, those with most interest to most people. If you have done a thorough research job, and have a very small shopping column ad, you can only *capsule* the *news facts* that your research has uncovered. This gives even more of a *news feeling* to your ad.

Each *news fact* must be boiled down to an ever briefer form. What is the single most universally interesting news fact about your product? What is the second? The third, etc.? Your headline often comes from the most exciting news that your research uncovers about your product. Your headline is a capsule of your number one news fact. It may be one word or several lines. Only by selecting any headline as a working headline, can you get started. Only by writing down *enough alternatives*, one after the other, can you make the best headline choice.

From a list you will have prepared of various alternative headlines and subheads, you must make the final best choice you can. Your experience with your big ad headlines will be a great help.

You must give *priorities* of importance to each *news fact* you boil down. Just arranging your news facts in this *news priority* causes your ad to take form. Editing is trial and error. Word by word, sentence by sentence, paragraph by paragraph is the only way. Sometimes, the revision comes in a rush, sometimes with painful slowness. Generally, the more thorough the research and the more saturated and impregnated you are with news facts about your product, the faster your news story rewriting builds. But it's far easier than in your bigger, more complex ad.

When you have completed paraphrasing the copy of your model ad, paraphrase its layout. Do so exactly as instructed for a page ad. This time it will be far simpler. Make your "copywriter's layout" 50 percent larger on the layout pad just as you did before. Follow the layout of your model ad as carefully as possible, but indicate any variations you have made just as you did on your page ad. Keep the same spacings between paragraphs, same margin on either side, same indentation, and allow the same space for pictures as your model ad.

For a small space ad *outside* a mail order section, use an equivalent size model that runs widely *outside* such sections. Most small ads successful outside succeed in an appropriate mail order section. It takes more digging to find your successful model outside, but it's worth it. In bigger circulation publications, your model will tend to be an ad that pays out both ways. Often, it's harder selling.

After you have written successful ads, you will begin using your own past successful ads as models for future ads. You will make more and more of a study of successful mail order offers and ads. You will adapt much from them, but in your own way. Once you've written and produced your first full page "hit", you'll have quite a different viewpoint on smaller space ads.

I prefer to write my full page ad *first*, even if I don't produce and run it first. To write my full page ad, I am forced to saturate myself with my product story so thoroughly that smaller space ads come faster and easier. They become tighter and more effective.

The art of first cutting and then capsuling to get down to smallest space is a discipline to acquire. But the result is superior to the first effort at writing a smaller ad *before* the full page ad. I have found that writing a nine line and picture editorial shopping column for an item is far improved after writing a page ad. Even in a one, two or three inch ad, the essence of the full page ad can strengthen it greatly.

Often, one picture element developed for the full page ad, but not thought of before, creates a dramatic impact for a smaller ad. Often, the heart of the headline of the full page ad becomes a magnet headline for the smaller space ad. Subheads supply meaty copy for small ads. Captions, even without pictures, are sometimes good copy phrases for smaller ads.

I like to start with a page, then write a half page, a column, a half column and a shopping column write-up. By the time I've finished the small ads, I've often found improvements for the full page ad, too. The smaller the advertisement is, the shorter and more to the point must be the ad copy. I keep cutting and capsuling. I keep searching for key copy words to excerpt.

In a very small ad, I may only have a paragraph or two of copy. My sentences sometimes become phrases. My connecting words become fewer. My sentences may drop a noun and start with a predicate. Each word must work. None must be lazy. Each must be specific. Often, my smallest ad is scarcely more than the headline and subheads of my largest ad.

I then write my smaller ads *two* ways. One is a version of my full page ad cut down to however small my small ad is. For the other, I select a model smaller ad and paraphrase by excerpting from my full page paraphrased copy. Either way creates a better ad for me than starting from scratch. Then, I often merge and combine into one far better ad.

The more research I do and the more I paraphrase, the more I also originate entire ads.

Often, you'll go back to original research for more appropriate word choices. You may conclude that your smallest version is totally inadequate. And originating your own copy can come fast as soon as you master paraphrasing of ads. It's still a matter of doing more research than others, studying with care the advertising of successful mail order products and applying what you care to, to your own ads.

Try writing, without a specific model, a tiny classified ad of several lines. Write your own original shopping column edit. Create a very small shopping column ad, without a model, entirely in your own words. Try larger ads. Work up to a Time magazine size page ad. Originate each time. Then cut and capsule to smaller ads again.

Done in this simple progression, creating your own original advertising won't seem hard. In giving my suggestions at each step, I may have seemed to make too much of writing a simple classified ad or any other first creative task. However, it has only been to emphasize how much easier writing more complex ads can later be, when you have mastered writing simpler ones.

Let's now take up producing finished ads.

Chapter 8

Producing Finished Ads

*. . . without. . . or with an art director. . . ad production
problems. . . "translating" into size variations safely*

By now, you may know the exact cost of running your test ad in a
publication. You're probably not familiar with its possible production
costs.

These preparation costs often start with the use of an art director,
an artist who makes "layouts" by roughly sketching out your intended
ad. If you are small, an art director usually can help you as a production
manager to carry through the execution of the ad.

You may place your advertising through an advertising agency
with an art director and art and production department. If so, you will
turn over to their specialists the problems of completing your ad. You
may work directly with a free lance art director or art studio. You may
work with an advertising consultant. All this we will discuss later in
more detail.

Total costs of ad production can be quite a shock. You may have
no choice but to do everything in the simplest way. You may try to
avoid the use of an art director and most other professional costs of
preparing an ad. If so, don't be too concerned. Many moonlighters have
started with almost no preparation cost for their first test ad. Many firms
have started out successfully in mail order without the perfect advertising agency or formed their own. Many firms without an agency have

137

operated without either an art director or expensive preparation costs.

This is most feasible for simpler, smaller ads. A very small ad with no illustration has the very least production cost and best chance of coming out closest to the effect anticipated. Paraphrasing a simple, small ad with or without a picture gives you a good chance to work without an art director. The more precisely you paraphrase, the more this is so. Your model ad provides the layout and guide in setting type. You can make a simple paste-up of a photostat of the picture, headline, subheads, body type, and of mailing instructions or coupon with your logotype. The less crowded your model ad is, the better chance your ad has of coming out correctly without an art director.

The paraphrasing of a page ad is the best way to get a "feel" for writing ads of any size. But your first test will probably be a small ad you have paraphrased. It is safer to try without an art director and perhaps, without an expensive typographer. For your page ad and particularly a complex one, I recommend that you work with an art director. As you make money in mail order and create more big ads, your art director will become more and more your right artm. The creative contributions will pay his or her way at each step. And the more you get into the preparation of your ads, learn about production methods and do the work yourself, the more you will save in preparation costs. You will also achieve better results. In some kinds of ads, you will become more independent. In others, you will not feel safe without using an art director.

I know one mail order man who profitably spent hundreds of thousands of dollars in advertising without an art director. He wrote all advertising himself. He owned his own house advertising agency. One employee acted as media buyer, production manager and forwarder of all advertising material. He has a talent for keeping ads extremely simple and not crowded. Ads were usually set in type by the publication without charge. His mail order business has always been quite profitable.

Moonlighters with little or no money can deal directly with the publication production manager instead of an art director. The smaller and simpler your ad is, the more feasible this becomes. Saving money by doing without an art director and a good typographer can sometimes limit the desired effect, take longer, and require more effort and know-how on your part. The smaller and simpler your ad is, the more feasible this becomes.

Newspapers usually set type without charge, but charge for photo engravings or linecut plates. Magazines usually charge for type setting.

138

A typography shop stocks a wide variety of type faces, sets type with care and is expensive. If you can't afford an art director, you usually can't afford a good typographer. If you sell a luxury product, a fashion product or prestige product of any kind, it's dangerous not to use a good typographer. Newspaper set type while often adequate is seldom elegant. This can provide a slum setting for a high style product.

Each way to save money on type setting has limitations. A small local newspaper is often a very low cost type setting source. The choice of type faces is very limited. Type setting is sometimes sloppy. But it's a start.

Certain shops with simpler IBM computerized type setting machines cost considerably less than full scale typography. Most of these shops also have quite a limited choice of type faces, but variety of choice is growing. The effect is usually more finished than the newspaper setting job, but substantially less than that of a top typographer. Both newspaper and IBM typesetting are usually slower than a typographer. The IBM typeset cost is usually, far less than the regular typographer and more than the small newspaper typesetting job.

One solution is to use the expensive typographer for headlines and subheads and the IBM typesetting for body type. There is also available headline and subhead photo type in a variety of sizes on adhesive backed paper. These can be pasted down letter by letter. The more you learn about production, the more money you can save.

Just as you can choose simple products to go into, you can confine yourself to the simplest kinds of ads. I know one very successful mail order man who only sells a product for which he can create a very simple ad with the smallest possible production cost. He avoids complicated ads because with each slight additional bit of complexity in an ad, preparation cost can go up.

Paraphrasing your page ad simplifies layout and production problems and saves preparation cost. The more closely you have kept to the exact number of words, syllables and characters of your model ad, section by section, the simpler should be your art director's job. Show the model ad, cite it's success and explain the success of other paraphrased ads. If mail order experienced, your art director will instantly agree to follow it.

If limited financially, you may use the art director solely to follow the paraphrased layout exactly. This will save his time and your money. If your art director *improves* your ad, he will need extra time. This will cost you more money but might increase results sharply. As you succeed and create other ads, it should pay to get even more time from him.

Layout work is only part of the cost of making an ad. It costs just as much to set type for bad copy as for good. Sometimes, it costs even more because bad copy is often needlessly overlong. It costs as much to retouch and then make a plate of a bad picture as of a good one. The paste-up cost is the same for a bad or a good ad.

If you've worked to *write* copy as suggested, you have painfully gone through many partial rewrites to perfect each paragraph. The art director's equivalent of a partial rewrite is an overlay. It would be fruitless to have endless rewriting by a copywriter and no revision of a layout. Yet, often this occurs. Usually, this is because an art director is given the problem of making a near impossible production deadline. Often, the high hourly cost of the art director makes the cost of layout after layout seem prohibitive.

This is not so. By laying a tissue overlay on the first layout and sketching in an alternative layout of part of the ad, a dramatic improvement can sometimes be achieved in *three minutes*. The more your art director understands what you are trying to achieve, the better prepared he is to make such quick, creative contributions. The cost of properly *orienting* your art director *before* the layout is an hour or so of billing time. If you total the cost of making the ad, including typography, engraving, paste-ups, photostats, messenger pick up and incidentals, you can usually get ample overlays and even additional layouts for only 20 percent to 30 percent more total cost.

Your art director must be convinced of the advantages of overlays and be willing to make them. Without this additional overlay and layout time, your ad becomes more of a lottery ticket. With overlays you can improve your ad together, step by step. He must help you in this way to marry words to layout and pictures or you must perform the function yourself.

As you work more with your art director, it may become advisable to get together earlier with him in planning and creating your newest ad. My suggested method of writing your full page ad assumes that you are just starting on your own as a copywriter and would waste more of your art director's time and your money consulting before you finished your ad. Until you finish your ad, you might not be properly prepared. I'm assuming that you've not yet gained a close rapport with your art director. Usually, it comes *after* you've worked together on ad after ad. When you first approach him, if your ad is finished to this degree, you may get more consideration as a professional, and more cooperation.

Have your art director read your copy and glance through your

140

research notes and list of picture ideas. He may see picture possibilities which you have overlooked. *His* layout may soon *transform* your ad. If you can afford it, ask him to make two layouts. He can follow *your* version fairly faithfully, but make his own entirely *his* way. In his version, he can use more space for pictures, less for words, change the ad in emphasis on headline and subheads, *enlarge* some words, make others smaller, whatever he feels best.

The more professionally you have done your work, the more he will respect it and faithfully carry it out. However closely he follows your "copywriter's layout", he will add little touches which one by one will improve your ad. Keep an open mind to each layout change he suggests. Each time, encourage him to do it two ways, first your original way, then with an overlay, his way. You may find that you prefer his when you see it. If each seems equally effective, *favor his.*

As soon as he realizes that you're giving serious consideration to his ideas and that you're not always adamant on your own, more of his ideas will begin to flow. The ideal is to stick to your guns concerning your copywriter's layout until you see it fully laid out, while encouraging overlay after overlay of his alternatives and a complete layout of his own.

When he completes the two versions, take them home to study carefully. Your own version faithfully carried out may surprise you. If your paraphrase contained more copy than the model, it may look cruder and cheaper than expected. It may not seem as clear. His version may be superior. If your version is an exact paraphrase, it usually will "work". His version, as a whole, may be impractical. But it will give you ideas. It will usually contain elements you never thought of, but which "work" exceedingly well. Sometimes, fitting elements of his ad into yours, or vice versa, improves it. *Consider* other ways of improving your ad.

Try your own copywriter's overlays. Crystalize your thoughts on possible layout revisions. Look again at other ads. Keep studying both versions of layout and copy. Your art director may contribute a change of emphasis that quite alters and improves the effect of your ad.

If you like your version best, stick to it. It is expensive to test two different page ads, different enough to require resetting type throughout. If each version seems to have a strong chance, consider testing both. Consider whether either version can be strengthened by using parts of the other. Consider any overlay ideas for each.

Seeing the layouts may stimulate rethinking on copy. Any worthwhile ideas can be worked into an alternative copy section to be considered. Read the ad as it was, and with your substitute insert section. Select the version which "feels" most right. Hopefully, your art director has also looked over both versions and has some suggested overlays completed. If so, give consideration to his creative contributions. Otherwise, his suggestions may quickly dry up. Don't compromise simply for public relations. Make your own final, command decision.

Rework any copy section or changes that the final layout requires. New picture ideas will require new captions. Any layout idea that devotes more space to any ad element will require revising the layout and appropriate copy block. Supply your art director with final complete copy. Include all copy revisions requested by him, to conform with your final layout.

Now, he (or when you're bigger, your production manager) specifies type for every word from headline to coupon. He calculates whether your entire copy will fit and if not, how much needs cutting. If you've done a good job of paraphrasing, the principal cuts required will come from agreed layout changes. Cut your copy as your art director or production manager requests. Type setting can now be ordered.

Now, the type proofs come back. For full page ads with simple formats and short copy, the problem is simple. But for a big crowded ad, complex and tight, you can still expect a surprise or two.

Handwritten corrections (if your handwriting is like mine) can cause typographical errors. Any mispellings will be faithfully reproduced. If your art director failed to calculate or miscalculated his typography arithmetic, the effect will be glaring and costly. If done reasonably correctly, there will still be minor corrections. There may be "widows". A "widow" is a single last word of a paragraph, carried over as the only word of the next line. Cutting just one word from the preceding line is the equivalent of cutting an entire line of type elsewhere.

Some corrections you can make from the typographer's proofs. You may find more errors when your art director makes the "paste-up" of your ad. All type will be pasted down. Photostats already made to correct size of each piece of art work, whether drawing or photograph, will be pasted into position. Take your first real look at your ad. If you have paraphrased your model ad closely and followed your art director's instructions for copy changes required, you should be happy. This assumes that you have a competent art director.

Let's take up the selection of the right art director and the most effective way to work with him or her. Being aware of problems and disasters that may occur, you can often avoid them.

You may avoid much costly grief by going into partnership with an advertising specialist. A top art director, copy writer or production manager might consider becoming your partner and contributing professional work.

If you can afford it, you may prefer to hire the best specialists. On the right fee basis, you may secure an advertising agency more suitable for you. You may hire a top mail order advertising consultant. You may hire a really outstanding mail order advertising art director. You can leave to others much of the problems of art and production. However, you will feel better knowing more about what you are paying for. Going first class *can* pay off faster. But in mail order advertising, it can cost you at every turn.

You may not be able to afford an advertising agency or consultant or get the one you need. If so, use an art director as needed and at lowest possible cost. If you decide to select one, get a recommendation from a successful mail order firm, or a friend in the advertising agency business. Check the nearest substantial department store. They can't have "cheap" looking art, yet buy anything at fairly rock bottom prices. The store's advertising manager may give you several good leads. Look for commercial artist's situation wanted ads. You might run a classified ad addressed to art directors, art studios and artists. Look under "commercial art studios" in the yellow pages.

There are untrained and trained art directors, hacks and "pro's", inexperienced, tired, old, fresh, those full of vitality and knowledgeable ones. Art studios can be "factories" or quality outfits. If you start with little or no money, you're fortunate to get anyone competent. But have confidence in yourself. Find good talent and sell yourself as a prospective growing client.

An art director in a larger advertising agency makes layouts only and does not work on finishes. An art director in a small agency or free lancing outside often does both. Some art directors are thoroughly trained in graphics, including a considerable knowledge of typography, engraving, printing and various processes involved. That's the experience you need.

Later, you will prefer your art director to do no finishes and just work with you creatively. At first, you can't afford that. You want him to help you get the best ad at lowest production price. You pay him for his services, partially in the fees for "finishes" he does for you and partially for layouts.

If you could find a young man or woman starting out, already thoroughly trained professionally, yet willing to bet on you as a future client, that would be ideal.

But most learn "on the job". Beginners often are the blind leading the blind. Their work is often slow. When hours are added up, only the appearance of your ad is cheap. Decisions they make on your behalf may give you nightmares, delay you and cost you far more than any savings you may think you're getting.

Seasoned "hacks" give you mediocre to poor work. But there are many excellent art directors, artists and art studios. Art studios are where beginners turn into professionals. Beginners supervised by professionals work far faster and mistakes are caught by superiors.

Check other clients of the art director you are considering. Look over samples of his work. Select the best art director you can get. Only trial and error can determine if the chemistry will be right and whether he or she turns out as you hoped.

Cost per hour is not as vital as would seem, certainly after you get your first success. It's better to do without an art director than select a cheap but poor one. Location is important. An art director needs to be in a large enough city to have a one hour photostat service, overnight typographer and engraver nearby and preferably, messenger service to his door. The less you know about production procedures, the more vital it is that your art and production manager be technically well informed and up to date on the broadest variety of production problems. If you have no production manager and no production background, it's vital that your art director be technically capable of being your production manager.

The art director properly selected and worked with can give expression to your copy and copywriter's layout or help to create an ad quite different than you visualized and far more effective.

If your art director is an old hand at creating and producing mail order ads, you'll get your ad laid out quickly and professionally. The better your art director is, usually the higher his or her hourly cost will be. If your art director has no mail order experience, this is not necessarily bad. You may get a still fresher, more interesting layout. The ideal is that your art director have a selling sense, as well as an art and layout sense. Your art director should be a good creative partner to you, translate your ideas into layout, and create his own. He should be able to give and take. If he has a professional knowledge of production processes, he can recommend the one most practical for execution of an ad. He should have a sense of frugality in production costs.

Because an art director's time is expensive, there is a tendency to

144

rush in, race through an explanation of the problem and race out. Often, the art director is busy at another job and cannot start on your project until later. Anything that you've told him verbally may never have been clearly understood and later, largely forgotten. The layout he comes back with may reflect this. The art director may want to get away from *you* and work by himself, then show you what he's done and sell it to you.

Try to protect the art director's time and your own. Remember, the meter is always running. Every anecdote you tell is costing *you* pro rata, what may be a stiff hourly fee. The hourly fee, however high, is usually quite reasonable for actual "board work"—making layouts and executing ads. Organized preparation for "board work" can only make it more effective. Before you meet your art director, assemble everything needed. Keep it in one neat package. Don't get charged for fumbling through your own brief case. Make notes beforehand of exactly what you want to go over with him. If you waste an art director's creative time, your creative costs will quickly go sky high.

Every product has a different picture potential.

Some are ugly and some, stunning. A great photograph can create desire for some, but have less effect for others. Each product has the possibility of being shown to advantage in some special way. For some, full color is magic. For others, black and white is superior. For some, a single picture, a before and after shot, a use sequence can indisputably· prove product claims. Picture research requires detective work. The more picture research you do, the more tools you bring your art director.

Often, a copywriter comes up with a picture idea that might be great. Sometimes, his lack of knowledge of art and photography result in his having a vague and fuzzy concept of how his picture idea will look. The art director, with far more professional knowledge, is more capable of visualizing whether such a picture idea can "work". He's often apt to be far more prolific with picture ideas. His will be on the average, far more practical.

Artists and copywriters are natural adversaries. Artists firmly believe that a picture is worth a thousand words. To some artists, copy is primarily a design block to be balanced with other design features. To such artists, the ad is a poster. As artists, they may not think in business or in sales terms. Most artists feel that most copy is too long and that a copywriter's layout does not give sufficient picture emphasis, leaves insufficient white space, gives an unnecessarily cramped and crowded effect and cheapens the effect of the ad and the product. Yet, this

145

different viewpoint can *help* you to get the best from your art director.

Some copywriters are picture people who think like and work well with art directors. They conceive a picture idea or grab one from the art director and build their ad from it. Usually, they are headline people, too. With the right picture and headline idea, they work out their ad. Sometimes, art directors develop a talent at writing or directing writers as well.

But generally, copywriters are word people. They want pictures to attract attention, to prove, demonstrate, emphasize or otherwise increase the effectiveness of their words. *A stubborn attitude on the part of both art director and copywriter can stalemate their joint effort.* A dominating copywriter often deprives the art director of contributing his true talent. The reverse is also true.

A *compromise* in which each yields some points can sometimes be too many cooks spoiling the broth. But being adversaries can *improve* the creative product, provided each respects and tries to be receptive to the other's viewpoint.

Assuming that your art director is professional and a perfectionist, you should gradually find a way to work together effectively. As your art director grasps more of what you are trying to achieve, he can contribute more. It is important that you both *believe* in what you are jointly trying to do. He may be professional, but think you're not. He may feel that you're merely *torturing* the ad, spending time and money uselessly, making the ad *less effective;* at the same time, you think you're improving it. And he could be right.

When starting to write, *feel* your way. If your art director is an old veteran of mail order layouts, let him be the *senior* of your team. Even if not, *respect* his opinion. One thing the new copywriter learns, but sometimes slowly, is that *emphasis* requires *contrast. Everything* can't be big. At first, you want to get across too much at one time. In the New York commercial art studios, there is the old phrase, "Smash with class", to sum up the apparent meaning of the client's instructions.

There is eternal conflict between the *smash* of a "buckeye" layout with accent on everything and the class of good taste which is in turn *restraint* in color shading, design blocks, type faces, art and logotype.

So be reasonable, at least at first. As you go through the creative process ad by ad, you'll gradually find *conviction* and *assurance.* You're becoming a pro and as you do, you'll become more senior in your creative team.

It's a pleasure to watch a top art director and an equally good copy writer work together as a team at the board. They've been through the

146

wars together. Each knows the other's way of working. The art director almost intuitively knows the effect the writer wants him to achieve, just by reading the copy. The writer can visualize in his mind what the artist is going to do as the first rough sketch starts on the board. Each is relaxed and can joke with the other. Each can disagree without offending the other. The art director first indulgently does the layout the copywriter's way. Then in a quick movement, he tears off a tissue from the pad, puts down his overlay and, with a few deft motions, shows his first recommended change. The copywriter smiles and admits it's better. They've made their first change.

I've seen two stars together for hours, the copywriter's chair pulled up close, but the copywriter usually standing, looking over the art director's shoulder. Not many words are necessary. The copywriter will say, "Let's try an overlay where you hit the headline harder". The art director has his overlay in scarcely a minute. Or the art director will suggest, "Let's put in a before and after picture back here." Again, the overlay is done in minutes. Each wants the ad to be the best they've done together. Sometimes, they'll disagree. And sometimes, I've gotten them over it by suggesting that we test each of the two alternative approaches. The overlay usually settles the argument. Before the overlay, it was just an idea. After the overlay, they usually jointly agree that the change should or should not be made.

Your object is to develop that kind of relationship with your art director. If he is not mail order oriented, explain very briefly how scientifically it measures results. He may be intrigued. Get across that the two of you are a team and how your work together can greatly affect results. Consider offering a bonus over and above the art director's regular fees if your joint efforts create a "hit".

Art directors are human. They're often under pressure. If you come to an art director with a deadline, his eye may be half on the clock. If you come to him without a deadline, he's apt to push your assignment gratefully aside while he goes back to other rush assignments. It's important to come to an understanding. You have to gamble board work time. He has to reserve board work hours. If you've labored mightily to get your ad this far, it's not right to rush it through the layout phase. The overlays should determine when the layout is right.

This ad may be your main project at the time and one on which you are prepared to concentrate. He may be under pressure from other directions and simply be thrown from the layout problems of your ads to those of others. He may be so battered by all the layout problems he has contended with that he can't think of any of them in off hours.

Art directors can sometimes be tired and careless. I have known art directors, who, when jammed up (often the case), would order type and specify it, but omit the necessary calculations to know beforehand whether the type will fit. Sometimes, too, an error is made in calculating the number of words that can fit in a given space.

The result is often overset. Your ad looks great except that, as you read it, you find it ends *partway through your copy*. The rest is neatly set in type on the art director's paste up next to your ad. Now, you can only make corrections at the expense of resetting, probably your entire body copy, and possibly even subheads and heads. It can all be your fault, giving too tight a deadline, rushing in too late and interrupting other jobs, fighting too hard for all your copy when your art director is just too weary to explain the inevitable result. It may be your art director's fault for being careless or lazy or not meeting the reality of the situation early enough. It may be a case ·of insufficient production knowledge of all concerned, the blind leading the blind.

Then, the art director gently says, "cut 10 percent of your copy". It may be 20 percent, even 30 percent or more. But often after type is set, the situation can still be saved without completely resetting the copy. Headlines can be smaller. So can pictures. Captions can be shortened and smaller type used. Subheads can be cut from three lines to two or even one and made smaller. Body type can start with the original size called for and drop a size later on. Copy can be cut and often improved in the cutting.

But it calls for give and take between art director and copywriter. It takes more overlays on the layout pad to get the visual effect. A look will often help make the decision of further cuts or smaller type. The earlier it takes place, the easier, more effective and least costly the solution is.

When you get your proofs back, everything may fit but look far more jammed than you expected. It may cause the ad to seem difficult to read.

You may have pushed your art director into accepting more copy than he would have recommended. Often, your art director is torn. His art training rebels at a jammed ad. But he also feels very much aware that crowded, jammed ads have often succeeded in mail order. He doesn't want to be personally responsible for your ad's failure by insisting too strongly on your adhering to his standards, particularly before he gets to know you and work regularly with you.

Your art director has visualized accurately how the paste-up will look. But seeing the paste-up of your first full page ad, you are probably somewhat surprised. Let us assume that the copy sent to the typographer was clean and correctly spelled. Let's also assume that the type calculating was correct and there is no overset. But now your ad looks more crowded. Yet, the more of a quality product you are selling, the more of a *quality effect* you desire. Your art director may not have realized how important this is to you.

Now, you need his help to keep the selling effect of your ad, and get more of a quality effect as well - even at this late date.

Look at your headline and main subsidiary subheads. Here's your biggest change possibility and *least costly* per square inch to make. Each word of type usually costs the same to reset - big or small. You want to "open up" your ad and give *more* emphasis to the headline itself. Write out alternate shorter headlines. Often, the effect of your headline can be dramatically *enhanced* by a last minute change.

Do the same with your main subhead and main subsidiary subhead. Preferably, just simplify and shorten your present one. Try for *shorter* lines and *wider* margins. Ask your art director to pencil in an overlay to get the effect. If it looks hopeful, he can reset an alternative version. He may even be able to get most of the words from extra proofs of present type. Then, the alternate can be pasted up as an overlay.

You quickly see which "works" best. Often, such a change quite transforms your ad at trifling resetting and art expense. You may even be able to make your main headline, if shortened, *bigger* and still "open up" your ad.

Look at your subheads interrupting copy. Each three or two line subhead that you cut to *one* line saves at least one or two lines of copy. How much more depends on how much bigger than your body type your interrupting subhead type is. Try to cut even one line from several words to one or two. If you do, you create air ... white space ... in bigger margins on either side. Often, your interrupting subheads are improved by the cutting.

You and your art director may be pleased with your headline, subheads and type but you may be disappointed with your picture effect. The pictures you have substituted for your model ad may not be equally effective to those in your model ad. And only when you saw the photostats of your art in your paste up could you fully realize the difference.

If your picture is bad and if your art director is a hack, he may try to sell you on how good it is. If he's a perfectionist, he will insist on whatever steps are necessary to save the situation. He may be normally a very conscientious craftsman but right now very tired or with his mind on other, urgent past deadline work. I've seen copywriter and art director work virtually all night to get out ads, when both have been physically exhausted. Again and again, I've seen one last extra change "save" the ad.

It may simply be "cropping" the picture, "blowing it up" a little larger plus retouching highlights or a last minute substitution of one piece of art for another. It may require reshooting one or more photographs. It may be substituting a drawing for a photograph or paying for a new substitute drawing by a specialized artist. The less your experience, the more dependent you are on your art director to achieve the finished effect you seek. You'll either get on each other's nerves or be an effective team determined to get a final ad you're jointly proud of.

Most problems in the execution of an ad come from rush ... and the use of the wrong specialist for part of the job... or one not properly oriented.

A taxi driver has to contend with people in a rush, often too late in starting to ever reach where they're going in time. To survive, a taxi driver has to be a philosopher. He may turn, twist, dodge and race in traffic to help you reach your impossible goal. *But to keep his sanity, he must keep himself removed from your emotional trauma about your situation.*

Production people have to have a somewhat similar approach to life. They are inclined to be sympathetic but philosophic. Some are hacks, some perfectionists and some in between. But they deal with clients who give them all manner of problems. Their customers batter down their prices, push them to difficult deadlines, misunderstand their technical limitations and are often incoherent in explaining requirements. The more you learn about production processes, the more you'll understand what your specialists are talking about, the limitations *they* work under and what you can expect from them.

Just one poorly selected or oriented specialist can spoil your entire ad. Your production process may be *wrong* for the medium you are using. A photograph that will look effective in a magazine may look like *mud* in a newspaper. The artist or photographer selected may be superb in his or her field, but quite unsuited to the assignment. You may strive to achieve a Tiffany effect and use an engraver great for discount stores, get cheap work for a cheap price, and destroy your ad.

You will need to assemble specialists for the job who each take pride in contributing to the final effect. It takes time, recruiting effort, trial and error in selection, and accidental luck. It takes fair treatment, ample time for a given job, thorough but not long winded explanation,

150

and often, incentive. But you will assemble your winning enlarged team, if you're determined to do it.

Chapter 9

Translating A "Hit"

Various size ads needed . . . improvements . . . risks of changes in newspapers and magazines . . . switching to color

If you have a "hit", it's exhilirating, but also worrisome. You want to make all the money that your successful test has made possible.

An axiom of mail order is that you should never change any element of any successful mail order advertisement in any future advertising schedule, except for new tests of variations. This means every word, picture, layout element, or slightest variation in offer. And it is true of every direct response method used by non-mail order people.

For one of the most able mail order men and businessmen I have ever met, Arthur Murray, we handled radio and later TV advertising. Arthur Murray mastered mail order. He originally sold dance lessons by mail and then applied the same techniques to build the biggest chain of dance studios in the world, at first franchised and later company owned. When he had an unsuccessful franchise, he would almost invariably find the same cause. The franchise owner had decided to change the successful advertising that, in city after city, was pulling inquiries and walk-ins into the studio and substitute his own. Occasionally, Arthur Murray would arrange to have a successful franchise owner step in and help operate a "sick" franchise. He told me that the first step was simply to go back and run the exact, tested ads that worked so well everywhere else. And often, that one change was enough to convert the loser into a winner.

Some changes are slight. Some are major. All are important. Simply running the identical magazine ad in a newspaper is a change that might not work, even if run exactly the same way.

Many of the biggest mail order money makers I know will avoid like the plague *any* change in a "hit" ad without a split run test. Of course, they *can't* always avoid it. Occasionally, they are forced to make a minor change without testing. Most feel that even the deletion of two or three words from the original coupon (for a smaller coupon) can imperil the success of the changed ad.

Your main picture photograph may look great on the glossy paper of a magazine and lose detail completely on the newsprint of a newspaper. The smallest type of your body copy may be quite readable on the glossy paper of a magazine and become fuzzy and far harder to read on newsprint.

In a newspaper, black headlines become grayer. Newspaper regulations often require greying out of more than a minimum allowed blackness. Often, drawings need be substituted for photographs. Retouching becomes more important. A mat will lose more detail than a plate. Poor engraving will lose more detail than good. A greater perfection of production detail is needed at each point.

You want to avoid risk. You prefer to run your original ad without change. But if attractive media opportunities open up, some may require changes in your ad. Each change *is* a risk. Try to make *minimum* changes with *maximum* care. Try to avoid too many deadlines, too fast. Make haste slowly . . . with "meticulous speed".

Not all magazines have the same page size, although "7 x 10" pages are becoming more standard. If smaller, you have a copy cutting job to do. Any perceptible cutting may change the effectiveness of your original ad. The ideal would be to make a small test of each such modification before running a major space purchase. I'll explain later why this is not always feasible.

Each substantial change is a "translation" of your original ad into a different form. You want to make the safest "translations" at the lowest production cost into other needed size variations.

Work as hard on each modification as on the original ad. Have your art director make overlay after overlay of various possible rearrangements. For some size variations, you may find a way to run your original copy intact. You may improve your ad, increase the power of your headline, subheads and main headline.

Any cutting or adapting needs to be done with extreme care.

153

Usually, the main body copy can be cut only slightly. However, it often can be set in part or in full in a smaller type face. The headline copy sometimes can be shortened somewhat. You may be able to shorten and further simplify main subheads. The main picture element needs to be kept. Sometimes, it can be reduced. Sometimes, a secondary picture can be dropped. The coupon can often be shortened somewhat. The copy of supporting boxes can be cut most. Sometimes, a supporting box can be eliminated.

In reducing from a Time Magazine size page to a TV Guide size page, such surgery can be considerable and affect results considerably. Expanding from a Time size page to a TV Guide sized double page is quite a different layout problem with quite different dimensions. You and your art director may see how to *improve* the layout effect dramatically. You may find it a *more difficult* layout problem. It will depend on how suitable your headline, main subheads, and mail illustrations are to a double spread, and on your and his ingenuity to modify and adapt them.

You may have *another* picture ideal for *horizontal* cropping that is far more effective. Or your pictures may not "work" as well in a horizontal layout. After revision, your double page may be considerably modified from your original page. It should incorporate your entire original copy. Try alternate layouts. You may surpass the effect of the original Time sized page.

In a Parade size Sunday newspaper magazine section your Time size ad can often run as a three-column ten-inch high "junior page" with no changes required. You may want to run a vertical half page (slightly smaller, higher and narrower). You may consider a vertical two-thirds, a three-fifths page, a four-fifths page or a full page. Each change of dimension can give a different layout effect and be both a problem and an opportunity.

It's a very simple change from a three-column ten-inch ad to the almost two and one half inches more space per column, required by a three-fifths of a page. The same copy can obviously be used. The art director can enlarge and rearrange headlines, main and main subsidiary subheads slightly.

Or with no resetting, simply putting more space between lines, he may be able to open up the main copy block. This creates more white space between interrupting subheads. He may be able to re-crop the illustration a little more vertically. At little expense, he'll probably achieve a better effect with the same basic layout and identical copy. It's also quite safe.

The half page is narrower and about the same number of square inches. If not, you may have some copy cutting required. Do it with care, and your cuts should not affect results too much. If you go to four columns, you attain a more open ad. If you go to five columns, your tight 7'' x 10'' ad can be greatly improved simply by rescaling and rearranging the layout. The proportion of headline to copy and illustration to copy can be somewhat bigger. Their size can be actually larger. You can go to a slightly larger type face in your main copy story and perhaps put in more space between lines. You may be able to add more white space above and below your interrupting subheads. Or you can, of course, put in more copy.

But why not stick with the exact copy of your 'hit'' ad and simply get the added power and quality effect of the larger page? Each change is a risk.

We often will convert a successful Time magazine full page ad to a somewhat larger newspaper ad, to make it easier to read the small type. Often, a *different* photograph with less detail to lose does better in newspapers.

Turning your copy and layout concept into a professional and finished advertisement is seldom simple or easy. In four color, it's more difficult, complex, speculative and far more expensive. We try to be cautious with color. Sometimes, we start plans for four color advertising, but limit our gamble to color photography only. We may start with color photography by staff members, just to feel out color possibilities.

The next gamble is to have a top color photographer take on the assignment. If you are not an art director and do not have professional knowledge of color photography, selecting the photographer can be speculative. A poor art director can select a poor photographer.

The *right* photographers and artists, each for his or her specialty, *can* one by one become trusted members of your enlarged creative team. If you start with the *right* art director, it's far easier. If you're working with the *right* advertising agency, the team may already be there.

Often, the more superb a photographer is, the more *specialized* he is. Some specialize in black and white, some in color, some in studio shots, some in outdoor photography, and some in special areas of *these* kinds of photography. But the biggest difference is between poor, mediocre and superb photographers.

Amateurs and mediocre beginning professionals, even if they charge nothing or very little, can be worse than the most expensive. The pressure for low cost photography makes hacks worse. They become

155

picture factories. You get your low price. They devote little time. The effect is usually disappointing.

The cost of the best in anything is always a staggering surprise.

Superb color photographers are often expensive. But there is always the dream of finding not yet recognized, superb talent. Just running any color photograph in any national publication, in an ad that does it credit . . . and gives him or her credit . . . can start off a new star. To get superb work at low cost, you're helping launch a career. If not qualified, the color picture may be bad. You may get little for your money.

A *top* photographer can be more cooperative than you expect. Expensively equipped studios can have a high overhead. Occasionally, to start off a promising client, and at a time *between* two big assignments, a top photographer will go substantially below his or her normal price. If your job is fairly simple, it may be fitted in *after* another job is finished in otherwise unused hours. Sometimes, a top outside photographer will have an assignment with all travel expenses paid by a big client in just the place *perfect* for your shots. And sometimes, he'll fit you in for a far more nominal fee.

If you can explain your situation frankly . . . and if the photographer *likes* you . . . and does not feel that you're taking advantage of him, he may go along with a lower price. Remember, you can always afford to add an incentive bonus for *extra* payment if your ad pays out. If your ad pays out, keep your word. Your photographer may be pleased and surprised and willing to gamble again.

The *right* color photograph makes *right* color reproduction *possible*. It does not *insure* it. The quality of the paper printed on, the printing process and the quality of the color plate or color separations, all affect color reproduction considerably.

A bad color photograph will look bad anyway. A good color photograph will, under certain circumstances, look far worse than you expected. The first question is whether color retouching is required. For some photographs in some situations, color retouching *is* required. This can be more expensive than you ever expected. Time and money are important factors.

Color separations and color engravings take time and craftmanship. More time and more craftsmanship costs more money. If you try to make a magazine closing date with inadequate time available, craftsmanship is not possible at any price. If you try to cut costs, there are those who are eager to serve you. They can sell you either color separations or color engravings for less, by subtracting more time and craftsmanship than the price reduction. Cruder, more primitive color *processes* also cost less. But superb color reproduction worthy of superb color photography is an art. Poor color can harm the effectiveness of your ad and often be *worse* than black and white.

Color processes are constantly improving. Different processes on different paper surfaces still vary in quality. Color on newsprint is not the same as on glossy paper. For certain purposes, color on newsprint is highly effective. For others, it is very disappointing.

Color is more complex than black and white. More can go wrong. This is true for reproducing other forms of color art as well as color photography. It takes an artist more time and costs more. The artist may be unsuited to the assignment. It's harder to be frugal and use color. Using less than four colors is less expensive. It can be effective. But attempting to achieve the effect of four color with three color or a two color reproduction can be a big letdown.

An art director usually can visualize the final effect ... before proceeding. You may have more difficulty. Less than perfect color reproduction and less than four color reproduction can still stop the eye and often increase readership. Sometimes, it can also cheapen your product and make it look less attractive than black and white. If you change your mind in black and white, tear your ad apart and start over, it's expensive. In color, the expense of such changes can be a small catastrophe.

Color can be overwhelmingly effective. It can glorify your product. It can give more picture detail. It can be the difference between mail order profit and loss. Until you have considerable confidence in the judgement of your advertising agency, art director or yourself, be *careful* with it.

We've started discussing creating advertising by taking up newspaper or magazine advertising. . .quite arbitrarily.

You may find your first "hit" in any form of mail order advertising: publications, TV, direct mail, radio, or in variations or hybrids of mail order advertising.

Any successful test in any form of mail order advertising has a chance to succeed in another form. A product may be more suited to one form of advertising. A product that succeeds in one form of advertising may fail in another. To succeed in *one* form is an accomplishment. To succeed in *all* forms is a near miracle. It is possible today to "translate" mail order success into more forms of mail order advertising than formerly.

Newspapers and magazines with adserts, free standing inserts and other hybrids become a direct mail medium and can use a variation of a successful direct mail piece. Direct mail co-op mailings with post cards offer the equivalent of small space in magazines or newspapers and can often run the identical copy. Radio, TV and even newspapers are sometimes successfully used as a *support* media for an enormous direct mail campaign.

"Translating" a successful ad into another form of advertising is far easier than creating an advertisement or commercial from scratch for an entirely different product. Many years ago, Huber Hoge and Sons specialized in radio and TV advertising. Sometimes, we would be given sucessful newspaper, magazine or direct mail advertising to "translate" into broadcast commercials. We were spared the research. And from your first successful test for any item in any form of advertising, your creative job will be much simpler in any other form. We must try to "translate" it into each other feasible form of mail order advertising. Let's first take up direct mail advertising.

Chapter 10

Direct Mail

Package enclosures ... inserts ... loose postcards
... bound postcard publications ...
multiple mailings ... samples ... solos

Direct mail advertising is any advertising which you receive in the mail.

Direct mail is the infantry of mail order ... the queen of battle. Direct mail has sold most mail order merchandise for years. Of all forms of mail order, direct mail is more complex, more swiftly and constantly changing and more confusing to the newcomer.

In recent years, direct mail has become more expensive. Costs have gone up more per thousand than for a page of advertising in many leading magazines. It never stops. One staggering postage increase follows another. Paper prices shoot up when business is good and rarely go down when business is bad. Printing keeps costing more. Costs in the mail zoom up when response from the mail drops down. Yet, profitable use of direct mail has soared.Moonlighters can sometimes still start with little investment and make money.

Here's why it's still so profitable. Credit cards, computers and telephones changed the mail order world—most of all in direct mail. They and automation created a direct mail revolution.

Credit cards took away risk and financed credit for medium size and smaller companies. Computers and telephone credit checking gave mail order credit managers a scientific right arm. Computerized list selection gave safer names to mail. Individual credit checks were made faster and at lower cost. Automation slashed mailing labor cost.

Bigger companies began to sell mail order using direct mail, including many Fortune Five Hundred companies. But entirely new ways of using direct mail made it profitable for small mail order moonlighters, too.

Direct mail began to proliferate and to create new hybrid media. The flexibility, forms and variations of direct mail have become as varied as the most innovative mind. It is the medium of the unexpected.

Newspapers, general magazines, radio and television are shotguns. Direct mail is, more than specialized magazines, the rifle. The computer has revolutionized aiming that rifle. You can reach whom you want with less waste duplication.

Creating direct mail advertising usually requires more time and work than other forms of advertising, but is less frustrating. It has less limitations and is more versatile. You can use more of your research, tell far more of your product and giveaway stories, in more detail, and put in more of your customer's own words. You can show more documentation of use and laboratory tests, show more before and after, and use pictures to better dramatize and glorify your product and giveaway.

You can select paper texture most perfect to reproduce desired color effect. In huge mailings, the ratio of cost of color to black and white has become *more* favorable. You can do many unusual things. You can send a sample of a textile material, include a recorded message from a celebrity or put in a perfume. You can vary direct mail in more ways. A computer letter can be personalized to a degree and at a low cost, unimaginable years ago. You often can be more personal in style.

The computer helps you do more and more. It compiles, keys and credit checks lists. It eliminates duplication and nixies (names of people who have moved with no forwarding addresses). It corrects addresses from old to new. The computer selects names from lists, types labels, bills statements and types collection letters. It welcomes new club members and expels others. It helps rent and manage lists.

The computer keeps track of customers for recency, dollar volume of purchases and classification of purchases. It personalizes letters with mention after mention of the recipient's name in the letter. It intertwines in a personal story book the first names of your child and friends along with the story. The computer will even judge contests and score aptitude tests and then send inquiries the results.

Direct mail is ever different. A lush color piece can come electron-

160

ically sealed into a transparent plastic film or envelope. A personalized letter can adhere to a super size, brightly colored postcard, doing the job a color broadside usually does inside an envelope. When business mail comes in every brightly colored variation, a new winner will come in a brown unmarked envelope. Or, in place of elaborate selling material to business firms, another "hit" will come in the form of a several page interoffice memorandum on plain blue paper backing without a single illustration.

A direct mail kit can include a coin, a stamp or other gift to bribe you to open and read it. It can be addressed in simulated longhand ... by machine. It can be printed in and mailed from Rome, Italy, or anywhere in the world. It can come in an engraved envelope as if an invitation, from a member of the nobility of any country. It can be a simulated telegram. It can come third class with stamps affixed by machine to look like first class. Patented envelopes turn into letters. Patented postcards tear out from letters.

Its post office cancellation mark can be that of an odd and obscure small village like North Pole, Alaska. It can be a first class, personalized letter. It can come as a simulated newspaper, newsletter or magazine. It can be a collection of postcards or one oversized double card with a tear off return order card.

In countless ways, the outside envelope can tease and tempt you to open it. It can seem to be enclosed with a bill or a check. It can offer a free gift, announce a contest or promise a saving. And inside the envelope, the variety is even greater as we will soon describe. But nothing has aided direct mail to overcome leaping costs more effectively than its constantly increasing ability to sell higher cost items.

The trend to higher price items for direct mail has been underway for decades. The legendary direct mail offer of the Bell & Howell movie camera and projector blasted off by breaking every record for sales volume of higher priced merchandise via direct mail. One record club, it is said, made a profit of $1,700,000 simply by mailing the original Bell & Howell mailing piece to their members with a special letter recommending it. People became accustomed to buying more expensive mail order items by direct mail.

The average price of items sold by direct mail has gone up and up (even subtracting inflationary factors). As incomes have gone up, people have grown accustomed to buying more expensive products and services by mail order.

Direct mail can present such products in more detail, color and variety. Direct mail can aim at lists of higher income people specifically

161

interested in the need the product supplies and who have bought higher price mail order products from others.

The rewards of success in direct mail have increased enormously over the years.

The chances of failing in direct mail have increased too. A bigger percentage of all tests fail. It's possible to project success so much further that more test failures can be washed out and still make a handsome profit overall. The standard full color mailing piece of yesterday with broadside, letter, return card, return envelope and giveaway flyer, all in an outside envelope, has become the big time "solo" piece. The economics of using it in color often require a million mailing. Smaller tests, at two or three times the cost or more per piece in the mail, usually lose or at best, break even. Only the million mailing projection can bail out the "successful" test. The advantage is to the giants and against the moonlighter. Some mailing pieces are so elaborate and lush as to bewilder a mail order moonlighter.

How can a mail order newcomer possibly compete with these and endless other offers of the giants? How many can give huge prizes in a contest? How many can print enormous pieces in rich color? How many can give six swatches of material? Who can send an actual record in the mail? Or who can guarantee to buy back a coin collection in five years at the identical price? What mail order newcomer can proceed in the huge volume required for any such operations? Who can afford the expense even of the top direct mail creative talent required? And how can you possibly paraphrase for your own products such incredibly complex and super lengthy mailing kits? It seems like competing with loaded dice. More and more, direct mail has become the domain of the mail order giants. Yet, more and more direct mail nooks and crannies keep coming up ... ideal for moonlighters to get started in and prosper in at low cost ... and risk, as we will shortly discuss.

In the wonderful world of the handful of super giant mailers, many factors tilt in their favor.

Lists costs per thousand often drop substantially for a full list rental. Giant mailers develop giant lists and can then swap lists. List rental costs then drop to that of mailing their own lists. These lists may include hundreds of thousands of specialized names suitable to mailing a specific new offer. For the first million mailing that web press color usually requires, the list rental cost may be low indeed.

New computer efficiencies of list compilation and revision are best used for biggest, most frequently mailed lists. These are the lists owned and swapped by this same small club of giant mailers. In this magic world, the offers themselves are swapped. Each successful offer of a giant mailer can be "syndicated" and offered to other members of the informal giant mailer's club in a manner quite lucrative to each party.

One giant can buy the merchandise from the other and mail the other's offer to his list. Often, a giant mailer develops a warmer, more clubby feeling with his own customers than with any outside "cold" list. By substituting a warmer, more informal letter on his letterhead recommending the offer and leaving all other elements the same, results from the same list can often double or triple.

Thus, it is more profitable for one giant to sell merchandise to another than to rent the other's list. Using a letter and recommendation from each giant to his own list makes a "cold" list hot. It is also by the same alchemy more profitable for the other giant to *buy* merchandise and make a profit selling to his list than simply to rent his list. This combination of factors often makes mailings safer and more profitable for those in the "club" than those knocking on the door.

In the old days, a small mail order firm could do its direct mail to a surprising degree all on its own. Its own girls could type labels on addressograph or equivalent plates. It could buy simple printing equipment and print and mail on the premises. It could maintain its own lists and rent or swap names directly. Now, a mail order moonlighter can be baffled even by the zip code separation job the post office requires for third class bulk mail. Personnel cost has soared so high as to make handling your own direct mail prohibitive in labor cost.

Only automated equipment can offset these costs. A small, new mail order firm cannot amortize such equipment's cost. The small firm has the same problem with computerization. New ways of putting names on computer become obsolete because still newer ways are always being developed. The answer is to use outside specialized services. But to get started safely, feel safe entrusting yourself to others and decide *whom* to turn to is not easy. Yet, you can. Become more familiar with what others do. Observe the giants and gain their assistance.

Smallest moonlighters can profitably use direct mail, often helped by the giants who have no realization that they are helping. We *can* learn their secrets from them. Gradually, as we do, we realize that giants are not impregnable, they are not perfect nor do they hold all the cards for mail order success. We small fry do have a chance. Just let them start helping us.

How would you like the biggest, richest and most successful mailers to give you direct mail seminars at no cost? How would you like

163

them to teach you their latest improvements in technique almost as fast as they develop them? How would you like to learn from them and never stop learning from them how to make far more money for yourself?

All you need to do is *read the mail*. Simply get on more and more lists. Get more and more friends to forward to you their direct mail. Then read it, compare it and analyze it. Almost every direct mail piece you receive teaches something. As varied as direct mail pieces are, all have much in common.

The copy tries never to get in the way of the quick decider, yet tries to overcome every objection of the slow decider or of those in between. The giveaway is even more essential in direct mail than in any other form of advertising. A giveaway featured on the envelope often is the most effective way to get it opened. A broadside (brochure) featuring it at the top gets looked through. A letter starting with news of a giveaway has a good chance of being read throughout. It even helps to get an order card read thoroughly.

The envelope yearns to be opened. The broadside wants to be seen and glanced through and the letter wants to be read. The order card, often assisted by return envelope, begs to be checked, initialed or signed and dropped in the mail.

More than in any other form of advertising, the giveaway gets more readership of the selling message throughout. As a mail order product becomes more familiar and accepted, a giveaway can be profitably featured more often. In some cases, the giveaway can take the spotlight away from the product. Even in a full page, you could never have enough space to tell as exciting a story about the giveaway or do it such justice.

In newspapers and magazines, an editorial ad often has a better chance because readers think it is an article. A direct mail piece often has a better chance of being opened if it appears to be something more welcome in the mail.

The envelope is the opening battle. Will it be thrown away unopened or will it be opened and glanced at? One reason to select a plain brown envelope for a business "solo" mailing kit is economy. More important is its similarity to vital business correspondence. It might be from your lawyer or accountant. It might be an interoffice memorandum. It has a plain but important look with no word on the envelope front or back. The first glance when it is opened may determine whether it will survive to be read or perish in the waste basket.

That glance must be converted into reading more or the battle is still lost. Sometimes, just revealing part of the picture of the giveaway, as the envelope is opened, tempts you to look underneath. Often, the most prominent words you read are "FREE" and "FREE TRIAL." It doesn't seem too dangerous to read on. Each direct mail kit from a giant is teaching you how the "giants' club" operates.

As soon as you create your own direct mail piece, reading the direct mail pieces of others will have far more meaning. You'll watch out particularly for duplications where you receive the same piece two, three or more times. You'll find in some cases they are split run tests with some seemingly minor element in the piece different from another.

Recently, I noticed two seemingly identical direct mail pieces from one company. One was a computer personalized letter with my name and address mentioned several times on the first page. The other was an obvious form letter with no more personalization than the name and address seen through the address window.

It's exciting to discover the split-run tests of others. Keep watching for them. You become the judge of the contest. Sometimes, you can even *ask* the company which won. Some say nothing. Some are friendly and helpful to mail order newcomers, not competitive. But, either way, you keep on learning. Over a period of time, you often can discover the winner. It's the *survival* piece.

Little things about each direct mail piece you receive begin to interest you. You begin getting a "feel" for direct mail. Some mailers almost always keep using in their mailing pieces some identical techniques. Some prominently feature telephoning in orders, yet others don't. You wonder why, if one giant finds it works, does another giant make a similar offer and leave it out. Some mailers use their own numbers and others, an 800 toll free number. Some solicit calls in office hours and others twenty-four hours, seven days a week. One business publishing firm always give its address, telephone number, TWX and Telex. You may order or inquire in any of *four ways*.

Not all the giant mailers get all the benefit they could from their direct mail. Our experience indicates that featuring the telephone substantially increases orders; that the 800 toll free number outpulls an offer to phone your own number collect; and that accepting phone orders twenty-four hours a day, seven days a week, outpulls limiting order handling to office hours. Many giants continue the somewhat less profitable way.

You're motivated more than most employees of the giants. You watch latest trends more intently. Your interest spurs you to come up with ideas for profitable changes. Being small, you often have tighter control, can watch tests more closely and implement changes faster.

Notice that, for higher priced products, copy is often longer and the mailing kit more elaborate ... and note the reverse. As postage, paper and printing goes up, so does the price of merchandise offered by direct mail. Notice how tax services often mention the per issue cost without mentioning total cost, and state inconspicuously that they will bill the full amount in fifteen days.

Notice that, when you buy anything by mail from any company, you begin to get direct mail on other offers from that company and from other companies, too. Years ago, giant companies began to discover they had a fortune in their mailing lists. Banks began to loan big money on them. I know one businessman who sky rocketed to success in a series of acquisitions, originally fueled by one loan on his mailing list.

How do you get into the "giants club"? The answer is simple. Become a giant.

The fastest way to do so is to start in a very small way. The best way to start is the simplest. Direct mail is a huge field. You can drown in an ocean of decisions as to how to get started. You can spend a small fortune in production bills and get a result that can greatly disappoint you. You can lose a lot of money getting started the wrong way. That's why I start discussing not "solos", but package inserts, billing inserts, loose postcards, bound postcards and the simpler ways of getting started in multiple mailings.

The next step is to become a small ally of the giants. Play the mouse to their elephant in a mutual aid society. Every executive of a giant wants to be a hero, but not a dead one. Each test you get under your belt makes you more of a potential meal ticket for one of them. Even a microscopic test success has meaning and deserves a greater confirming test. Let a giant project your successful test.

Some talented entrepreneurs confine all their risk taking to creating an effective direct mail kit and proving that it's profitable on a very small scale. From then on, they are "syndicators" offering the right to the giants to use the mailing kit and buy merchandise from them. An important step to becoming a giant is associating with them. If your offer works, you become a supplier to them. You can go on your own, later.

The next step is to work harder than the employees of the giants. If you do, water can seek its own level. If you search harder than the employees of the giants, you may find or originate a better offer faster. If you do more research, you may come up with more exciting facts. If you are more of a perfectionist, you will create better copy and layout and produce more effective finished advertising. All this comes more out of your heart and your head than your pocketbook.

You can overcome advantages of big mailers by developing better offers and better direct mail pieces than they do. A giant is a giant employer. The work is done by employees. Employees are usually specialists. Often, they're great in their specialty and lost out of it. No employee can obtain as great a personal reward as a far smaller entrepreneur off on his own. You have an incentive no employee will ever have. If you're a partner in an advertising agency, you can usually make more money than important employees of your biggest client. Even as a moonlighter, you're an entrepreneur. He or she isn't.

Innovation can seem more dangerous to the career of the company's top employee than playing it safer. The bigger the giant in any field is, the safer the employees of that giant like to play. The giant is slower, more ponderous and subject to internal politics. Many genuinely exciting offers never get off the ground. The giants have great muscles and can be muscle bound. They have all the tools, yet often do not use them. A giant publisher can occasionally forget it owns plates to a very saleable book. And the same is true in other fields. The giant tends to make offers similar to those other giants make, although some never copy. The giant tends to paraphrase the techniques of others *without* introducing freshness and individuality, although some are most distinctive. The giant tends to have higher overhead, although some are extremely frugal. The giant tends to pay more for specialists, services, advertising production and a host of other costs just as a Cadillac buyer may pay Cadillac prices for every repair and part thereafter. Yet, some giants have tight control of such costs.

We can compete with the giants if we always remember we are not giants. We can get into direct mail gradually. We can benefit from the latest direct mail techniques. We can understand the latest changes and their effects. Let's get back to fundamentals. We simply want to create the most effective direct mail advertising possible and send it to the most suitable list, at the right time and at lowest possible cost in the mail.

We want to get into direct mail with the least risk. We want to benefit most from the customers we gain. We want to take out the confusing gobblygook of the experts, benefit most from new method advantages and do it all in the fastest, simplest way. We want to make money from direct mail advertising and avoid disasters due to misuse of new methods. We want to get away from complicated words and foggy terminology and cut through to hard facts. It's not as complicated as it's

167

made out to be. Let's try to simplify it.

A computer is a very fast filing clerk. It files more things in more ways. It pulls them out of the file faster. It can group them very fast. It can check the files very fast, look for something and report back fast. It segregates names faster and better. It aims your direct mail rifle more accurately. Some of what it does is better and cheaper than done without it. It does some things not feasible before. Some things it does can benefit some firms and not others. In direct mail for smaller users, it is usually best used outside through a specialized service rather than in your location.

The complicated or slang words describing new computer abilities translate into simple words. "Merge-Purge" (and dozens of name variations) simply means taking out duplications. "Hot-line" names mean recent names. And so it goes. A moonlighter can understand new techniques and can find a niche to succeed in.

Start by saving and filing your own direct mail research—every piece of direct mail you receive. Save everything in the envelope. If you have a credit club card, a charge card, a bank card, save every mailing and every billing insert. If you buy anything by mail, save each package insert.

If you're in business, you'll get far more direct mail advertising. Junk mail can mean money in the bank to you now. Keep it all.When you get a fat package of postcards keep the entire package. When you get any multiple mailings with different literature from different manufacturers, keep it too. Get your friends to keep theirs for you. Write in for literature from companies offering it, particularly for products similar to yours. Particularly look for and keep in one file a series of mailings.

Keep separate files for single package inserts, multiple package inserts, single billing inserts and multiple billing inserts.Do the same for single inquiry follow up mailing pieces, series of follow up mailing pieces, "solo" mailing pieces not inquired for, multiple mailing pieces not inquired for and so forth. Have still more people collect for you. Each is on certain mailing lists the others are not. Not only will your collection grow faster but you will begin to get duplicates of the same mailing pieces. The more duplicates of one mailing list you get, the more lists the offer has been mailed to. If you get duplicates of one offer for a period of time, it is probably a successful offer.

Let's consider several kinds of direct mail which are the easiest to create and have the lowest initial testing cost.

The enormous growth of direct mail has created new forms of

direct mail. Billing inserts and package inserts have always been the safest, cheapest, and most lucrative per dollar way to sell anything mail order. Now, they are used in a far bigger way. Multiple billing inserts and multiple package inserts make extremely low cost tests with maximum chance of success feasible. Co-op multiple mailings give surprising volume, yet can be tested at very small cost. Computer personalized letters for appropriate offers can be profitably used in runs of 25,000 or so and tested with virtually no production cost. Simple "solo's" can pull without color. In black and white, the problem is far simpler. Fifty to two hundred and fifty thousand mailings usually get close to maximum economy per thousand.

What should your first direct mail test be? Let's assume you are successfully selling one mail order item in newspapers and magazines. You are mailing packages every day. Total volume is beginning to mount cumulatively to quite a few thousand. You hope to sell over twenty thousand in the entire year. Let's consider starting with a package insert in your own shipments.

You want the most practical package insert for your situation. The extra business is quite profitable if the cost per insert is quite low. But volume is limited. Total gross profit is limited. It can only grow if you ship more of the original item. This is speculative. For any mail order item, sales may stop at any time. You may sell through the year less than expected.

Your time is limited. You work hard and have much to do. You can afford very little advertising production expense and time for the limited profit potential. You don't want to neglect the opportunity. The ideal is to have an ad for a second successful mail order item. Just photo-offset the ad with a typewritten coupon change. Even if the ad is breakeven or a slight loser, if the item is related, you should have a package insert winner.

If your package is big enough, insert your full ad reprinted on one side. Keep the other blank. Any waste of paper in a tiny test is not worth rearranging your ad on half the paper size on both sides. A small, quite light package may require reprinting on tissue thin paper. We have done so quite successfully with a New York Times size full page ad reprinted on one side and folded several times (by the printer).

For a tiny package, you may find it necessary to print half your ad on one side and half on the other. This is the first big difference between publication and direct mail advertising. Here's how to try it for a Time magazine size full page ad set in three columns. Cut a photo copy of it horizontally in half. Underneath headline, main subheads and top illustrations and boxes, cut out the second and third columns of body copy of the top half. Switch with the entire first and second columns of the bottom half. Paste the new front combination on one piece of blank paper and the new back combination on another. When you read this, it may seem complicated. But when you do it, you'll find it quite simple.

Now, comes the finer scissors work. The front will have too much and the back, too little. The ad will, however, read consecutively from front to back. Make more photocopies of the new front and back combinations. Scissor out all overcopy at the bottom of the second column of the new front combination. Cut out the third column at the top of the body copy and pull it down to make room for the overcopy of the second coluon. This means much more overcopy at the bottom of the third column. Scissor it all out.

The new rear combination will not have enough copy to fill the first and second columns. Cut out the copy in the second column and pull down to the bottom of the column. Cut enough from the bottom of the first column to fill the empty space at the top of the second column. Cut out all copy left in the first column and pull to the bottom of the column. The overcopy of the new front combination should fit perfectly in the space now open at the top of the first column. The new front and back combinations should each be exactly half the ad space and together should contain every word and read consecutively. It's taken no rewriting and cost no money. Just photo offset. Further changes might greatly improve it but can come later. For your first package insert test, I suggest only one. At the right bottom of the new front combination, type in paranthesis the word "(over)".

If you don't have a mail order ad but do have a second item, proceed as if creating a publication ad. Find a model ad for a product of similar quality selling to similar people. Paraphrase exactly as previously shown. But write a *quickie* mail order ad. Cannibalize any trade, consumer advertising or literature for your product to get type and illustrations for reproduction. Use as much as possible. Fill in with typewritten copy. Make a copywriter's layout. Get someone neat (perhaps yourself) to cut up the literature and paste in position on white paper. Make your own typewritten coupon. Put in a department number as a key. If higher priced, offer it with a credit card option. Keep it on one side unless small package size requires putting half on each of a half size piece. If you have no other items to include, put in a re-order insert for the original merchandise. Put in an offer of a savings incentive for customers to buy bigger sizes or multiples of your item. An insert reorder can average 50 percent more than the original order received for the item. Your insert can be two or three mimeographed paragraphs or a simple letter. Either way, include a coupon.

If your package is still too small, you'll have to take an existing small ad or write a still smaller ad. If the item you're shipping is larger, you can add a Dear Friend and Customer letter. Write your letter as though to one single customer for the order.

Your logotype is important now. Your stationery should make a good impression. Don't use cheap looking stationery, especially with a quality product. Use *appropriate* stationery. If you advertised the product you're shipping under a name different from your company name, print stationery to conform to the name used.

People feel friendly after buying a product they look forward to using. If you talked to each personally, you could talk in a friendly personal and simple manner. Do so in your letter. Try to get across the personality of your company in your letter. Explain the extra pride you take in finding or developing your product or products. If your business is in a small town, capitalize on it. People expect more frankness, honesty and integrity from others they do business with in small towns. But be yourself. Don't be folksy if your're not, or extroverted if you're an introvert.

Write in the style you usually write. Read your own letter carefully. Make sure it includes the points you want to get across. Be sure it has an introduction, body and conclusion. Keep sentences and paragraphs short and to the point. Start with a very, short opening paragraph to key interest. End the same way to hold your point. A rewrite or two should straighten it out. Keep it fairly short.

Include in your letter the story of how you located the item for which you're enclosing literature. Write how unusual you feel it is and your own experience using it. Cover in the letter the most important advantages you've already covered in your photo offset sheet. If you have an appropriate model letter, paraphrase it. If not, do the best you can. Ask for the order. Give a reason why you are making the offer. Offer an incentive with your P.S.

For both insert and letter, try to combine extreme frugality in preparation costs with effective presentation. Spending money on art, engravings, color separations, expensive typography can take away all potential profits and leave a deficit. With little or no preparation cost, package inserts are great. With excessive costs, they're sometimes not. Photo offset in one color as few as one thousand and start inserting.

When those first orders come in, you begin to realize the surprising profit potential you have been missing up to then. For a printing bill of

$58, you might make $240. For a printing bill of $520, you might make $4,650, and so forth. It could be far less or even more.

Just a mimeographed form for re-orders only can do this. For a trifling extra cost, you have gotten a tasty extra profit benefit. There's nothing in mail order that you can do that can give you so attractive a ratio of profit earned to money risked.

Let's hope you are surprised at the success of one of your package inserts. You feel you could do more with it. What should you do next?

What you need now is a package insert to suit the packages of other firms. If successful for others, projection volume could be big. You can now produce your insert somewhat more professionally. But, before going ahead, consider the *next* step which might be billing inserts. The same insert might work in packages and in bills. Let's presume that you are selling entirely for cash or through credit cards and do not send out bills to mail order customers; but others do who will enclose your insert?

For your first test, keep closely to your successful package insert copy. Billing insert sizes are more standard than package insert sizes. The usual sizes used by credit card companies are excellent to go by. The cost per thousand for another mail order firm to insert your advertising is often the same for a somewhat smaller or larger piece. If you sell your product to another firm which inserts your advertising, a longer piece benefits both. Therefore, a somewhat longer piece is preferable.

Credit card companies generally use three basic sizes. One is called a single panel. It is usually 3¼" by 7". The square inches on both sides together add up to about the same as in a Time magazine sized half page ad. If your already successful package insert is small, for your first test of a billing insert, choose the single panel size. Stick closely to your proven package insert copy. If you don't have a successful package insert, but do have a successful publication and close to the same square inch space, use it. In either case, reset your copy after layout and type specification by your art director. It will look better, be more acceptable to other mail order companies and, hopefully, pull better.

Project as a package insert and test as a billing insert. Let's hope it succeeds both ways. You can keep projecting to bigger volume in package inserts and you will also have a "hit" to project in billing inserts. If a new offer, it's also worth considering translating into still other forms of advertising. If you have not yet tested magazine or newspaper advertising, let's translate the successful package and billing insert into an ad. If it's a one panel insert, you can probably test in a

172

one-third Time size page ad and keep almost all the copy. It's comparatively simple to make this conversion or test a page with ample space for all copy. If you succeeded with a single panel, there's little risk in going to a double panel insert. It might pay out far better. It will give you *two* sizes for billing inserts and for package inserts, suitable for smaller and larger packages. It is also a test of full page 7'' X 10'' copy and layout (Time size). Because everything on both sides of your double panel insert can later be easily rearranged for layout onto a 7'' X 10'' page. All copy will fit. All elements can be used. The rear of the double panel needs some rearrangement. A subhead may be converted into a second headline on top. Such rearrangement wasn't worth the trouble on your first home made package insert. But now, you have more of a track record and the stakes are far bigger.

More picture elements can be put on top as well. This can be a longer picture or an extra one. The production cost to translate the double panel into a 7'' X 10'' ad will be far smaller than to create the 7'' X 10'' ad from the start.

Proceed with the double panel insert, just as we've discussed for a full page 7'' X 10'' ad. Now, the research, the writing and rewriting, and the work with your art director are all worthwhile. Be a perfectionist. Do it professionally. If your one panel billing insert was in black and white, stick to black and white. Still keep art and photo costs down. To get still extra space, you can go to a three panel insert but all companies do not offer them. In the three panel insert, you'll have about 20 percent more space than for a Parade size full page ad.

When you project package inserts and billing inserts in bigger runs, you can consider color.

The credit card companies print enough billing inserts each month to use a web press. Because they usually use a standard size one panel, two panel or three panel insert, they can arrange for one web press printer to print a number of panels up on the same web press. This means that you can use color with less expense per thousand on smaller runs than normally.

You can test as few as 25,000 inserts or even 10,000. If you have color material already, the production and test expense may not be to great. The first step is to have color photographs and transparencies of good color quality. The next is to have color separations of the right size. Even if the size is wrong, the separation can be reduced or enlarged at not too great an expense.

As in magazines or newspapers, cost per thousand will still be far lower on bigger runs. Inserts printed on a web press in 500,000 lots will

173

sometimes be closer to the cost of black and white inserts than the cost of color to black and white in some magazines.

Loose postcards! Who would have expected it? A package containing fifty or so postcards is mailed third class. People open it, glance through the cards, pick out one or more, fill it in and drop it in the mail.

Wonder of wonders! This is profitable in many cases for individual advertisers. Each card has advertising and often a coupon on one side and return address on the other. Usually, these packages of "direct response cards" are mailed to a specialized list and most often by a trade magazine.

It's one of the easiest, simplest, fastest and least expensive ways to get started in direct mail. It's one of the hybrids, part direct mail and part publication. A half column ad in a Time sized magazine can be reset to fit comfortably on one side of the postcard. If you have a successful half-column ad, it's a simple and often a safe "translation".

If you have no successful half column ad, simply paraphrase from the most appropriate model card. One package of loose cards can give you plenty to choose from.

It's worth spending time with a layout pad to prepare alternative copywriters layouts. It's not too risky to prepare without your art director. In style, it's closer to the shopping column editorial. The printer can set type. People seem to enjoy getting these collections of little postcards and thumbing through them. The mailing becomes a market place. The more specialized the list is and the advertisers are, the more this is apt to be so.

It's called a direct response publication and is sold like a trade publication, often by the same space salesmen. Each postcard is news. The more real bonafide news your product is, the better chance of profitable response it has.

The more technical and professional the list mailed is, the more factual and businesslike should be the copy treatment. The return card is particularly productive for inquiry advertising. We have also been successful in completing the sale with it.

I would recommend testing a successful half column magazine ad as is, only giving more space to the photograph. If you have no small space copy, follow the copy writing and layout method as though for a half column ad. If you then succeed with your original postcard mailing, it's easy to translate it into a half column ad in an appropriate publication.

Before you test loose postcards, you may already have a successful full column magazine ad in a publication reaching a similar circulation.

174

Or, if you don't, you may find that when you write copy you require twice as much copy as you can fit into the advertising side of the postcard. In either case we have sometimes successfully run our advertising on both sides of the card. However, you do not always gain more with larger copy than you lose, giving up the return card.

Do not leave off a coupon in any case. With advertising on both sides and a coupon on the reverse side, the reader must drop the card in an envelope, address the envelope and mail it. With the return postcard, the sender need only mail the completed card.

In preparing copy for both sides, either use successful copy for one column or write as though a one-third page ad. Put the words "turn over" at the lower right bottom of the front side. It helps to use some picture element back as well as front. It's wise to give near headline value to a subhead at the top of the reverse side. This attracts readers who passed over the front side.

A postcard can be read horizontally or vertically. Most cards in a loose postcard package are set up vertically. This is about the right size to fit in a vertical half column ad. But some cards are set up horizontally. This means that your vertically cropped picture, which may be at the top of your half column ad, will probably go to the right of your advertising half of the post card. Your copy will probably go on the left and have wider but fewer lines and therefore, require resetting.

Your headline set horizontally on the postcard will be changed in effect. A three line headline becomes two and a two line headline often becomes one. You *need* a coupon on the card and may have had none in your half column ad. Making room for one may require cutting copy. If you use advertising on both sides of the card, you may have room for a little more copy even than in your one column ad. Your coupon will be on the back side only. You'll have a little extra space on the front side. If you have a *successful* one column ad, rather than adding copy, use *more* space for headline or picture or both.

Loose postcard packages are usually black and white on light cardboard stock. Black and white photographs will usually have better reproduction than newspapers and worse than magazines. This growing form of advertising is ideal for the specialized product appealing to a specialized list.

From the success of loose post cards grew the first bound post card publication.

We have used bound post card publications even more successfully than loose postcards. They are often more flexible. Often, they are printed in color. Often, a post card publication has a four color front cover.

The postcards are printed horizontally three to a page with perforated lines around them. Each can easily be torn out and mailed. But more alternatives are available. Most bound postcard publications have several non-perforated pages in a shopping column format. These are used for inquiries only with a "bingo" card. This works well for specialized equipment when mailed to the same kind of specialized list. The number of words varies. A picture to illustrate your product or service usually runs alongside the copy. Follow my suggestions for writing a shopping column but conform to the number of words and lines allowed.

With a bound postcard publication, you can also effectively use a double card or triple card.

A double card on both sides can often carry the full copy of a Time size page. The layout has to be changed and copy reset. It requires more picture element emphasis. There should be pictures on front and back. The subhead going across the top of the back of a double card is even more of a headline.

Use your successful page ad with the least possible changes. If you do not have a successful page ad, follow my instructions for writing one. With your art director, simply modify to the requirements of front and back as described. A double panel credit card billing insert can be used almost as is.

We have used the double postcard successfully. But a triple post card is sometimes more successful. In this case, the front side of all three postcards usually will take 80 percent of the copy from a Time sized full page. Sometimes, the entire copy should fit with very little change if any. It will need to be rescaled to somewhat different proportions and about 10 percent smaller. If you have to cut, follow my instructions for cutting a space ad. Fight for every word, but yield to your art director if he feels some cutting is necessary. Probably it will not be. Use the postcard on the bottom rear as a return card. This will leave you two half cards to fill. We recommend using them for one or two other items with one coupon.

You may have copy and layout ideal for a triple card on both sides. This could be a successful "solo" piece with a horizontal broadside that is approximately the same size. You may be using a newspaper freestanding insert that can be reduced to the triple card size. A successful full page magazine section in the Family Weekly and Parade size should fit nicely when rearranged for both sides of your triple card. If the post card publication is printed in color, it will usually be on a web press. Its color reproduction on cardboard stock will be better than newspapers but not as good as the the magazine section of a newspaper. It can usually use the same color seperations to reproduce from.

If you have no proven ads near this size, prepare copy as though for a Parade sized page with this exception. Get particular help from your art director in laying out the *back* as well as the front. If possible, put in *more* picture elements. Keep the back page from having an all-type appearance. Make the subhead on top of the back page still more of a headline.

Another alternative is to create an ad and coupon for one half card only with no return card on the back. We have done so successfully. Another is to feature one or more items on *each* side with a coupon for all items on *one* side only. Generally, the lower the price of the item, the less the space size you should consider. Even a *half* card may be too much for too low cost an item. It is possible to feature three or more lower priced items on each *half* card. The ideal is a low cost item which can be ordered in larger quantities. Add-ons in the coupon for multiple orders, bigger sizes, or deluxe models can be very important to overall success.

For each alternative, adapt your successful magazine ad from the nearest equivalent size. Or write copy from scratch as suggested in the instruction for writing such a size ad.

Constantly rising postage has caused multiple mailings to be used more and more. Multiple mailings are far more flexible than bound postcard publications, or loose cards. They usually include inserts of various sizes. The very diversity of sizes and types of inserts in one envelope make it more interesting for the recipient to go through. Insert material can range from the equivalent of a single panel credit card insert to the main broadside of a "solo" piece. Each can be in black and white, or in black and white and one or two colors. Or it can be in full four color reproduction. You supply the printed piece to the company organizing the mailing. You usually pay just as much for your share of inserting, addressing, mailing and list rental, regardless of the size of your insert or whether it is in black and white or full color.

Whether you have separations, plates and complete mechanicals and their size can best determine which size you use. If you have production material, full color in larger space mailing inserts will only cost more for running costs of printing. If you have used color success-fully in billing inserts, it won't be such a big step to use it in a multiple mailing . Your art director should be able to guide you to do so most frugally. The volume potential in projection can be huge. If cost of

177

inserting and mailing is no higher for the larger piece, it becomes tempting to go ahead with one. You can do so in steps, starting with a less complex piece. You can use the largest package or billing insert you have as your first multiple mailing insert. If you pay out with present smaller material in a multiple mailing insert, consider creating a still larger one.

Go through your solo mailing kits. Look for a broadside that seems an ideal model. Study your most successful inserts and ads. Re-read your research. List all your picture and copy box ideas. Start to paraphrase your model broadside using all your advertising and research. Take your time. Meet with your art director. Show him a number of broadside models and be sure he agrees that you have selected the best model. Go over your picture, headline complex and layout ideas with him. He may have a big improvement for you and help you crystalize your layout and thus, your writing plan. Don't take too much of his time yet. It can be expensive and premature. Include a coupon in your broadside regardless of your model. Discuss how to lay out the rear page of the broadside. Consider paraphrasing different elements from different broadsides and combining them.

Don't be too worried if you can only afford a black and white brochure or only with flash color in type, borders and backgrounds and not full color art. Often, in a multiple mailing black and white is *contrast* to one lush color piece after another. Often, flash color has great emphasis.

Construct your broadside in segments. Take one step at a time. Take days and weeks. Try each day to make it a little better. Try to see your art director next when you have completed copy and made your copywriter's layout. It will be less costly, more helpful and speed his job. Follow through as though for a page ad but expect more problems because it's a bigger job. Have more overlays made. Rewrite more. Perfect and test.

If your broadside works, the next step may be to include a letter as well. In some insert negotiations, you may not have to pay additional to insert and mail your letter. Your sole extra cost might be to prepare and print your letter.

Go through your library of solo's again and pick out a model letter to paraphrase. Select a size letter that will fit comfortably with your broadside and be acceptable to the insert program that you are considering.

Notice how your model indents, spaces between paragraphs, changes paragraph construction and how wide its margins are on each

178

side of paragraphs. Notice how your model underlines, uses capital letters and alternate colors. Avoid a model that uses pictures. You can try that another time. Notice the color and texture of the stationery and how the logotype and signatures are used.

You'll find your model letter far easier to paraphrase than your broadside and far easier than paraphrasing a page ad. Be thorough. Keep improving it. Take your time. Come back to it from time to time. Now test your double insert, broadside with letter.

You now have an arsenal of direct mail weapons.

Most kinds of inserts in a multiple mailing are simply variations of some other kind of insert or advertisement you know how to prepare, and so are many kinds of inserts in magazines and catalogues.

Some of your same pieces can be used in different ways. The same single, double or triple panel insert can be a package insert, billing insert or in a direct response publication. You can translate a Parade size page ad, Time size page ad, a half, third or sixth page ad into direct mail or vice versa. You have a size range from one side of a postcard to a big brochure and letter for multiple mailings.

You can make your original test in the form of advertising where you can start at least cost and risk. You can translate any success in any form one by one into other forms, often with only minor modifications.

You have learned a lot that you can apply in many ways. You can now see that much of what is made out to be quite complicated can be quite simple. Yet, the direct mail projection of these forms of advertising is *huge*. You have already created by far the hardest parts of the "solo" kit. To try for the biggest time projection in mail order all you need to do is finish one.

The "solo" kit has the biggest jackpot in direct mail to win and the biggest chance of losing. In the good old days of low postage, cheap paper and printing,the "solo" was far more the standard. Today, in its more lavish form, the "solo" reaps richer rewards than ever dreamed of but for a smaller and smaller proportion of the largest mailers. It's not often for moonlighters.

The "solo" kit in its more elaborate form in a four color outside envelope can contain a lush four color inside broadside, a two to four page letter in various colors, a return envelope and a return card. Often, there is also a smaller broadside on the giveaway offer. Sometimes, there's a lavish color booklet demonstrating the product in use, cataloging more advantages or giving more documentation by experts and testimonials by users. Sometimes, there are even more insert pieces. But more and more, even for giant mailers, cost limitations usually keep the "solo" kit to the first five basic pieces mentioned above.

The rich "solo" kit needs a lot going for it. It's lush four color is usually, hopelessly overpriced per thousand except on a web press with a million run minimum. At this volume, every cost but postage nose dives down. Envelopes sometimes drop half or more in cost and the main color broadside even more. The most automated mailing house in the country is ten minutes away. At this volume its charges to insert, affix labels and mail are lower than it cost us many years ago inside our plant. But here's how to create a simpler kind of solo more practical in smaller volume for moonlighters.

If you've already paid out in multiple mailings with a broadside and letter, now get the most perfect model outside envelope and inside order card., You can paraphrase each quickly. If either does not quite fit your offer, modify your paraphrase accordingly.

You've completed a simple "solo" kit. You've avoided the most difficult and costly problems. Your additional production cost is trifling. You've stayed away from color or already proved that it has been profitable in multiple mailings. Your broadside and letter are smaller and simpler than in most "solos". If you're already projecting your broadside and letter for multiple mailings, you can print extra copies for your "solo" test at lower cost per thousand than otherwise. You can test a return envelope later.

To many businessmen, the daily office mail is most important.

They look in the mail for orders, bills, important letters and opportunities to save or make money. They know that such opportunities can come in third class mail, as well as first class. A wise secretary watches out for her boss when she opens the mail. She is paid to screen out time-wasting people and junk mail and to get to her boss, people or mail he really should see personally. Simple, business-like looking mail often gets opened and read by secretary and boss, when more lavish but less to the point mail gets thrown out.

If you do not have a broadside and letter, but do have a basic offer that you feel is suited to direct mail, try creating this simplest of "solo" kits. It's ideal to use in mailings to professionals, technical specialists and best of all, businessmen. Select a model successful kit in black and white with simplest layout and illustration. If it has a plain brown envelope with no copy or printing front or back, choose and do the same. From this and other models, select the most appropriate return order card as a model and paraphrase it word for word, as far as your offer allows. It's just a little more complex than paraphrasing the coupon in your ad. If your offer has a giveaway, look for a fairly simple flyer on a giveaway as part of one of your model mailing pieces. Paraphrase it as clearly as possible. Paraphrase your model's broadside letter and return envelope if any.

In your paraphrasing, take one small segment at a time. For that segment, substitute word for word your copy. It may take a long time on one paragraph. The next may come right away. Don't get discouraged with a slow start. You'll pick up speed later. If you're translating an already successful ad, it will come far faster. If you're already saturated with research for that ad, your direct mail paraphrase may almost write itself. Take it easy, go at your own pace. But finish it professionally and test it. Giant mailers often paraphrase closely their own successful mailing kits for their next mailing. To do so, many actually build their new product and offer as a paraphrase of the old. Shorter, simpler direct mail kits that fit your product can often be paraphrased just as publication ads can be. For a larger, more specialized and complex direct mail kit, there is less chance to paraphrase it effectively throughout.

You are more likely to find the perfect model for *one segment* of your direct mail kit here and the ideal model for another segment there. Paraphrasing parts of model mailing kits and putting your paraphrases together is more practical, faster and safer.

The right model coupons, guarantees and envelopes are easily paraphrased. Broadsides (brochures) and letters are more specialized and individually suited to specific offers as is lengthy giveaway copy and involved giveaway layout for very specialized giveaways. This simply means deeper digging for right models. Find the right one for each. As soon as any successful development in direct mail is tested, it is often paraphrased by the same company and by others. The surest road to direct mail success is this combination paraphrasing of successful mailing kits.

Your first combination paraphrase will be your hardest. It will force you to think, dig deep into research and to seek models. It will improve your writing structure when originating. Your sentences and paragraphs will become shorter and crisper. Searching for equivalent "color" words will help you paint product advantages more appealingly. Searching for equivalent picture ideas will develop an art and layout sense. Following the model forces a discipline on you. It tightens your layout arrangement and puts it in order.

If you paraphrase a good part of one direct mail piece, patch in paraphrases of parts of other direct mail pieces and begin to fill in with entirely new portions of your own, you're beginning to originate. The paraphrasing you do will bring ideas out of your own. Constant revision of research notes will create original and effective selling sentences and paragraphs. Frequent analysis of picture techniques of others will give you picture ideas of your own. Salesmen, demonstrators and users will give you approaches and ideas that may be unique. In direct mail it is far easier than other forms of advertising to depart from your paraphrase and to begin to originate your own copy.

Direct mail is so flexible that it is subject to infinite combination and variety.. Variations come easily and naturally from thorough research and sufficient analysis of direct mail copy and layouts of others. As you paraphrase techniques of others, you will master them and start to develop your own copy and layout ideas. This will lead to more innovations and quite different direct mail kits of your own. You start paraphrasing, word for word, simpler direct mail kits. You go on to paraphrasing partially from one piece and partially from another to combining with elements of your own. You proceed easily to creating your own entirely.

The direct mail letter is an excellent starting place to create your own style and approach. Observe most outstanding direct mail letters. Usually, they start with news of the giveaway, avoid mention of price and payment as long as possible, emphasize the no-risk trial privilege and tell important advantages in order of importance.

They favor the word ''you'', they picture in words the reader using and enjoying the product and they often tell how the product was developed over difficulties. They often ask for the order a number of times even before telling the price. They may simply ask the reader to fill out the ''reservation'' card and return it. They usually avoid such traumatic words as ''buy'' and ''pay'' while emphasizing words like ''try'', ''test'' or ''see for yourself''.

The words may paint product use and benefit with vivid color or be practical and factual. But they will be simple and sentences and paragraphs short. White space, ample leading between lines, wide margins and alternating wider and sharply indented paragraphs will be used for easy reading. Judicious use of typewriter type with an alternating second color and occasional underlining of words will help as well.

Words, sentences and paragraphs beckon the reader into more text. Subheads, underlined words, indenting and key sentences and paragraphs in color *capsule* the story for those skipping through. Letters open and close with short paragraphs. As you saturate yourself with the direct mail letters of others, you will naturally revise your own letters in these ways with your own personality added.

Reading the broadsides of others can also spur you on. You're told by the craftsmanship of each effective piece to work harder. You can recognize the research it took to write each piece. Digging deeper for your own research, more rewriting and editing is the answer. If an offer seems irresistable, make yours more enticing. When you see a near perfect giveaway, check if you have *any* giveaway or if you can improve it or its presentation.

When you read an almost irresistable guarantee, strengthen your own. Can you match the credit terms that tempt you? When you see others give a reward for quick action, *plus* a "cash up" incentive for quick or full payment now, check whether you can. If others take telephone orders and feature credit cards, do you? Should you use the 800 toll free number?

Are you using the rich color words of others? Are you asking for the order soon enough and often enough? Do *your* words, sentences and paragraphs tempt the reader to go on to the next? How does your layout, quality of art and caliber of copy reproduction, choice of paper, kind of envelope compare? Each point of analysis leads to a question about your own work. And each question forces an answer that becomes an absorbing lesson.

The broadside and letter must be read and believed. The order card must seem tempting, riskless and urgent to attain immediate action. Broadside and letter should complement one another and be independently sales effective.

Introduce more and more of your own innovations into your direct mail. Gradually, you will need to rely less and less on paraphrasing any model. Your approaches will be more varied, fresh and original.

You'll consider a bigger kit. If you buy a larger ad, your cost goes up proportionately. If you enlarge your direct mail piece, your cost rarely goes up in proportion. More space used in black and white is less expensive than less space used in four color. Pictures can cost more than words if they involve expensive photography, art and production. Greater complexity can cost far more money than space.

When you develop a quite original direct mail hit, you'll start paraphrasing your creative mail order success. You'll want to project proven success into more products. Once you learn how to sell profitably a certain way, you'll probably go into another product ideally suited to the same technique.

The more you originate your own broadsides and brochures the more dependent you will be on your art director. The right art director can greatly help you keep costs down while greatly increasing the creative effectiveness of a direct mail piece. The wrong art director can escalate your direct mail costs and slow final completion to the point of disaster. A direct mail piece can be made ever more complex and ever more expensive. It needs creative discipline to keep costs in line. Your art director needs to be a thorough professional in production or you need a production manager as well. Your art and/or production manager needs to have a business head and you do, too. So, originate broadsides, brochures, booklets and entire direct mail pieces cautiously. Start simply. Be frugal.

If your art director is guiding you and can't estimate in advance the probable cost, your bill may surprise you. Direct mail can cost you anything. Originating can *multiply* the cost. If your art director is a "taxi driver", solely concerned with his hourly rate, and philosophic about your costs, beware! If he's ignorant of production costs or hasn't a business bone in his body and you're unfamiliar with direct mail costs, stop before you start. With the right art director and/or production man, you can watch costs *and* be creative.

When you complete your first paraphrased direct mail piece, you'll know far more about direct mail than before. After you work with your art director on your first piece, hopefully, you'll work better together on the second.

As in space ads, the creative secret of getting full benefit from your art director is getting more and more overlays after first layouts. As suggested for space ads, make your own copywriter's layouts and overlays, too. Doing so helps you understand what your art director is up against and helps him work more effectively.

Your art director may transform any idea of yours into something quite different and dramatically improve it. Your art director may come up with picture ideas far better than your own. Little by little, step by step, and quite naturally, you'll become a creative team originating more and paraphrasing less from others.

Confidence comes fast with success.

Confidence gives creative sureness that speeds completion of new projects and proliferates success. The endless variations of direct mail format will no longer bewilder, but become so many keys to *more* success. You'll develop a reflex "feel" as to which format is best suited for which product and offer.

As you develop a strong creative team of art director, copywriters, photographers, artists, retouchers, printers and production people, projects will go faster and the finished job will become more predictable.

You'll feel at home in any type of direct mail. You'll write and layout with your art director a giant postcard, tabloid newspaper or

184

specialized small catalogue. In each case, you'll start with paraphrasing and gradually originate more and more yourself. You'll come up with quite original concepts of entire direct mail pieces unlike any others.

You will be a direct mail professional combining innovation with a thorough knowledge of what works in different situations. You will successfully compete with and probably profitably work with the giant mailers. Best of luck!

185

Chapter 11

Specialized Mail Order Sales

The mail order two step...inquiry getting and closing...
telephone selling... specialized catalogues

Many moonlighters have started in business with a tiny classified or small display ad to secure inquiries.

Often, they have profitably converted inquiries into sales with a single and simple, direct mail follow-up. Sometimes, they have profitably converted inquiries to sales with a telephone call.

Inquiry and conversion advertising has *two* steps: the advertising that gets the inquiry, and the advertising that completes the sale. Often, a tiny ad at little expense is all that's necessary to secure inquiries. The direct mail follow up material used by moonlighters is often simple, too. The same paraphrasing method can be used for both ad and follow-up material. Sometimes, the ad and follow-up together can be simpler to paraphrase from than a one step full page ad for a lower priced item.

Usually, creating advertising to get the inquiry and to close it, is more complicated than creating a one step ad. It is also more rewarding. The same small ad will often pull inquiries profitably again and again, sometimes for years. The same follow-up literature which converts a certain percentage of inquiries into sales will, under similar conditions, often do so indefinitely. The combination will often pull for a longer period and for bigger sales volume overall than a page ad campaign asking for full payment. You could be creating a business for years, or for a lifetime.

Let's take up the kind of inquiry and conversion advertising most practical for moonlighters. It's a small, simple inquiry ad and simple black and white, one time follow-up literature. If profitable, we can go on to bigger ads and more complicated direct mail follow-up kits. Done in the simplest way, inquiries can be quickly converted to sales, bringing in money and making operation practical for a moonlighter.

Inquiry and conversion advertising can sometimes be practical for moonlighters and sometimes not. It can be used to signal and later sell those interested in an intriguing field such as science, toys, basket weaving, fly fishing or whatever. In such cases, the follow-up is often a specialized catalogue. Sometimes, for an exotic subject, such a catalogue has been typed out, photo offset without any pictures and mailed out. Or the photo offsetter has been provided with homemade photograph illustrations. The more intensely interesting the field and subject matter, the more primitive and simple literature has been able to pay out as a start. Here, you must have a catalogue of the rare and unusual. Your research for desirable and unusual items in a fascinating field, should dig up colorful background facts on each. Your catalogues should be fun to read. Often, the primitive simplicity of your crude catalogue can give it a personality. Many successful moonlighters have started in this way. Knowing your field can make all the difference.

Inquiry and conversion advertising can sell an item that's harder to sell in one step.

It can sell a more expensive item, and often a specialized one. Only a small percentage of the circulation of a mass magazine might consider buying it. A big ad would be costly and wasteful. A little ad at small expense can *signal* those interested and get inquiries. Follow-up direct mail can convert inquiries into sales. Sometimes, such direct mail kits can be simple. Those inquiring for professional, technical or business equipment, for instance, desire detailed, factual descriptions more than lush expensive art, color, and typography. Simple black and white material can often be used.

Presenting your product's case more effectively rather than more lavishly can be most important. This kind of presentation can be quite practical for a moonlighter. Often, such an imported item has been successfully sold in another country by the inquiry and conversion method You may need only to translate highly professional follow-up

188

material into English. Photos, art, even color transparencies may be available from the exporter at no cost. Literature may even be available in English. Sometimes, a tiny ad with such proven follow-up material available has rapidly catapulted a moonlighter to a substantial business.

Inquiry and conversion advertising is also used to recruit others to help sell your product, product line or service. It may be on a commission basis or to act as agents, franchise dealers, distributors or in any way to buy your product, product line or service for resale. This kind of business has often been practical for a salesman moonlighter with a flair for sales management. There's one simple requirement. You must have case histories of those who have made enough money reselling the product to interest others to do so. Once anyone starts making exciting money reselling your product, telling others the facts is all that is needed. You will need to collect inquiry ads, recruiting help in selling, with a similar offer to yours. You'll need to collect follow-up literature to inquiries. You'll find it simple to paraphrase. Again, simple black and white advertising is often all that is needed. Fewer moonlighters have succeeded this way because items easy and profitable to resell are hard to come by. Advertising misstating such resale earnings is fraud and leads only to government grief.

An effective salesman or sales manager can sometimes come up with a successful sales technique, often a demonstration technique, that he can teach another salesman. For a moonlighter this can build a business soundly if the technique described can be passed along by mail. Advertising for a business selling products mail order for resale requires *three steps*...getting the inquiry...converting the inquiry...and providing sales help and tools to the dealer or agent. Sometimes, none of these steps need be complex or elaborate. Each can be paraphrased and each can come naturally to a good salesman or enthusiastic inventor or promoter. Often, big businesses of this type have been started by moonlighters in the worst economic periods. When jobs are hard to get, more people want to sell something at their own risk.

Inquiry and conversion mail order businesses can be too complex for most moonlighters to consider. Sometimes, a series of up to five direct mail follow-ups is required to convert inquiries into sales. Sometimes, such literature is lavish, complex and expensive. Sometimes, further complicated steps, to benefit from inquiry and customer names, become necessary to obtain overall profit. If so, more capital and logistical organization can become necessary than is possible for most moonlighters. The direct mail kit or kits that convert an inquiry into a large sale can be more complex than many direct mail kits that complete

189

a smaller sale. Let's stick to the kind of inquiry and conversion businesses that are simple, and more practical for moonlighters, at least to start.

You want to start with an item that requires just one simple black and white follow-up. If it is profitable and inquiry volume builds, you can develop a more complex follow-up. If this works, a second follow-up can be tried. The original cost of getting the inquiry has been covered by the success of the first follow-up. Results from the second follow-up can fall off somewhat and still be successful. Several additional follow-ups may each show a profit and improve overall conversions.

For a muscle development piece of apparatus, a single follow-up mailing has pulled an average of 17 percent conversion to sales. An entire series of five follow-ups for the same offer has brought the conversion percentage up to 39 percent of inquiries. Be cautious. Expand your follow-ups carefully. Test each. Crawl before you walk. Walk before you run.

Gradually, you can consider, create and test more ambitious and complex direct mail follow-up kits. You may even go into more lavish color pieces. Just take one simple step at a time and pay for each step out of the profits of previous steps. To print and mail a single direct mail kit needed to follow up an inquiry usually costs a small minority of the advertising cost to get the inquiry. To create a more convincing direct mail kit it can be profitable to spend more per kit than if mailed to cold names. Four color direct mail kits, printed in smaller runs than practical for cold name mailings, can be profitable used as follow-ups.

A double purpose direct mail kit can be created. It can justify its production cost by its use as a follow-up of inquiries. It can be tested on cold names as well. If this is profitable, it can be printed in the big runs usually required for cold name mailings and used for both purposes quite profitably.

But *start* an inquiry and conversion business that is *simple*. This requires a small ad, a single follow-up and black and white only.

How do you find this kind of inquiry and conversion situation? It's simple. Clip and file small inquiry ads for simple moonlighter type businesses. To get a file of follow-up literature, send in inquiries. In future years, when *you're* successful in your inquiry and conversion business, you may spot inquiries from would-be moonlighters; if so, remember and understand.

When you send in an inquiry, key your name and address. You can then recognize any follow-up to your inquiry. We'll explain how, later. Make up a simple form. Fill in the date that you mailed in your inquiry.

Fill in the date that your inquiry is received. Fill in whether the reply is by first class, third class, or bulk rate third class. Enter the weight of the envelope and cost of postage of the mailing kit reply. If there are further follow-ups, enter each in the same manner.

File all follow-ups received with your form in one folder. You will know the frequency of any follow-up series, and the number of direct mail kits in the series. You will know the price of the item, terms, giveaway, additional ordering incentive or any price reduction later offered. You will be able to estimate probable printing, direct mail processing and postage costs.

Enter offers from the company advertising the original items on one form. On a different form, you can enter offers from probable renters of your name. File away specialized catalogues, special sales or even co-op programs sent to your keyed name.

Keep separate folders for specific inquiry and conversion offers. You can keep two groups of folders. One can be for simpler, one time follow-up offers. One can be for more lavish literature with a more complex series of follow-up direct mail kits. You need (to start) only concern yourself with the first group.

Try to find ideal models to paraphrase. Try to start with a paraphrase of both inquiry and follow-up for the same item. It may be more practical to select as a model for your inquiry ad, advertising for one product and as a model for your follow-up direct mail, follow-up advertising for another.

Avoid any model with advertising obviously based on misrepresentation. Consider only legitimate models. Try to avoid an unsuccessful model. Select one which has run widely and continuously for years. Paraphrase as previously instructed. Be a perfectionist. It will allow you to revise both ad and follow-up with improved effectiveness.

Selling with the inquiry and conversion method is constantly becoming more difficult for some kinds of items and easier and more profitable for others. Changing conditions make the obtaining of inquiries for and follow-up of many lower priced items less profitable. It makes getting and converting inquiries for some higher priced items more profitable.

For many items, formerly too expensive to sell in one step, inquiry and conversion advertising is now too cumbersome. It's also too expensive and is no longer necessary. The same item can now be sold through credit cards in one step. At the same time, entire new categories of items have become profitable to sell with inquiry advertising. These items are *more* expensive than formerly possible to sell via inquiry advertising. The average price of merchandise which can be profitably closed by direct mail follow up has been going up. Even in somewhat, worse economic times, there is a greater willingness to buy more expensive *classifications* of items by mail, classifications formerly, only bought in a store. Credit cards have helped. More confidence and trust in mail order has also helped.

Inquiry ads and direct mail conversion kits have special creative requirements.

Advertising must produce inquiries at low enough cost and convert inquiries into sales in high enough percentages to be profitable *after* all costs of product, ad, follow-up material, postage and processing.

The object is always to get advertising cost per inquiry *down,* volume of inquiries *up,* and to *improve* the percentage of conversions. Without inquiries, you cannot convert to sales. With poor quality inquiries, your conversions can drop precipitously. Desirable inquiries are genuinely interested inquiries. The higher the price of the item is, the harder it is to convert the sale and the more important it is to get an *interested* inquiry.

The wrong method of sharply lowering inquiry cost and greatly increasing inquiry volume may cause a *sharp drop* in the percentage of inquiries converted to sales. Even getting inquiry costs at one half or one third of your former cost can be *unprofitable...* if conversions come in at a sharply lower percentage.

How you create your inquiry ad greatly effects inquiry costs, volume and quality. How you create your follow-up material greatly affects the percentage of inquiries converted into sales. Inquiries can be obtained with shorter copy than can orders. Often, short copy produces genuinely interested inquiries converting to a higher percentage of sales than inquiries from longer, hard sell copy. But short copy often includes less qualifications and less pre-selling as well as possibly less overselling. Low pressure, long copy sometimes can produce more qualified inquiries with a higher percentage of conversion than shorter copy...and sometimes produce lower cost inquiries in greater volume.

You can get more inquiries with more dramatic product claims and more urgency. Featured offers pull more than not. Any device that makes it easier and lazier to mail back an inquiry pulls more.

New ways are constantly being developed to obtain inquiries in bigger volume and at lower cost as are new ways to improve percentages of conversions into sales. New ways to obtain still further benefits from the use of inquiry and customer names are being developed just as fast. The art of getting and closing inquiries is getting so complex, it has become a big business for big companies. There are mail order advertising agencies and consultants who specialize almost entirely in inquiry and conversion advertising.

You may start very simply as regards both your ad and your follow-up. But, as soon as you succeed, you will want to advance to even more productive methods. Don't attempt to learn everything at once. But keep up with changing techniques. Keep answering more ads...and filing different follow-up techniques.

Let's discuss ways to get more inquiries and how each affects conversions.

If you use direct mail to *get* inquiries, a return postcard or envelope which can be dropped in the mail without postage will pull more. Postage is paid by the advertiser. An enclosed postcard will have the original address label affixed to it so that the label can be seen through the window envelope and the original direct mail kit. The recipient often needs only to check a box in the return card and drop it without postage in the mail. Inquiry response can soar. But prank and crank mail increase, too. Usually, you are better off with a lot lower inquiry cost and a little lower conversion rate. But sometimes, it's vice versa. Careful testing and entering of test results is necessary.

A patented device, which makes it easier for a recipient of a letter to *pull out* a return postcard, increases inquiries. A perforated double postcard in direct mail makes it easy for the recipient to rip off the second post card and drop it in the mail without postage. Usually, inquiry quality holds up fairly well. But this device must be tested for each offer to make sure that it does not cut conversion.

The telephone is the most *immediate* way to get an inquiry. The featuring of the telephone in advertising can sharply increase inquiry volume and cut inquiry cost. Persuasive urgency, combined with a toll free telephone privilege, can jump inquiry volume. But inquiry quality can be *lowered*. Telephone inquiries need to be tested before going all out. The telephone can be invaluable as an aid to getting more inquiries that do close satisfactorily...particularly, when a WATS line toll free 800 number is featured.

As explained previously, a WATS line is merely a method of getting a reduced cost per call and the use of the 800 number in return for a specified monthly guarantee. A small guarantee gets a small saving. A big guarantee buys the calls wholesale. You must get a big volume of telephone inquires continuously to justify using it. If you don't use the WATS line sufficiently, you lose money on the deal. If you go into it cautiously, by stages, you won't. The telephone company can give you full details.

The 800 WATS line number preceding your own can be featured in your advertising and answered twenty-four hours a day by you or your staff or when your line is busy, or doesn't answer, by the telephone answering service. You can indoctrinate the personnel of the answering service, as well as your own staff, and perhaps better because they are inquiry answering professionals.

Properly used, the telephone can sometimes make inquiry ads, commercials and mailing pieces pay out when they would otherwise fail. The telephone can create business that would otherwise not occur. It can *secure* inquiries and become its own inquiry advertising. Specially trained operators can telephone compiled lists of prospective buyers and warm up their interest. Then follow-up direct mail kits can be forwarded.

The telephone operator can take an inquiry and convert it to a sale at the same time. The same operator can get credit card numbers to check and even check them with the credit card company in minutes. The same operator can take a direct billing order from a big company and even take credit references.

The telephone can do most of what any follow-up literature can do, plus a lot more. It can do almost all that a salesman's personal call follow up can do. With WATS lines, using a telephone can compete cost wise with elaborate mailing piece costs and at a fraction of a salesman's personal call cost.

In print or on broadcast, a star personality can ask readers, listeners or viewers to call in. A recorded message from a star personality can give the effect of personal response from the star to the telephone inquiry. It can be introduced and followed up by the telephone salesman or woman. This has been done with great success. If you can ever have an association with a name personality, it could benefit you.

The telephone can be used particulary effectively for an add-on offer. The add-on may not even be mentioned in the ad but be offered on the telephone as an alternate privilege.

I know one businessman who has done over one million dollars in sales over a number of years with *no* advertising cost by a combination of free publicity and telephone follow up. He has personally secured substantial publicity for some of his products in a number of magazines. The stories describe some of his items with price, name and address. When orders come in, he phones each on his WATS line and jumps the average order from a little over $30 to a little over $70.

194

The telephone can help you to get more value from inquiries for higher price items. Your coupon can specify a blank for telephone number. A special rate WATS line can be used to follow up inquiries.

The 800 WATS number can be used effectively to call back big ticket customers and offer other big ticket items to them. A skilled telephone sales person can build up a rapport with such customers and develop a clientele who appreciate news of a new intriguing product or service or a special reduction, perhaps first available to them.

The telephone can be invaluable to get more and convert more inquiries.Emphasis on replying by telephone can increase response to *any* advertising. But every time that you do *anything* that lowers inquiry cost, a re-check of inquiry quality is advisable.

Each technique or device to produce more inquiries can also cut the percentage of inquiries converted to sales. "Bingo card" numbers are listed in magazines with each number representing a booklet obtainable merely by circling the numbers. A bound in return postcard is often included with the number. The reader can circle various numbers and drop the card in the mail without postage. Sometimes, huge volume of near worthless inquiries are produced. "Adserts" are postcards attached to magazine pages. Insert cards are bound into a magazine next to an ad. Either can triple inquiries and worsen the percentage of conversion.

Any device that tremendously increases inquiries runs the risk of decimating the percentage of conversions. Usually, a way can be found to use the device effectively, but proper controls must be set up.

From one issue of a mass circulation publication, "bingo cards" produced respectively for three different free literature offers, 26,000 inquiries, 21,500 inquiries and 16,300 inquiries. For a fourth offer requesting 60¢ for a booklet, the same bingo card produced 201 inquiries. There was no advertising cost for any of the inquiries; but for the free inquiries, conversions were so negligible that follow up cost alone was prohibitive. The inquiries enclosing 60¢ converted to sales satisfactorily.

Bingo cards producing huge volume of worthless inquiries can be unprofitable whatever the advertising cost or at no advertising cost. Yet, bingo cards properly and selectively used in publications where qualified prospective buyers have been accustomed to them have helped to build inquiry and conversion item businesses. •

Bind-in cards and adsert cards, despite stratospheric cost, have produced a torrent of inquiries at substantially lower cost per inquiry. The percentage of inquiries converted to sales has dropped too. The net

195

advertising cost per converted sale has often still been profitable with huge additional volume.

Take-one cards in buses, trains, subways have sometimes produced a deluge of inquiries and a desert of conversions. But, used in certain areas for certain products and services, they have produced low cost inquiries that did convert in satisfactory percentages.

There are countless ways of producing inquiries. Book matches, laundry cards and time tables have produced inquiries at low cost which have converted satisfactorily. Literature is passed out in the street, slipped into cars, left on doorsteps, given out in public places. And sometimes it works. New methods are being devised as you read this page. Each can be considered, but used only after being carefully tested.

Offering anything free pulls inquiries, but the wrong free offer or the right one presented wrongly can reduce or destroy inquiry quality. The more *related* a booklet you offer is to your product, the better the quality of your inquiry will be. It may also cut the number of inquiries sharply. The more general the audience is, the more important it is to *charge something* for the booklet, but not always. The same booklet can be offered free, for 10¢, for 25¢, for 50¢, for $1.00 or whatever. Each increase usually raises the advertising cost of obtaining inquiries by cutting inquiry volume, but improves the conversion percentage. Inquiries sent in for unrelated free gifts and followed up by direct mail may convert no better than if the same direct mail was sent to cold names. The higher the price of the item, the harder it is to convert the sale by direct mail and the more important it is to get an *interested* inquiry.

Changes in offer and copy can modify inquiry cost and percentage of conversion inquiries in many ways.

The more *related* a booklet offered is to the product, the better will be the quality of your inquiry. The more your copy dramatizes product advantages, while soft pedaling costs of product, costs of product operation and product limitations, the lower your inquiry cost will be, but also the smaller the percentage of closure.

If a product is complex and slow to assemble, spelling this out may discourage inquiries. Glossing over it may hurt conversions, if your follow up literature *does* explain this. If neither your inquiry advertising nor follow up literature indicates sufficiently these points, *returns* may be higher than expected.

Sometimes, a copy approach can lower inquiry cost, jump inquiry volume and improve the percentage of conversions simultaneously.

196

Sometimes, a full page ad can tell more of the product story, more dramatically and with more conviction. The headline complex may have more excitement and the body copy and proof boxes more credibility than smaller ads. Before receiving follow-up literature, the inquiry is partially *pre-sold*.

Emphasis on an offer can vary considerably. It can be buried or featured.

A few words of tiny, agate type buried in the bottom of the copy can whisper the offer. Or blazing headlines, big illustrations jumping off the top of the page and copy carried through from the opening to the close can *shout* it. Or the offer can be modulated to anything in between. The same variation of emphasis can occur in radio, television, direct mail, magazines, newspapers or any media.

From pianissimo to fortissimo, you can "play" your offer like a concert musician for whatever purpose you determine. The quiet, buried offer will only be seen by someone who has read the copy through and perhaps been qualified by it. The headlined offer will reach far more people, often with dramatically lower inquiry cost and far greater volume of inquiries. The whispered offer attracts the genuinely interested offer for better conversions. We prefer to use the emphasized offer to get inquiries in volume at minimum cost per inquiry.

In the same way, the offer itself can be varied in *desirability for instant action*. You can be the mail order cook, and vary your recipe ... putting in more sugar ... or cutting it down to a minimum. You can offer a booklet alone, or with something else. You can mail a booklet and an item usually $2, but offer booklet and item for $1. You can offer the booklet FREE, with a $1 value for 50¢. Or, as mentioned earlier, you can charge for the booklet alone knowing that at each increased level you get less replies, but presumably more qualified ones.

Your situation can determine your decision. If you're in mail order alone, you may go for the jugular. As you begin to sell the trade more, you may wish to be discreet about the emphasis on mail order. You may vary your approach by the media. You may want all the inquiries you can get from the New York Times, but want to screen the quality of inquiries in a more mass publication or on radio or TV.

You can vary offer emphasis and desirability as you wish.

If you advertise your lowest priced model only, such as "from $39.99" for an item people expect to pay $100 for, you will get inquiries at low cost.

But if your average model sells for well over $100 and your lowest price model is not practical for the average person then, when your

197

literature and price list arrives, conversions may be poor. If you give your full price list range in your advertising, you may sharply reduce your inquiries and increase inquiry cost accordingly, but conversion percentage may be far higher.

Increasing the believability of your inquiry ad produces more inquiries and can *improve* the percentage of inquiries converted to sales. A picture of real people using your product with their testimonials strongly featured can do so. Photography, art and often color can increase desirability and inquiries. What is needed is a constant "feel" for changing inquiry cost and the changing quality of higher or lower cost inquiries. Ways of getting leads are always wearing out. The quality of inquiries can vary because of media, geographical area, copy, offer, competition or general economic conditions.

You can also increase the volume of inquiries at will. With printed literature, it is possible to follow up a torrent of inquiries or a rivulet. And often, any new way of producing a torrent of inquiries, in time, dries up to a rivulet. It is often immaterial where the inquiries are geographically. They can be followed up just as easily. And within a range varying for each product, the quality of the inquiry can *vary* as described above.

It's a matter of starting and stopping, turning off and on, slowing down and speeding up. Simplistic, standard solutions are not flexible enough. What works now, fails tomorrow and vice versa. But you're at the controls and can turn the proper dials to adapt to changing conditions if you have a "feel" for it.

The president of one of the world's largest mail order advertising agencies has stated that the day of starting on a bootstrap a catalogue business like Sunset House is over.

He has said that the future of mail order would largely be with Fortune 500 and other big companies. This may be so. But as moonlighters, we are interested in nook and cranny catalogues, in fields obscure and small and perhaps, even seasonal enough as to hold no interest for the giants. We can find one big enough to give a moonlighter a good living. And we might find a small, brand new field just about to skyrocket into giant growth. We might get in on the ground floor with a specialized catalogue for that field.

Every new hobby, interest and activity has the possibility of a specialized profitable catalogue. The first creative task for such a catalogue is the conception of it. As a moonlighter you are limited in money, time and logistical organization. You can only start a catalogue in the simplest way as many, many successful catalogues have before

198

you.

Send for and file unique catalogues in special fields. File separately the very simplest which are most intriguing...those on plainest paper with simplest type and most homemade illustration (or with the least or none). Most amateurish catalogues fail. But you are looking for those that are fresh and original with a real personality. You are looking for one to paraphrase for quite a different field, not to copy. It's your creative job to come up with an exciting new field and concept in which your catalogue has an original reason for being.

It may take you considerable time to come up with the right concept. It may depend on your background or that of a partner. You want to marry your concept to a paraphrase of the right model catalogue. Let's hope it's in a quite different field. You want to be sure that you are paraphrasing a successful catalogue. Investigate it. Get a Dun and Bradstreet rating on the company. Speak to space salesmen from publications that sell the company advertising. Phone the company; explain that you are starting a catalogue that is in no way competitive and only seek advice. Very likely, you'll get frank answers to questions and can get an idea if the catalogue is successful.

Once you have concept and model, you will need to research your potential item possibilities for your catalogue. The freshness of your item copy will depend on the freshness of the items you can secure.

The dice are loaded against small ventures as regards printing cost, mailing cost, advertising cost, list cost, merchandise costs. Your concept, your field, your execution must be so superior as to overcome these disadvantages. You can't compete on the giants' own ground. But if you realize your limitations, you do have a chance. In field after field, a fresh concept for a highly specialized catalogue can succeed.

Retail distribution has limited choice of most kinds of items. Someone intensely interested in jig saw puzzles, fishing flies, books or tape recordings, or endless other specialties has difficulty finding a wide enough selection. Specialized catalogues keep coming into existence to fill such needs. Some prosper.

Try to create a specialized catalogue in a field where you already have a successful specialized item. Then, you can start your catalogue as many other successful catalogues have - as an enclosure with an item. You want a successful item in the field and in the price range of the items you expect to include in your catalogue. It is only worthwhile to consider the catalogue when you are selling your single item by the tens of thousands. The mortality in catalogues is very high. The soaring costs of postage, paper and printing discourage catalogue experts. But building a simple, specialized catalogue as a package insert can sometimes overcome those difficulties.

Once you get one specialized mail order item that sells, you're in a position to build a specialized catalogue. You start with an insert in your mail order package and feature the items you have that are most related to the first successful magazine items. Your first one page black and white insert, if successful, can quickly become a several page folder. The next step is mailing your inserts to your customer list. Soon you're expanding to mailing to outside names, other company's customers for items as related as possible to those you are selling. Your catalogue is growing fatter now, and more frequent, from Christmas catalogue to spring and summer as well. Later, if tests prove out, you can convert to color. You may never need to.

Catalogues may become quite unlike anything now visualized, whether on microfiche, TV recording, photo copy produced at home by telephone or by facisimile reproduction from your TV set. Some new forms of catalogues may be far beyond the ability of a moonlighter to participate in. As a moonlighter, you want to get started safely and get in on the ground floor of the simplest new catalogue development.

The telephone can be used particularly effectively with catalogues. The phone orders can be solicited by advertising in the catalogues, themselves. Specialized catalogues can be mailed cold to compiled lists and then followed up on the WATS line.

The more successful your first steps into the catalogue field are, the more potential expansion possibilities you have and, very likely, the more help you will need to attain those objectives.

If the field is quite small and projection quite limited, your choice and problems will be less. If the field is growing rapidly and you're successful to start, you may have the chance to build a good sized business. A catalogue can grow very rapidly. At this point, professional creative help can pay off for you. The right advertising agency or consultant with plenty of catalogue experience can open your eyes to one step after another to increase your catalogue profits and volume.

Let's hope you need such help. Now let's go into radio mail order.

Chapter 12

Pulling Money From The Air

Radio mail order ... writing commercials backwards ... avoiding "print" words ... radio commas, headlines and coupons ... time compression

A radio commercial can be simpler and easier to write than any other mail order advertising.

It is not difficult to write, even if you've never written any other advertising. I wrote radio commercials which sold profitably millions of dollars worth of products through mail order for years before I wrote for TV, publication, or direct mail, mail order advertising. It is not as easy as formerly to pay out profitably on radio for a mail order item.

Radio was yesterday's TV, eagerly and closely listened to. Radio, today, is less intensely listened to and is more often background to other activity such as getting dressed, eating breakfast, driving a car, cooking, homework or whatever. Today the radio is more often on while not attentively listened to.

Today's mail order commercial needs to get attention, be listened to and understood throughout and to obtain action. Just to achieve comprehension requires careful clarity. Your radio commercial must get across verbally what you're selling, your offer and price, and where to write or telephone to get it.

In military instruction, the difficulty of getting across clearly to anyone the simplest verbal message is always emphasized. And each

201

time you stop your car to ask driving directions you can realize this. You may not be prepared with pen and pad to write them down. If you're like me, you may only remember the first part of the instructions and forget the rest almost immediately. To get the instructions straight, you usually need to have them *repeated* to you. Even if directions are repeated, if at all complex, they're still hard to grasp. A very hurried repetition helps little if at all.

In publication or in direct mail advertising the reader has the option to pass over, glance at, read casually or read thoroughly. If interested, the reader can act at once or tear out and keep the printed message for future study, consideration and action.

Let's suppose your own mother is listening eagerly to a mail order radio commercial you have written. With loving attention she may never understand what you are saying. Many people are more attuned to absorb information through the eye than through the ear. A radio commercial happens quickly. You rarely are prepared with pen and paper. Suddenly, it's over and the listener may not have even clearly understood the mailing or phoning instructions.

That's why complex forms of radio commercials are usually impractical for mail order. That's why complex choice mail order offers are usually unsuccessful in radio. And it's why commercials shorter than one minute rarely work on radio for mail order.

Have you ever taken advantage of the one minute rate for long distance telephoning? To keep within sixty seconds on one telephone conversation can be a frenetic experience. Even if you're calling to say "Happy Birthday", one minute seems short. If you're calling someone you don't know on business, just identifying yourself, your company and it's product takes precious time.

Listen to radio mail order commercials when you hear them. Sometimes, for a while, the same commercial is run on the same station at the same time each day. If you hear a mail order commercial and own a tape recorder, tune in the next day and tape the commercial. You can even telephone the station and ask for the exact time the commercial will be on next. Keep listening to and taping more radio mail order commercials. Play them back a sentence or so at a time and write them down. In five minutes or so, you can write down an entire one minute commercial. You'll soon assemble a number of radio commercials both on tape and written out. Selecting a model and paraphrasing is simpler in radio than in any other form of advertising.

Notice which mail order commercials use dramatization, music or sound effects for background or even use more than one voice. Notice which are less than one minute. Most will be *without* dramatization, *without* music or sound effect background and use *one* voice. Almost all will be one minute or more. And if less, they will ask for inquiries and not orders.

Now, listen carefully to the offer and mailing instruction portion of the commercial. Hear how often the product name, the price and the address or telephone number is repeated. Now time this portion. You'll find that instructions for mailing *or* telephoning in a free offer usually take fifteen seconds or so, if not rushed and are clear and understandable. This usually includes one repetition. If the instructions are to send in money, they take several seconds more, if there is no choice of size, color, or price model. Any choice of telephone or mailing in an offer requires more seconds. If you add a third repetition and then slow directions at all for more clarity, you add more seconds. You can quickly realize that the mailing instructions are the minimum part needed for the commercial. If you time them and subtract the number of seconds used from the commercial length allowed, you can get the number of seconds you can use to introduce what you are selling, describe it and convince the listener to take action. You, at once, understand that a minute commercial is the least possible to do the job. It is simple to convince a new writer of this by asking the writer to write the commercial *backwards,* that is to write the mailing instructions first, then time and subtract from total time allowed.

In publication advertising, if you want to make the ad smaller without cutting copy, you can make the size of type *smaller*. In radio, you can only make the announcer speak faster. Faster spoken directions are sometimes *harder* to understand. A voice that speaks faster tends to speak louder. A commercial with rushed almost shouted instructions is not just hard to understand, it is high pressure. It psychologically causes listener resistance and tends to *reduce* the number of orders or inquiries produced. Loud fast instructions are not friendly. Bear in mind that your commercial is just part of a clutter of various commercials that *no one* has a burning desire to hear.

For this reason, it is wise to keep your commercial simple. Your offer should be one way with no choice. It is wiser to ask for mail only *or* telephone only. It is wise to *slow* up for mailing or phone instructions and to repeat product name, price and address or phone number *three times* if possible.

This will probably take at least twenty seconds and leave almost forty seconds of a minute commercial for your actual selling job. This means eighty slower to one hundred faster spoken words. To convince anyone of anything in this time with this number of words is difficult.

Every word of your commercial must do its share. An unneeded word or even a lazy word is sabotage of the money the commercial is costing you. The simpler the approach of your commercial, the better chance it has. It should be warm and friendly. You can't talk in stilted language. Don't use "print" words more natural to read than to speak in conversation. They are not simple enough. You want to talk as neighbor to neighbor. Read the commercial aloud which you are paraphrasing. Try to substitute equally natural spoken words.

I try to write a radio commercial to one individual listener as I would talk to one person on the telephone. Listen to announcers on country music stations and black announcers on black music stations. They have naturalness, a colloquial quality, friendly talk, warm phrases and a rapport and informality with their audience that's hard to match.

Capsule your entire product story naturally, even if longer than the commercial time allowed. Then cut to the required size. Don't cut sentences. Cut words as though each was your right arm. But don't cut as you would an ad or direct mail piece. Don't cut out the word "and" and substitute a comma. There are no commas on radio. A comma is an instruction to an announcer to take a breath. A breath takes as long as the word "and". In radio you can't cut connecting words as easily as in print. You can't be too abrupt.

Type your commercial all in caps with lines triple spaced with wide margins on either side and with no punctuation. This makes it easy for your announcer to read and easier for you to think of as spoken.

It is wise to simplify your offer and mailing instructions to the utmost. It's easiest to start in radio by translating an already successful ad or direct mail piece. Generally, a mail order commercial should open in a natural manner, warm and friendly, and not too fast. The pace can then pick up very gradually. The close— giving mailing instructions should begin to slow. When name of product, price and address are mentioned your selling voice should slow most to be extremely clear. Keep listening to your model commercial.

When you write *your* commercial, read it aloud to yourself. Tape yourself reading it. Study it as you listen for pace, rhythm and clarity. Announcers often write excellent commercials because they are writing naturally - the way they talk on the air. If you have a friend with a good speaking voice, tape him or her reading it. Avoid a high voice or a nasal voice. Try to get someone with warmth in his or her voice to read it for you. It will help edit copy.

Be careful to write the clearest instructions you can. Then make this test. Telephone a friend or acquaintance who has never heard of your product. Start by asking him to listen carefully to your instructions and then to telephone you back and repeat them to you. If he or she can't get your instructions straight, what casual listener can?

Once you realize the job your radio commercial has to do, it is easier to write. You'll find you're not as limited as you might fear. There are announcers who can talk faster without sounding louder. They can increase their speaking pace almost imperceptibly without raising their voice. Listeners can clearly understand almost three times a minute the pace that a human voice can normally speak at. There is now a science of word compression by which a spoken voice can be retaped at a faster pace. It is possible to take each breath and pause out and retape at a faster, yet even rate. The result is more words per minute, clearly understood and without a feeling of high pressure.

Voice, music and sound effects, background and dramatization can sometimes be the equivalent of art and layout. The right mood music and voice accent for a travel commercial can be the equivalent of a rich color page.

A taped testimonial from an actual user can be highly effective. A taping of a famous personality recommending a product can be even more effective. On stations where a station personality has a strong following, a strong first person recommendation by the personality will be especially powerful. An interjecting voice can be effective in citing documentation.

As in other mail order advertising, it's wise to stay with a tested commercial message. If your commercial runs frequently, alternating openings gives freshness for those who have already heard the commercial but not acted on it. But work on each opening. Each is the equivalent of a headline and subhead. A *worse* opening will *cut* orders or inquiries. Work to make *each* alternate opening *more* and not *less* effective.

Radio will work for some mail order offers. You will find it surprisingly easy to grasp what is needed and write as required.

I only mention any creative writing at all in my method in case you like it, take to it, and are good at it. The rule is still to do what you like and are good at and associate with others for what you are not. You can forget radio, get a competent advertising agency or find a partner who has mastered it.

Good luck and enjoy it.

Chapter 13

The Mail Order Gold Mine

TV frustration...fortunes to make...
easy commercials to write, nightmares to produce...
playing safe the TV paraphrase way

A TV commercial can be the most effective of all mail order messages. It can be so powerful that it not only sells the product profitably mail order in huge volume, but creates store demand as well. If you have proprietary rights to your product, this may give you a lifelong business. A TV commercial has everything in its favor. It has sight, sound, and motion. A close up of your product can take up the entire screen. It can demonstrate your product in use. It can do all this in full color (to over half the viewers). TV demands viewer commitment. Many leave the room when a commercial comes on, but many more keep watching and listening.

A TV message can be pictorially dramatized in many ways. A zoom lens can leap to a close up. Pictures can pop on the screen, fade out...and be successively replaced by one after another. Pictures can jump one by one into a quarter of the screen to create a montage effect. Key words of commercials can be supered on the screen on pictures already there. The announcer can talk right into the living room. He or she can occupy the entire screen or part of it...with supporting pictures and printed words.

Mailing or phone instructions can be shown in print on screen and spoken by off screen voice as well. Double reinforcement helps make the instructions, price, address and phone number clearer, faster.

But of all forms of advertising, TV can be more frustrating, more difficult...and more disappointing, when you compare the commercial as you see it on the TV screen with what you attempted to do and expected it would be. This is simply because there are more ways to be disappointed and more kinds of mistakes that can be made.

It's easy to write into a TV commercial the effects you see each night achieved by sophisticated commercials. It's hard to achieve those effects *professionally*...particularly for very little money. But TV mail order can be so powerful, so profitable, so huge in volume that you want to participate. And if you have secured the rights to an item perfect for TV, you should.

Don't attempt to do TV *alone*...if you have no money or are not good at it. Associate with someone else who is. Limit your objective. You have the product. You can ship it or have it shipped. Find someone to gamble the TV advertising for you. The most obvious candidates are those already successfully selling mail order on TV. They're making money. You haven't started. Usually, they *need* new items to test. You may have one you believe will sell on TV. Often, they have a successful background as professionals in TV broadcasting. You can make money from them...and *learn* from them. The simplest plan for them will be for you to sell them your product or take a royalty on it. They may be willing to buy it and also pay you per unit to pack and ship it. If they prefer a royalty and you are already paying a royalty, you add your royalty on top. This may or may not be acceptable.

You must be willing to make less if you associate with someone who takes over your risk. You may be able to make a deal giving up TV mail order sales only...only for a specific period...and only if a certain minimum income is produced for you. You earn less but learn more while risking nothing. And if you're starting moonlighting with little or no money, you have very little choice. Once you make some money and gain some TV know-how from your association, you can try your next item on your own.

The next alternative is to get others to take the risk on making the TV commercial while you take the risk on buying TV time. The risks in *testing* a TV commercial can be small. The risks in making one can be big. Many try to eliminate risk in buying TV advertising by trying to get PI's (no risk advertising) and paying so much per order received. We'll discuss this later. But the real risk in TV mail order advertising is the risk in making the TV commercial. It's far better to take the small risk of testing it on one or more stations and if successful buy cautiously thereafter. But first get someone, or several, to take the risk of *making* the TV commercial.

Occasionally, a TV station will produce a TV commercial for you and test it, both at the station's risk, charging you a percentage of sales. This is rather unusual. And it's not easy to get anyone to take such risk. Sometimes, you offer a limited royalty such as a small percentage until a performer, producers, actor, facilities owner, crew member gets an agreed fee bigger than the standard fee for such services... or a far smaller perpetual royalty. Most won't touch it. But if allowed, it is a way and perhaps the only way you may be able to start. If agreed to, you'll get substantial motivation for all concerned to produce a profess-ional job.

Any professional wants to get the highest fee possible for his or her work. But many capable professionals at some time in their careers gamble their professional abilities for a share in something. Many a lawyer or law firm owns stock in corporations in return for work done.

However, let's now assume that you can afford to take your own risk of making a TV commerical. A TV commercial can be extremely complex or far more simple. No matter how much money you have the best way to master making TV commercials is to start simply. If you can produce a simple commercial that works you can go on to a more complex one. And if you start moonlighting with little money you can only afford to go on TV in the simplest way. So, let's not get into sophisticated production. Let's discuss the simpler kinds of TV com-mercials most practical for you to start with.

Some of the simplest and most effective TV commercials are demonstrations. Many were successful for years before going on TV. They might have been in stores, at fairs, on the boardwalk or house to house. A demonstration on TV can be *more* effective than in a store because close ups occupying the entire screen can show more clearly what is happening. The demonstration is cut to the essence, usually about one minute and thirty five to forty seconds, leaving twenty to twenty five seconds for the mail and phone directions.

A demonstration TV commercial can be so simple that it is filmed exactly as it has always been done, but cut down to the required size. In some cases, there is no other action, art, voice, camera shot or even slide, except for mailing and phone instructions. Many a salesman owning a small company has gone on TV and delivered his own sales talk cut down to commercial length with no real production assis-tance...and has been successful. In many cases, the same demonstration commercials are effective for years.

The reason is often that a demonstration "hit" has been translated into TV. And the less tampering with the already successful demonstration, the better chance it has had to succeed in TV as well. Many products are extremely well suited to demonstration. The problem is to find a really effective demonstrator. Often, this requires manual dexterity plus natural salesmanship and showmanship. An able TV announcer or actor may lack the necessary dexterity. But sometimes, a TV actor or announcer who likes a hobby or sport (even if not really good at it) can demonstrate superbly anything connected with it. It is wise to have a real expert check him or her at each point.

Many product salesmen are *not* natural demonstrators. Others are superb. If a salesman is a natural demonstrator, but has never been on TV, often he or she is *not* bothered at all doing the same demonstration on TV. The same is often true of the product inventor. If someone has demonstrated a product for months or years, then it usually is easy and natural whether off or on camera. Some demonstrators and salesmen have surprising potential for being entertainers as they demonstrate on TV.

We've found natural talent many times in TV demonstrations by fishermen, artists, cooks, beauticians, dance instructors, home repair men, sewing experts musicians, teachers, authors and hobby authorities, in many fields. We've also found many authorities who knew their subject, yet came over poorly on TV or froze and became awkward. It takes trial and error. Usually, you can determine before filming or video taping if your candidate is or is not suited to TV demonstration. And if you do find someone who can successfully sell or demonstrate your product, it may give undreamed of TV success. That someone might even be *you*.

Very likely, Julia Child was as assured, natural, amusing and convincing her first time on TV as in later shows. She probably had this talent for years before her TV appearanace, and noticeably enough for anyone to observe it. She might even have considered going into business with you on your kitchen product if she believed in it. And there are other great demonstration talents waiting now for someone to associate with.

Public TV has brought back how-to instruction programming and cable TV has, as well. This trend will continue as more VHF, UHF and cable stations are available providing homes with more alternatives to movies and serials. Even today, the items that often sell most profitably mail order on TV are demonstration items. We've built entire TV programs around demonstrations: art instruction shows, gardening shows, dressmaking shows, and so forth. On cable, these shows will become more and more welcome. On cable, as earlier on TV, longer TV demonstration commercials will be acceptable...and I mean longer than today's two minute TV mail order commercials. We will see a renaissance of demonstration. And remember, a demonstration by a superb demonstrator has the least chance of anything going wrong.

You may not believe in long commercials. But try this test. Watch mail order commercials on TV...on any old movie and some new ones. Tape the voice and sound. When you see a mail order commercial you can phone the station and get the exact times it will be on next. Play back the tapes and time them. Write down the words on the *right* side of a yellow pad. On the left side, write down a description of each change of scene that happens on the screen and each super and fadeout where words are superimposed on the screen or taken away. Keep watching, taping, and transcribing until you have a collection of TV mail order commercials. Time each and note which are two minutes, which are one, which in between and which less than one minute. These will be your models to paraphrase.

You will find that the big majority are two minute commercials. Those that are less are usually asking for inquiries only. Now, notice which ones are most elaborate with dramatizations and lavish production, and whether big name performers are delivering the commercial. Notice which are simplest with slides and off screen voice only or with one person on screen doing all demonstration and selling and with slide only for support and mailing instructions.

You will find that many of the most repeated TV mail order commercials are the simplest. Now, notice how mailing and phone instructions are handled. You will find that many commercials ask for both mail and phone orders. You will find that many commercials offer a choice of a less and more expensive offer. The combination of seeing instructions in print on the screen and hearing them simultaneously allows this slightly more complex handling compared with radio.

You can keep your TV commercial simple...and make a profit. But even if simple, it is usually not practical to make a TV commercial as you go on the air or just before it. Too much can go wrong. The production staff of the station is either not available or so rushed with other duties as to be unable to get into your problem. Even displaying your product on camera, demands effective lighting, and effective lighting is often slow trial and error.

For the beginner in TV, videotape is far easier to work with than film. It can be seen immediately after being taped. Mistakes can be seen. Scenes can be immediately retaped and corrected...or eliminated. Videotape can vastly simplify making a good TV commercial. But still the more elaborate the TV production you attempt, the more opportunities there are to *destroy* its effectiveness. Each added complication that you put into the production of a TV commercial session is pushing your luck a little more.

Next to a demonstration only, a slide commercial interspersed with several simple action shots and all with off screen voice is the best bet to get what you expect with least accidents. Even then, to make one two-minute commercial using a competent crew takes most of one eight hour working day. Making *two* two-minute commercials in an eight hour session is not easy. The logistics of preparation to get full value from these eight hours can be considerable.

Otherwise, when you get to the TV studio, you may be in for a surprise. You need to bring to the studio in ample time each slide, each prop and contingency plans for what might not work. Each component part of your TV commercial has a possibility of not coming off properly. A picture you think is great may look poorly on the screen, even one of your product in use. Your producer or director may or may not be as effective as you hope. When you arrive, you may find nothing in particular happening, no one particularly concerned, and your TV commercial hardly geting under way. Soon in the day, you may realize that it's going to be a race to finish the commercial at all. You're aware of your hourly cost for the studio and crew. You feel helpless. You're in the hands of others. Each suggestion you make might *worsen* the overall effect and get you into expensive overtime as well. That's why careful selection of a TV commercial to paraphrase and careful paraphrasing of it is so important.

Being thorough and careful from the writing of your commercial to the day of production can greatly lessen chances of anything going wrong. In writing a TV commercial with off screen voice, the first tendency is to use too many words and too few pictures. A slide that overstays on the screen can slow the commercial considerably. If you have little or no motion on the screen and do not see the announcer face to face, a mostly slide commercial needs fast change of pace. Keep to the action and timing of the model you paraphrase.

Sometimes, a very large advertiser with an ample budget for elaborate commercials will use one with nothing but stills. This is because such a commercial is a complete change of pace from a more sophisticated one. But in such a commercial, one slide after another will pop on the screen. This can be very effective.

211

For this reason, one of our alumni (and one of the most successful mail order operators on TV) usually writes his two minute TV commercials with *twenty* slides or action shots. He usually allows twenty five seconds for mailing instructions, using only three to four slides. He usually avoids telephone orders, preferring cash only. Each slide or action scene averages six seconds. Four to five of these shots will be motion shots, usually quite simple such as a hand picking up the product or the product in use. He intersperses these throughout. The rest are slides. He will use approximately two hundred off screen words, running from three to fifteen or so per shot. He will super words on the screen in about fifteen of the twenty shots. He supers one to five words to a shot. In total, he gets thirty to forty words on the screen at times throughout the commercial. Several of these times, he will fade out several words and super in other words.

We favor slightly less pictures, words and supers. Naturally, each product and commercial has its own requirements. Either way it's fast moving...and subject to possible mistakes. That's why so much preparation to avoid error is required. Sometimes, it's possible to view certain important shots in advance at a cooperative TV station. This is particularly important for a product shot. If such a shot does not come off, the entire commercial could be unproductive. Your art director can be of tremendous help in creating a TV commercial and preparing for it. This can be so, even if he or she has previously had no experience in TV. But tell your art director how important it is to paraphrase...and do it. Accustom yourself to working with a storyboard sheet or creating your own when you write your TV commercial. It causes you to put TV picture ideas next to words and helps you work with your art director. Use the same number of words with each frame as your model commercial.

It's wise to compare costs producing a TV commercial by different talent, producers, studios and in different cities. Los Angeles, Chicago and New York are expensive production centers. There are competent crews in lower cost centers elsewhere. There is a risk anywhere, of less than competent announcers, actors, camera men or directors. There can be more risk where experience is less, which can occur in small cities. If you at first associate with others more professional in TV than yourself, at their risk, you will quickly learn where and how they make professional commercials at reasonable costs.

TV can be extremely powerful in using real life testimonials, if you use them correctly. Just going out with a tape recorder and interviewing *enough* customers at their homes or offices, will uncover some

212

so natural and convincing that you could not write anything yourself, or pay anyone to act the part, anywhere near so effectively. Giving the same testimonial on TV is more difficult. None of your customers giving testimonials may come across on TV. Many may even be unwilling to take the time required to go to a studio and make a commercial In such a case, it may be necessary to dramatize with commercial talent the testimonial for which you have a release. Be sure you identify it as dramatized, in whatever manner the latest rules of the FCC and FTC require. Just ask them.

Featuring the telephone on TV gives urgency and maximum immediacy of action. The toll free 800 number is particularly effective and simple to present both audio and video.

If your paraphrase works, your TV projection can make so much money and run so widely that you may become a desired advertising account to the right advertising agency. If you lack money, but do have a successful commercial, you can attract partnership or association from financially responsible experts.

But be discreet. The right experts or consultants can make you rich... and the wrong ones steal your item and commercial. Let's discuss finding the right agency or expert.

Chapter 14

The Experts

The ideal advertising agency...finding...
winning...pleasing...working with one...
being your own...the same for a consultant

Obtaining the *right* mail order advertising agency can change your mail order life.

The right agency can compensate for lack of mail order marketing experience on your part...or augment your own know-how. The less advertising and promotional background you have, the more important the right advertising agency is to you.

The chances of a mail order moonlighter getting a top mail order advertising agency are almost nil. Large advertising agencies desire large accounts. Getting any competent mail order advertising agency to accept you is difficult. Small to medium advertising agencies are sometimes tempted by smaller accounts they hope will grow. Sometimes, they do not have the time for their smaller accounts to cause them to grow. This is sometimes a surprise to those who have the impression that it is possible to get part of the 15 percent commission back from the agency.

Far from trying to get advertising talent to work for less than full commission, the problem is to get real advertising talent at all, and if you get them...to motivate the talent to *work* for you. More incentive, not less, is needed. Some small mail order firms give a partnership to outstanding, creative advertising talent. Some give minimum fees

214

against commission. Some give a bonus on successful ads. I've been paid a royalty on sales by substantial companies, as have others. Of course, you can get part of the commission back from an advertising agency which places the ad for you but does no work other than mailing in the order.

A new agency is often more willing to speculate its time and talent by taking on with no minimum fee, a smaller account it has confidence in. New talent is constantly starting up shop on its own. You may be fortunate enough to select the right, young advertising agency at the right time. When starting out, an agency is more willing to use its best efforts to make a success of your business. But a new agency may be tempted and take you on because it wants to *list any accounts* to start. It may not have time to work on your account.

More small advertising agencies can give you excellent media selection help than give top creative help. Less time is required for the first. There are few very small advertising agencies expert in each form of media. You can often get excellent media buying advice on one form of advertising. This is fine if you concentrate on that form to start. Sometimes, you can combine selecting a quite small advertising agency, quite strong in media, with offering to pay for free lance copywriting as an advance against future advertising agency commissions. Or you can create the ad yourself and get the agency to help in media.

As soon as you have your first successful test in any form of advertising, you become more interesting as a prospective advertising agency client. As you develop more hits and project each, you become a bit more desirable. Agencies which had no interest in you before may now consider you as a client. The more you grow, the higher up the ladder you can go in getting consideration from desirable advertising agencies.

The more successful advertising agency you wish to interest in your account, the higher is their overhead. If your account is small, either be prepared to pay a minimum service fee to a larger agency or seek a smaller advertising agency. That minimum agency fee can be the safest money you'll ever gamble. It may enable you to get top talent instead of mediocrity.

Getting the right agency to accept you is a step toward your success. Winning their interest and confidence that you can be a big client can greatly speed your success.

The difficulties in creating your own advertising are powerful reasons for working with a competent mail order advertising agency. If you are starting off with very little money, this may not be possible.

215

You may have to begin largely doing your own creative work. You will probably start with a quite small advertising agency, if any. Even if a small agency creates advertising for you, you may be disapointed.

A smaller agency is tempted to secure more and more small clients. Each may get less and less time. A retail store can train a copywriter to write very fast. So can a radio station, a printer, or a creative service doing quick jobs for small advertisers. The one common denominator of such work is that there is no time to *think*.

Very small advertising agencies are often a combination of artist and former salesman for space, artist and printing salesman for direct mail and announcer-producer and time salesman for TV or radio. Usually, the emphasis in such small advertising agencies is on the salesman-account executive. Often, there are too many accounts, too little time and limited professional training. The objective can be billing for the agency. It may not know how to get the most from each advertising dollar for the client.

For any size advertising agency, the weakness of being a client is that you cannot be the only client. You share the time and talent with others. If you're a small account, you may get *Junior,* being broken in on YOU! If you get the agency's better talent and your billing is much smaller than other clients, you may get much less attention and thought from them. Advertising agencies must make money. They must make a profit on time and work invested. They must make money NOW and not gamble on futures to too great an extent. A smaller agency can give more time but cannot escape the basic economics. Generally, a smaller agency, with lower overhead and lower-cost executives and creative people can profitably give more time for the same billing. But the most talented mail order advertising people usually earn more. If you get the services of lower-cost mail order advertising talent, it is usually less effective for you. So, there are frustrations and drawbacks in dealing with large and small advertising agencies until you're a large enough advertiser to be profitable for top advertising talent to deal with you.

Pleasing the client can produce more short term billing and agency commission than improved creativity. Sometimes, a copywriter, art director or account executive develops an extraordinary ability to "sell" creative work. He or she is a showman, setting off the work to best effect, usually only after a persuasive "pre-sell". Creative ability that might have been improving the advertising has been devoted to selling it.

When your account becomes big enough to interest a leading mail order advertising agency, your real growth opportunity will arrive.

216

A top mail order advertising agency can be an exciting clearing house of mail order opportunities. So many tests are being made so fast that new information of what works is pouring in. Newspaper and magazine salesmen and their bosses are meeting with the agency executives as are station representatives. Publishers, TV and radio station managers are coming in on periodic trips to touch base with the agency. You, as a client, are getting access to the newest techniques uncovered, the newest exciting media buys. Often, opportunities arise for joint ventures or cross mailing inserts, list swaps or whatever, with other clients.

Check on any agency you consider. Call several clients and ask if each is satisfied. Call several publications or broadcast stations and talk to the credit manager. Explain that you are considering the agency and have heard good things about them, but that you would appreciate any information on how promptly the agency pays its bills.

If you get to be a larger account and are considering a larger agency, check on them more thoroughly. Be diplomatic but ask how much percentage they add to production bills...the greatest sore point with clients. Ask the agency what functions it charges for and what it gives for its commission. Try to avoid future surprises.

Look over the creative work of the agency. Meet those who will work with you. Be frank about your present size. Don't exaggerate your hopes. But try to impress them with your honesty, competence and sensible plan for your business. Discussing your business with their specialists can be revealing. Judge the common sense of any observation, reactions or suggestions that each gives you.

Ask for financial statements of any advertising agency that you're ready to select. Clear them with your accountant. An underfinanced agency can hurt you. You may be asked to pay an advertising bill *twice* once to an agency and if it goes bankrupt, once again to a publication or broadcasting station if it was never paid by the agency. Check if any of the partners have been involved in a previous bankruptcy in any business. This can be a bad sign. Such a history can repeat itself.

What is the company's policy on competing accounts? Do they handle accounts you feel are competitive? How much information about your business will be passed on by agency personnel? Check their clients for the agency's reputation for discretion in such matters. Ask who would be your account executive. The definition of an effective account executive is that to the account he is the agency and to the agency he is the account. He may turn out to be a salesman trying to get you to spend more. Or he can be the key to harnessing the maximum abilities of the agency most effectively in your behalf. Of all the agency personnel, he must be the most discreet. For he will learn more about your business than any other. Be sure he does not handle any account in the agency you feel at all competitive. The chemistry between you and him or her will be most important.

Don't rule out any agency for a single reason. Consider all factors. The most understaffed agency with a very talented one man owner enthused over your growth potential may be better than the top agency who looks at your account with a jaundiced eye. Using *any* advertising agency exposes you to danger of vitally secret information about your business getting out. Some super secret mail order men have a house agency solely for internal security. More feel that the assets of dealing with the right agency outweigh such liablilities.

Many mail order firms do have their own "house" advertising agencies owned by them, but recognized by all media and receiving their 15 percent and 2 percent cash advertising agency commission. These firms seldom set up their "house" agencies just to save money.

Sometimes, the principal owner or a partner is an advertising agency man and if so, is often an egotist. He wants things done quickly his way. He wants creative people to report to him. Sometimes, the mail order firm is too small to be interesting to most advertising agencies. Instead of paying a minimum service fee to an agency, the mail order firm sets up its own. Sometimes, it's just a self defense against the choice of an agency inexperienced in mail order or getting Junior in an experienced one.

Few mail order companies I know use a house advertising agency to save money. The main advantage is getting what you want done, when you want it, and getting moment-to-moment control of your advertising. There is a difference in the economics. An advertising agency tries to take the long view but must make a day to day profit on motions made and time spent. But on your own advertising, you are solely interested in profit overall, not commissions earned. In one case, we spent five months of a top copywriter's time to write one ad but made $100,000 from it in the next forty days. We'll discuss later how to organize your own advertising agency.

If you are an advertising man gone into mail order, it will be hard for other advertising people to satisfy you. If you are a superb businessman without advertising background, why not team up with equally superb mail order advertising people? Why have a fool for your client? As far as getting a kickback rebate of some of the advertising agency commission, it may appeal to a non-advertising-background

218

businessman but it takes the heart out of any interest in creative work by the agency. It is usually less profitable for the advertiser. But if you are an advertising man who would like support in some advertising area, it might work. This could be so, if you write your own advertising, but need the agency's media help. I would personally, still recommend giving full commission and pushing them to make up for your writing contribution in other ways. So, act according to your own talents and situation.

Start your agency relationship with a test of their advertising for your product. Proceed cautiously with projections. Try to put yourself in the agency's shoes and then be a good partner to them. The proof of the pudding, for both you and the agency, will be in the eating. And once you start a good relationship, keep it. Don't be a "tap dancer", dancing from one agency to another. If you're fortunate enough to find a competent agency, handle it with care.

The right agency has the right team for you. You want to help that team to work for you. But your efforts to contribute creatively to their work could drive them out of their minds. Proceed with care. Try to simplify and not complicate their work.

Any research that you do helps your advertising agency create better ads. It can dramatically increase the percentage of "hits" they create...and their total billing from your account. Incidentally, it can *multiply* profit you get from advertising they create.

If your account is small and you are not on a fee basis, they are always trying to determine whether to keep working on the account, probably at a loss but in the hopes of future profit, or to drop it. You could push them over, either way, by personally helping or hindering them

Don't dominate. A determined client can get advertising that pleases him, but far inferior, creatively to advertising that the agency could prepare for him.

Working with your advertising agency should be *supportive* to them and time saving for them. Start with your account executive. Make him realize that you feel you can help him and the agency build billing and profit. Then gradually convince him that this is so. What you innocently propose may be upsetting. Each creative specialist has an ego. An advertising agency, no matter how objective it collectively tries to be, has ego, too. Any offer to contribute creatively can be taken as a reflection on the agency's creative ability, and perhaps the first step to a more partial use of the agency, perhaps even leading to a future request for a partial kick back of agency commissions.

Working creatively with your advertising agency requires spending time in their offices with their specialists. It sometimes upsets the internal procedures they have set up. The more you're in their shop, the more you see their problems that perhaps might embarrass them. The man you're talking to may be getting an angry phone call from another client. Just seeing how much time they devote to other clients, and how little to you,   can disturb the illusion all clients and agencies like to preserve of an organization working primarily for one client, *you*. You can be like a guest walking into the bedroom you weren't expected to see...with unmade beds, clothes scattered and bathroom in disarray.

So, to be easy on them and be a good account, the chances are that, initially, your advertising agency can do more for you than you can for them. You want to correct the balance...and more. In this way, you can hope to attain a relationship where your account is desired...and the loss of it to be regretted. Your account then becomes desirable to other agencies...and in turn, more desirable to your present one where you wish to stay.

Just expressing your appreciation of *any* work they do is important. Your account executive, in one way or another, personally benefits from the growth of your account. Your first job is to prove your *competency* to help him and the agency. Let him realize your respect for the agency's ability. Simply *present* him with your own copywriter's layouts and copy as a further step beyond research.

The account executive, himself, may be quite realistic. He may be quite aware that your present billings are not attractive enough to the agency for him to get much creative time from the agency for your account. He may *appreciate* your contribution. The proof will be in the pudding. Your research material alone may be tempting and provocative to the copywriter assigned. He or she may be a junior writer anxious for a chance to write a "hit". Your research and your rough ads may be more help than that writer is getting from other clients. It may result in a "hit", even if credit should go mainly to *their writer*.

Now, there will be *requests* for more research material and more consideration for any rough ads and layouts you contribute. Now, you will have a chance to meet the young copywriter, who from your material, scored a "hit". There is mutual appreciation and the beginnings of mutual respect. If the net result of your meeting with the writer is that the next "hit" is written faster, with more projection of advertising billing for the agency, you will find the agency more receptive to more help from you.

Now, you can meet the art director, the production manager, and

220

eventually get in closer cooperation with them. It's a slow *step by step growth of a relationship*. And at each step, you must prove competence to additional specialists to win respect. Gradually, you'll be invited to sit in at a photo session, to meet with artists, retouchers, engravers and other specialists. Each step will have the same requirement. *If you save them more time and help them make more money, you're welcome*. If you waste time and hinder them, you're endangering your relationship. And you must be a diplomat at all times.

Most advertising agencies are strongest in space and broadcast advertising and weakest in direct mail. Many do not handle it at all. Many mail order firms accept the idea that the agency should make its 15 percent on space and broadcast advertising, but not on direct mail advertising. It's very hard to pay out in direct mail advertising. Adding 17.65 percent to costs to average out at 15 percent is not worthwhile to some mail order firms.

Some mail order firms believe that the right direct mail consultant can advise them all they need to know for an agreed flat fee, and that they can perform all actual functions. And in any form of mail order, a top talent executive who has spent his life developing a new successful technique for big mail order advertisers can, on a part time basis, sometimes be a gift from heaven to other mail order advertisers.

The woods are full of mail order consultants. Many are simply between jobs, fired from one and looking for another, with a feeling of dignity by hanging out their shingle. But some mail order consultants can be invaluable, particularly in direct mail.

Selecting the right consultant can be more difficult than picking the right advertising agency. First check his biographical sketch. How long has he been a consultant...and for whom? Exactly what function does he perform? Does he advise only, create copy, make list or media schedule recommendations? Which big companies or agencies has he worked for? Was he on their payroll...before he was a consultant? When did he learn his trade from them? How recent or obsolete is his present know-how?

Ask his clients if he has been worth the fees they have paid him, if he has tangibly increased their business...and if so, exactly how. Ask if they feel he's familiar with the very latest techniques. Ask exactly what he has done for his fees.

Talk to him about his career and your business. See how you get along...and how common sense his reactions are. I know one mail order consultant who has a fantastic background. He is fascinating to talk with. But he's mentally lazy. His first meeting is his best. In successive meetings, he has less to contribute. After a while, he's squeezed out like a damp towel. He's a poor buy for a yearly fee, but a tremendous bargain at a stiff fee for several meetings. Just one suggestion from him has sometimes made tens of thousands of dollars for his client. But it's most apt to come in earliest meetings.

Select your consultant carefully. Go carefully into the relationship. A quick cancellation privilege of any regular retainer fee is desirable. Different factors can change the worth of the relationship. He's only one person. He may be unable to deliver effectively to you. He may become too successful in getting clients to be able to service them. He may contract an illness. He may undergo an upset in his personal life.

So, try to select the best on the most flexible basis.

If you're starting out without adequate capital, but you succeed in securing the rights to an outstanding product, you might consider proposing a partnership to the right direct mail consultant for direct mail only. You might provide the product, do the fulfillment and take the risk on the actual mailing costs, but give a partnership for direct mail only for the creative work. It might make you rich.

And now, with all this help (or self help), let's discuss just how good advertising should be.

Chapter 15

The Money Making Laboratory

*The perfectionist concept...post mortem
lessons...continuous testing...perpetual improvement*

In this course, I have asked you to master your product and its field, to study and analyze successful mail order advertising closest to your product and field and to apply lessons learned.

Adapting your advertising to a "model advertisement" you select is the method I've successfully used to start young men and women in this field. Most had no prior copy, advertising or mail order experience whatsoever. It's the method by which I taught myself.

Step by step, you will familiarize yourself with more and more successful mail order advertising. More and more, you'll see how to apply it to your own. My hope is to help you to apply *your own* actual experience to originate your ads more and more without formula or model.

My interest is to get you to create a successful mail order ad in the shortest possible time and start making money. I'd like you, as you make money, to make a continuing laboratory study of improved creative techniques...simply by analyzing actual mail order sales of each ad you create. I want you to become a perfectionist, not a hack. I want you to make this hobby a mail order university.

A perfectionist can't stand any of his work that is less than perfect in his eyes. A hack is always happy. Time after time, working with

223

talent in radio and TV, I've seen the same reaction. The more top the talent is, the more they worry about each tiny facet of each phase of their work...and the more endlessly they go over and over it, again and again, to correct it. The happy faces that come out of the studio after a TV show, radio show, taping or recording are often the hacks. The tense, worried ones are...the stars.

I've gone out with a top Viennese photographer to various locations day after day to get desired shots and seen him again and again refuse to pull the lever of his camera! "The only thing that will come out is what I see through the view finder. If it isn't right when I look through the finder, it won't be right when I develop the picture!"

We've sent a crew of three to take color pictures outside for one of our products every sunny day for seven weeks. They have taken over 2,000 shots and selected only a dozen or so for our advertising material. Great art directors make initial layouts and then, one tissue overlay after another, change parts of the layout endlessly until completely satisfied. And great copywriters, working with art directors insist that they do. I've seen bitter fights between the copywriter and art director version, ended by testing *each*.

What I'd like to get across is that the way you work creatively is only important in that it should be the way suited to *you*. But accepting mediocre work from yourself, your copywriters (regularly employed or free lance), your consultants or your advertising agency is condemming you to mail order failure or at best—mediocre success

How good should an advertisement be whether publication, direct mail or broadcast? An advertisement must be the best that can be made.

Like a good product, a good advertisement can always be made better. The Model T Ford was a good car, the best that could be made for the money at that time. It went forty miles an hour. You could have it in any color, provided it was black.

Later, it was not good enough. Today's Fords are great cars, the best Ford can make for the money at this time. But, soon they will not be good enough. Never give up on improving your advertising.

Every sports record was made to be broken. Your advertising can also be made better. Year after year, products thought to be perfect, are radically improved. And advertisements, like *anything* created by the human mind, are capable of constant and infinite improvement. The mind does not have the physical limitations of the body.

Yet, improvements in advertising often do not keep pace with improvements in products. This is particularly true in good times. When advertising billing is huge and the advertising agency business is booming, new clients can become more tempting than improved advertisements. When ads make money in mail order, it is tempting for the mail order company to stop worrying about further improvements of the advertising.

Even in good times, mail order advertising often fails in initial tests. In times of business adversity, almost all tests can fail. Fortunately, adversity is the mother of improvement.

We have, for our clients, spent many millions of dollars for hundreds of products under the stress of having to make a profit keyed to the advertising. We have had to work under laboratory conditions where the exact sales produced by each form of advertising and each separate advertisement were measured exactly in dollars and cents.

It has taught us the hard way that advertising can constantly be improved. Over many years, we have keyed separate advertisements for over 50,000 individual mail order situations.

These tests, in each case, recorded exact sales of a separate advertisement in print or broadcast. These tests covered most units of advertising space from a one inch ad to a seventeen page section with return envelope.

We like to think of ourselves as a money-making laboratory. We try to be a laboratory devoted to the development of new techniques to sell more goods at less advertising cost. We think of all our work as one large continuing experiment to determine exactly what it is that makes certain advertisements more productive than others, and to insure more effective advertising, a bigger share of the time.

Others have more experience, with bigger companies, spending many more millions of dollars. Others are technically, far more authoritative in specific fields of business, mail order and advertising. Books have been written in far more detail on each of many aspects of mail order and advertising.

We have worked for large companies. In this course, my concern is the practicalities of making money in mail order for the smallest moonlighting entrepreneur. We have already been through the mill ourselves. Thousands of times, we have observed what happened with a specific advertisement.

We have observed what happened when we changed a headline, layout or copy approach and when we cut or expanded copy. We have observed case after case of seemingly slight changes, slight shifts, slight improvements which had startling sales effects.

We try to keep all factors constant but one. We avoid testing different headlines *and* different prices at the same time. We try to be

225

scientific. Scientists can often measure *exactly* what happens each time they change one element of a chemical formula. You can become a mail order scientist measuring *exactly* what happens when you change one element in an advertisement.

There have been tremendous improvements, in recent years, in mail order testing methods. Yet, many advertisers and some agencies still do not realize exactly what could happen in sales if they slightly changed certain elements of the mail order advertising.

Test after test, for product after product, has shown conclusively that the apparent difference between overpoweringly, effective advertising and ineffective advertising is far slighter than most people have any inkling. Again and again, seemingly slight variations have made the difference.

That one extra test could make the money, even for a tiny ad. In an inch ad, just putting in a thick dotted line border will sometimes improve results 20 percent or more. This simple addition attracts more readers. In a tiny ad, *bigger* type in the headline can make a 35 percent or more difference. It usually, more than pays to make a small ad bigger for this purpose. More white space around the headline helps, too. Often, a several line headline asking a question, will stop readers and increase orders.

Of course, it's *what* the headline says that determines readership. Just changing to a stronger, more universal product claim can make the difference. In any size or form of ad, there are many ways to improve results.

Execution of any ad, direct mail piece or radio or TV commercial *can* sometimes be far from the great expectations of the layout, script or audio-video sequence sheet. Fighting to insure that the final effect equals or surpasses your expectations is an unending battle.

Each specialist concerned must realize how vital a contribution he or she can make, to perfecting the presentation. Artist, copywriter, announcer, actor or actress, producer, director, special visual or sound effects man, each can help, or hinder, the final effect. Utilize the special advantages of each form of advertising you employ...whether newspapers, direct mail, radio, magazines, television...or whatever.

In any mail order or direct response activities you go into, I urge you not to stray from the straight and narrow path of mail order success, once you've found a successful test. Just keep doing what you did the first time successfully, and in the same identical way. Never stop testing improvements, but only change your main advertising when you've proven a new changed advertisement or form of advertising.

Never fall in love with a business, a product or an ad. The day you get your first copy of a publication carrying your latest test is usually a thrill. As you read the ad, mesmerized by your own copy, it seems absurd that the ad should be anything but an overwhelming success.

When an ad fails, it's hard to accept the results. The first reaction is to blame the entire thing on the unconscionable slowness of the post office. The next is to search for any reason for the surprising lack of mail; any reason that is outside of the fact that it has bombed out. Your beautiful ad has collapsed.

Take your time. Give the post office every chance to produce a belated avalanche of mail. But, finally, read your ads, both sides of a split, again. You will see them with a new eye. Try to analyze why readers didn't buy. They didn't want it, didn't understand it, or didn't believe it.

Try to analyze why they might not have wanted it. Does it seem too expensive, too difficult to assemble, too difficult to use, too impractical with too limited benefits? Does it seem to have too *specialized* an appeal? Is the copy clear? Is part of it confusing? Is it offensive? Does it talk woman language to men, grown-up talk to children, or hip talk to adults? Does it offer easy enough terms? How about the photographs and art? Did they do what you hoped for in the ad? Would you now use a different picture idea?

Examine the ad, element by element. Then go home and sleep on it. Put it aside for days, weeks, or months. But don't necessarily give up on it. Your work may yield future benefits. One of the biggest hits we ever had got 40 percent of break-even on its first test. A partner (one of the top copywriters in the country) had written it. The next day, he rewrote it. The next week, we retested it. And in the next few months, we made several hundred thousand dollars. It could happen to you.

Let's get a little deeper into the science of testing and projecting.

227

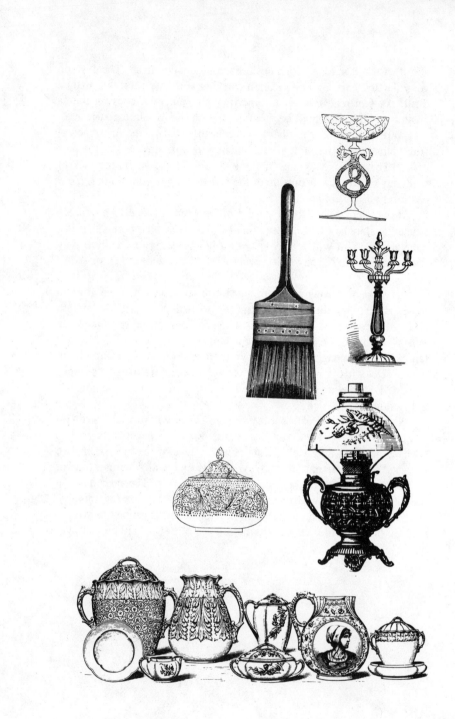

BOOK IV

Selection and Negotiation

Tactics of tiniest tests...strategies
of safest projections in newspapers, magazines
direct mail, radio, TV advertising

卌 卌 卌 卌 卌 卌 卌 卌 卌 卌
卌 卌 卌 卌 卌 卌 卌 卌 卌 卌
卌 卌 卌 卌 卌 卌 卌 卌 卌 卌
卌 卌 卌 卌 卌 卌 卌 卌 卌 II

Chapter 1

Psychology By the Numbers

*Measuring human behavior
reactions...probing firm and flexible rate
cards...asking...analyzing...deciding.*

Testing in mail order is the art of buying information. You are trying to find the answer...whether a certain product, price, approach, or offer can make money. It is based on the surprising science of human behavior reactions. If, out of a thousand people, three or five or twelve can be induced to take a certain action, the same proposal made the same way to another thousand similar people will usually induce approximately the same percentage of people to take the same action. Without that, we'd all be broke. Because of it, you or anyone who gets the "feel" of this science sufficiently can make a mail order fortune. The secret of testing is the ability to buy information at least cost. All too often, cost of tests are higher than necessary, often for newcomers ...and often, because of advice from interested parties.

Tests are unprofitable to advertisers, advertising agencies and services involved. All concerned, if asked advice, try to be objective. Yet, a small struggling advertising agency may advise a somewhat larger test ad for a somewhat larger commission. Space salesmen, asked for advice, have difficulty recommending a smaller rather than larger advertisement or a later rather than earlier one. Coming rate increases, closing dates, the possibilities of losing a position, become reasons to do something that maybe you shouldn't. List brokers, printers, artists,

231

TV producers, time salesmen, all want to help but are tempted to recommend what's good for them, which means more money.

The business of mail order is based on testing items and then fully projecting the successes. The art of mail order is to test in pennies and project in dollars. Every unnecessary dollar spent in a test is the enemy of that art. Spending any more money on one ad test than needed limits other tests.

Ever lower cost testing is the answer and ever closer to maximum projection of hits. If losses on a number of tests are extremely low and projection of one success is major, the profits of the one success can easily wash out all losses of all losing tests and make a handsome overall profit as well. It's amazing how tiny an effective test can be.

Different forms of advertising such as newspapers, TV, magazines and direct mail advertising sent through the mail are called media. Selecting the right media for *your* advertising and getting the right position and the best advertising rates is also an art.

Doing this has been much of my job almost all my business life. Before I bought advertising, I sold it for newspapers, magazines, bus cards and direct mail. I have bought radio advertising and TV advertising both on individual stations and networks. I have bought advertising in newspapers and Sunday newspaper magazines and in general magazines, specialized and trade magazines. I have bought direct mail lists, printing and paper, billing inserts and package inserts. I have bought the hybrid media of direct mail co-ops in newspapers, magazines, and mailings, packages of loose postcards, bound postcard magazines and who knows what.

In buying advertising in any form, much of the secret is getting *all* and not just some of the facts needed, analyzing these facts and *acting* on them in the buying decision.

Every time, the method needed to make the right buy is very much the same. If you carefully research the facts and analyze them correctly to buy even a classified ad, you can gradually apply the same approach to larger and larger media buys, each time to your benefit.

Making the right media decision is a matter of media research. This means asking more questions, insisting on getting *full* answers and judging whether these answers make sense. One of the shrewdest buyers of mail order advertising in the country (an old agency client of ours) has made some of the soundest decisions in media I'm familiar with. He simply insists on getting *more* facts, *all* the facts needed for a media decision. This can be a lot.

Each form of advertising has its own most important questions to

232

ask. But, whatever form of advertising you are buying, the selection procedure is much the same. Pitfalls to check into vary by media, as do the comparison points most important to investigate. The need to dig is the same. For each medium, deeper digging means safer buying.

Patient telephoning to other mail order users of the medium considered can uncover important information. Simply ask: what did they sell? How did it pay out? How did results compare with results advertising the same product elsewhere? Often, this way you will get some other good buys to consider, too.

In selecting each form of advertising, skilled professionals can help you buy advantageously.

But, even in media selection, the small agency's resources will be limited. A larger agency specializing in mail order has specialists in different media. In television alone, a top mail order advertising agency can have a number of knowledgeable buyers. The quite small agency will probably have one buyer for all media. The bigger the agency, the better the deals they are in contact with. Unfortunately, they are usually reserved for bigger clients.

As previously explained, your problem as a moonlighter is that it is not profitable for such agencies to handle your account. You may get a smaller agency excellent at media buying, particularly if you find a good one just starting out. You may simply sell your product to a top mail order firm. You may select just *one* form of advertising to start off in. If so, you may get a small advertising agency specializing in that one field. You can succeed in that field and go on to the next.

But, however you proceed it is wise to familiarize yourself with media selection. If you use an advertising agency strong in media selection this background will be helpful. If not, it will be necessary.

As a small moonlighter, if you use an advertising agency, you *may* end up with a beginner to work with. He may know little more than you do. Or you may get little time from an experienced media buyer. With possible billing small, your desire for lots of information may seem premature to him or her.

If you deal directly with media, you will probably be assigned the newest, least experienced and least informed salesman. He may know nothing of mail order. He may have no idea whether advertising your product in his medium is sensible for you. The temptation for all concerned, including yourself, may be to make a *quick* decision, particularly for a small buy. The very fact that you are dealing with others almost as inexperienced as yourself makes your questions seem an unnecessary waste of time. The salesman wants to make his sale or go make another sale.

Yet, only your dredging up necessary facts from him and others can help in your decision. Your job is to sell each person you work with on yourself. Each media salesman you deal with may be able to help you either directly or indirectly with answers you seek. Just cultivating each person involved can help get you more answers. If you don't have ample money, it's vital to devote ample time to make each dollar spent, less risky. Asking questions, getting answers and analyzing them is the way to do it. The decisions are usually just plain common sense, once you have all the necessary facts.

Let's consider what you need to know to make a sound media decision. Advertising costs money and delivers readers, listeners and viewers. The numbers of readers, listeners, and viewers are calculated in determining how much to charge for advertising. In magazines and newspapers, this is usually on the basis of the total *paid* circulation: subscribers and newsstand buyers. However, research is often done and quoted on numbers of actual readers (rather than buyers), including "pass along" circulation. This is usually for the purpose of justifying rates. Mail order media buyers usually simply calculate the cost per thousand paid circulation.

Radio and TV rates for individual stations are different for different arbitrary time classifications. These rates are usually based on the amount of listeners or viewers averaged out for each time classification. Research surveys to determine the actual tune in of listeners and viewers are quoted to justify these rates.

The rates are determined by human beings and not always with perfect logic. A small moonlighter making his first test has little chance to negotiate a better than quoted rate. He can decide whether to pay it or not advertise. For larger advertisers, the "rate card" is adhered to strictly by some individual media and less so by others. A magazine publisher will sometimes be more flexible than a newspaper publisher and a broadcaster more so than a magazine publisher. We'll discuss negotiating rates later.

All you have learned so far will help you in making sound media buying decisions. The item you select will be more logical for one form of advertising than another. The advertising presentation that you develop will give it a better chance in one form of advertising than another. The price you sell at will help determine the most logical advertising medium to select. The right price can differ in different media. The price ideal in one medium can be suicide in another. The medium that you advertise in must be suited to the item and price that you sell it at.

The "National Enquirier" is a "shot gun" mass medium. For total number of people reached, it's a rare bargain. The lower cost product that you advertise in it, the bigger percentage of the total circulation can afford it and the more you can cash in on this bargain.

A "solo" piece in direct mail is a super accurate rifle, hopefully aimed at exactly the prospects you're after. It costs far, far more per thousand reached. Usually, higher priced items ideally suited to the list do better. With each postage and printing price increase, the average price of successful direct mail items goes higher.

Radio and TV require the low price common denominator item that the National Enquirer does. The average newspaper and mass magazine is suited to a slightly higher priced item. Highly specialized magazines sometimes are suited to the same priced items as those successful in direct mail to similar audiences.

Even the same people can best be sold *differently* priced products when reached in different ways.

The American Express credit card has five million members. You can reach members via Travel and Leisure Magazine, via inserts in bills sent out monthly or via "solo" direct mail kits mailed out separately to the list.

To reach a thousand members via the magazine costs about five dollars for a page ad. To reach the same thousand members via billing inserts with the same message costs about fifty dollars. To reach the same thousand members by a direct mail "solo" piece costs about two hundred to three hundred dollars or more.

The most desirable retail price of an article offered in the magazine is lower than via inserts and substantially lower than via the "solo" direct mail piece. This is so true that American Express direct mail specialists in their own mail order division have told me there is very little correlation between what sells successfully in the magazine and what sells successfully via their "solo" pieces.

This means that each mail order article you sell, by its very retail price, is *limited* somewhat as to how and where and to whom it can best be advertised. Trying to sell the *right* article at the *right* price but in the wrong place for that price is trying to put a square peg in a round mail order hole.

Media testing works hand in hand with product selection, developing price and offer and advertising creation. Here's how.

235

Chapter 2

Split-Run University

*The mail order laboratory ... testing
half circulation one way ... half the other
keying results ... limitations*

In mail order, partners need not argue about advertising. It is simpler to test. It is easy to try out either partner's preferred way in regards to copy, price or offer; each tested in a separate ad and keyed separately. Then, count the mail.

On television or radio, it's possible to select two different times with about the same viewing or listening audience and try one commercial one way and one, another and compare results. We've done it many times. In publication advertising and in direct mail advertising, it's possible to do so more accurately with a split-run ad. Half the circulation gets ad "A" and half gets ad "B". The best offer or ad wins.

Anything in the ad can be tested this way: two different headlines, two different prices, giveaway or none, two different giveaways, two different pictures on top, different terms, different body copy, a buried offer of a free booklet deep in copy versus none or whatever. In each case, all other elements but the two being tested can be kept identical. Testing, keyed and measured, has taught us most of what we know. We never stop testing and learning.

Tests teach us how changes in ads can increase profits, often seemingly slight changes and surprisingly big profit jumps.

A first test is sometimes quite a borderline success. Every mail

236

order man can tell you stories of an apparently minor change made in a later test that skyrocketed results in the more successful half of a split-run test. Many mail order fortunes have been made this way.

For a publishing client, we once created a mail order ad we were proud of. It made quite a modest profit. But it was losing money and here's why. In a split-run, an improved advertisement, telling a more complete story, upped sales 22 percent and made 56 percent more profit than the first advertisement. And yet, this improved advertisement was still losing money. Here's why. A further improved advertisement with a new approach in a split-run jumped sales exactly 320 percent and earned 600 percent more profit that the second advertisement. And yet, this further improved advertisement was still losing money. Here's why. A still, further improved advertisement, without changing a word of copy, made 82 percent per dollar more profits than the third advertisement. This was the advertisement used in the final projection of this campaign. Had the original advertisement been run through the entire campaign, profits would have been $7,800. The first revise would have made $11,400. The second revise if projected would have made $66,500. By running the third revise of the ad in the final projection, actual profits were $105,000.

In each test, the offer was the same with every ad element frozen but those of copy, layout and illustration. In each test, the publication and position were the same. Each ad in each split stayed approximately within the same product claims. But for the ad creating 600 percent more profit the presentation was in editorial style. It was a complete departure from a book ad without even a book illustration. For the ad creating a further 82 percent improvement, the editorial style was also used but changed somewhat. In this split, every word of the copy of each ad tested was identical.

For the second ad, our art director carefully studied the typography and format of the paper selected for the test. In the rearranged ad, the headline and main pictures were actually made smaller. The type was reset to conform even more to the newspaper's own style for its stories. That was all. I have seen this same sort of transformation of profits in other cases as well. Continued improvement of advertising produced continued improvement of profits.

For other editorial style ads, we've taken special news type photos of the kind more often used in such a story. For different papers, we have kept headline ad subheads to sizes used in that publication. In each case, we've used the closest equivalent type face permitted to that of the publication. We've split-run the more editorial ads against somewhat less editorial ads. In each split, the version of the ad most authentically identical to a news story in that publication out–pulled the other. This was so, even when the changes were not too great. We never stop split-running possible improvements for ads. And we never stop being surprised at how dramatic those improvements can sometimes be.

We ran a full tabloid page split run test to determine the most profitable price to sell an article used by automobile owners. A prior test had been slightly unprofitable. Identical copy and layout was used for *both* sides of the split. Only the price differed. In one half of the split, the price was *50 percent higher* for a slightly more deluxe product. Every other paper carried the alternate advertisement. The unchanged price half of the split broke even. The other half produced one more order and over 50 percent more revenue. Advertising cost was the same. Product cost was almost the same. The higher price half of the split made a good profit. It was run elsewhere at an equally good profit. Simply raising the price transformed a formerly unprofitable campaign into a good profit one.

You can only consider selling on any terms but cash if you are financially and logistically equipped to do so. If you are, it's still wise to test alternate terms to determine which will produce the most profit for your product. We often do. We keep price and other factors identical and test alternative terms such as:

Cash vs.cash or credit card.

Cash or credit card vs. cash or direct credit one payment.

Cash or direct credit one payment vs. cash or direct credit time payment.

Cash or direct credit time payment vs. direct credit one payment or direct credit time payment.

Let's assume that cash, or cash or credit card pays out, but cash or charge, or charge or time payment pays out significantly *better,* assuming reasonable collection and returns. In this case, we immediately start projection of the cash, or cash or credit card offer. Meanwhile, we *wait* for verification of the hoped for answer on collections and returns. If collections and returns are each in line in the cash or charge, or charge or time payment offers, we switch to the winning terms.

For direct credit orders it takes considerable time to get the answer on collections and returns, particularly on time payments. Orders may come in at a low selling cost. A good percentage may take a cash option (for a saving or giveaway in return for full cash payment). You may have a satisfactory collection history from similarly priced items sold via similar circulation or lists. If so, its worth considering projecting

238

before verifying. We, being small and conservative, prefer to wait. We like to verify that we really are collecting the money. We like to be sure that bad credit figures are within our original estimates. We like to know that returns are within our estimate percentage. If all this is so, we can then go ahead.

Factors that are vitally important are these. Does the copy *oversell?* If so, bad credit and returns can be out of line. Does the product *completely satisfy* the customer? Otherwise, bad credit and returns can be catastrophic. Is the collection series used too weak or too strong? If too weak, bad credit can be overly high. If too strong, it can step up returns. That's why we prefer to wait for final test answers. It's slow. Conditions may change radically while we wait. But, overall, it's safer.

One point to be particularly cautious about is price competition in a fast changing situation. A highly successful mail order offer sold through many top mail order companies was an excellent quality electric adding machine, selling for over $200 on credit or time payments. The collection and return percentages were found to be within estimates. As the offer went into a tremendous national projection, orders poured in. But even as the shipments were being made, the new chip calculator adding machines, far more desirable for far less money, were suddenly being advertised widely. Returns, by customers of the over $200 adding machine were stratospheric. *Did emphasis* on the guarantee and return privilege in the advertising contribute to these big returns? Probably so. But who could have foretold this situation?

Simply changing the space size tripled profits per dollar spent in advertising for one client, a thread company. For this client, we tested four space units. One was two inches. One was a 56 line single column advertisement. Another was a 200 line ad. This was a 100 line on two column advertisement. The last ad was a full tabloid page 1,000 line advertisement.

The basic offer was identical in all advertisements, although more items in the line were featured in the larger space advertisements. The 56 line ad was more profitable per dollar of advertising than the two inch ad. The 200 line ad was more profitable than the 56 line ad. The full page tabloid ad was by far the best per dollar. The increased sales per dollar of the biggest versus those of the smallest were about three to one.

For other products and other clients, other size units have sometimes proved most profitable per dollar of advertising spent. Finding the best size advertisement for your product can make a big difference in your mail order life.

239

We ran a split-run test for an automotive safety product. One of the advertisements featured a problem and solution illustration. The difficulty this product guarded against was illustrated and the product's use was clearly illustrated. The headline was a simple promise. The other advertisment featured an exceptionally, dramatic accident photograph. It was a real stopper. The headline was a powerful fear headline. Both appeared in alternate copies of the same newspaper on the same page. The product, offer, publication and body copy were the same.

Fear lost. The non-fear ad pulled 48 percent more sales than the other. It produced 65 percent more profit. We've been afraid of fear ever since.

Often, a price reduction ad is successful. But never assume so. A price reduction ad yields you *less* gross profit per sale than selling at the higher price. It may give less gross profit from your advertising or even cause a loss. So, each price reduction ad must be tested before being projected.

Different elements of ads can be tested in a split run by freezing all other elements. Featuring a giveaway can be tested. The results can surprise you. Often, giveaways are selected *without* scientific testing. Time is short. It is assumed that the giveaway *must* help. One is selected arbitrarily and all tests made on other elements.

The benefit of a giveaway should not be taken for granted. Offering a giveaway can actually *reduce* sales or gross profit compared with offering *none*. And if one giveaway is *proven* to increase gross profit, another may do so even more. Each should be tested, with all other key elements of the advertising as identical as possible. One giveaway may take less advertising space or time than another; and no giveaway takes less space than any.

We like to test a giveaway first on its own...selling it, itself, as a mail order item. If it won't sell by itself at a price it's rarely an effective giveaway. If it does sell by itself and we sell it widely enough as a mail order item, then we have established a known retail value. We can then state that it has sold nationally at this price, but is now a *gift* with the purchase.

Often, a giveaway, self liquidator or partial liquidator can also be tested as an add-on at full retail price. An add-on can help considerably or *hurt*. If you get as many basic orders with it as without it, plus some add-ons, you're ahead of the game. But sometimes, tests show *less* orders and less total gross profit, with the add-on than without. This can be so if a large size of an item costs far more. The add-on can sometimes cause the prospective customer to decide that he or she *needs*

240

the large size but can't afford it and that the regular size is *insufficient*. The same effect can be caused by an add-on of a deluxe version that is a good deal higher priced than the regular model. The deluxe version may seem to be the good one, but the price may seem more than the prospective cutomer cares to pay while the offer of the deluxe may cause the prospective buyer to conclude that the regular model is *inferior* and decide against it. Each add-on must be tested before projection is safe.

Here's what happened when we tested the use of a cash-up offer. A cash-up offer to prepay shipping costs ourselves has pulled 75 percent cash on an average $100 order. In this case, it cost us about 4 percent to pay shipping costs ourselves. At the time, we were paying 3/4 percent monthly for bank money. The average credit customer took about 80 days to pay. Being paid in cash saved us about 2 percent for the period. It also resulted in that much less bank money borrowed. Net cost to us was therefore about 2 percent. Returns are always a lower percentage for full cash payment customers than for credit customers. This is because, when the bill comes, the urge to return comes, too. There is no credit loss on full cash payment. Credit loss on charge customers on this item ran 4½ percent. Costs of billing through the credit cards were averaging 6 percent. Therefore, the cash-up *made* money rather than cost money.

For the same offer described above, telephone orders were later actively solicited by our advertising. Telephone costs were absorbed by us in a WATS line 800 plus your telephone number. The percentage of full payment then *dropped* to 25 percent and the charges via credit cards went to 75 percent. You can't, as yet, send cash via telephone. But the volume of orders increased substantially.

A cash-up usually works and usually is a necessity for a small business projecting advertising widely on a high ticket item. But, in some cases, a cash-up can *hurt*. The incentive may be too substantial and too *heavily emphasized* in the advertising. Most people may feel that they cannot now send the full cash payment and that buying on credit is *too expensive*.

So be cautious, don't make the incentive too big, don't play up the incentive too much, and test that the cash-up *really* works, and how well, before you project.

A guarantee can be broad and simple or very specific and detailed. How will each affect sales? Testing can tell exactly. Our tests have proved that far more mail order profit is lost by failure to emphasize and repeat the guarantee than by additional returns as a result of a guarantee.

241

Our tests have also proved that a simpler guarantee is good business as well as a builder of good will. But test it yourself.

Compare simplicity with the added protection to you of spelling your guarantee out in maximum detail. Simplicity probably means more sales and customer good will. Spelling out limitations probably means less orders, but a smaller refund percentage.

Make a split run test in publications or direct mail advertising with all elements identical *except* the guarantee. Run the simpler guarantee in one half the test and the more qualified guarantee in the other half. If the simpler guarantee wins, run a confirming test. If it still wins, run it in enough advertising to get over five hundred purchasers. Key the guarantee certificates differently, thereafter. Watch defective returns under the guarantee. If, after the guarantee period, defective returns are within your estimate, then make the terms of the guarantee your permanent policy. If not, your alternatives are to *tighten* the guarantee or drop the product. Usually, the defective returns are the product's fault and the simpler and broader guarantee only spotlights them. Otherwise, with the broader and simpler guarantee any disappointment is rarely great enough to increase returns.

It is practical to make clear and reasonable limitations in your guarantee. It's important to do so for higher price items.

Department store customers sometimes return purchases…more so for more expensive items, still more if bought on credit and most often for items bought on time payments. A mail order buyer from an unknown firm may be more tempted to return a purchase. Often, the return is only after being billed for months.

No company can risk shipping unlimited amounts of high ticket items as a perpetual *loan* to people who constantly postpone their final decision as to whether to buy or return the item and meanwhile don't pay for it. The longer payment is postponed, the greater is the possibility that it will never be paid. In this case, the inertia is against you. The first reaction, by such a customer to a strong credit collection follow up system, is to return the item. We have emphasized earlier, that only after determining from test orders that the percentage of returns and bad credit is within anticipated estimates, is it safe to project.

Because inquiry and conversion selling is more complex, it requires more testing. You can never stop testing ways of lowering lead cost and increasing lead volume. And with each success, you must become suspicious of the effect on lead quality, and test that too.

Going to four color can be overwhelmingly, more effective or the disappointment of your life. Extra color costs must pull proportionately

242

extra orders.

Some products seem overwhelmingly suited to color. Garden products seem so. Yet, for a fertilizer, we arranged an unusual split-run test half in color and half in black and white. We pulled more orders from the black and white version than from the identical ad in four color. In black and white it had an editorial look. In color, it did not.

Color can be a temptress luring us into test costs that we did not originally contemplate and perhaps cannot afford. A product or product use picture can look so stunning in four color that its black and white advertising seems drab and lifeless. Only a test of full color versus black and white can *prove* how much of a difference four color will really make.

The cost of any testing in color escalates. The cost of running a color ad can be substantially more than that of running the same ad in black and white. Even where running in color produces more orders, your color ad can lose money by not producing *enough* more orders.

For moonlighters, the sound plan in considering color advertising is to crawl before you walk. Test black and white advertising. If successful, project and make profits. If tempted by color *then* test in color with *part* of the black and white profits. If your product seems to require color and black and white advertising is useless, only test if you have the money to lose or can get around the cost in some way.

Sometimes, you can get your four color test *free*. A catalogue may purchase your item, photograph it at its own expense in four color and run it in four color as part of a four color page. Sometimes, extra color shots are taken and the rejects can be obtained for nothing or for very little.

It's sometimes possible to save much of the risk of color tests. You may have available to you at no cost the color separations or engravings or at least color transparencies and not realize it.

If you import, your exporter may have them. If you buy from a manufacturer, he may have them. You may have them for another purpose for retail packaging, in trade literature or in a direct mail piece. If so, you may be able to save much of the production cost of testing color in your advertising.

Some publications run mail order shopping section color pages where you can test a small space color ad with minimum production expense. This is often a safer way to explore the possibilities of color for your product.

When you project a successful test, you may need to make changes to fit different sizes of ads. It is important to avoid changes without

243

testing and to not make any change carelessly. Radical changes can create quite different ads, which can have quite different results.

A magazine you are considering may be smaller or larger than the page size your successful ad ran in. You may be offered a bargain in a somewhat different space size. You may have a right hand coupon and be offered a left hand page at a bargain. You may be offered a premium position if you will put your coupon *on top* so that it will not be back to back with another coupon.

The more radical the change is, the more dangerous it can be to run the changed ad without testing. The bigger the publication is, the greater is the possibility that such a change may be needed. You may be trying to meet a closing date deadline. You may not realize the possible effect of a change on your mail pull.

You may be considering a TV Guide size page vs. your successful Time magazine size page. If the reduction cuts copy, it may be wise to test the smaller version before running it widely, you might consider running a TV Guide-size double page in place of a Time sized single page. In a magazine like TV Guide you can test a single page in several small local editions vs. a double page in several small local editions. Both tests can be in the same issue.

Many smart mail order men test even minor changes before projecting them. Be cautious. Go a little slower. Better be safe and test than sorry. But it's time now to discuss some of the practical limitations of testing. Mail order is an *imperfect* science.

Given more and more time and money, mail order can be more and more of a perfect science. The problem is more often a slight shortage of the necessary time and money. Time is always short. Tests may not be worth your while if test costs become too excessive. There is always a race to get a "hit", project a "hit", make a season, beat competition or whatever. Testing takes time. Testing more elements takes more time. Test information gained after a competitor has won the race often has little value.

Every test costs money. Production cost for many ads tested is greater than advertising cost. A split-run test of two completely different ads can double test production cost. For elaborate color ads, production cost often runs far ahead of advertising space cost. Small ads usually can't be split-run except in geographical splits.

Testing in newspapers is more difficult than formerly. Less newspapers offer split-runs. Many of these newspapers have increased their production charges (aside from advertising cost) for split-runs. Newspaper advertising costs for mail order advertisers have often risen

244

higher, proportionately, than have magazine advertising costs. Therefore, fewer newspapers now have acceptable costs per thousand for mail order advertisers. Newspaper pages per issue have increased greatly and proportionately more in advertising pages than in editorial. Therefore, small ads now have more tendency to become lost in newspapers.

We avoid geographical splits where part of the circulation in one geographical area carries one ad and the remaining circulation runs the alternate ad. This is because one part of the circulation might go mainly to lower income areas, and another part mainly to higher income areas and the split would teach us nothing. We use "true splits" only, in which special presses print every other copy with the alternate ad. This means that, for a split run ad in a newspaper, every other copy of the paper on each newsstand, wherever sold, will carry the alternate ad. In this case, exactly half of the circulation, in each geographical area, gets each alternate ad.

If, as a moonlighter, you only advertise in small space in newspapers and magazines, you may never get into split runs at all. It is only possible for ads larger than a minimum size, varying by publication.

Production charges are usually higher in relation to space advertising cost for minimum size split-run ads. Split-run direct mail tests can sometimes be practical in small circulation.

As a moonligher, your tests will probably be small and sometimes inadequate for a final decision. A successful small test needs to be confirmed by a more adequate bigger test. If, in a split-run test in a newspaper of 50,000 circulation, one ad is 25 percent better, it's worth confirming test.

Retest the same split in one or more papers (not the original paper) comprising 150,000 to 250,000 circulation. If the same half is again successful, split-test once more. This time, test still different papers comprising 700 to 800,000 circulation. You will then have split-tested a total of a million circulation. If the last test confirms, project the winner.

In direct mail, follow a similar procedure. Elaborate color mailing kits are far more expensive per thousand in small runs. Therefore, large mailers jump to a million mailing after the very first test. That's why for most moonlighters, full color direct mail is prohibitively expensive.

If a test that you expect to succeed fails, don't be surprised. It happens. But take nothing for granted. Results very occasionally can be *tilted* by conditions in that area or at that time.

Houston, Texas was hardly touched by a major recession when the rest of the country was suffering. A winner in a test in Houston was a *loser* nationally. Conditions were not the same. Check conditions at the time and place of your test. Did anything unusual occur? When a president is shot, marches into a far-off country, or starts or stops a cold war, mail order results can fall off for a few days or weeks. Check the position in the publication. Check the weather. Super hot weather or a snowed-in condition cuts mail orders. Check the competition that day and for weeks before. What looks like the same product at half the price can decimate your mail order results. Was there an error in the coupon? Was there a contradiction in the terms? If in doubt, retest.

Test in *several* sections representative of different parts of the country. Too small a circulation split run test may not be a sufficient sample. The more expensive an item, the less orders you need to pay off. The smaller the number of orders involved, the less adequate is the sample. We run in at least a million circulation to confirm the results of any initial test.

Being overly frugal in test ad production costs may destroy your test. Your ad may look entirely unlike your layout, if you resort to publication set typography. Your pictures and art may be so bad as to keep people from buying. Watch your money, but be professional. One half of the split may be a more professionally *finished* ad than the other and *tilt* your results.

We will test a lower price item first in a circulation of one hundred thousand or more. We prefer to test an item selling for $50 or more first in a circulation of several hundred thousand. A less than adequate test is better than none. If it fails, not too much is lost. If it pays off, there is little further risk to run a confirming test. The poor results of too small a sample test can cause you to stop further testing. But giving up on testing is more apt to come from poorly made tests or failure to analyze properly each test. The more soundly you select, research and create an ad for your product and the more sensible a media selection you make, the safer your test becomes.

Avoid spending too much on your test. Budget for yourself an allowable total for test expenditures. If you're small, you must do so or go broke. This means that you will never have enough money to test all the things you'd like to. Start testing with part of your savings. If successful, project your success and confine future testing to a percentage of actual mail order profits already made. This is realistic. It means each success that you get and project creates a budget for more testing.

Here's what makes mail order an art. First, it's the ability to select most important elements to test. Second, it's to project most safely without unlimited time and money. You should also avoid giving up

246

after inadequate tests or after any test of any ad you have doubts about.

We try never to give up on anything we have faith in, yet not to throw good dollars after bad. We try to put aside an unsuccessful test for a time. Doing so clears the head and gives perspective. A later post mortem going over product, copy, offer and conditions and time of test can sometimes cause us to come up with a new approach. Periodically, we do this. The more faith in the product we have, the more frequently we take another look. Sometimes, months or years later, we come up with a successful test from our earlier failure. Conditions are constantly changing, giving one product less chance and another, more. If we observe change and analyze which of our old failures have a new chance because of change, it becomes time to consider a new test.

Ideally, testing should be objective. Your faith in the product is subjective, but it is a most important ingredient. But wishing for success can cause misinterpreting of test results. There is no point to testing if you cannot face the facts of a test. A failure must be faced as a failure. If you test and fail and project anyway you can lose a lot of money. If you test in too elaborate a fashion because of conviction that it will pay out, you will risk bigger loss than necessary. If you keep testing a proven failure, you will probably keep failing.

Some very successful mail order people drop a product after an unsuccessful test as though with burnt fingers and never test it again. They have found that on the average there is less risk to test something new and different.

You can get *testitis,* testing anything and everything and falling in love with testing itself. This can be an expensive hobby that can put a moonlighter out of business. Testing is only for the purpose of coming up with a *hit* with the least money and in the fastest time.

A moonlighter starting out may have very little money. Only some of it can be risked testing. Thereafter, even if you have success, profits may come slowly. Testing will need to be very limited indeed. Each test will need to be kept to smallest cost and risk. Of all the tests you'd like to make, you only make some and at first, maybe only *one.*

Our method is to establish *priorities* for testing. We constantly make "A", "B" and "C" lists for tests of those items, offers and ads we want to test. Those we feel have the best chance we put under "A" and so forth. Changing situations may cause us to move a test candidate from one list to the other or to drop it from all three lists.

By selecting our best "A" list candidate for our first test we feel we have a better chance and keep testing risk down to a sensible minimum. If we're making more money, we test more and if less, we test less. If we're losing money we stop testing because at this point we would be using *principal* and not income to test.

A mail order moonlighter must keep tests small and occasionally stop testing completely. When you make money again, start testing again with part of the money. It's necessary to *earn* the *right* to test. If a free write-up makes $1,000, you might take $300 of it to test with. A sale to a catalogue house may make an unexpected modest profit. You can then spend some of it for a long desired test. We have been able to keep testing without taking principal for a number of years and we hope to keep it that way.

Trying to make it happen can cause test losses. This might break the heart of a determined salesman, but it is so. You may *want* a test to succeed and need it to succeed. But fighting for a test to succeed by a certain date or in a certain way or place can cause a test to become less scientifically and objectively conducted. Christmas items don't sell as well in July. Few people fish in December. Advertising too late or too early for many seasonal products can bring in very little response, despite your desires.

So, take it easy when you test. Try not to be too intense. Try to work on another project when your important test is coming up. Watched pots sometimes don't boil. Tests I count on to succeed often fail. Ones I never expected to make it, pay off. We don't decide. And what difference does it make which works, if any test does? The idea is to go with the tide, not to command the waves.

The purpose of testing is to come up with something to project. And when you succeed in a test, the time comes to project. A development engineer sometimes seems never to want to make the product. He seems just to want to keep improving it. The same can be true of a mail order man fallen in love with testing. At some point the airplane must fly. The time comes to run the ads that are succeeding. We try never to stop improving our advertising, but only with part of the profits and only aside from projection of the most profitable advertising we already have. And when a moonlighter succeeds in a test, he needs to *go*. He needs those profits quickly. But he needs to go carefully and thoroughly.

Let's consider the safest ways to start.

Chapter 3

Moonlighter Adventures in Space

Truths ... surprises ... quirks ... buying
newspaper, magazine ads from classified to pages
... favored positions ... "remnants"

Don't pay for it if you can get it FREE.

The safest way for a moonlighter to start is with free advertising.

You've written an effective shopping column "edit".You want some publication to run it free. Start by going to the library. Glance through current magazines. Note which have shopping columns. Some give the shopping column write-ups almost entirely to advertisers. Others seek intriguing new items from non-advertisers. Experience has taught them that they often create advertisers this way.

McCall's Needlework and Crafts keeps looking for interesting craft items. Some publications have no connection between editorial and advertising. Parade, for instance, with 18,000,000 circulation seeks out new items with no interest in gaining advertising and no tie in, but entirely maximum appeal. Orders are addressed to you. A tiny Parade write up can make several thousand dollars profit, a nice mail order nest egg to get started with.

Make a list of prospective shopping columns. Now, start your selling job. Personally talk on the phone or bring your write-up personally to the shopping column editors you're after. Call the advertising department of each publication you're after. Talk to a salesman for the mail order shopping column advertising section.

Most magazines with shopping columns use the "edits" judiciously as a reward for those buying and as a lure for those considering it. The shopping column editor is often, closely connected with the advertising department. If not, both will tell you. In any case, you want to impress either with your item and yourself. Be frank. Explain that if the write-up pays off, you may advertise later but need the editorial help now.

Talking to either shopping column editor or sales department manager may get the write-up faster. Either or both may like you and your item and feel you're business-like and should succeed. If so, there may be leeway to give you that first write-up *free* to help you on your way. Try all magazines most appropriate for your product. Trade magazines will usually give any intriguing related product at least one free write-up. The simplest and safest way to start is a free write-up offering your items *for sale* with orders to you.

If you have effective follow up literature and if your item sells for over $30, a free write-up asking for inquiries may well be even more profitable. Only do this in a small magazine once, until you see that your inquiries can be closed with your literature in sufficient percentage to be profitable after the cost of mailing. Be particularly cautious of "bingo card" inquiries. These are post cards inserted in the publication and addressed to the publication with numbers printed on it. Each number is also printed at the end of each ad and write up. The reader circles the numbers of write ups and ads he or she is interested in. The post card requests more information. The publication's computer service types up labels for each name for as many numbers as circled and forwards them to the proper company. In consumer publications, "bingo" inquiries are sometimes of too poor quality to be worth mailing literature to. But in trade magazines, such inquiries often do convert into sales.

How would you like to make your product a major editorial item?

Years ago, the Curtis Publishing Company sold $1,700,000 of one such mail order editorial item. It was a creative stitchery kit for a grandfather clock. In creative stitchery, I have seen magazines like American Home sell $70,000 worth of a new creative stitchery design mail order from an editorial feature in a single issue.

Such items are featured by the magazine as an editorial service to readers. A real effort is made to bring an item to the reader as a value and a bargain. It is usually featured in full color, often in full page space. I've seen a science magazine feature a boat kit with a picture of a one-man speed boat on the front cover and a story on the kit inside with fabulous results.

The editorial department selects such items. If you're a designer and they like your work, they may give you design ideas to complete. They want you to make a fair return and will offer to work with you again if a promotion succeeds. They're extremely knowledgeable and cooperative and often help you develop a greatly improved product. They use the finest photographers and writers to picture and describe your item. The color separations and color plates alone that they invest in for your product might be otherwise beyond your reach. But they are paying for everything and you are not risking anything.

Warning! Their interest is in *talent*. You must really have a flair for design and an exciting concept in the kind of items they feature.

Some moonlighters have gotten modest extra earnings simply by submitting an occasional item for consideration for a free write-up and never buying advertising. As enough orders and names come in, a customer list starts and other offers are mailed to the list, sometimes building up to a simple catalogue.

More and more magazines run regular major editorial promotions quite aside from their advertising departments. Women's magazines, shelter magazines and more and more specialized publications are running pages and double spreads on mail order items often with surprising results.

Consider starting with a classified ad. A surprising number of tiny and small mail order enterprises have started in just this way. Let's suppose you have an item you've written such a classified ad for.

Go back to the library. Glance again through magazines. This time look for those which carry classified sections. Look at Grit, the science magazines, Work Basket and every magazine you can find carrying such ads.

Look at the business opportunities columns of the New York Times and the Wall Street Journal, at outdoor magazine and underground newspapers. Look for those which carry items most similar to yours. You'll find some selling extremely specialized and quite low cost items. Others seek inquiries for exotic or specialized items or catalogues. You'll find it fascinating to read these tiny ads. Just one can launch a new venture.

Reading such classified ads is a perpetual course on new items, copy, and media. Note which ads repeat regularly in issue after issue. Not only are the items probably profitable, but the publication probably is quite logical for similar items. In this way, note each publication that seems logical for your item.

251

Now phone or write the publication. Ask for rate cards for classified ads and case histories of successes. Ask particularly for the names of the longest, running advertisers. These publications usually sell their mail order classified ads mail order. Therefore, they can send you full information. Now, of those publications, which seems *most* logical for you with strongest success stories? Select the *cheapest*. It will probably be a very small risk.

However, please note that most of the classified advertisers who repeat the most are for *inquiries,* not sales. Your chances for success with an inquiry offer followed up professionally at modest cost are probably several times greater than your chances of selling any item outright.

This possibility is dependent on whether you have such an offer and have created effective direct mail follow-up. A tiny mail order firm selling fishermen fly-tying materials may be able to get qualified inquiries in considerable quantity using classified ads in fishing and outdoor magazines. The same firm might fail if it attempted to sell the fly tying kits in one step in the classified ad. To succeed, a superior line of fly tying kits is needed and equally superior follow-up literature for any inquiries secured. One without the other is useless.

You will need the same. Tiny ads in classified are great for smoking out people genuinely interested in highly specialized activities. If you've come up with such an activity, whether a catalogue for left handed people or for paddle tennis equipment, you can get started with a classified ad. Your follow-up material and catalogue can be the simplest, even photo-offset typewriter type with no illustrations. If the interest is there, it will work for a start.

Don't worry how small your beginnings are. A mail order test success can be on a microscopic scale and lead to a big business. If you haven't any money, don't worry about the size of a sample. Three hundred photo-offset, simple letters can pull enough orders to self liquidate and show a profit. Of course, it's an inadequate test. But who cares if you have no alternative?

A four line classified ad in one day's insertion can pull $1, $2, $3 or more orders for a booklet you write, type and photo copy yourself. Gamble your time more than your money. Work for months to get the perfect item. Labor over the copy for weeks. Do it yourself or team up on a profit sharing basis with the best mail order copywriter you can find. The more you risk your time, the less you'll risk your money.

And the tiniest display ad that produces a profit for $27 risk or less can be run more places and repeated. The tiniest success can quickly make enough profit to pay cash in advance for your next tiny ad. And as soon as you have provable success in several publications, you can get advertising agency credit from someone who has faith in you.

Let's consider what to investigate in buying various kind of display advertising ... ads bigger than classified ads.

You might expect that any advertising in a newspaper or magazine would cost the same for anybody. It often doesn't. One kind of business may pay one price. Another kind may pay another price. Small users of each kind pay one price and large users another. This varies in application. Sometimes, the lower price is for running more total advertising, sometimes for greater frequency of advertising and sometimes a little of each and each rate card may have its own odd little quirks charging a higher rate for this classification and a lower rate for that one.

One newspaper in a city may have a more favorable rate than a competitor in one classification and a less competitive rate in another. Various newspapers under the same ownership can have quite different policies on rates for the same classification. When free standing inserts (usually a postcard thickness brochure) were first put into newspapers for advertisers, one newspaper of one ownership charged over twice as much for each thousand inserts as another paper of the same ownership.

Retailers with substantial lineage contracts usually have far lower rates than one time mail order advertisers and often, substantially lower than large mail order advertisers. Retail rates in one city may be far lower than national rates and in another city, far less so. Lowest retail rates in the main section of a newspaper can be far lower than lowest national rates and in the magazine section of the same newspaper be virtually the same as the lowest rates for national advertising. Retail rates are usually quoted net with no allowance for an advertising agency. National rates are usually quoted *gross* with *15 percent* commissionable to the agency. And with little trouble you can organize your advertising agency and receive that 15 percent.

Newspapers normally will set type for your ads without charge. Magazines will not. This is because newspapers have a staff to set type. Magazines do not but must buy the type setting. Both usually charge for engravings.

In newspaper or magazine advertising, your first objectives are to create the most effective ad possible and to place your ad in the most perfect publication for it. If so, the first appearance of an ad is an adequate test.

Running more times usually gets *worse* results each time, contrary to space salesmen talk about the cumulative effect of repeating. The

253

only time you will see cumulative build-up of orders is when you do not key repeat ads separately. Cumulative effect helps store distribution products but not in mail order. The first page ad usually pulls best, the second usually worse, the third usually still worse and so on.

I have known some mail order men who have profitably repeated by reducing ad sizes. They ran the biggest ad the first time. They repeated with an ad perhaps 60 percent of the size of the first. They then repeated again with an ad perhaps 50 percent of the size of the second. This has worked well in a market place such as the garden section of the New York Times. We seldom like it because it requires more production cost than we care for and we find it difficult to follow as a formula widely with uniform results.

An exception to such drop off can be a seasonal item. If you run too early, results are worse. If you run two or three months in a row ... in January, February and March for a fishing item, for example, your March ad will pull best, February second best and January least. This is not cumulative effect. If you skip January, you will do better in February and March. If you skip January and February, you'll do still better in March. A very strong seasonal item will still benefit from running each of the three months. But there is no point in testing the same ad more than once in the same publication.

Big ads drop off more than small ads. Very small ads drop off the least and therefore can be repeated the most.

Position can mean profit or loss for an ad. Not asking for any position usually means obtaining the worst position, although sometimes you get a pleasant surprise. One position can produce dramatically more orders than another. A full rate plus premium cost in a premium position can sometimes be more profitable than a remnant rate considerably below rate card cost for a "back of the book" Siberia position.

Position is so important for pages that many page ads can only pay out in prime position and will not otherwise. A backcover may cost 30 percent to 40 percent more than inside space yet produce 50 percent to 150 percent more for it. And some backcovers cost only 25 percent more or even less. Alert small mail order advertisers who pay out in a small specialized magazine may have a chance at a backcover just by asking for it. Most publications often favor the holder of a premium position for the same month or week of the following year and will give it to the same advertiser if the advertiser orders enough in advance.

This means that stability and advance planning can pay off for small, new mail order advertisers. New publications constantly appear.

Each if successful is an opportunity for a prime position franchise for years to come. Some mail order advertiser who fails to come up with new winners will relinquish his positions. Therefore, while it first seems that large advertisers monopolize most desirable positions, this need not be so. I've seen my products on back covers of huge circulation publications with giant advertisers *inside,* simply because I patiently waited in line but kept *asking* for the position, particularly immediately after I anticipated the possibility of a major company cancellation due to an automobile strike, etc.

The smaller an ad is, the greater the response variation can be for a good or bad position. This is far less so in a mail order shopping column market place. In a magazine like House and Garden, page after page of the mail order section together build into one big mail order catalogue. Each small ad helps the others. Readers browse from ad to ad. The desired position is most of all to be *in* the section. Outside the section, the difference in position of a small ad on an individual page is most important. Inside the section, an ad has a better chance overall and there is less difference in the pulling power of different positions on the page or an earlier or later page in the section.

Small ads outside of a mail order section suffer more from poor position on a page. Position on a right hand page is favored. Position on an outside column is preferred and the higher the better. Upper right hand position is favored. The "gutter", inside left hand column bottom on a right hand page or inside right hand column bottom on a left hand page, is least effective. It not only is less read, but is more awkward to tear out. However, the editorial matter on the page greatly affects pulling power. Gutter position next to a top editorial feature can be *excellent.*

Page positions favored are back cover, then second cover (back of front cover), next third cover (inside of back cover). After that comes the page facing second cover which may be page number one. Then comes page three, five, and seven. Some favor page facing third cover ahead of these. After that it's usually the earliest right hand page. A bound in postcard will usually make a magazine flip to that page when opened, thus creating a premium position. If the postcard is with a single page ad, the ad on the left hand page opposite seems to benefit as does the right hand page following the bound in card page.

In a newspaper with many sections there are wider choices of position and of rate. In the New York Times you might place a small ad in the mail order section which is at the end of the sports section. You may run in the New York Times magazine mail order section at a substantially *higher* cost. Or you might run it further forward in the New York Times magazine, outside of the magazine mail order section, but at the same magazine rate. Or, if a specialized product like a garden item sold mail order, you might put it in the garden section at a different rate. If it were a garden book, you might choose the garden section or the *book section* at a still different rate. If a boat item, a business item or a stamp item, there are other sections to consider and so forth.

We find that products for men often do well in the sports page mail order section and those for women do well in the magazine. We find that smaller ads in the magazine do better in the mail order section of the magazine, and bigger ads do better outside of it. We find that small ads and large ads in the New York Times do well in the most *related* section, garden items in garden section, boat items in boat section. We find that small ads can do well in such a section *and* in the magazine section as well, even on the same day. The Sunday Times is such a job to read that many tackle just part of it, often resulting in non-duplication between two sections for a good deal of the readership. A book on any how-to subject may do well in the book section. The magazine is higher priced, but is read by more purchasers of the Times than other sections and is worth the higher price. Other big city papers have similar differences.

The fatter a magazine is, the more likely you are to suffer from a "back of the book" position. This is usually combined with a higher cost per thousand for mail order advertisers than some other magazines. Less successful magazines often give better position and a better mail order rate per thousand. Sometimes, for this reason they pay out better than the favorite.

Each advertising buy you make must not only be in a publication, on a station or whatever, that has produced profitably for others, it must be suited to *your* kind of product. Some products are suited to a highly specialized hobby publication and do very badly in a general publication. The great opportunity for you is the existence of many specialized places to advertise in. There are magazines for virtually every interest. Direct mail lists are more specialized still. There are items that do beautifully in sewing magazines but nowhere else. The same is true for shelter magazines (House & Garden, etc.), for outdoor magazines and those appealing to men only, women only, young women only, teen-agers, young boys, children, business men, or covering other special interests.

We have sometimes lost money trying to turn a nice small profit-able offer, proven successful in special markets, into a more universal mass offer. Some offers will succeed in small space and fail in big ads. Some items sell mainly to rich people, others mostly to low income groups. It's amazing how comfortably profitable it can be to sell something only on WQXR or in Ebony Magazine or just in Cosmopolitan, just in Work Basket, just Grit or perhaps only projected into the closest and most similar media. Limited objectives can give you limited income year after year, perhaps lifelong. A lot of mail order losses come simply from pushing a good offer further than it should be and into places it shouldn't be. Any mail order moonlighter is best off to limit objectives to start. The empire can come later.

Newspapers are usually firm in their rates. This means they usually get the rates they quote and will not bargain for more reductions. For a newspaper (or magazine) more advertising means more pages, less advertising, less pages. They are not caught with unsold space. Sometimes, some papers will quote a "remnant rate" for pages in their magazine section. A "remnant rate", sometimes called a "standby", is an ad that gets a lower rate if at the last minute before closing date it is needed to fill out a section of pages otherwise requiring editorial material. Other than that, newspapers, while keeping their rate card, may wink at some ways of getting around it. A mail order advertiser may pass on a saving to another advertiser by having an ad for another run under his contract. He may do this on a reciprocal basis benefitting from someone else's lower rate in another publication. Or he may do so just to help earn a volume rate.

Sometimes, in ways not officially noticed, the smaller mail order advertiser gets a rate that a higher volume would usually earn. Other than this, the attitude is of shock if the idea of bargain rates is broached by the advertiser to the newspaper. It's harder to request and get a desired position in newspapers than it used to be, even for bigger space ads. Fewer newspapers are profitable to use for mail order. Those that pay out are less typical of other newspapers or of magazines than formerly. National ads in newspapers are far less read than local ads.

Magazine sections of newspapers often have a better chance, often with special mail order sections at special rates. Some have quite major differences between a one time mail order rate and the maximum discount mail order rate enjoyed by large mail order advertisers.

If you're interested in magazine advertising, just looking at and reading each magazine you're considering is the first step. Notice the kind of advertising in the magazine as well as the editorial content.

Many magazines have an absolutely firm rate. Some offer a "make good" ad "if needed". Some offer up to twelve and even fifteen

257

shopping column write-ups for a page ad. Some give a guarantee that you will get enough orders to avoid loss on the advertising cost of the ad. In this case, you pay for the ad at the regular rate. The publication agrees to run make-up ads without charge until you receive enough orders to avoid loss. Some will offer an outright "P.I." In this case you pay so much per inquiry or per order and in no other way.

Magazine rate cards vary from the simple to the complex, from one rate for everybody with reductions for total advertising run and for frequency, to almost as many classifications as newspapers. In magazines, the rate cards sometimes begin to bend a little. The smaller the magazine, the closer to break-even or more in the red it is, the more flexible it becomes regarding rates. Most big newspaper organizations are richer and stronger than most big magazine organizations and more stable in their profit records. There are often more changes of management in magazines. New bosses come in more frequently and are *fired* more frequently. They, therefore, grasp at straws more frequently.

There are few *struggling* newspaper organizations. There are quite a few struggling magazine organizations. They need and want help and are open minded. Attitudes about rates vary with the necessities of the moment. Many magazines sell regional editions in various parts of the country. They sell these at a higher cost per thousand to advertisers who acquire them. Often, a certain page is sold to advertisers in much of the country but not the rest. The remainder of the circulation is sold as a "remnant" or "stand by" at a reduced rate. This is so of national magazine sections appearing in newspapers. The discounts offered vary widely by publications. Originally, they were quite large discounts and big bargains. Often, they were actually available for full circulation and sometimes in premium, even back cover (when otherwise unsold) positions. These were the happy days. You may find discounts substantially less, rate card rates far higher and positions worse with a premium position almost never available.

You need to run in the most appropriate magazine possible. You're looking for a magazine used by mail order advertisers with products similar in price and selling to similar people. Every newsstand you pass is liable to include a magazine for you to consider. Simply going to a library and looking through every magazine that seems logical is a good first step before talking to the publication salesman. From ads in magazines, make a list of the advertisers of mail order products which seem to appeal to the same people your product does. Then, call them up.

First, write down on a yellow pad the questions you'd like to ask.

258

Don't call people your product is directly competitive to. Tell others that your product is not competitive, but that you'd appreciate their advice. If they're busy, don't bother them. Years ago, I found that I had to restrict such conversations to clients. But for a good part of my career, I have been able to spend some time answering such questions. Quite a few people will help with answers. Call only those who repeat their ads in a publication.Explain you are considering running and how important it is to you. Ask if the publication you are considering has been doing well for the advertiser, whether results are falling off and how it ranks with other magazines used. Try to get the names of the best other magazines used in the order of effectiveness for the product. Each call you make is teaching you more.

Talk to the salesman for each recommended magazine. Get the rates for each. Calculate the cost of running your ad in that magazine. Divide the cost by the number of *thousands* of circulation for that magazine. Ask if it is ABC circulation. This means checked by the Audit Bureau of Circulation, an organization subscribed to by leading magazines. It checks and vouches for the *honesty* of circulation figures quoted by magazines. Compare the cost per thousand circulation for your ad size for magazines considered. Check the rate discounts for running more times and for maximum frequency. Check discounts for dollar volume. You may find that the advertisers you talked to are using their favorite magazine at a far lower rate than you will pay for your first test.

Check if it has a mail order shopping editorial column. Usually, in such a section, if you buy an ad, you can get a write-up. Find out the *smallest* ad you can run and still get the free write-up. Find out if the magazine will run a write-up *first* with no ad to give you a test of its pulling power. You may get an extra free test in one magazine in addition to the paid test and free write-up in another. The smallest ad you can get a free write-up for may be your safest bet. If after writing copy you feel you need an ad bigger than the smallest ad that will get a write-up, ask for *two* free write ups. The larger the ad you are considering, the more write-ups you might ask for. Some magazines have given an advertiser as many as twelve (I know of one case of fifteen) write-ups for a page ad. Of course, it varies with the strength and situation of a magazine. One may do now what it did not do months before and perhaps won't do later. For more free write-ups you need more items. If you don't send in write-ups with glossies, you won't benefit.

The magazine that has pulled well for others with a better cost per thousand than others and which offers the most write-ups free seems best. But check if you're being quoted the regular *national* rate or the lower mail order rate. If you have a book, does the magazine have a special book rate which is sometimes even lower than the magazine rate? If you have a page or whatever size required, does this magazine have a remnant rate? If so, what is the reduction or discount from the national rate? Check the position you will get at each rate.

Some magazines have special representatives who act as special mail order salesmen for a number of magazines. Perhaps you will deal with them. They can be particularly helpful. They understand mail order. They're realistic about the rates required in each magazine to give mail order a chance. Some have their own mail order companies. Sometimes, you can sell your product to them or get them to advertise your product at their risk. Sometimes, they will sit down with you, work out the number of orders you need to break even, gamble themselves up to that point and split profits in some way thereafter. This way you get a risk free test. If it works, they will then help you run in other magazines. Once you get to know them, you learn a good deal quite fast about buying magazine space, particularly as you compare what each says.

Chapter 4

Buying Direct Mail Advertising

From package inserts to "solos"...testing pyramiding...
selecting printing...envelopes...
paper...processing sources
renting...swapping names

If you use direct mail, the printer you deal with may have no idea whether the cost of his printing is "in the ball park" or not. He may know nothing of mail order. The kind of printing he specializes in may be impractical for you.

Printing costs vary tremendously. Different printing equipment is suited for different purpose. The small town newspaper printer, who can set simple type at a small fraction of the cost of a sophisticated typographer, can print a very small run competively. For a somewhat bigger run, a small quick copy photo offset house is usually cheaper. Neither can compete with a bigger, faster photo offset press. There are printers that can give superb quality in color reproduction, but specialize in runs of 20,000 to 150,000. Many such printers do not realize that for most items their costs are so high per thousand as to make it impossible to use direct mail profitably. The use of a high speed web press that turns out rich four color pieces with a little less quality can be (in an enormous run) a fraction of the limited run color cost per thousand.

The envelope man you deal with may be a retailer buying from an envelope wholesaler who in turn buys from an envelope manufacturer. Any printer you deal with may have equipment that's wrong for *your* purpose and not realize it, himself. Your art director may be quite unaware of any dollars and cents requirements of mail order, yet help you select your printer. But your dogged asking of questions can provide the answers you need. Just telephoning mail order advertisers who use direct mail can give you priceless information..

If you talk to such a direct mail user, who has a mailing piece of similar size and treatment to yours and mailed in similar volume, you can usually find out what his experience has been. If his product is not competitive to yours, he will often answer questions frankly. By calling small, medium and large successful users of direct mail, you soon learn current costs in the mail usual for the kind of mailing you're considering

You also, often get specific names of printers, mailing houses, type setters, artists, engravers or whatever you need to know, competent, near by and competitive in mail order. And as you start to deal with suppliers experienced in working with mail order people, each can teach you more. You learn whom to use and what to pay them.

Testing in direct mail is often, most practical. Keying is simple. Lists are keyed by computer on the label for very little cost. You can split to your heart's content, not just two ways, but three, four, five or as many ways as desired. You can take the identical list and split it as many ways as you desire for as many tests. You can split price, terms, copy, picture or whatever. All that is required is to use enough names for each split to be a representative sample. Small splits of a thousand names or so are liable to reverse themselves, if you run another thousand. Usually, one thousand names is not an adequate sample.

The number of names you need to test to get a satisfactory split varies with the price of your offer. The lower the price of your offer, the more orders per thousand you should pull and the smaller the list of names need be for a satisfactory test. The reverse is true. As direct mail grows more expensive, the average retail price of a successful offer goes higher, too. Less orders are then needed per thousand. This means a bigger list is then required for an adequate test.

Today, the average successful offer needs to pull 1 percent to 2 percent. This means ten to twenty orders per thousand. A minimum of a hundred orders are desired by most direct mail testers for each segment of a test (and several hundred are desired) to give a representative sample. This means each segment of a test should be 5,000 to 10,000 names as a minimum, depending on the price of the offer.

However, we would prefer to make a less than adequate test rather than not test at all. Further, we would prefer to start very small in any direct mail test. We would rather test in all 5,000 to 10,000 names. Start with simple black and white tests. We use the small local newspaper to set many such tests with very small production costs.

Usually, at first we test one basic mailing piece and separate lists only. We select one to 3,000 names for each different list for the first test. If successful, we go on to 25,000 to 40,000 names, then to 80,000 to 125,000 and then increments of 200,000 to 300,000. If a seasonal product, we may have to go faster. As soon as we begin buying 10,000 or more names of one list at one time, we begin breaking them down into splits. At first, we make tests of 2,500 to 5,000 names each. When we buy 20,000 or more names of one list, we make larger splits or more splits of the same list. We begin to test 10,000 names for each segment as a confirming test for an earlier, smaller and less adequate test.

We prefer to start out tests for direct mail as package inserts in our own packages. Using the local newspaper to set type and print, we can sometimes make our first test for under $100.00. We usually are not shipping enough units fast enough to provide enough circulation for split-runs so we test one way. A package insert usually pulls better for us than a direct mailing to outside lists and sometimes better than a mailing to our own lists.

Assuming you have a low priced, very related offer, a single package insert might pull 4 percent to 10 percent.

For a higher priced, quite related and equally appealing offer, your package insert might pull somewhat better than a reverse percentage of the price comparison. An item three times as expensive might pull 40 percent as much and so forth. Unrelated offers would probably pull as little as a half or less of these percents.

If you do ship your 20,000 packages, this means that you might sell 800 to 2,000 low priced very related items. An unrelated, higher priced item might pull 160 to 200 pieces. Other factors will cause this to vary. If your customers are happy with your product, more will buy. If they're unhappy, far less will buy. If they know your firm, more will buy. If not, less will buy. If you sell a high price product, a bigger percentage will buy a higher priced item from an enclosure.

Consider these points. First, do you have any other products of your own? If you don't, it's probably not worth your time to look for one yet, just for the insert. If you do, is your product at all appropriate? We don't put a package insert on our inflatable boats with our dress form.

Don't waste your time putting an insert for a $3 item into a package of a product selling for $300. Instead, select either a needed accessory selling for $20 to $100, a related item selling for $100 or more, or a

263

more expensive unrelated item. The higher priced the item, the fewer the packages you will ship and the more trivial will be the sales of a very low priced item. Further, you have a tremendous asset, if you have a customer for an expensive item. Don't waste it. He or she is a prospect for higher priced, higher quality merchandise. And don't destroy the relationship by offering him or her junk. Offer quality to quality customers. Stay away from junk, anyway. You'll be happier and make more money.

If you're shipping a higher priced item, particularly if sold on credit and far more so on time payments, a resell insert on the product *already bought* can cut returns and bad credit.

A successful test can be projected to inserts in other firm's packages of related products. We now try to convert our package insert to a billing insert for use in other firms' bills. Both package inserts and billing inserts can be projected widely. They are an ideal method for the moonlighter to get started in direct mail, project gradually and make good money.

Another low cost test can be a loose postcard or a bound postcard mailing. For a specialized industrial or technical product this can be an ideal way to start in mail order. It's also a simple translation for a half column ad. We've found it particularly good for office products and executive gifts. It has had great success with products sold to doctors. It's been very successful in producing specialized inquiries in volume at low cost and closable in profitable percentages. Most such mailings, are to credit checked firms or high income professions such as to doctors. Therefore, more expensive products are salable and it is safe to give credit. And by selling only for cash or through credit cards, it is not necessary to sell on credit. This is a perfect way for a moonlighter to start.

Black and white loose postcards often give a low cost split-run test. They're ideal to test offer variations, half and half. Or you can split-run test advertising on one side with return postcard on the other versus advertising on both sides and no return postcard.

In running an inquiry ad in a postcard publication, be sure to test the inquiry quality by keying the conversion coupons in your follow-up material to the postcard publication. If disappointed in the percentage of conversions, stop. If satisfied, continue.

In a postcard publication, we have succeeded with a single card on one side with another advertiser as the other side. Each had a coupon. There was no return postcard. We have done well with an ad on one side and return postcard on the other. We've succeeded with one item on each side. Sometimes, we used a coupon on each side, sometimes only on one. In neither case we used a return postcard. We have succeeded with a double card and even a triple card using both sides for one item and return card. Here's a suggestion.

If you buy a triple postcard in a postcard publication for one offer only, try to persuade the publisher to keep the top two, rear half cards for his own use or to sell to another advertiser.

If you use the front side of all three cards, you can use a full page Time magazine size ad and use the bottom card *rear* as your return postcard. It can be quite successful.

The next safest and lowest cost test is in billing inserts. If you go into billing inserts, you can start where you can be the only insert. If this works, try multiple billing inserts. If this works *very well,* try multiple mailings. In this case, you pay substantially more because you are paying a proportionate share of the mailing plus a proportionate share of a profit. You also can anticipate pulling *less* because almost *all* bills are opened and much third class junk mail is not. And the package of different direct mail brochures will be considered junk mail by many. However, a share of a multiple mailing is still safer and far cheaper than a "solo" mailing where you are the only advertiser. It points up how very safe and attractive billing inserts and package inserts are.

If you have a proven and desirable offer you may not have to gamble the entire test and perhaps not at all. One credit card company for very selected offers will insert for a 30 percent percentage of sales and this includes their credit charge. You supply the insert which can cost you $10 a thousand. For a thirty thousand test, your total cost can be $300. If you have a big gross margin, you can make an excellent profit with very little risk. There are millions of credit card company names. You could earn $25,000 to $50,000 yearly with just one insert on this basis run widely by credit card companies. They are very selective and yours may never be chosen. It's best to approach them after you have a *proven* success story.

These new kinds of direct mail are very important to the mail order moonlighter. You can get started testing with very small sums of money: $100 to $500. Yet, you can project to huge totals. Getting in ten million package and billing inserts can be done if tests are successful. You can expand a little at a time. There's not too much risk after the first successful test. Multiple mailings are bigger volume and you can get more circulation. Of course, these big projections are only possible for fairly universal appeal products. The more specialized your product, the more limited your potential projection is.

In direct mail "solos", safest, quickest, low cost testing is to your own lists as soon as you acquire names. If you sell a quality product and not junk, you have satisfied customers. They should be good direct mail names. They need to have bought items in the price range that you can normally, profitably sell mail order by direct mail. This means items selling for $30.00 or more. The higher price the articles are, the more valuable the names can be to you. But to benefit, you need to find or develop other mail order items in the same price ranges or higher.

If you get inquiries from any form of advertising, what you do with your inquiries once you get them can be important. A single follow-up requires you to show a profit, after initial advertising cost and follow-up cost. If a series of follow-ups works, then you need only make a profit, after advertising cost of the inquiries and the entire follow-up series. But presumably, you are doing additional business on each follow-up. If you are actively building a list and have a consistent program of mailing the list with other offers as well, you are further amortizing your original advertising cost of getting the names. If you run an annual or semi-annual sale of offers mailed to them earlier at full price, you may get further benefits.

If you work your customer list, first with package enclosures, then (if sold on credit) with billing enclosures and then with mailings of other items, you get another plus. If you ask customers for referral names and get good ones in this way, you get another bonus. If you consistently build your list with customers for the same or similar products and "clean" the list by mailing it yourself first class and correcting addresses with the help of the post office, you will start to build list rental income. This, too, affects your decision as to how much you can afford to pay for the original inquiry which makes it all possible.

Much of the art of direct mail is getting a core of good names and then mailing the list. Of course, for a small moonlighter to develop a big list of high ticket items can take a long time. More probably you will first succeed in space or broadcast with a lower priced item. This list *might* be responsive to higher ticket items. It is not safe to use it for another single, low cost item. It also might respond to a specialized catalogue in the same field of products in the same and somewhat, higher price range. It also might be responsive to a multiple mailing of different insert brochures for products in the same and somewhat higher price ranges.

The smaller your list, the more vital it is to keep production cost the lowest possible. For small lists, this usually rules out any catalogue. The multiple mailing is still practical for a list of a few thousand names.

Use simple photo offset of existing advertising for your own proprietary product or products and complete your mailing with literature you do not pay for but get from other mail order people. This literature should not have another product company address on it. If you pay nothing for such literature with no one else's address on it, it is well worthwhile to insert it on a very attractive basis to the cooperating company taking only 25 percent of sales as your share.

The larger your list gets, the more important it is to *use* it always assuming you are securing satisfied customers. As your list gets larger and more profitable to mail, you will prefer, more and more, to photo offset your own literature of other people's products and work on *higher* percentages of sales. You will begin to *combine* this with including inserts of others with their address printed on it but charging them $25 a thousand or so, to insert their literature. This becomes practical when your mailings are big enough to be handled by an automated mailing house. Your costs of inserting will drop to a fraction of a cent for each of a number of brochures. Therefore, the $25 a thousand figure can be quite profitable. You will also try to develop more proprietary items to mail to your own list. On proprietary items, you will have your best gross profits.

If your list keeps growing still further, you can go in either of two directions. You can convert your multiple mailing into a small catalogue. Or you can organize a co-op multiple mailing, selling others for $25 a thousand for sharing costs and retaining your own *proprietary* items with maximum margin. The ideal is to get enough participants to cover your entire costs and even a small profit. Then, all gross profit from your own items is free and clear. You can't lose and can only *make* money.

At this point, *exchanging* names with others mulitplies your potential. If your names are on computer, the running charge from the computer house is usually very little. On a swap of lists, this cost of running off the equivalent labels of your names for those you receive is your total list cost for renting such names. You can swap just some of your names and *test* those you exchange your names for. If profitable, go ahead with the entire swap. Do this carefully, list by list. Surprisingly quickly, you multiply a number of times your total list to mail to. Your volume and profits grow, too. Usually, your own customer list will remain most profitable to use.

Your own list will usually be the safest to mail to for your first "solo" if your list consists of customers for products selling for $30 or more and particularly for a very related item. Otherwise, you may be

267

able to swap your list for names of such customers. If so, it's even more important that such a list be quite related to the item you are advertising in your mailing. If you neither have a list nor can obtain a list on an exhange basis, you will need to rent an outside list or lists as a test.

"Solo" direct mail costs a number of times as much to reach each person as any other form of advertising. For some, it still makes money. Part of the reason is that a "solo" usually contains far more advertising material. But by far, the major reason is the selectivity possible; the rifle approach compared with the shotgun. And much of the reason the "solo's" continue to work in direct mail *despite* rising costs is the increasing ability of the direct mail user to select lists of names more scientifically, the most perfect for his offer and with the least waste.

But proper selectivity is still a matter of human judgement. Poor judgement or careless selection throws away the advantages available for scientific selection. Now, more initial "solo" tests fail than years ago. But successful "solo" tests project to far bigger volume. As a moonlighter, you may not have previous knowledge. You may not yet have skilled advisors. You may feel quite confused about how to go about making the safest, wisest selection for your first "solo" test. But you do have *time* and *motivation* to make a sound decision.

In considering a list, investigate what item those on the list bought. A list of buyers of a single specific item very related to the product you are selling is preferable. Sometimes, a specialized catalogue list is excellent. Otherwise, be cautious when considering a list of a variety of items. Be sure that all those items are fairly equally related to the item you are selling. Sometimes a list owner mixes different lists into one. It gives a larger total list to rent. Revenue is greater. And list users like big lists. It means if a test works, they have a big volume to project to. But if the list is really a *mixture* of lists, this is not really so. The mixture can be an unfortunate one. It may include lists that are good, mediocre and poor. It may include lists of buyers of good products and poor products, of satisfed customers and resentful ones. It may include buyers of products very related to the product you are selling and buyers very unrelated to it. On a modest test, you probably can only use one to half a dozen lists, so why not pick only the most perfect for you? Why not play safe and select buyers of a single product most related to yours? Next, investigate how these names were obtained. What kind of advertising was used where? If sold in magazines and newspapers, which were used? If sold on TV or radio, was it secured by telephone or by mail? Was the article sold for cash or on credit ? If sold on credit, have the bad payment names been left on the list or deleted? If sold via direct

268

mail, what specific lists were used?

Generally, names of purchasers of higher priced articles are preferable, but only if the article you are selling would appeal to such people. Names of customers who bought from the Wall Street Journal are sometimes preferable to those who bought from the National Enquirer if *your* item appeals to better income people. Generally, those sold through magazines and newspapers are better names to mail to than those sold through TV and radio. Generally, names of those who bought through TV and radio, but *mailed* in cash are safer than those who bought C.O.D. Generally, those sold on credit via radio or TV are *poor*. If sold on credit via radio or TV, those sold via telephone are generally *worse*. However, if sold on credit and if bad credit names have been later *deleted,* the names are usually better than cash names because they are candidates to sell safely on credit.

Names that are very fresh, obtained just in the last few months, are most responsive. These are called "hot line" names and get a premium rental price. However, they are the best buys and safest to use. Their only drawback is that, even if successful, other names on the same list must be carefully retested before any major projection of list use. Names that are one year old generally pull better than those two years old; names that are two years old generally pull better than those three years old or older. Lists of names must be "cleaned" regularly by the list owner or the list quickly gets hopelessly out of date. Theoretically, a constantly cleaned and renewed list can be kept constantly up to date and productive for all names. The secret of list buying is to buy a small test of any large list and increase in gradual steps, feeling your way at all times. Some list owners mix several years, state that the entire list is constantly re-cleaned and refuse to break it down by years for rentals. For your first "solo" test, we recommend that you do not select such a list. Later, if successful, you have ample time to include it in future tests.

The list business is built on trust. Cheating by either party can occur. The list owner can misrepresent the names as being newer than they actually are, can represent that TV names are magazine names, can adulterate a desired list by *adding* less desirable names, and can even include *duplicate* names (if not caught by a merge-purge computer). The list renter usually gets the labels he rents in his possesssion, where he can *duplicate* them and thus *steal* them. Fortunately, most people are honest and you *can* trust them. But in a business built on trust, it's wise to deal with *trustworthy* people. There *are* others. Lists from bigger companies are more likely to be as represented than lists from tempor-

269

ary promoters.

Rental prices per thousand vary considerably but are usually about the same as *similar* lists based on type of item, price range and recency. In making a test, often the last thing to worry about is the cost per thousand of the list you are testing . It's not a huge sum for a small test.

Some big list owners,Dun & Bradstreet for example, have a high price per thousand for a small test and a dramatically lower cost per thousand for the full run. Other big list owners have sometimes agreed to a better price per thousand when offered a flat price. If you ever mail in huge volume, you, too, may discover savings.

In renting magazine names, "expires", who no longer subscribe, are usually considerably less responsive than current subscribers. We have often found magazine subscribers less responsive to related merchandise offers than buyers of related merchandise. "Compiled" names gathered from directories are usually, less responsive than buyers. Buyer names are far more responsive than inquiry names. Premium names who mail in box tops and cash for bargains are usually far less responsive than mail order purchasers of merchandise at more normal prices. Inquiry names secured through "bingo" cards are usually far less responsive than inquiries for the same products obtained in the same magazines through coupons. "Bingo" card inquiries in trade magazines are usually of higher caliber than "bingo" card inquiries in general publications. "Take one " card inquiries are usually, far less productive than inquiries in publications and magazines.

Renting names scientifically boils down to common sense. If you sell anything successfully in any magazine and wish to sell it successfully in direct mail, you don't have to look very far for desirable lists. Simply notice what firms advertise mail order similar price products or services in the same magazine. Those who repeat are probably successful and probably sell to the same kind of people as you sell to for your product. Other publications they advertise in successfully might well work for you. And their customer list is a very logical one for you to consider. Often, too, *your* list is ideal for them and you have the natural makings of a *swap*. Otherwise, you can consider them for your test purchase of names.

Another common sense step to being safe is to investigate which firms repeat their rentals of a list you are considering. If a firm selling a product in the price range of your product to the kind of people you sell to repeatedly buys one list, that list may be good for you. The fact that a firm repeatedly buys a list, if selling a product quite unlike yours sometimes has little bearing on your problem. A sex book that succeeds on a list may not indicate success for a stitchery kit.

You may buy your lists through a list broker. There are excellent list brokers available. Often, they will work patiently with small mail order entrepreneurs on small tests. If they have faith in you and your product, they will do so. They have seen many big direct mail users start as small ones. The good list brokers are very knowledgeable. They have information about myriads of lists instantly at hand. They can save you lots of time. Most list renting is done through them. They collect their commission from the list owner, but work for you. They usually are also list management firms as well. Any one of many of them usually will manage *your* list (if large enough) if you desire it. There- fore, a small group of list brokers and managers usually work with and know each other intimately. They can be a big help to you.

You may buy your list through your advertising agency. Here, you have the advantage of a firm hopefully, already thoroughly oriented to your product, market and problems. More advertising agencies who specialize in mail order are taking over such responsibilities. But this is more true of larger mail order advertising agencies. If you select an advertising agency, dicuss this with them and judge their ability in list selection for yourself. If you set up your own "house" advertising agency for yourself you may also select you own lists and make your "house" agency your "house" list broker, saving 20 percent but taking all responsibility on your shoulders.

It's actually easier for a moonlighter to get help from a top list broker than from a top advertising agency. Therefore, if you can't find an advertising agency you like and set up your "house" advertising agency, it's probably safer and wiser to work with a list broker. A top broker will be teaching you a lot about direct mail each time you work with him or her.

Now, let's investigate your use of broadcast advertising.

Chapter 5

The Time Bazaar

*Negotiating by the book...and for help...
deals...PI's...on AM and FM radio and
on VHF, UHF and cable TV*

If the rate cards and policies of newspapers and magazines seem at all perplexing, enter the wonderful world of TV and radio. There are almost ten thousand broadcast stations including VHF, UHF and cable TV and AM and FM radio. Most of these stations actually make money. And some make a lot. But some lose, some break even, and some worry that they won't keep making present fat profits.

In good lush years, I've heard a broadcaster call his license "a license to steal". It seemed so easy to make all that money. But even in a fat conglomerate a broadcast station which year after year cranks out fabulous profits can start to produce thinner profits or indicate it might even go into the red. Sometimes, this can cause all the flexibility in rate negotiation of an Arabian rug bazaar. If earnings drop, managers' heads will roll. Prudence calls for an open mind to ward off such an eventuality. Holding *too* firmly to the rate could produce a dead hero.

This is so because of the basic economics of broadcasting compared to that of publishing. In publishing, there are out of pocket costs for each extra page printed, notably *paper*. But in broadcasting once the overhead is covered, it's hard to find what it costs the station to run an extra paid commercial. Extra gross dollars tend to become extra net dollars. A broadcaster can't add or take away time. Any unsold time

272

from sign on to sign off is available for use. He can't get any more. He can't make it less.

How would you like broadcast advertising without risk? Perhaps no misinformation about mail order is more prevalent than of the easy and big money believed waiting for anyone making PI (per inquiry) or per order arrangements with media.

Radio and TV stations often are believed by mail order newcomers to be waiting and ready to gamble their facilities for the asking. The truth is otherwise. A very, very small percentage of our total mail order sales comes from such arrangements, although we appreciate them. We prefer to buy our tests at our risk and usually to project them that way as well for reasons I'll explain later.

It's hard work to arrange PI's. Most radio and TV stations will reject your proposal. It's frustratingly slow work, as well. A test can be quite delayed. You're possibly on a waiting list. A station that does run your commercial may be so poor in it's response as to not even be a fair test as to whether your item can sell at all on TV. Further, to get a station to take a risk on the *production* on an untried commercial for an untried item is even more unusual. If *you're* paying for the production, you might as well pay for the test.

But there are *some* radio and TV stations which will make *some* PI and per order arrangements. And *some* stations will gamble on the production as well. So again, if you gamble your time and some telephone calls, you will have an excellent chance of getting some broadcaster to gamble on your product. Per inquiry advertising can be dangerous. Phone orders on a C.O.D. basis can have high refusals and on a charge basis, phone and mail orders can have a high percentage of bad credit.

Be particularly careful about TV and radio inquiries. Radio and TV are the ultimate mass media. They have great immediacy. The telephone featured on radio and TV can zoom inquiries. At once, the mail order man must get a *caution reflex*. Inquiries can even come in from applicants who can't afford, or even *use* the product or service or who completely *misunderstand* what it is. Test such inquiries carefully. Make sure conversions are satisfactory before taking on a big broadcast schedule featuring telephone inquiries.

What station gives such deals? Only when the deal is made do you know for sure. And asking whether such an arrangement *can* be made can be an insult to one and acceptable to another. But if you're turned down, you're no worse off than you are already.

Why are such arrangements more prevalent in broadcast media

273

than in newspapers and magazines? I say it's because a radio or TV station is like a hotel, while a newspaper or magazine is like an accordian. A publication can be expanded or contracted at will. A thinner paper simply uses less pages. There's no real reason to gamble. But there are twenty-four hours in a day, no more and no less, regardless of how much advertising the time salesman brings in. And until the moment a public service announcement is read on the air, the time is usually for sale. This can lead to a certain flexibility in sales arrangements.

The top management of a station, with whom Huber Hoge and Sons spent over $100,000 a year on a percentage basis for a client, has told me why it has been such good business for them. "We don't want to be sold out on a rate card basis. It can only mean our rates are *too low*. We'd rather raise our rates, have 5 percent to 10 percent unsold time and make deals with people like you."

And the Lord be thanked for small favors!

How do you go about it? The first step is to write or have written a TV and/or radio commercial.

Lists of susceptible stations are sold to the unsuspecting for $50, or more or less. Ignore such lists. But don't ignore the list of any friend who *currently* is on the air on PI stations. A station can get "religion" at any time and refuse all future offers. Or a rate card station can "go off the wagon" and start taking a PI deal or so. Policy can shift with the manager, the last quarter's financial report or last week's time sales.

Get your hands on the radio and TV Standard Rate and Data books. Find an advertising agency friend and beg for a several month old copy of each. Now, look through it. Ignore the TV network stations of the largest cities. They would be slightly surprised at your proposal. In radio, independent stations are often more important than network stations. In radio, markets beyond the top fifty will rarely pull for mail order. On TV, often the smallest markets will pull. Now, compile a list or three lists, "A", "B" and "C". Your TV PI prospects will be largely non-network in large cities and any station in small markets. You'll gradually notice certain prestige time sales representatives that are the same for a number of the largest stations. They will usually influence stations *against* PI deals and stations represented by them will be more dubious. Now, guess which will be easiest and put under "A", next easiest "B" and next "C". Ignore the ones that seem most difficult.

Now, write a persuasive letter about your offer. Emphasize your product's quality as well as pulling power and your ability to ship *promptly* and answer complaint correspondence quickly. Now, send your letter. Next, try to follow up by telephone. Be a good Fuller Brush man and don't get discouraged if most turn you down. The first acceptance and you're in business. Now, wait for results. If a dismal failure, and on checking you find others have done far better on the same station, *forget your offer.* If successful, telephone every other station on your list and tell them your good news. And congratulations!

Warning: Few mail order offers still work on radio. More and more listening is from a car and you can't write an order while you're driving. On T V, the majority of all successful offers are just record offers. And many other offers fail. But if you do hit, you'll hit big. At least, this is a way to find out without risk.

Broadcast time rates are different for different classifications. These classifications are usually: peak evening for A rates; Monday through Friday daytime for B rates; early morning, late evening, Saturday, Sunday and daytime for C rates. However, any station may choose to charge somewhat differently and have more classifications. In each classification the rate for one spot is a good deal higher than in buying a schedule of spots. Ten spots a week is usually substantially less per spot. Some stations have the equivalent of remnants in weekend schedules. Time for Saturday and Sunday, unsold as of business Friday, is sometimes available at a lower rate to standby advertisers. These advertisers provide in advance filmed or video taped spots to the station with an authorization to run, if time is obtainable at the special rate.

Let's consider buying radio advertising. An adequate radio test will usually require five to ten spots. This is so because the radio audience is often more fragmented. Commercials are even shorter. It's even harder to get the mail and phone instructions straight. Yet, one of the most successful mail order men I know still prefers to test with one to three spots on a good station at a good time.

Many radio stations get good radio audience ratings by appealing to teenagers. Teenagers don't buy much mail order. Constant contests with incentives to listen and to *say* they are listening when called by telephone can increase audience ratings more than audience. Housewife circulation is sometimes casual in listening and less apt to buy mail order. Adult circulation, aside from housewives, is concentrated in very early morning and in "drive time" (8 to 9 AM and 5 to 6 PM). While driving, it's harder to order by mail.

This means that radio does not produce the mail orders it once did. But it can still produce mail orders and inquiries profitably, if used correctly. Specialized radio has held up best. Black radio is a more recent medium with loyal and intense listenership more comparable in pulling power to the old radio. Offers most suited to it, often pull the best.

Classical stations like WQXR, AM and FM in New York have become scarcer but are productive, particularly for specialized offers. We have sold many thousands of opera appreciation books this way. Country music stations do well for *highly specialized* offers. All news stations have mostly adult audiences and are ideal to use for a broader variety of adult offers than other radio stations. Some of the old, clear channel, 50,000 watt stations have continued to run more *talk* shows and kept a following of older listeners. They still pull for offers suited to this group. Records and tapes do not sell as well on radio as on TV. This is partially due to the fact that nostalgia albums appealing to a somewhat older audience have often sold best. Old movies on TV provide this audience better than teenage record shows on radio.

One difference between TV and radio is that TV in smaller markets can be very productive for mail order. Radio in the same smaller markets is far less effective for mail order. Successful mail order AM radio is best on a station with a good position on the dial, middle to low; with strong power, 50,000 watts; as close to clear channel, no competition anywhere on the frequency, as possible and top rating.

In recent years, this has been less possible. Top audience in a metropolitan area is often on a lower powered station with a worse frequency. This means the signal does not go out as far. Proliferation of stations have cut the huge, scattered out of town audience of the old big power stations. FM has taken away a great share of AM audiences, which in turn was already cut tremendously by TV. The audience is fragmented and not as productive for really big volume mail order purposes. FM radio started out with almost all classical musical stations, but could not get sufficient audience. Now it has big audience for teenage rock music and a gradually widening audience. FM has not hung up mail order getting records for adult products remotely like the old AM radio. It *has* hurt AM listening. FM can be used profitably for mail order for highly specialized offers suited to the station used.

Use radio—but *selectively*. You can test for very little expense. But be *cautious*.

Now, let's discuss buying TV advertising.

An adequate test on television can be *one* broadcast of a commercial at a good viewing time on a good station. The less the viewing audience and smaller the city, the more necessary it is to test more than one spot. If you are running a schedule on a station for a successful offer, dropping in a test for one to three times for a new item can be practical. If you are not running a schedule on a TV station, you may pay a high premium to run your TV commercial only one, two or three times. A schedule of ten spots may be so much less per spot as to make the ten spot test more sensible. All ten spots will cost a minority of the cost of making the commercial. Therefore, it is tempting to run the full schedule for a test. Also in TV, there is advantage in some continuity. A viewer may not get the price, address or phone number straight the first time, but get it clearly the next.

To investigate a television buy, this means obtaining listener ratings preferably from more than one audience rating service. Such ratings are based on scientific samples of typical viewers who are asked which station they are watching or did watch, depending on the system used. First, it's necessary to get the actual audience for the station considered at the time considered and for each competing station. On TV, programming is changed *seasonally* quite considerably. A survey of summer listening has to be further checked for upcoming *fall* program changes. Therefore, it's now necessary to get any information possible on upcoming program changes. How long does the station considered plan to run the program considered to carry your commercial? If it is substituting another this is a new ball game. What is *that program? Is it a new* program? If now on the station at another time what is its current rating? If it only runs Fall through Spring, was it on at this time last Fall? If so, what were the ratings last Fall? If not, *where* was it on and what was its rating? If on at another time, what is its competition and what does it precede and follow? What *will* it precede and follow and *compete* with this fall? If the spot is between shows, what does the spot precede and what does it follow? How long is the spot? What other mail order advertisers have used and repeated spots on this program? And what have they used elsewhere on the schedule of this station?

As TV has grown more successful, time has been sold in smaller and smaller time segments. The segment used most is a thirty second spot. Stations usually have far more thirty second availabilities open than one minute availabilities. Gradually, one minute spots have been priced less attractively than thirty second spots. The biggest stations in the biggest cities often do not accept two minute spots at all. But some do. Independent stations in big cities do so more often. Network and independent stations in smaller cities are more willing to run two minute spots than those in larger cities. UHF stations in all cities are more open

277

to doing so than VHF stations. And cable outlets are more willing than UHF stations. Yet usually, only two minute and occasionally one minute spots pay off for mail order on TV.

Each of these kinds of stations has a policy based pretty much on its local situation. The bigger its audience, the more advertising revenue it has; the more profitable it is and the sounder it is financially, the more firmly it adheres to its rates. For bargain buyers, boom times shrivel up buying opportunities. Bad times open up opportunities. Managers are given some autonomy or sometimes take it anyway, but are sometimes fired if the results of their decisions are bad. A new broom sweeps clean often setting up a policy veering away from that previously followed. The same station can therefore religiously adhere to rates, then under a different manager, give rate bargains or guarantee results and then under still another manager, tighten up again. The same station may refuse to sell two minute spots, then sell two minute spots for mail order, then refuse all mail order commercials in any length.

It depends also on the behavior of mail order people. If a mail order firm advertises on a station, ships months late a defective product, then is publicized in local papers as being a fraud pursued by the post office, FTC and Better Business Bureau, and caps it all by going bankrupt and not paying the station, the station's eagerness for other mail order advertising can cool.

Attitudes of stations toward mail order constantly change. Some decide they'd rather gamble completely in mail order, but control it completely. They will demand that you supply them with a stock of merchandise that they themselves will ship instantly to any complaint and that you deposit a substantial sum, as much as $5,000. Then, they guarantee to produce enough orders to give you a profit at no risk at all. In such cases, the station quickly becomes sophisticated and wants a higher percentage for themselves with less for you. Also, they quickly form opinions about which kinds of offers have a chance and which don't. Again, this entire plan might last for a few weeks, months or year or so, and then be abolished completely; usually, with the arrival of a new manager.

Essentially, stations are attracted to mail order as extra income and constantly frustrated by disappointments and difficulties working with mail order firms. They are inclined to work with the firms they trust and have found honest and competent in past transactions and stay away from the rest.

This means particularly the mail order advertising agencies representing old, live solid accounts. If you can become the client of such an

278

agency, a lot of your problems are over. But if you are a small moonlighter with little money, this is not too probable. If you have a good product, you may interest an agency to go into business with you or a mail order firm active on TV to buy from you. If you have a product and an effective TV commercial, you can bargain better with them or despite problems, you can get started yourself. If you see mail order commercials on a TV station, try talking to the station. Tell the station your situation. Be frank. Explain that you are not familiar with their rates, that you believe you could succeed, but that you surely can't pay off if you pay a higher rate than others. Try to talk to the station manager or sales manager and work your way down. Show your commercial. They may *like* your product, your commercial and *you* and help you get started. Even if you are overcharged for your test, it may be wise to make the test. When your commercial might have paid off quite well at a bargain rate, it may pay off marginally at the higher rate. If the test does this well, the station may suggest a bigger schedule but at a far lower rate for each spot. If they don't, other stations may.

TV can grow from small test to bigger volume quickly. If a station manager sees an advertiser pay off on his station, he realizes that it probably can increase the schedule and keep running for a while. If the station is making a profit, this added revenue increases that profit with almost no extra cost. An alert salesman, sales manager or station manager usually knows how well a mail order account is doing. The mail is usually addressed to the station. It becomes obvious that a bigger schedule is feasible, if at a competitive price per spot.

Generally, the salesman has to go more by the book than the sales manager and the sales manager more than the manager. But an aggressive, competent and trusted salesman can often sway the sales manager and manager. If a salesman sees that his commission on his account depends on management cooperating with you in some way, he may turn his salesmanship on management to gain cooperation for you. If your offer is paying out exceptionally well, if the availibilities are open for a good schedule and if there is pressure for more business at that time, the chances for cooperation grow.

American business goals are based on beating last year, last month. This means if a business keeps sales for February of this year above February of last year and so on, the business is ahead of last year consistently. Inflation can cause overhead costs of salaries and expenses to be higher by a known percentage. Each business must beat last year by that percentage to come out the same and by more than that percentage to be at all ahead. Along with other duties, station managers are hired to beat last year by more than the inflation increase percentage. If they don't, they risk being replaced. Responsibility is subcontracted by manager to sales manager and by sales manager to individual salesmen. A salesman who produces can usually keep his job, even if salesmanager or manager or both are replaced. Such a salesman is a big asset to the *new* manager or sales manager.

Your successful schedule of additional spots can help beat last year's figures. It can help safeguard a job and get a bonus. Therefore, salesman, salesmanager and manager are tempted to be on your side. They want each mail count to be good, just as you do.

Some successful mail order advertisers and accounts capitalize on this situation. They do not bargain, ask for special advantages, guarantees, PI's or whatever. Instead, they turn the responsibility of paying out over to the station. They give a budget for one week for a small market for $200. They ask the station to select times and to give whatever spots are reasonable for this sum. They offer to increase this budget to $400 the next week if the first week is successful. The next week, if successful, the budget is increased to $700 and so forth. They simply tell the station how many orders are needed to be successful. The station can run a schedule at card rates, give a bargain or simply run enough spots to pay out. The mail order man does not attempt to influence the station decision. There is nothing on an order, in a contract or in any correspondence referring to anything but normal station rates. But the temptation exists for the station to give more, to get a renewal or increase of schedule.

The end result can be that, in weeks, from a tiny test a small entrepreneur is running a major schedule, yet never gambling more than a single week at a time. If he watches the mail counts carefully he can cancel the first week the orders slack off. If so, he can usually only lose in the last week part of what he has made to date on that station. In a quite large city, a schedule can quickly get up to several thousand dollars a week. The larger the city and the more varied the audience of programs run on, the bigger the schedule can be and the longer it can run.

The ideal in mail order is to make a "buck for a buck", or better. This means the objective is to make a dollar in profit for each dollar spent in advertising. To have a margin for possible sudden losses, you should be making at least fifty to sixty cents for each dollar spent. Pyramiding of TV profit can come quickly.

A small station with a $200 test can make $200 the first week. Increasing the schedule and running from week to week for even five or six weeks can bring expenditures up to $2500 to $3000. Profits may drop percentagewise. But your only real risk was the $200 to start. The increased schedule and renewals had far less risk. A larger station starting with $500 might make $4,000 to $5,000 in the same period. A very big station starting with $1,000 might make $8,000 to $10,000.

Profits on a number of stations can pyramid quickly, from $2,000 in a week to $7,000 to $19,000 to whatever. Entrepreneurs starting with a few hundred dollars have become small capitalists in months. If a schedule is substantial and mail slacks off, it is possible to recoup at the end of a schedule with a "close-out" offer. This means announcing at the end of the commercial that the offer is going off the air on this station at the end of the week or in a week, in five days, four days, three days, two days, one more day and this is the last time. People who have been considering buying are tempted to get it while still available on this station. Response can double and triple over an average week in the last week on this basis. It is not wise to do this if you hope to go back on this station shortly. Conservative station practice would not wish to take the schedule. If you closed out your offer with the plan of going back on the station anyway ... and then did so, it would be considered misrepresentation by the Post Office, FTC and Better Business Bureau. In other words, any closeout offer like any sale or going out of business announcement should be real and legitimate. But if you *are* going off the air and *say* it, mail will be better the last week and you will improve the schedule's overall profit.

In the course of one campaign, projecting a test to a successful schedule, you can soon become quite professional as a buyer of advertising. Water seeks its own level. Stations want business and, to get it, will do for you what they do for others. You will quickly learn which stations are currently not deviating from published rates and which are. You will learn the different varieties of station transactions. Some stations prefer some form of guarantee or PI arrangement because it is a simple way to have automatic renewal and increase of a schedule, as long as results continue. Other stations are shocked at the idea. Some have policies in between. A station manager may make a practice of "helping where necessary" with extra spots, but will never say so in writing. Others will never say so even verbally, but still do. Others will infer they will or might help, yet not really mean it.

There is always the chance of misunderstanding. A salesman might *think* his station will help, but top management won't. A manager might intend to help, but the very next week be forbidden to do so, generally by ownership, or he might lose his job.

281

Often, a young new mail order entrepreneur will be carried away by apparent big success. He increases his schedule rapidly. His bills come in. Orders are fair, but he has been promised make-goods (he thinks). He begins to get some bills far out of line with orders received. He's convinced that his friend Bill or Joe will reduce the bill or get more orders for him.. He pays a bill or two and puts the other bills in a drawer. He isn't facing the facts. He's losing money and the stations have no intention of bailing him out. And suddenly, he can't pay his bills and can't continue. Don't let this happen to you.

The key is to avoid *fuzziness*. I remember as an advertising agent attending lunches between station, client and station manager. At the end of lunch, client and station manager shook hands and said, "It's a deal." I asked, "What deal?" Each then stated the opposite of the other. The station manager would prefer a schedule with no deviation from rate card. The client would like 100% protection that he cannot lose. Each talks sympathetically to the other and often avoids a confrontation. The station manager wants business, but not to risk his job. The mail order firm wants orders, but not at a loss.

The careless, loose mail order operator gets into misunderstandings and *loses* money. The prudent, thorough and careful mail order operator knows where he stands. If he is taking a risk, he knows it. If he thinks he's protected, he has it in writing legally. If you sign a contract with a station and have a verbal understanding that you will get extra broadcasts, this will not stand up legally. You can be billed according to the letter of the contract. You can even write the station manager a letter confirming a previous verbal agreement by him to give you more broadcasts if needed. This still won't hold up legally. You still must pay as billed. Any contract change or addition must be signed by *both* parties. Otherwise, the original written contract stands as the sole written agreement.

Despite this, some new mail order entrepreneurs keep getting in trouble, thinking they are protected when they are not. Be careful. Say what you mean and keep your word. Forcing a station manager to put in writing the protection you want could risk his job and lose the deal. Gambling with him that he will keep his word, has authority and won't be overruled or fired before the transaction is completed *is reasonable*. But you must realize it is a gamble and you must be able to afford that gamble. This means if there is a risk, it should be for a limited amount of money that you can afford to risk, preferably a one week's schedule. Then, if misunderstandings come, up they should be clarified *before* further risk. You should not risk a *blank check* of a continuing schedule.

282

Preferably, you should only order in writing one week at a time. If you do have a written agreement for a continuing schedule, make it subject to cancellation by you. If sufficient orders are not coming in, cancel instantly.

The young entrepreneur who is intoxicated by seeming success is inclined to let schedules continue. If lazy or careless, he may not be aware of correct mail counts or may not be methodically acting on them. Success on one station does not mean automatic success on another. One manager may do what he says in addition to his written commitment. This does not mean that another manager will. Assume the worst. Be content with less profit watched more carefully. Limit your objectives. Go a little slower, but more safely. Be *thorough*. Pay your bills promptly. Clear up misunderstandings as soon as they occur. Do so in a fair manner. If you get bills one way and pay them another, even if you are shaving off small amounts, you are building up to more misunderstandings. It is better to take your losses from a misunderstanding and be more explicit thereafter. The best plan is to call whomever responsible at the station. Then reach an equitable compromise if possible, put the compromise in writing, have it signed by the station authority and pay the revised bill.

In business, you can deal with some people on a continuing, mutually satisfactory basis and cannot do so with others. Avoid the latter as fast as you compare their words and actions. Others will judge *you* similarly. Build your reputation. Be proud of the products you sell or drop them. Keep your copy honest. Ship on time. Do what you say. Pay your bills. Be competent and make and protect your needed profit. However small you are to start, on this basis you are desirable to deal with.

As station managers find you trustworthy, they will trust you. Your products will be preferred by them. All this can happen surprisingly quickly. In a few month's time, you can become a larger advertiser than you might have anticipated. Mail order on TV can actually make a new mail order entrepreneur hundreds of thousands of dollars in one season on one item. If you operate with prudence, the risks are surprisingly small to accomplish this.

Just remember that doing so is a rarity. You may never achieve such success. But others have and you can too with the right item, the right commercial and the right approach.

Now, let's discuss the "hybrid" media.

Chapter 6

The "Hybrid" Media.

Publication forms of direct mail...
direct mail forms of publications
...cable TV catalogues...mixed media

The recently developed "hybrid" media have become a big opportunity for big mail order advertisers and can be opportunities for smaller advertisers as well. First, it was return postcards bound in next to advertisements of the same offer. Next, it was free standing inserts, (brochures on postcard stock) with an actual return postcard perforated at lower right. More recently have come multiple mailing envelopes in a newspaper section.

At first, such advertising seems just for giants but this is not always so. I've seen our products in a sixteen page section with return envelope, run as a specialized catalogue in a specialized magazine. It was an advertisement bigger than that of any giant company in the issue. Yet, I've seen the orders come in to self liquidate and make a profit.

In some big city newspapers, free standing inserts can be run in only a small minority of total circulation, in most desired suburbs for instance. They can then be expanded city-wide in the future, if warranted. The advertiser supplies the inserts and pays for insertion.

However done, inserting of direct mail material in publications will continue to grow. It simply becomes a logical projection of a successful direct mail brochure and an alternative to list buying (and postage, envelope and mailing costs). It is not a big risk to insert an

284

already successful brochure in a smaller city newspaper or part of the circulation of a larger city newspaper. If this is successful, projection can be enormous.

Organizers of co-op multiple direct mail pieces inside an envelope in a newspaper are becoming publishers of alternates to syndicated Sunday newspaper magazines. It is possible to supply a simple insert for such a multiple envelope and to test it in very limited circulation. This becomes practical even for the small mail order moonlighter. Organizers of co-ops in newspapers or by mail become tempted to go into the mail order business themselves or to take risks and share profits. The smallest moonlighter may secure rights to a product and create an exciting brochure for it that may appeal to such a co-op entrepreneur. It could become another opportunity for the smallest moonlighter to start without risk.

It's hard to tell *what* some of the new hybrid media actually are. A great book publisher started a bound co-op publication, mailed to its list and sold advertising in it to other mail order firms. Is it a magazine? Whatever it is, it is an opportunity for small mail order firms. You can buy a page in a small run or an even smaller space. All orders come to the publisher in a return envelope bound into the publication. For each customer ordering products advertised by any participating mail order firm, the publisher adds a free gift. The publisher forwards orders and money to participating firms.

Executive Mart is a bound postcard publication going to a big list of executives with premium buyers mixed in. Any moonlighter or anyone else can advertise in small space in Executive Mart for inquiries at no risk. He just pays per inquiry and sends literature for follow-up. Or he may buy a return postcard with advertising on one side selling an item or items. For us, it's worked on item after item. We give a choice of four credit cards or cash. If cash, the card is put in an envelope with a check by the customer. Three postcards are printed on one side of each page. Each card has printed on that side the advertiser's address with a post office permit number so that it may be mailed free and postage paid at the other end. The customer can sign an order and drop it in the mail.

These new forms of advertising custom created for mail order have been jumping up faster and faster. In some cases, direct mail uses a publication for its delivery. In others, it *becomes* a magazine itself, a participating catalogue that you can take a small share of the cost and risk in. An Executive Mart achieves printing savings which a quite small catalogue cannot achieve and passes much of them on, to mail order firms participating.

More and more bigger trade magazines are organizing direct mail co-ops of loose postcards, bound postcard publications, or multiple brochure mailings to their lists without the burden of editorial costs. Such co-op mailings can often be safer to advertise in than the equivalent trade publications. Don't close your mind to *any* new form of mail order advertising, however unusual. But investigate each carefully.

Investigating these new media requires the same thorough questioning technique, as for any other form of advertising. There is a cost for each that can be calculated per thousand. You quickly see that some bound postcard publications cost far more per thousand than others. Some are far more expensive per thousand in black and white than others in full color. Some packages of loose postcards have far more postcards to share readership than other packages. Some packages charge over twice as much per thousand postcards as other packages. The cost of inserting a free standing insert is different per thousand in different publications. So is the cost of an adsert postcard affixed to the back cover of different magazine sections. And so is the charge for inserting a return postcard next to your ad in magazines. Sometimes it's simply an effort to get a sharply higher rate per thousand for quite similar circulation.

Only thoroughly researching each hybrid medium buy can indicate if its cost is reasonable and probably safe. When mail order advertisers selling products of similar appeal to yours run repeatedly in any of these media buys, it's safer to consider. Telephoning other mail order advertisers can give more answers and make your decision sounder.

Chapter 7

Barter Advertising

Direct and indirect...misconceptions
...benefits...risks...broadcasters and publishers
...safely buying it...barter gamblers.

Barter in advertising is as old as advertising. The owner and printer of the first newspaper was happy to pay a bill by giving the equivalent in advertising. And it's been happening ever since. For any publisher or broadcaster, barter is an alternative to rate cutting for last minute unsold space or time. Originally, barter was directly between the owner of a product or service and the publisher or broadcaster.

Later, barter also became indirect. The publisher or broadcaster would receive a product or service from a company which would get space or time in return and then swap or sell it to some other firm. Years ago, a group I was a part of, in return for acquiring an interest in a broadcasting network, received over $500,000 of broadcast time. My assignment was to arrange to exchange the broadcast time for advertising space in magazines. We then ran mail order ads in the space in magazines with cash orders coming to us. At other times, I have arranged to purchase big blocks of broadcast time at 50 percent discount and then swap it for advertising space. We traded card rate for card rate. Thus, it became a way to buy advertising space in excellent publications at half price.

Most publishers and broadcasters exchange some space or time for something. Some do not. Some only exchange in very specific situa-

287

tions. Some swap in a wide variety of situations and on a very large scale. Barter or swap is interesting to you only as a means of getting advertising space or time for less cost or risk. Sometimes, this is possible.

Today, large companies exist which do nothing but barter something for advertising and then resell the advertising at a discount. Naturally, their effort is to purchase something for very little, barter it for advertising which therefore costs them far less than rate card, then to sell it at under rate card keeping as big a profit for themselves as possible.

TV programming is the biggest field of barter. Many TV stations always want and need more programming than their cash budget will normally allow them to buy. Older, weaker and more specialized programs are offered on a barter basis. It is attractive to many stations to pay for them by giving broadcast time. On a series of programs, a station will sometimes give one third or one half of the spot availabilities within each program to the program owner. The owner will try to sell these spots to a national advertiser. For strong programs, he will do so at full price. For new and weaker programs, he may sell at a bargain price or gamble on the time he owns.

Biggest and most successful "program packages" will not have to sell at a bargain or gamble. But anyone can become a small ".program packager". Any show produced by anyone or any station and video taped can be offered to other stations on a barter basis. There are many small TV "program packagers" who have time to sell at a bargain or to gamble with if they choose.

A small mail order moonlighter might have a chance to deal with such a small TV "program packager". If the product is related to the program, it can be very successful. It can be the basis of a partnership between packager and product owner either on a percentage of sales with no risk to the moonlighter or a separate corporation partially owned by each.

There is little chance of doing business with the large program company. As a moonlighter you're too small. Most barter companies want to sell large blocks of time for real money to substantial companies. They seldom wish to gamble with the time they have acquired. And if they did, they would probably consider you too small. However, nothing ventured, nothing gained. If venturing is merely making a no risk proposal, you really can't lose. If you have a product that is extremely related to a specific program, it might pull extremely well and the big owner of the program just might see the potential. The barter

288

company likes to line up purchasers first and obtain necessary time as needed, thus having no inventory risk. But often, the barter company can't avoid program inventory risk and sometimes its acquisition of space or time is hard to sell. Normally, it would simply sell for less to move it out. But it's always possible that at some time the barter company will gamble with the time. Not being in the mail order business, it may do so on a percentage of sales basis. It might deal with you if your item pulls and if you're content with a smaller percentage than others he can deal with.

A surprising number of firms and individuals have blocks of bartered broadcast time. Far less have publication space. Caution! Broadcasters and publishers are not foolish. Naturally, their interest is to obtain good value in what they get and to exchange least desirable time and space for it. There is a continual battle between those offering anything for space and time and those giving space and time. Barter companies try to barter merchandise at full retail price for full rate card. Publishers and broadcasters try to barter advertising at rate card for lowest wholesale cost. Program packagers have offered programs for a cash price to a broadcaster or for *four times* the cash price for time valued at rate card. The outcome has varied constantly. When a publisher or broadcaster needs cash badly, a broker will sometimes put up a big block of cash prepayment for a very big bargain in space or time and then resell it at a discount, but still at a good profit. With better business, barter is less attractive to media.

The result is great confusion. Sometimes, space or time available through barter for a lower cash price is a bargain. Sometimes, it's just about what you'd get if you bought at best rates directly, and sometimes it costs you *more* than if you dealt directly. This is particularly so in broadcasting. There are adventurers, dreamers and frauds in the barter field. Some offer lists of stations on which they do not actually have time. Some did have time but don't now. Some have restrictions on their time which make it impossible for you to get a two minute TV commercial or even to sell mail order at all. But don't be concerned. Some new opportunity will turn up.

A given situation makes some way of buying advertising advantageous for a while. Then this situation varies and something quite different becomes the advantageous way to buy. It's everchanging. Fortunately, there's usually some new way to buy advertising advantageously enough to make money in mail order. It can be something you would never expect. The opportunity may be available for a day, a month or for years. It may stop at any time.

Chapter 8
Mail Order War

Fighting off "knock-offs"...and winning...
making competitors say "uncle"

From the first thrill of a new "hit" in a test result to full projection, the name of the game is speed and secrecy. Because in mail order, it's easy for someone else to steal a good part of your success.

A competitor can apparently duplicate your product. His looks like yours in the advertising. Yours may be top quality and his junk, but the customer doesn't see either until after he's bought it. Customer inertia can cut your competitor's returns, at least to a "profitable nightmare". A patent is a "license to sue". A good percentage of patent claims originally granted are denied in the first lawsuit. It is slow, expensive and dubious.

Later, we'll discuss how to beat your competitor to the punch; but why suffer him even in the first place? Discretion and secrecy can make the difference much of the time. Every salesman who calls on mail order people, each mutual friend, even your own employees can pass on the vital information that you have a "hit" to "knock off". You, yourself, can mention your first success to your later loss. Until you give the fact away, only YOU know for sure, so keep it quiet.

In considering any kind of mail order advertising buy, ask what *direct* competitors have used it. Find out how often, and how recently. Ask if any are scheduled to run before or in the date of issue you are considering. If so, it's important to find out what price your competitor sells his product at, what are the terms, if there's a giveaway, what are the claims and what is the guarantee. It's necessary, if at all possible, to see the competitive advertising.

A competitive ad with about the same price, giveaway value, terms and claims will affect your results badly if run before your ad runs. If run more than once, the effect will be worse. If run very recently, the effect is worse. If it runs the day your ad runs, it will be a good deal worse. But if the competitive ad has a lower price, has a more attractive giveaway, gives better terms, a stronger guarantee, has better copy, or simply stronger claims, the effect on your ad's results will be the worst, particularly if run close to your ad date and catastrophic if in the same issue as your ad. You simply *increase* your competitor's orders at your expense.

But if *your* ad offers a lower price, etc., *you* may win. But price alone may not be the deciding factor. If you're up against severe price, claim and offer competition, one strategy is to *avoid* the competition. As soon as your tests warrant, race into media your research indicates he has not yet bought. Direct item competition then becomes a race to get there first. It sometimes happens that without realizing it you and your competitor *share* the market, almost as partners, one getting first into one publication, one in another or one racing first into TV and the other jumping into direct mail. Each pushes in the form of advertising he feels safest in using, based on past experience.

Such competition can become mail order war. If you have a fine quality product, you do not care to have profits you're entitled to turned into big losses because someone copies your ad and ships a far inferior product that can only disappoint...looking for a profitable nightmare by going way under your price and at your expense. On TV, we were advertising America's finest roses for Jackson and Perkins. A competitor offered seven times as many roses for two-thirds the overall price and ran big schedules on the stations our Jackson and Perkins garden programs were running. We had a council of war and instructed our TV garden personality to give a little lesson on the difference between grades of roses. He held our quality rose plant up for a close-up of size, root structure, thickness and sturdiness. He held up the next more borderline grade and showed how much thinner and weaker it was. He then held up the cheapest bargain grade and showed the measly roots and skinny trunk and weak structure. He called it a "garden cripple" and threw it to the ground. Our offer did better than ever and our competitor had to get off TV stations we were on. But when you're a

291

mail order moonlighter, duck any such mail order war. It's far too dangerous and that's why it's important to get a mail order product that does not yet have direct competition. Test it as fast as prudence permits and project it *before* competition rises up.

In mail order war, you may have to sue legally. You may be sued legally. We'll take up the selection and use of lawyers as we next discuss the day to day operations of a mail order business.

BOOK V

NUTS AND BOLTS

Recommendations and warnings ...
what to do and not do in
operations from moonlighting
start to big success

293

Chapter 1

Alone or Together

*The pro's and cons ... selecting a partner...
negotiating a partnership*

As you make a hobby of making mail order money, you will find a quiet satisfaction unlike that in any job.

In your job you are a cog, perhaps quite small in a quite large wheel. In a mail order partnership the partners are the wheels. If entirely on your own, you are the big wheel. In either case, the daily round of your own business can become a pleasure and a joy.

Your part time business and hobby can become a stepping stone to a full time business, either shared or entirely your own. To make it secure and increasingly profitable, your enjoyment of and interest in routine activities can be vital. The most brilliant mail order man or woman can go bankrupt fast, simply by neglecting little things that seem minor but can be all important.

Let's discuss the nuts and bolts of daily mail order business operation. Each moonlighter will start and operate his or her business somewhat differently. Some will be amply experienced in business. Some will have had no previous business experience. Many will start with very little money. Some will become quite successful and may grow far beyond their moonlighting beginnings. We'll take up various eventualities. If any does not concern you, just skip through.

Some moonlighters will be best suited to being sole owner, more to partnership and many to either. You may feel equally suited to partnership or to sole ownership. Your first decision will be whether to go it alone or to team up with others. Before deciding, consider these advantages of each choice.

Your solely owned business may give you more satisfaction. You are sovereign, the sole ruler of your moonlight empire. You are also alone and may be lonely. But you have no friction because you need not please anyone but yourself. You are truly your own boss. You are flexible. You can act at once without consultation. You can still go into various forms of joint ventures with others on individual transactions. It's simpler. It's also more work, strain and risk. And it's slower. You may have limited time and money.

Advantages of partnership can be greater. A partnership may be far more suited to you personally than going it alone. You may gain partners perfect for you. Even if your partners have shortcomings, you may be far better off with them than without. With partners, you will have more combined money to risk and more man hours available.

Partnership can be a way to get help without risking more overhead. A partner doubles the facilities of the organization. Several partners build a larger organization of just themselves. Partners, between them, may provide first equipment. One may already own a typewriter, another an electronic pocket calculator and another a simple photo copy machine. One partner may even be in business and as his contribution, allow the partnership to use his facilities. One partner may have storage space, another a little machine shop in his cellar and another have needed skill in advertising or product design. One may be the inventor. One may be a salesman who can get a mail order product going in the stores as well. One may travel to foreign countries and be able to negotiate sole import rights. Or one may already have the rights to an item which he will contribute to a partnership.

You can gain and learn much from your partner or partners. You can move faster and possibly achieve success earlier. Your first success as a moonlighter probably will mean faster success the second time around. Each success then accelerates progress to the next. Your partnership can be your start. If it's a great partnership, you may continue in it lifelong. If not, it may be a more temporary joint venture. And when you part and divide up, you may have a nest egg starting capital for your solely owned business to help accelerate its growth. Caution! Look before you leap into any partnership.

Even if you and a neighbor take a flyer together on one ad in one paper for one item, it's best to consider the future implications. Thinking and talking things out *before* can go a long way towards a long happy relationship *after*. Otherwise, misunderstandings can sow seeds of future disputes, bitterness and possible financial loss to you, all started the moment the business began. A partnership is a business marriage with lots of emotion potential in it.

It is also possible in business to marry in haste and repent at leisure. The agreement that you make with a partner can be a mortgage on your entire life. As a potential partner, many of us look better than we do in the realities of partnership. We're often disappointed in each other. And business divorce can be as painful, emotionally tearing and expensive as a broken marriage. Too often, no provision has been made for the terms of splitting up if the partnership should not turn out. It's wise to start a business partnership as a trial marriage with a clear cut agreement for a severance division of products and assets or a mutual buyout clause. Business divorce can then be amicable, without shock or bitterness and may never come at all. Mail order usually involves a continual development of new items. A dividing up of items at severance, one to one partner and one to another, is not unreasonable. When analyzed years later, one might have gotten better items than the other. But more important is going ahead on your own again and ending a bad relationship.

Partnerships sometimes fail when one is far more able than the other, when one is unstable, dishonest, far more financially pressed, lazier or when objectives of one are far different than those of the other. Good businessmen can be poor partners and simply strip each other's gears. Ego is the greatest enemy of partnerships. Social friends or relatives are often the worst partners. The best partners who, have usually known each other in business or hobbies or interests before, are working individuals and each contribute his or her share. The ideal business marriage in mail order is between two or more partners, each compensating for the other's weaknesses and benefitting from the other's strengths.

A dreamer and doer partnership can be perfect. The dreamer can develop concepts and the doer can carry them out. But dreamers and doers often do not have sufficient respect for each other. Are you a dreamer or a doer? At first, in your own business you'll have to be both. Maybe you'll develop the ability to be both permanently. More likely, you should consider partnership with your opposite.

Before you go ahead with any partnership, talk out with him or her possible, future friction points. Each partner going into partnership instead of on his own is surrendering some sovereignty. Each risks losing by the association. Consider these points. Who will do what? If fifty-fifty partners, what will happen when you and your partner disagree? Who will sign checks? If your partner signs checks for more than the bank account, unless incorporated, you are personally responsible. If both partners must counter sign each check before it is valid, it may be safer. But if so, and you disagree and one won't sign, will it stop the business?

Suppose one of you is financially better off than the other. Should one draw money from profits before the other one? Suppose one has a very demanding job and travels on business as well, while the other has a lower pressure job with far more time off for moonlighting. If one works far more in the moonlighting business, will he accept the fact that the other doesn't and can't?

Should this be a fifty-fifty partnership? If so, who will row the boat? If not, who will own less than half? And if one will, how can he or she be protected from being taken advantage of by the other? If the business succeeds and one suggests hiring or taking in his unsuccessful brother-in-law, what will be the attitude of the other? If the company succeeds and there's a company car, who will keep it after hours? What happens if one partner gets a job in another state or country?

Money partners putting in limited sums once, are one time contributors usually resented from the day after the money is paid in. But money partners able to finance future needs can help build a Rock of Gibraltar solidity. If you can contribute more in other ways but lack money, the right money partner can speed your success. Before you start, discuss with your partner future eventualities. Determine your own financial needs. You'll make a better deal if he can loan to the company instead of invest. Discuss what will happen if the partnership makes money and financing needs grow. Will your money partner put up more money, guarantee a bank loan or take a smaller share if more money men are needed? Think out if you will appreciate your partner less if your partnership does so well that it is self financing.

If you have ample money, would *you* like to be a money partner to a mail order man or woman? If so, be careful. If neither you nor your partner have a "feel" for mail order, your chances are poor indeed. If your working partner has it, your chances are better. If you have it, they're even better . If your partner is frugal and hard working, it helps. My advice is to extend your risk over a number of smaller tests rather than one or two bigger tests.

But what will happen if success comes? Consider this carefully in advance. Will he resent you? Can you get your share of profits out? Will

298

he draw too much? One way to operate that may be good for you is on an arms length basis. Help him get started and own nothing in his business. But have all orders for each test come directly to a box number controlled by you. Bank all receipts and parcel it out on an agreed basis. Pay first for merchandise costs, then shipping labor and postage or freight costs, then advertising bills, then yourself and the money loaned. Then divide profit on an agreed basis. Nothing goes for overhead or his draw. That comes from his share of profit. Control the projection of successful tests the same way. Only gamble one season at a time. If successful, try again and perhaps with others as well.

One man I know has backed entrepreneur after entrepreneur in mail order over the years. He's never greedy and usually takes 20 percent ownership, often for backing someone in a desperate situation. He has helped some mail order men within days of their own disaster to make a new start. He has taken any promising young man who has done well in mail order as an employee, but only when out of a job and backed him the same way. Gradually, he has developed minority interests in dozens of mail order companies and mail order suppliers too. He doesn't breathe down the back of any of them. Usually, the actual cash he has put up has been quite small. He has seldom lost on his credit guarantees. Usually, he has been able to develop some activities between companies he has an interest in that contribute to profits. He now has such partnerships all over the world. Many only needed a $5,000 to $15,000 investment. Some of these companies now do millions of dollars a year. Gradually, he has pyramided profits and gambled up to $150,000 at a time.

As a money partner in mail order, you can go on as small or large a basis as you care to. But developing a "feel" for mail order is one key. The other is to be fair to your partner when you start and later on. Put yourself in his position. If the business is turning into a bonanza, ask yourself how you would feel if you were him. Once he's on his feet, he may feel he's creating profits that become capital and that he's a money investor equal to you. Further, he may feel that he is contributing skill and know-how and endless working hours that you are not. Once the company is prospering, if he feels he can make more money in any other way, he may want to unload you.

My suggestion is to only take as a partner someone you feel is a real mail order "star". Then, make sure you're right by working with him. And if convinced, *hold to him* on any basis that makes sense. If from time to time you renegotiate, increasing his percentage and decreasing yours, he may make money for you *all your life* and for your children, as well. Or consider bringing in *more strong partners* contributing for them proportionately *more* from your share than his.

Any partnership can be adjusted as things change. Partnerships tend to grow and take in more partners. Younger partners tend to increase their roles. Older partners like to taper off. From time to time, ownership adjustments can and sometimes need to be made.

A really good partnership can be perfect for you. The monies gained from participation in good partnerships are overwhelmingly greater than those lost in bad ones. A bad partnership is more often an exception, an accident, but it could happen to *you*. You want the benefits. You want to protect yourself from the dangers. If you select your partners carefully and discuss possible conflicts with them thoroughly, the chances are that you can have a happy productive partnership.

Usually, the longer that you have known, the possible partners, the more probable will be the smoothness of your relationship. Check on a potential partner and ask him or her to check on you. If you find any background of instability, over-suspiciousness, a tendency to quarrel or sue others, laziness, selfishness, previous bankruptcy or shoddiness, simply back away from that partnership. Just a little checking on an affable acquaintance may dig up such background. People rarely change and partnerships are best avoided when such background is uncovered. Don't look for perfection. Don't go by one or two bad reactions. We all have faults. But if the concensus of reports is negative, stay away.

Fortunately, there are more potential good partners than bad ones. And most who check out as good will be good. If so, it becomes a matter of chemistry. Will we like each other and work well together? Sometimes, even with no bad reports, one partner goes into business with the other with some misgivings. Usually, if you don't feel right about a partnership before you start, it's better not to start.

Once you have partners, be understanding in working with them. Try not to be jealous when your partner contributes or bitter when he doesn't. The chances are that you'll contribute more some of the time and less at other times. A renegotiation of partnership interests each time could be a strain. It is impossible to avoid all risk of partner incompetence, instability or dishonesty. Many shrewd businessmen feel that the best plan is to accept the fact that there is risk and simply get out of a proven bad partnership quickly. If you form a corporation with partners as fellow shareholders, you reduce the personal risk of a partnership. An embittered partner could still sue you personally, but you would not be ruined personally by the bankruptcy caused by an unstable partner.

Try to choose as a partner someone who can contribute as much time as you can, someone who does not have to draw money faster than you do and someone who wants to go at about the same pace and in the same direction as you. Try to make a policy that each partner draw the same in salary and expenses whether trips, cars or lunches and that the partnership avoid hiring relations or friends of either partner. Many smart businessmen feel that, aside from this, mutual trust is the answer. Each should have sole check signing privileges and each should accept the other as a fifty-fifty equal partner. If so, it is often advised to divide jurisdiction, give one the final say on advertising decisions and the other an inventory decision and so forth.

If there's a will, it's amazing how smooth and comfortable a partnership can be. The right partnership can create synergy, a more total mutual benefit than the sum of partner abilities. Each can stimulate the other.

With an advance agreement, most problems might never occur. That's why getting a lawyer as soon as you decide that you want to go ahead is well worth the cost. If you can't afford a lawyer, it's wise to postpone the partnership. Often, it's possible to agree to share income or profit *without* forming a partnership. Your future partner may be just as happy for you to act as sole principal while the test is going on. You and he can agree on a simple deal with a simple letter. You can pay him a percentage of profits after all out of pocket costs, charging nothing for overhead or pay him a royalty. A lawyer would advise that you have a lawyer draw up a legal contract for you. But many would make that first test just with a simple letter. If so, the letter should *limit* the sharing to results of the first ad. Then, if the ad succeeds and it seems to be a business, you may feel it important enough to afford a lawyer. Most businessmen would. Or you and your associate may choose to go ahead ad by ad according to the terms of the letter of agreement with you owning the business but sharing as agreed.

To summarize, analyze whether *you* are suited to have partners. Check thoroughly on your future partners *before* they're partners. Work out in your agreement exactly what will happen later if you split up. And then, go ahead and make it work.

Chapter 2

Simplest Starting

Least paperwork beginning steps...survival tips
through initial tests

It's quite a thrill to hang out your own shingle and get underway. Most mail order moonlighters start by picking an unincorporated company name and product name (if needed) to use in their first ad. In many states, the law requires that anyone doing business under any name not their own must register it at their county clerk's office. The form to fill out is usually simple and the fee nominal. A proprietorship or partnership can usually be registered in this way. Some moonlighters test first and register later if the test succeeds. Lawyers recommend that you do register and use a lawyer to avoid error by county office personnel.

Most businessmen would advocate incorporating quickly. Any growth from here on in will mean obligations and risks. If you operate as a proprietorship or partnership you are personally obligated for company obligations. If the business goes under, you can go under personally. This could be the result of a business disaster that you could not have reasonably foreseen. If you don't want to risk your family's future, as well as your own, it may be wise to consider forming a corporation. Most partnerships are actually in corporate form with each partner a stockholder.

Some cautious people would not even run their first ad before incorporating. Most mail order moonlighters incorporate later. Take

302

your choice and maybe your lawyer's advice. Lawyers usually recommend that you incorporate right away, guided by a lawyer. Books are available at your library which tell you how to incorporate for little money without a lawyer. We have used a lawyer each time at a cost of several hundred dollars, including the pretty kit needed of stock book, minute book, stock certificates and corporate seal.

Organizing your business either way is quite simple. You don't need a license to be in the mail order business. Alone or with others, you need to determine whether to organize in unincorporated form or as a corporation. You may prefer to postpone forming a corporation to start, until your test succeeds unless your lawyer advises it.

When you run your first tests, there's no assurance that *any* will pay off at a profit. Any expense other than these tests you may regret later, if the tests all fail.

The word for any starting business is *survival*. Most that start don't survive. The way to survive is to *limit your objectives* to reality. If you work at too hard a pace you will endanger your health, upset your marriage, risk your job and take away all the fun that you can have in mail order. Crawl before you walk, walk before you run and you'll *survive* to run far faster than you may realize. Let's begin in the simplest way possible.

As a moonlighter, you can start without a staff if you do everything yourself or have it done as needed. You don't need to print any stationery, billheads or business cards. That can come later.

First bills can be paid by personal check (unless otherwise advised by your lawyer). First stationery can be plain paper with a rubber stamp for name, address and telephone number (your own). First merchandise can be ordered on blank standard purchase order forms from any stationery shop. Just stamp and fill in. If you prefer orders not to come to your home, simply rent a post office box and pick them up.

As soon as checks and money come in, you can deposit them in a new account in the name of your business. If a proprietorship, your bank can tell you the simple procedure. If others are principals with you, it will be wise to get a lawyer and form a corporation before you run your ad. The bank account can be opened accordingly.

Whether you use a lawyer or not, if you incorporate and open an account, the bank will require written designation of individuals properly authorized to sign checks and will give you the necessary legal forms to fill out.

Your object is to test and *avoid* buying anything or hiring anyone for even part time hours except when absolutely needed and out of

303

profits. For first tests you can operate from home using your telephone without buying or renting any equipment. Some letters you receive do not need to be answered. Most others can be answered by telephone.

You can type your own letters or use a temporary secretary hired by the hour or day to come to your home. You can keep your own books coached by your accountant. If your business is very small, your only financial statement need be a business tax return prepared with your accountant at the same time as you prepare your personal tax return. Or you can even get the IRS local office to help you without charge, just as it may do with your personal return.

As soon as you advertise, help can come in the mail. Letters will usually come from a publisher, broadcaster, printer, mailing house, etc. soliciting advertising. But read each letter carefully. You may get a pleasant surprise if you have the sole rights to make or to sell the item in most ways. A catalogue house may be intrigued by your ad and write of their interest in running it. An advertiser may be interested in it as a premium. A mail order firm may want to advertise it on TV or in some other way and buy it from you. A store may want to buy some. A publication may want to do a story on it. Alert follow through can turn mild interest into a sale with a profit more than wiping out any loss your ad may have had. Or it may be pure profit on top of the profit of a successful test.

Before you advertise, make sure you have the right product and advertisement. Then, worry about shipping it.

Let's assume that you have an item and are scheduling a test. You've packed it carefully in a shipping carton or padded envelope. You've found out it's acceptable for shipping at the post office or by United Parcel Service. You've compared the costs of each.

Before the test, ship one to a friend. Ask him or her to open it up, check for breakage and ship it back the same day. If you have breakage at either end, try to determine the cause. The package may be crushed indicating too weak a package. The item may not be wedged in or cushioned firmly and properly. This may have caused breakage due to the item shaking loosely within a strong container.

In either case, hold up the test. If a crushed package, repack in a stronger carton or heavier, more thickly cushioned jiffy bag. If loose in a carton, take special care to cushion with tissue, newspaper or plastic material. Now, send two packages as corrected to two friends with the same request as before. If each arrives in fine condition, go ahead with your test. If there is still breakage in either package, either way, cancel your test and forget it. However, if you're still sold on the item and

304

convinced that you can correct the shipping problem, you can always go ahead and repackage or repack more carefully or both.

We have occasionally had breakage problems but almost always have been able to correct them. Sometimes, a spring in an action toy will be shaken out of place within the toy, causing it to jam. Sometimes, the manufacturer (perhaps you) can correct this. But sometimes, you've discovered that the item you selected is simply too flimsy for mail order shipping. Let's assume that your breakage problem is solved and that orders do come in. You will need to keep track of them.

Mail order is a science because results from each advertisement in whatever media can be measured.

The ability to key addresses and count separately mail addressed to each key makes evaluation of tests possible. It is vital in comparing the results of two or more ads in a split-run test. Whatever form of mail order advertising used can be keyed.

Keying each publication and direct mail advertisement can be done by printing a slight variation in the address. A key can be printed in a coupon and changed for each advertisement. It can be printed in the final mailing instruction at the close of any ad without a coupon. It can be changed in the mailing instructions of each TV commercial or each radio commercial on each station. If telephone orders are taken, different telephone numbers can be arranged with a telephone service and each used as a key.

Often, in direct mail each label is keyed with the same number series for each list used. If one list is broken into test segments, each is keyed this way. Otherwise, and always for multiple mailings, billing inserts and package inserts, the key must be printed on the order card, coupon or mailing instructions. The printer can change the key for each segment of the run as required (each five thousand for instance).

On radio or TV, mail is keyed by the station or box numbers. A key might be Bargain Books, WCBS-TV or Bargain Books, 1001 Grand Central Station with city, state and zip added. Another key might be "Best Sellers" with all else the same. A different simple word or phrase can be each key. Large mail order companies usually key each advertisement in whatever form with a special number sequence and enter mail counts for each sequence into their computers. As a moonlighter, you will probably key and enter mail as most smaller mail order firms do. A key will often be simply the initials of a publication and numbers designating the date. A key in the coupon of a Woman's Day ad would be WD-11 plus the last two numbers of the years. This would mean that the order came from the November issue of that year of

Woman's Day. A split-run test would usually add the letter "A" to the keyed address of the half the circulation with one keyed ad and the letter "B" to the keyed address of the other test ad in the other half of the split.

The smallest mail order moonlighter must key his mail for specific advertisements. He must count and enter it for each key into some kind of record. There's no thrill in mail order like counting the mail for an important test or big advertising buy. Entering keyed results can be simple and fast.

If each advertisement is properly keyed, every order coming in on a coupon can be quickly separated into the proper keys. The mail count for each key is entered into some sort of mail count sheet, book or books. If ads are unkeyed and results not entered, mail order becomes a lottery ticket. Advertising buying decisions cannot be based on past experience.

One big publisher I know mails book bargain catalogues in huge quantity with five hundred or more book titles. For years, he kept his mail count in a very primitive but quite practical manner. He didn't use computers, printed forms or specially trained personnel. He didn't enter detailed information about the orders but just the number of orders received for each book. His mail opening girls kept records on big blank sheets of white paper all entered by hand. It was all done fast. There was no mail entry record by days. But it was adequate. You could instantly see how the mail count for each book compared. At a later date, you could multiply total orders received for each book by its price. Different sheets were made up for different mailings and inserts in newspapers. Each was compared with the other.

A very able mail order man I know, who mainly buys TV advertising, enters mail count in almost as simple a way. He scotch tapes to the wall a big piece of paper ruled into small squares. For years, even when doing several million dollars a year, he has kept these charts on the wall in his own office. When he makes a test, he enters mail count himself. When he runs a schedule, an assistant helps. Even the squares are marked out by hand. Only numbers of mail count received are entered. The number of spots weekly, times run, and cost are written underneath the TV station call letters.

We try to keep mail entering simple and mail records easy to refer to and understand. We mimeograph our own form on 8½" X 11" punched sheets kept in loose leaf binders.

We print on top:

PUBLICATION _____ DATE _____ KEY _____

306

OFFER _____ COST OF AD_____

We rule out on the page enough vertical and horizontal lines to produce twenty-four small boxes vertically and twenty horizontally. Each square has room enough for one entry for one day. To start, we use the far left vertical boxes for the date and weekly totals. We can enter numbers of pieces of mail only or numbers of orders for each of several offers in the same ad or both. We use one column for each offer. We can also put in the dollar volume total each day of orders received for the key or for each item offered or both. We use each sixth vertical box for a cumulative total before filling in the next daily count.

We use one or more pages for each key. If we have several offers in an ad, we keep records for each offer for at least a hundred orders and preferably one thousand. Then, we determine the average order in dollars and cents by dividing the total dollars and cents for the key by the total number of orders. Thereafter, we only enter the number of orders received each day and assume each is an average order.

If our ad asks for inquiries for later follow up by our literature, we key each piece of literature mailed as follow up. We use the same key as for the inquiries. We can do this with a rubber stamp, handwritten initials or a simple code mark in ink. To determine profit or loss for each ad we can trace in this way actual sales converted from each ad. The same mail count sheet records inquiries and conversions in separate columns. If the conversion is for a standard price, we show number of conversions only. Otherwise, we show conversions in dollars and cents as well as by number.

However you enter your mail count, keep the records where you can quickly and easily refer to them. Looking over your own previous mail counts will help determine future advertising buying decisions.

Before you run your first test, you will have to decide on the form of payment your ad asks for. The simplest way to start is to ask for cash. This will be check or money order. If you ask for C.O.D. orders, get from the post office their C.O.D. labels and tags and fill them out by hand. Later, if you get C.O.D. orders in volume, you can have C.O.D. labels printed. Your ad may have stated the price and added "plus C.O.D., postage and shipping charges." The shipping charge can cover your labor of making out labels and tags, plus a reserve against refusals.

If you ask for credit card orders, first make your arrangements with each credit card company. Do so if your item sells for over $15. Master Charge and Bank Americard are by far the two most widely distributed credit cards. Start with them. You'll probably deal with a nearby bank franchised by one of them. Explain that you are not a store. Otherwise, an electrician may install electrical equipment which you don't need and which costs you money. Get the pads of little invoices to fill out and exact instructions how to fill them out and where to forward them. In several weeks, you will start getting checks from the credit card companies for orders which you have shipped to their members.

If C.O.D. money orders come in from customers, deposit them in your bank. Soon you will also get C.O.D. refusals back. These are C.O.D. packages which your customers refused to accept or were not home to receive. You may refuse to accept these packages back. In this case, they will be destroyed and you will lose the merchandise. Otherwise, you may pay postage both ways, plus the C.O.D. charge. C.O.D. orders using UPS work in the same way. However, rules change. Get from the post office and UPS their latest regulations and rates.

If you start moonlighting in a small town or village, you could become important to the post office. One mail order firm that booms in a tiny village can ship out enough packages and mail with enough increased dollar volume of postage to change the classification of a small post office. If so, the postmaster and in some cases other personnel can get a raise. Often, a tiny mail order firm is catapulted by successful tests into big volume shipments. This could happen to you and help them. And they can help you. The personnel of the post office you use may not be familiar with mail order. In most post offices, they are.

Years ago, when post office salaries were lower, it was always possible for a mail order firm to hire post office personnel after hours by the hour. It costs more now, but still can be helpful for a mail order moonlighter.

Ship promptly. If you use a drop shipper, ask for post office or UPS receipts. Only deposit a check after receiving this receipt. On any orders you ship, deposit checks after shipping. If you know the delay is a matter of weeks, write a note of apology on a postcard; rubber stamp your business name and address and mail. If you get any complaints of non-delivery, even after you have shipped, send a note or a postcard that shipment has been made. For an item of $50 or more, consider insuring for your cost in the mail. Do so at your post office. If a low cost item is lost in the mail, it is usually cheaper to consider the occasional refund paid as your insurance cost.

Read carefully any customer mail. It may show you how to repack or write new directions for an item or even tell you that you should give it up. Letters of praise can suggest new uses, give new advertising approaches and be invaluable testimonials.

308

Before using a testimonial in advertising, you need a release signed by the writer. Some lawyers draw up a release so legal as to frighten away testimonials and charge more than you care to pay. A simple short release may not be airtight. We have no standard one. We write and clear one each time with our lawyer. Some moonlighters make up their own. Others get someone else's standard release. The public relations or advertising department of a large company might be willing to show you its standard release for testimonials.

Let's now discuss organizing for safer growth.

Chapter 3

Organizing For Growth

First allies ... selecting your accountant
... bookkeeper ... bank ... lawyer ... forming an
advertising agency

Of all specialized services, an accountant is most needed.

The right accountant often really costs a small firm nothing at all. Used frugally and properly, the right accountant can frequently save you the cost of his fees again and again.

Today, simply coping with government forms is difficult for the owner of a tiny firm. The accountant can take over for you, filling out much of this necessary paper work and explain each to you carefully before you sign it. The right accountant can keep you out of financial trouble in many ways. He can warn you, but cannot stop you from unwise false moves.

He can help you select a temporary bookkeeper by the hour and often teach you or your spouse how to set up and keep your own books. He can catch bookkeeping errors, calculate all corporate taxes and often advise you on tax benefits you might not otherwise be aware of, and handle your personal taxes as well.

Our accountant is like a member of our family. He has been with us through good times, boom and adversity, when we were tiny and when we were a good deal bigger (although still small). He has helped us select and train personnel, buy accounting equipment (even a computer), approve and get credit, acted for us in tax audits and checked out order margins. We never conclude a royalty agreement, form a corporation, go into partnership or make an acquisition without clearing certain financial and tax implications with him. He has advised us how best to take advantage of a tax loss, helped us prepare cash flow estimates and assisted in countless other ways.

From moonlight start to selling out or going public, the right accountant can be your right arm. As soon as you start making money, he can help free you to make more money. He may gamble on a young tiny firm's future and charge very, very little to start. If you have very little money, find the right young accountant just starting out and be frank. If he likes you and has confidence in you he may become part of your team for a very modest starting fee.

A good way to select one is to call larger accounting firms and ask for recommendations of smaller ones. Another way is to call the professor of accounting at a good business college. Interview several. Check clients or recent employers for opinions. In talking to each perspective accountant, explain you can pay little now but will pay more as soon as able. Consider an older semi-retired accountant. He may be understanding about working for little. But get a good accountant and you won't regret it.

Your accountant can keep your books but will cost you more an hour than a bookkeeper would. A bookkeeper enters transactions. An accountant starts work with the bookkeeper's figures. With very little help from your accountant, you can keep your own books to start.

But let's hope that your mail order moonlighting business prospers. If so, you may soon prefer to pay a temporary bookkeeper by the hour and use the time saved to make more money. If you have kept your own books it will help you help the bookkeeper and help you keep a sense of control.

Tiny firms often get behind in their bookkeeping. Often, the owner plans to keep his own books but does it irregularly if at all and soon gets hopelessly behind. Sometimes, a tiny firm gets a bookkeeper for three hours a week, or so, for ten hours a week of work. Often, in either case, records get tangled, papers misplaced, errors are made and soon there's a bookkeeping mess to clean up. Roughly speaking, at this stage each hour of work undone or done incorrectly takes three to five hours to catch up. And usually, a regular bookkeeper will not attempt it. Only a higher cost per hour specialist in cleaning up such messes may then do so.

If you do your own bookkeeping do it *correctly* under your accountant's instruction and supervision, and do it regularly and promptly. Don't get behind. And if you use a temporary bookkeeper, see that books are up to date. If one leaves and you can't get another fill in yourself or if necessary, pay your acountant to come in extra hours even at higher costs per hour. Keep up to date and you won't regret it.

When you pay for an accountant and a bookkeeper, much of what you can ever find out about what they do is contained in your financial statement. Preparing a statement is legally necessary. You pay for the statement. You might as well know fully what it's trying to tell you.

A financial statement is the scoreboard of your business. Never can so few words say so much to anyone who understands them as in a financial statement. Your own financial statements can become a continuing course on how to make more money. In each new statement, you can see briefest but most needed do's and don'ts, easiest ways to cut overhead, where to get most profitable sales, how best to increase net worth. You get more value from your accountant. You can better understand what he's advising you. You don't have to ask him simple basic fundamental questions and get the answer at an accountant's hourly rate. You can now ask him for more advanced help and get it in the same time and at no more cost than when he had to explain beginning principals.

And of course, if you start selling the trade and giving credit, getting financial statements from those asking for credit is more practical if you can understand them. Understanding how experts rate financial statements can also help the firm asking for a business loan. I think that if you are in business you should be able to understand clearly a financial statement.

I may be prejudiced.

Business Studies, Inc. of which I am president, publishes a course on "ANALYSIS OF FINANCIAL STATEMENTS". Four hundred banks and the Small Business Administration use our course to train lending officers.

As soon as mail order brings you money in the mail, make up a bank deposit slip showing cash, money orders or checks. Keep a duplicate for whatever simplest bookkeeping records you set up, take your deposit to your bank and open up a business account. Let's hope that you will keep putting money in the bank and for some time not need to borrow from it or require long term credit.

Mail order done on a cash basis can bring in cash in time to pay inventory and advertising bills. Each profitable purchase can bring in cash to pay for the next. The safest procedure is to keep original test

312

advertising and inventory costs to what you have in the bank. If you have no money, you must start with free write-ups or risk advertising by someone else. You can only sell what is immediately available and buy inventory as orders come in. In either case, safest projection is to keep future advertising and inventory risk to profits made. You may proceed slowly but you will pay bills promptly *without* borrowing money.

As you grow and prosper you can develop good credit. Try to avoid the precedent of paying cash. If you have to pay cash, make the provision that on the next order you get credit. Make your first orders on credit *small*. Refuse any personal guarantee. But pay first credit orders *the day you get the bill*. You'll be surprised how fast you'll be considered good credit. Then begin to specify to your salesman that for bigger orders you want thirty day credit, and specify this in writing on each order. Pay in *three weeks*. Now for *occasional big orders,* ask suppliers for sixty day credit. Specify sixty day payment on the order. Always pay in *fifty days*. With some suppliers for occasional orders you can go to *ninety days*. If so, pay in *eighty days*. Continue to buy smaller orders for normal credit from suppliers, pay ahead of time and always take cash discounts you are entitled to. On the longer credit orders you will lose a cash discount, but this is a loan to your business. If at any time any supplier asks for any personal guarantee, explain that it is against your policy.

Officers and directors of corporations are often asked by suppliers and lending institutions to guarantee personally purchases and loans. If you sign your name to any such commitment, you are running a personal risk for your spouse and family. If your business grows and makes bigger purchases and gets bigger loans and you continue to sign such guarantees, you can dramatically increase these personal risks. You are taking away more and more of the personal protection that ownership of a corporation is intended to give stockholders. Don't do it.

When your account at the bank builds up, speak to the highest officer you can. Tell him that you want for your corporation the tiniest loan the bank will make, even $50 for one month. Explain that you cannot guarantee it personally. Explain that you want to build up a record of repayment with small unguaranteed loans.

Many banks will not make a loan to a business except guaranteed by assets or by a personal guarantee of officers or by both. You should be willing to assign business assets such as cash in the bank, inventory or receivables. You should not sign a personal guarantee (although many successful business men do). If your bank won't give you a tiny loan on this basis, it's worth looking for another bank that will. Switch your account, however small, to the first good bank that will make your corporation its tiniest loan with no personal guarnatee signature. Then, repay the loan in a few days. Three months, later borrow a little more for ninety days with *no* personal guarantee. Pay it back in forty days. Soon, you should be able to borrow your needs seasonally at competitive interest and with no personal guarantee signature.

Our company has built a very happy banking relationship. We have borrowed fairly big money for our size business when necessary and paid one percent over the prime rate largest companies pay with no personal guarantees. If you have partners, it's wise to insist that they also refuse to sign personal guarantees for your corporation. If you won't sign guarantees and they will, they become your money partners and may soon take over. If they are solely money partners and signing such guarantees is their contribution, that is another matter.

Does a moonlighter need a lawyer?

A lawyer can make an excellent case that you do from your start as a mail order moonlighter until you retire. Most mail order moonlighters make their first tests without a lawyer. We hope that you will succeed and grow. If so, you will need a lawyer, perhaps two lawyers: one as your business lawyer and one for patents and copyrights.

In each case, you will need an able lawyer whom you can grow with. To start, the cost of a lawyer can be small. Often, in a brief telephone conversation, a lawyer can give a legal answer that can save you a costly mistake. Highly skilled lawyers have played along for modest fees for years with clients whom they had faith in. Sometimes, it has paid off for them.

If you get a good lawyer, realize that his time is his money. You must protect it if you wish him to work with you. Usually, a lawyer needs facts on paper to give you a sensible opinion. Your work can save his time and reduce your legal bills. The right lawyer will be a realist. He will know your financial limitations and your legal needs. He will realize that as a tiny entrepreneur that you must walk a tight rope between not taking a step without a lawyer where one is really needed and not using a lawyer for one unnecessary minute. Get the right one and you can build together.

A successful big businessman uses a lawyer and accountant as a part of his team in on every deal.The right lawyer pays for himself in every negotiation. In any involved negotiation, the quality and caliber of the respective lawyers has much to do with which principal ends up with the best part of the deal.

Lawyers (and law firms) are like doctors. There are specialists and general practitioners. There are great numbers of lawyers greatly varying in training, specialties and competence. There are lawyers who primarily handle real estate, sometimes with little experience in many corporate problems. Young lawyers may be inexperienced. Older lawyers can be, if successful, very expensive and if unsuccessful, incompetent. Law firms may assign their most junior, junior to guide and counsel you.

You need a lawyer to draw up contracts acquiring sole rights to a product, possibly a partnership with others, help you deal with a government agency, perhaps advise you on procedures from avoiding advertising over-claims to complying with a department of labor regulation. You may not need a lawyer for months or a year at a time or need him on the telephone twice a week. You have no need of a patent or copyright lawyer until you are seeking or investigating a patent or a copyright. The more successful you become, the more probable it will be that from time to time you will need good legal advice.

Call a top law school. Speak to the dean's office. Ask for recommendations of top ranking graduates just started on their own. Ask a big law firm to recommend a small one. Ask a successful businessman friend for his suggestion. His request to *his* lawyer for a recommendation may get you a good one. A semi-retired lawyer formerly with a big firm background could be a great help if he might be tempted to work with you. He might be if convenient to him in hours and where you meet. In each case, it will depend on whether after meeting you, the lawyer or law firm *likes* you and believes in you. In any business, it's worth the time and effort to seek and find the best possible lawyer *for you* that you can possibly get.

A man who is his own lawyer has a fool for a client, but there is a narrow line between what your lawyer can best do and what you can best do in making an agreement. To use your lawyer as a father figure and throw the entire problem in his lap is not fair to him and can be expensive for you. There are lawyers who are superb negotiators and handle entire negotiations for their clients. But they are expensive and effective only if so familiar with your operation as to almost be part of it, and practical only for larger transactions. I try to work as part of a little negotiating team with my lawyer. *I* take responsibility for achieving agreement with the other party to all negotiating points I'm after. Only then, do I submit the agreement to my lawyer with a memorandum detailing exactly what I'm trying to achieve.

Lawyers are expensive. I try to have the best and use him the least. Essentially, I ask my lawyer to check that each point of agreement I've

315

come to in my negotiation says legally what I think it says. I count on him to avoid traps in any contract submitted to me in a negotiation. I rely on him for suggestions and advice in countless ways. I try to give him the facts on paper - all the facts - and get a fairly fast answer at modest cost. I believe that you can do the same.

What do you do if you don't want to work with an advertising agency? You can buy advertising direct from the publisher or broadcaster. Or if you start to advertise widely, you may choose to start your own advertising agency.

An advertising agency prepares advertising and buys it for an advertiser (called a client), but is usually paid by the newspaper or other media from which the advertising has been purchased.

Many years ago, an advertising agent (or agency) was a salesman for the media. The agent (or agency) received a commission of fifteen percent for making the sale. The preparation of advertising copy started as an extra convenience. When advertisers grew larger, an agent (or agency) began to act for the advertiser as the real boss, but got media to give the fifteen percent commission. The media did so, feeling they were still helped by the agent (agency). The agent became only known as an agency and usually built up an organization with creative and other services. The media then began to employ salesmen (media representatives) to call on the agencies.

So important were the agencies to the media, that the media often cooperated with them by refusing to give the 15 percent agency commission to an advertiser which tried to buy "direct" (without the agency). Different media associations often set up standards to determine whether or not someone stating he or she and associates was an advertising agency should be "recognized" as one and given the 15 percent advertising agency commission. In particular, it used to be difficult for an advertiser to organize his own advertising agency and receive "recognition" and the 15 percent commission. In recent years, this has become simpler, but some media, mostly a few newspapers, still require that an advertising agency be "bona fide". Even they usually accept the naming of *two* outside "clients" of the advertising agency as proof that the agency is "bona fide".

Media often have credit recognition rules with minimum net worth requirements for an advertising agency to be given credit. But most media will accept a check with order for the cost, less 15 percent, from any new advertising agency which fills out a form and often without the form. Many advertisers, even small mail order firms, have formed their own advertising agency. Often, this has only meant setting up a prop-

316

rietorship with a different name for the advertising agency than for the mail order firm. Sometimes, the entire procedure has been to register the advertising agency name at the county clerk's office (for a nominal fee), to print up some sheets of stationery and open a bank account. Quite a few small mail order firms have done so. Sometimes, a mail order man becomes quite proficient at advertising, enjoys it and after opening a "house agency" makes it an active one. He handles outside accounts and enjoys another way of making money.

Some media will grant recognition and give quite limited credit to a tiny new advertising agency with almost no "red tape" or stringent credit requirements. If you do decide to set up and own a "house" advertising agency, just talk to the radio station, magazine or whatever medium and ask for credit and recognition. Newspapers often refer you to their association which has minimum net worth and other formal requirements. Some newspapers and many other media will deal with any advertising agency individually. Each one which grants you recognition and credit even in a tiny way, if paid promptly, can be a credit reference for others.

The American Association of Advertising Agencies has set up standard order and other forms for advertising agencies. The use of standard forms for ordering advertising from media and other purposes can be quite helpful.

Who knows ... maybe you'll like the advertising agency business, too.Or perhaps you'll begin to value more the use of a good advertising agency.

Chapter 4

Overhead

What it is...your starting advantage...
costs to charge to business...controlling
overhead as you grow

A moonlighter can start with almost no overhead.

For first time tests, out of pocket expenses for overhead can be trifling. But some overhead starts with the first phone call, the first letter mailed and the first drive in a car anywhere on moonlighting business.

If you test an ad that succeeds, your business will become more active and your overhead will start to creep in and up. You will make *more* phone calls. Your spouse won't like the higher phone bill. You'll use *more* gas and oil, pay *more* tolls, use taxies, buses, subways for your moonlighting business and all costing money. You may buy someone lunch (and get some free ones too) or take an overnight trip for your moonlighting business. This could go on indefinitely. Make sure that all business expenses are accounted for so that the IRS can see proof of the deductions.

You will still have very little overhead compared with setting up an outside place of business with any rent, utilities, equipment and staff. But any overhead expense is something to *avoid* whenever possible. Each time you spend one cent for overhead ask yourself, "Wouldn't it be nicer to keep this cent as profit?" If you're making money, just avoiding spending a dollar can create a dollar profit.

318

When you perform all functions yourself, your organization is *you* and can do less than a larger organization. But you can make your organization larger with no employee commitments.

You can have mail keyed to box numbers at your neighborhood post office and pick it up and open it yourself. Or you can use a mailing house with mail addressed to a post office near them, have mail picked up by them, counted by them with counts to each key forwarded to you, mail opened by them, checks and cash recorded by them (with tallies forwarded to you) and deposited in your bank by them. Computer tape labels can be typed by them. Orders can be shipped by them from merchandise stored by them. You need only pay for each service per piece as performed.

List brokers can help you select lists to mail to. List managers can help you rent to others names you accumulate as you make mail order sales. Mailing firms can with automated equipment mail any number of mailing pieces up to the millions for you. Their machines do everything; insert, seal, stamp, collate by zip code, at far less cost than you would ever employ direct labor for. Your printed material comes to them from the printer and they take the mailings to the post office. You may not need to store anything.

Advertising agencies can prepare the advertising completely. Or you can employ free lance copywriters and free lance artists at so much for a specific job and pay for it by setting up your own advertising agency and saving the 15 percent commission.

You can buy products complete in the U.S. or import them or you can control manufacture without any factory. If you own molds or dies, you can turn over making the entire product to one supplier or to several, performing separate functions with one final assembler.

One of the biggest money making mail order men I know (another alumnus) has made millions of dollars in mail order as a gypsy businessman. There is *no* continuing overhead. Employees only exist month to month or week to week, paid generously but with *no* commitments. A lease is quickly cancellable. Inventory is bought hand to mouth. This is because mail order profits can be *ephemeral* ... here today and gone tomorrow.

For decades, my friend has every so often made his mail order killing, then folded his tent and vanished, sometimes for several years off on a favorite trip. He goes into mail order as others go into the market. He simply pulls out when the going's tough. And with this method, he's made more money in relation to time and strain and been a better father and husband with more time for his family than any really big earner I know.

You can follow the plan, modified as you prefer, expanding outside your home for a big campaign and back to your home for smaller continuity of volume. Of course, supervising free lance people and services is work. Depending on others can be disappointing, delaying and frustrating. But for anyone, the safest mail order approach is to start slowly and safely.

Some overhead is necessary. Much overhead, on second thought, is not so necessary. Avoid any overhead as long as you can. Then keep it as low as you can as long as you are in business.

The biggest overhead expense in any small business is often the salary of the owner or owners. If you have a job, can live within your income and need not draw at all from your new mail order venture, you are giving it a far better chance to succeed. Profits made that you don't spend as personal income can start building capital. The more you *need* to draw money *quickly* and *sizeably,* the riskier your moonlighting venture will be.

On the other hand, in operating a small business the owner sometimes forgets or neglects charging to the business small business expenses he has paid for personally. This is also bad. Whether it's a postage stamp, a phone call, gas money or whatever expense you've paid for, get it back from your business as soon as you lay it out. Your moonlighting business need not tax you or your family. Repaying such expenses is a reminder that your business must make the money to cover such overhead and a reminder to try to *cut* such expenses down.

There's quite a difference between the objectives of a job and business.

Many people successful in their jobs get into deep trouble in their businesses because they don't fully recognize this. And what a difference it is! In a job you want to earn the biggest income possible. In a business you want to build the biggest net worth possible. You are building an estate capital for growth and a cushion against business disaster. In the sudden changes of the economy, the skyrocketing inflation, the need for more inventory investment, the fluctuation currency of recent years, our conservative net worth has saved us at certain times when otherwise we might not have made it.

It's absolutely vital for you not just to make good profits, but to build net worth with those profits. A big earner going into business tends to draw big income from that business too fast. Many executives think that in going into their own business they've simply got a new boss, themselves, and draw big money which keeps their new venture from building capital. Many privately owned businesses, year after year, make nominal profits but provide big salaries to owners. But this is *not* a way to safely operate any business. The more you grow, the more capital you need. The winners in small business are those who draw *less* from their business, perhaps less than they would like, while building capital with *more* than average speed.

Most mergers are submergers, the one in trouble being swallowed without risk and on a bargain basis by the stronger one. And if you build net worth, one day you'll get that desperate phone call from an otherwise able competitor. And you'll grow more in one day than in years and safely.

So when others drive Cadillacs and live in super luxury homes, just point to your financial statements and say, "These are my pearls." And tell your spouse that all else will surely follow and in this way it will belong to you *permanently.*

Telephone bills can mount up quickly. Charge business calls and minimum service charges to your business pro rata. Longer calls get bigger bills. Make only necessary calls. Keep them short. Ask others to call back. Refuse collect business calls. Call at lowest toll rate hours. Write down what you want to say first. You'll reduce the cost accordingly.

Use the telephone to replace a lengthy letter or to avoid a trip. The telephone can make and save money. Used blindly, it's a blank check on your business. Every unnecessary phone call and phoning minute is destroying money that would otherwise build capital or give income. Whom do you want to get it? Ma Bell or your spouse?

Spending money on some kinds of overhead takes *time* as well as money. When you cut it out, you sometimes not only save money but *make* money with the time you also save. Much time as well as money is wasted in business entertaining. It's fun to have lunch as a business expense, but is it doing any good? For years, my wife and I have brought our lunches in paper bags to our office. We very rarely have a business lunch with anyone. The business saves money and with our time also saved, we are doing some job that would be otherwise undone.

For a mail order moonlighter, time is precious. There is no time to waste on rationalizing business entertaining. Avoid entertaining for business where possible, at least until your business is sound and sizeable. Travel can be postponed as well, in most cases. A car may soon be needed just for business or not needed for years or not needed at all. Location will determine this.

321

The cooperation you get from your local post office may affect this. If you have to mail your customers packages each afternoon, will the post office pick up for you or will you take packages to the post office? UPS (United Parcel Service) will pick up at your door for a small minimum weekly fee. UPS can be less expensive for certain size and weight packages. It also delivers faster and with less breakage for more breakable packages. Using UPS might save renting or buying a car. If you need a car for business occasionally, rent a car occasionally. If your business grows and you need one continually, buy or lease one. If your accountant approves, your business might buy a car *from* you, one you find yourself using mainly for business. Caution! Insurance for company owned cars *jumps* to far higher rates than privately owned cars. It may be wiser for your company to contribute so much a mile to maintenance and amortization as well as paying for gas, oil, tolls and repairs while you continue to own your car. Again, check with your accountant.

Next, comes professional fees for lawyer and accountant. Prudently used as needed, neither should be as high as your phone bill and yet they are far more necessary. We've already discussed keeping these expenses down.

A mail order moonlighter can start using part of one room in his home as his business. As the business grows, the space used tends to grow. Papers need to be filed. Sometimes, things need to be stored. A moonlighting business should pay some kind of rent and share of utilities (heat, light and power). If the business grows instead of getting a separate place of business, it's sometimes wise for the business to contribute a fair share of a somewhat larger home. You may then have a separate room as an office with room for files and perhaps storage space in your garage or elsewhere. It's realistic and fair to your family to pay something for the use of the facilities. It can be a token at first and raised gradually to what your accountant considers reasonable.

Later, you may have some expense in going to trade shows. Usually, there's no charge to attend, but expenses getting there and for lunches or even staying overnight are involved. When you grow considerably, you'll have more overhead expenses. You may have a secretary come in by the hour as needed, as well as a bookkeeper. If you store considerable inventory, you will probably insure it against fire and possibly theft. If you sell to stores, you will need product liability insurance to protect you and those who distribute your product against a possible lawsuit by an unhappy user of your products. You might join a trade association and pay dues. You might exhibit at trade shows. You

322

might subscribe to trade papers, specialized publications, courses and services, like a tax service. Of, course this is in the future.

If you're quite successful, you might rent a place of business or even buy one. If you do, you might have repairs and maintenance. You might rent machinery or office equipment (starting with a typewriter). You might hire some assistants, part or full time. Now, you would have real estate taxes, social security taxes and perhaps other taxes. Your company might be paying health insurance for your staff (including you). Little miscellaneous expenses would creep in from a little Christmas party for staff and suppliers to photo copy paper for a rented photo copy machine (also overhead) and stationery, printing and sundry expenses.

I don't calculate overhead exactly the way accountants do. For my purposes, I include depreciation of furniture and office equipment, automobile or building improvements., But advertising I consider in quite a different way which I will explain later.

To me, overhead is any expense, outside of advertising, that I cannot calculate per unit as needed specifically to make or to ship a product. Product cost, component cost, product assembly or manufacture, labor cost, cost of running a mold or die, packaging cost and packing cost is not overhead. And any other cost that can be fairly easily calculated per unit and is needed specifically to make or ship the product is not overhead.

Each of these expenses can be calculated at so much per completed unit. You can do the same with an allowance for the cost of handling returns, including refurbishing and repacking them (and cost of replacement packages). In each case, it's fairly simple to get an experience record of what percentage of purchasers don't pay or return the product. You can then apply, as a reserve for the cost of refunds and returns, this percentage to each order. Every businessman needs to know the total of all such direct costs and reserves that can be calculated per order. He needs to make enough gross profit on each order over all such expenses and advertising costs so that multiplied by total orders received, it can pay all overhead (operating expenses not applied to each order) and still provide a net profit before taxes.

Just looking at the total and the breakdown of overhead and operating costs is usually a shock for a small businessman. A mail order moonlighter starts with as close to no overhead as can be achieved in business. But it is vital for him to look at his financial statement at the end of each year, extract from it all overhead items and total them. Do it once and you will think quite differently about the price you need to charge for anything and the cost you need to get it for. Do it each year and you will be surprised at how the overhead varies in percentage from year to year. With us, it's varied from 9½ to 22½ percent.

In good years, overhead sneaks in the door without being noticed. After several good years, the "nut" (break-even point) is suddenly substantially higher. A bad year raises the percentage of overhead to sales, that is sales drop faster than overhead expenditures. A disaster year does so even more. But, bad and disaster years force slashing overhead. If sales pick up faster than overhead, the overhead percentage drops.

Once you get a "feel" for testing and projecting, you seldom have overall losses in advertising. If you test small, pyramid carefully and cut quickly when advertising fails, you can be surprisingly safe in your expenditures.

The essence of mail order strategy is to vary advertising risk and volume as results warrant. This means *irregular* volume. All you need is *regular* overhead at too high a level to quickly go out of business. Flexibility in overhead is all important.

Even after you succeed in a big way, management is best when small and tight. The more you do yourself, the less overhead you take on and the more control you get in every way. You can still do your own buying, check out your advertising claims personally, know your inventory intimately and eliminate most problems I've discussed.

A little restraint in overhead expansion may lose some immediate business but overall, *save* your mail order business.

Chapter 5

Moonlighter Mail Order Math

*Calculating overhead costs, margins and improving them
...setting price...determining ad profit and loss*

The average non-businessman, or business employee, is often unaware of the cost structure of any business. Amazingly shrewd businessmen often visualize quite a different cost structure in mail order than in their own non-mail order business.

Since mail order sales are direct to the consumer, it is expected that an article may be sold for less and still make more profit then if sold through the trade. This is seldom possible. Too low a sales price loses money.

The mail order pro will usually rule out selling any product with inadequate mail order margin. Margin is the difference between all it costs you to make, sell and ship your product and the price your customer pays for it. More factors go into *accurately* figuring costs than often realized.

We do not sell any product by mail order that we lack the margin to sell through the trade. For the trade we need enough margin to give 50 percent discount to retailers, or 55 to 60 percent to wholesalers and above this 5 to 10 percent to sales representatives. We must also pay for trade and consumer advertising, trade shows, store display and packaging. We have billing costs and collection losses.

It's hard to realize that mail order selling and handling costs can be

325

just as high, particularly when only simpler lower cost packaging may be required. But they usually are. Advertising cost alone is usually a number of times the percentage of selling price as in sales to the trade. Individual mail order shipping and handling costs are far more per item than for bulk shipments to jobbers or dealers. Returned goods percentages are far higher, because people buy before they see what they are buying. There are more damaged goods when shipped by mail in small packages. There is some post office or other in-transit mail theft. If sold on credit, there are often more bad credit losses than to the trade. Mail order administrative costs can be higher.

In mail order, the margin is calculated for each mail order and is called the "order margin". The order margin is the amount of dollars and cents left for advertising and profit after the item cost "in the mail" is calculated. Each direct cost to buy or make and ship it is included as well as allowances for spoilage, refusals, returned goods and if sold on credit, bad debts.

No one can operate a mail order business safely without understanding all such costs "in the mail" and how to calculate an order margin. Without an order margin, you cannot accurately determine the profit or loss produced by a mail order ad, even after all orders are received. If you calculate an order margin incorrectly or fail to be guided by it, you can go broke. Yet, it's easy to grasp and use. All that is necessary is to include *all* costs and allowances and to figure each accurately. Order margins become inaccurate when each such cost or allowance is not calculated or is miscalculated. Sometimes, those new to mail order are not aware of, haven't analyzed or prefer not to think about certain of these costs. Here is how we break such costs down for a mail order item.

We first calculate each cost of purchasing in the U.S., importing or manufacturing one thousand units. We can then realize more fully the possible savings in dollars achievable in lower competitive quotations.

The following is a breakdown of costs of manufacturing and importing hooks for a plastic fishing lure. Each cost is calculated for one thousand units.

plastic parts molded	39.00
set up cost	5.00
color change	2.00
inbound freight	4.50
hooks	39.70
ocean freight and importing charge (broker)	6.50
duty - 12.5%	4.38
inbound trucking	1.29
other hardware	7.90

inbound freight	.97
paint quantity needed	.68
inbound freight	.13
labor painting	53.25
labor assembly	49.00
Total unpacked item cost	214.30

Our item cost for each thousand sets of three is:

$$3 \times 214.30 = 642.90$$

Next, we calculate the costs and allowances of mail order processing and shipping. Our mail order offer is for a set of three lures. We will not use expensive store packaging but instead lowest cost mail order jiffy bags.

To ship each one thousand package of three lures we have the following costs and allowances:

item cost	642.90
mail order package	12.50
inbound freight	3.40
packing labor	7.50
mail order label	12.35
inbound freight	.13
typing label	40.00
sorting label zip	9.20
postage	120.00
mailing	10.00
allowance for returns 1.5%*	64.95
check cashing	50.00
royalty 3% of retail selling price**	118.40
excise tax 10% of wholesale selling price***	267.00
Total Cost for set of three	1358.33

*1.5% × 3.98 mail order retail price
+ .35 (4.33) =   .06495 × 1,000 =   64.95
**3% × 3.98 mail order retail price = .1194 × 1,000 = 118.40
***10% × 2.67 wholesale price = .267 × 1,000 = 267.00

Now, we want to convert each per thousand cost to a per item cost. To do so accurately and easily we need only move each decimal point three digits to the left.

The total cost for one package of three lures in the mail with all allowances becomes $1.35833.

Selling price is $3.98 plus $.35 or $4.33

We subtract 1.35833 from 4.33000 and get our order margin of $2.97167 let's call it $2.97. It is 69% of $4.33

We have not included advertising costs or overhead.

To make a profit before overhead on one ad run, we must receive

327

enough orders from that ad so that $2.97 for each order received from it totals more than its advertising cost...including its proportionate share of any advertising production cost.

Profits from profitable ads must total more than losses from losing ads. The difference between making and losing ads for one year must be more than all overhead costs for the year. After that, we must pay federal and state taxes before earning a net profit after taxes.

We have not included any state tax in the order margin. In New York it is 7 percent on the retail price. We are responsible for collecting this from each New York State citizen who buys from us and sending on the tax money collected to New York State. If we don't collect, we must pay it out of our pocket. 7 percent of $3.95 = $.2786. New York State orders average 10 percent of all orders nationally. A New York State business would include 10 percent of 7 percent of $3.98 or $.02786 in its order margin. Check your state for its sales tax if any. Check latest rulings on any liability in other states.

Any cost not included, or shown as less than actual, makes the total of estimated costs less. This causes the order margin to seem larger than it is. To determine the profit or loss for an ad, you multiply the order margin per order times the number of orders received and subtract the ad cost. An apparently larger than actual order margin per order causes the total order margin for the ad to appear larger than it actually is. The result can be a fool's paradise. Break even or loss ads are assumed to be profitable. Losing advertising can be happily expanded and losses multiplied. An accurately calculated order margin enables a mail order operator to exercise tighter control of advertising purchase decisions. An inaccurate one causes his business to careen out of control.

As explained, we first figure costs per thousand You may prefer to figure the cost per item from the start. For an item which you buy complete, it's simple. You are usually billed per item. Otherwise, divide the number of items bought into the amount of the bill. If you pay freight cost (trucking , parcel post, UPS or whatever) divide the number of items shipped into the total of the shipping bill. Figuring each other cost is almost that simple.

Postage is. It must be paid to the post office per item. An item that you buy complete may not come in a self mailing carton or cushioned envelope mailer. If it does not, include the cost of one and the labor cost to insert the item. To figure labor cost, pack a hundred cartons or mailing envelopes. Time yourself. Are you clumsy and slow to start? Will you and others be more dexterous later? Or are you speeding through at a rate you could never keep up, much less a goof-off assistant? Be neither over hopeful nor hopeless about future labor speed and cost per item. Make a realistic estimate and include it.

If you buy a finished product, an order margin may be lower (because of the profit of the seller). But you have a *known* cost. You get a bill and pay. When you buy components and assemble it yourself you have more variables, particularly in your labor cost. Your margin for a completed product is usually more accurate and stable than your perhaps, higher order margin when you manufacture or assemble yourself.

The more of the manufacturing process you do yourself, the more carefully you must calculate *all* labor costs per unit. If you buy a completed product, you usually get credit for defective merchandise received (if you check it). If a perishable product, you need to calculate the percentage of spoilage. There will be some spoilage of ingredients or components if you manufacture. There will be some overruns of components that do not match other components and hence, cannot be used.

Add up the dollar value of spoiled or impossible to use components or ingredients. Divide into it the dollar value of all such components or ingredients purchased. You now have the percentage of spoilage. Multiply this by the dollar value of such components or ingredients used in one item. Add the figure arrived at to the cost of such components or ingredients used in one item. It may be just 1 or 2 percent of a component, costing pennies. Calculating *each* cost this carefully gives you an accurate order margin.

As soon as you have any employees, even part time, you have extra social security costs to contribute. You contribute to unemployment insurance as well. Any employee working regularly gets a regular vacation while paid but not performing. According to law, in the smallest places of business there must be provision for regular break periods of ten minutes while employees are paid but not performing. The bathroom must be visited occasionally by any employee. If an employee works regularly and gets sick, will you pay him or her for hours or days off the job? In a little venture you may do so. And almost every employee is occasionally sick. Even small ventures often get an accident and health insurance plan and often life insurance as well, to which the employer contributes. And what about the cost of a foreman or supervisor who directs, but does not produce?

The cost of packing and any other labor is actually more than the hourly rate paid. Labor cost of packing, assembly or manufacture is

329

easily obtained. Just keep track of hours worked by each worker, multiply the hourly wage cost by hours worked and divide by the total number of items packed, assembled or manufactured. We then add 20 percent in our estimates for such contingencies.

If a mail order moonlighter performs any labor function himself, he may not consider it a cost. Therefore, he may not include the cost of his own time. But labor of any kind is a cost whether performed by owner, spouse, children, or friends for nothing. As soon as you sell your product in volume, you can no longer do all the labor required yourself. And you cannot expect others in your own family or whomever to help you for nothing forever. Even if you do all the work now, you'll hopefully grow and have these costs later, so let's estimate and include them. Calculate your time, or that of anyone helping you for nothing, at the hourly wage it will cost you to hire someone else.

Whenever you increase production and hire assistants and staff, there is a break-in period when labor costs are higher. A somewhat increased labor cost overall can be guestimated to average this out. In importing, be sure to include duty and brokerage, as well as freight and insurance. If your product is subject to an excise tax, figure a 10 percent excise tax will be one-eleventh of the jobber price which you would sell your product at, not the mail order price to the consumer. Check your accountant on this for latest tax rulings.

If you provide instructions for assembly or use, what was the printing cost per piece? Did the printer pay freight cost or was there any trucking cost to you (or parcel post or UPS)? Determine the labor cost of putting each sheet or booklet of directions in the mailing box or envelope. Again, do it, time it and calculate it, figuring the probable labor cost per hour.

Now, you get the idea. It's very simple, but meticulous work. You don't leave anything out. You figure each cost realistically. Do you have a giveaway? If so, what does it cost? What was the trucking cost to you per unit? What is the labor time and estimated cost to pack it into your package or envelope or ship it separately (including cost of its own package and extra postage if needed)?

Is anything else being shipped with this offer? What about advertising literature to ask customers for repeat or other orders? Again, you need to determine the printing cost, trucking cost and labor cost of including it per item.

What does an address label cost you? What is the labor cost of applying it to the package? What is the labor of typing the label? Do it, time it, calculate the rate and cost per hour and finally, the cost per item with necessary allowances. What does it cost you to open mail and sort it? Follow the same procedure. How about check cashing? The bank will cash a few checks without charge and more and more if your account reaches certain totals. As you get orders in volume, the bank will notice that far more checks are being cashed than normally. It will then charge you for each check it cashes over a minimum allowed free. Bank charges for check cashing vary widely. In Canada, we've paid as high as 25¢ a check. In the U.S., we allow 5¢ a check, although when our bank balances are fairly good we don't have to pay it. Your bank can give you a check cashing cost. Include it.

How about getting your packages to the post office? Time this and calculate the labor cost per package. Are you paying a royalty? If so, calculate the royalty per item. Just multiply the selling price of one item to your mail order customer by your royalty percentage. Are you getting some orders through credit cards? If so, what is the average percentage of sales made through credit cards that you are paying the credit card companies? It will vary by companies depending on their rates and your volume of sales through each. What is your labor cost of filling out the credit card forms, forwarding them to the credit card company and corresponding with them? Again, time the handling of a hundred credit card orders, calculate the hourly labor rate times the number of hours required and divide by the number of credit card orders handled.

What percentage of all orders are by credit card? Take a hundred orders (a thousand would be better), count how many are credit card orders and calculate the percentage. Now, take the total of the credit card company charge per item and your estimated labor cost of handling paper work with the credit card company figured per item. Multiply this total by the percentage (of all orders) which you have found credit cards to be. If credit cards are 40 percent of all orders, then the cost of selling via credit cards per order for all orders must be 40 percent of the cost of handling one order through a credit card.

It *is* a discipline. As described in these pages it seems complicated. Done step by step, it's tedious but really quite simple. Use your good common sense. For a handful of orders in a losing test of an item you're surely giving up, don't lose further money in endless detailed calculations. I simply wish you to be aware of all possible costs involved.

How about returns? What percentage of your items are being sent back for a refund? In this case, you get back the merchandise and give the customer a refund check including the shipping charge the customer originally paid. You have a labor cost in unpacking each return. Sometimes, the item is defective or has been damaged beyond repair in

331

shipping. In either case, it's a dead loss. Or the product is as good as new, but needs a new shipping container and repacking. Or the product may need some minor refurbishing to make it saleable again.

Returns are usually low and most returns are usable. As soon as first returns begin, it's vital to estimate fairly exactly the percentage of returns. It's important to get a fairly good guestimate of the percentage of returns that are reusable. Let's assume that returns are 3 percent and 80 percent of those returns are reusable, but require new labor for packing and new packaging. Let's just assume that the value of the usable inventory equals the labor cost of handling it and the cost of the new packaging. This value will be higher if the return percentages are low. Therefore, simply show a return cost of 3 percent of the selling price and shipping charges for one item. If however, returns for an item are above average and handling the returns is becoming a nightmare then costs of handling returns must be calculated quite accurately. This situation could occur from a defective product or from such poor packing of a delicate item as to cause great breakage. In this case, most returns would be worthless. You would be out the refund, plus most of the labor cost of processing returns. You must time the labor of handling a hundred returns and calculate the cost per return. You could then reduce it somewhat arbitrarily for the value of salvaged products. A 14¢ per unit handling cost might come down to 11¢ for instance. Add this to the refund cost. A perfectionist would add the labor of writing the refund check and any bank charge for the check. Now, multiply this figure by the percentage of returns and you get the allowance to put in the order margin for returns.

Estimating any allowance is a chore. This may have your head dizzy now. But if you make up an order margin, step by step this way, you will find each step simpler. If you sell C.O.D., figure the cost of handling one C.O.D. refusal (someone who turns the postman or UPS man away and refuses to accept the item ordered.) When the C.O.D. package comes back to you, you must pay postage or transportation *both ways,* to the customer and back to you, plus the C.OD. charge. You calculate exactly as for any other return, but include the C.O.D. costs there and back. If your offer had alternatives in model or multiples, first make up an order margin for each alternative offer. Then determine the percentage of each hundred orders for each alternative and average out. If 20 percent of your customers buy a deluxe model with a bigger order margin, subtract the regular order margin from the bigger deluxe order margin. Take 20 percent of the difference. Add this to the regular order margin.. You now have the average combined order

332

margin.

Usually, the first time a mail order moonlighter calculates his order margin, he leaves some costs out and calculates others at too low a figure. When he is first shown how to include all costs and calculate them correctly, he usually is surprised at how high the total of costs now becomes. And he is even more surprised at how much less order margin he has than he originally counted on.

An allowance for bad debts is a headache to figure for items billed directly by you. As a moonlighter, you will probably not sell on credit except through credit cards. However large you may become, you may never do so. And if you do, you'll be able to get help from a skilled professional, experienced in mail order credit collection. So, don't give up mail order after reading the next several paragraphs. I'm taking it up in this course for a simple reason. If you are financially able and logistically organized to do so, selling on a direct billing basis can be quite profitable. And you should understand it.

What do you lose if someone does not pay you? You lose the full retail price and shipping charge which you billed but did not collect. You lost the printing cost, envelope cost and postage cost of each bill, statement and collection letter sent plus the labor cost of typing and inserting each. Time the labor in typing the average bill, statement and collection letter. Add 20 percent for incidentals to the average hourly labor cost. Calculate the average time spent in billing and follow up for collection and the labor cost to do so.

When you grant credit, you tie up money. Either you are losing interest you could earn on this money or you are paying the bank interest to borrow it. Estimate the average time from receipt of order to full payment. Multiply the daily interest rate which you pay or would pay your bank to borrow money, by the average number of days tied up by the retail price plus shipping charge of one item. Include this as a cost per item.

Key the first five hundred bills sent. After six months, add up all payments received. Include in payments the net after collection fees of any payments collected by a collection lawyer or agency, if you have turned any over to one. Subtract the total of payments received from the total billed. Divide into this bad debt total the number of customers billed. This is your bad debt percentage. Multiply this by the total of retail price and shipping charge for one item. You have now calculated your allowance for bad debts for one item for a one payment offer. Include it as a cost per item.

For time payments, your collection costs are often higher. You

333

send more statements and collection letters. You may offer a cash-up or discount for payment in full after one or more time payments. If so, total your cost in the mail to give a single cash-up gift or discount, including postage and mailing labor. Divide the total of those billed into the total of those who accept the cash-up offer. Multiply the percentage by the cost in the mail of one cash-up. Include it as a cost per item. To calculate interest lost on money tied up, estimate the average unpaid balance over the average collection period. Otherwise, calculate interest cost as above.

Key the entire series of the first five hundred bills and statements sent as instructed. Add up all full and partial payments received including the net after fees of those through collection lawyers and agents. Subtract the total of payments from the total billed. Divide into this bad debt total the total number of customers billed. Multiply this by the retail price plus shipping charge of one item. Include this allowance for bad debts for one item for a time payment offer as a cost per item.

One cost included generally by large companies in an order margin is an arbitrary percentage for overhead (often 10 percent). I did so for years. But one partner I had, insisted on *not* including overhead in a margin. He felt that overhead, any overhead, should be fought and avoided where possible and that including it in the order margin made it seem allowable to spend it. We leave it out as well. For years, we've covered all overhead with income from activities other than mail order. We use mail order to create capital and help launch and increase trade businesses.

The optimist happily leaves some costs out and is sure that others will be lower next week or month. The pessimist grimly assumes costs higher than actual as he slashes the order margin to pieces. The realist veers toward the fears of the pessimist, but simultaneously notes down what can and must be done to come closer to the hopes of the optimist. Just writing down the order margin correctly can become a guideline to improving each cost involved. And often, the difference between mail order success and failure is implementing these cost improvements.

The shock of seeing each cost of a product "in the mail" can start you reducing that cost and become the first step toward scientific buying and cost control. Let's start.

Anything bought or made in hand to mouth quantities is often dramatically lower in cost in any reasonable volume. Bigger volume drives costs lower. Each labor step can usually be simplified and speeded up with sharply lowered cost simply by *familiarity, continued work* at the same thing and organization of tasks performed. Hands

334

grow more skillful. New molds or dies or just improved equipment may multiply production volume. Costs usually drop sharply as volume increases sharply. And mail order projection of a "hit"does increase volume sharply. The pessimist's order margin if he assumes that in volume, conditions will not change, may be far from reality. It can actually cause a success to be dropped. But the optimist's hopes need a realist to make them happen.

Reducing costs may increase profits, create a profit from a break-even or even turn a decided failure into a pronounced success. Reduced costs will sometimes make a reduced price possible to the mail order customer and sometimes jump sales far more proportionately.

If we buy for a tiny test like a tiny retailer, we're not going to get the price Sears Roebuck pays. But if we project a successful test in big volume, we can get a volume price. It's a chicken and egg problem. Often, only a low price to us makes possible big volume which is the only way to get a low price. Act small in tests. Think as big as is realistic for projections. Plan ahead what you will need if your test succeeds.

Explain your problem to your manufacturer. Get quotations for the larger quantities. Ask him (or them) to go along with the volume price for the test. Some will. If he won't, ask for a retroactive discount when you hit an agreed upon volume figure. Make it a figure that you can reasonably attain if you project. Can the manufacturer streamline the item, simplify it in some way for him, yet keep quality and saleability for you? Is there a slightly smaller model? Can he give you a lower price in this way? How about painting and decoration? Can this be simplified? How would it look in a solid color dipped, rather than a hand decorated design? Is the product now shipped fully assembled? Can it be shipped "knocked down" with assembly directions? How much labor cost will that save?

If you are buying a product packaged for store display, can the manufacturer pack it instead in a corrugated box or cushioned shipping envelope? This can save money for him. Can he pass it along to you? At least if he gives it to you for the same price, you're saving the cost of mail order shipper, its trucking cost to you and the labor of packing the item.

Check the postage or UPS costs. Is the package just over a certain weight classification? If four pounds and three ounces, just saving three ounces might save substantial postage. Again and again, we have slightly modified weights and sizes of shipping packages for substantial savings. Just dropping the store package and shipping in a shipping

335

container can cut weight. Shipping knocked down almost always saves postage. And each simplification can save product cost, shipping cost, labor cost and postage cost.

If an item is small, compact, light and expensive, shipping cost to you may be a factor not worth worrying too much about. But freight costs, whether truck, train, plane, ship, bus, UPS or Parcel Post, never stop going up. In most cases, it is worth while trying to make savings. If your item is bulky, not light and is inexpensive, then shipping cost to you and by you to your mail order customer is quite important.

First, determine the freight classification your item is shipped to you under. There are many freight classifications. An item shipped under an incorrect but expensive classification can cost considerably more than if classified correctly. For different situations different shipping methods are lower priced than others. You may be shipping parcel post and get a comfortable saving shipping UPS. You don't have to become a freight expert to make savings for your small business. You do have to ask questions and take nothing for granted.

In trucking, train, plane or ship freight the smaller the shipment, the greater is the penalty. For a small test, you must order in a very small way and freight cost will be high per unit. But you can determine how much you need to ship at one time to get shipping cost down to a sensible percentage. This is particularly true in imports. On a 25 percent duty item, duty freight and brokerage can be over 60 percent on a very small shipment when on a big shipment it would be 35 percent. Determine if you have a reasonable chance to bring in later the volume needed for a sensible shipping cost. To do so often means planning ahead. Such planning can save still higher cost emergency fill-in shipments by air or however.

On some items, "drop shipping" from your supplier can be quite a help. If you are located on either coast, you can save money *two* ways by "drop shipping" from a midwest supplier if his drop ship labor charge to you is no more than your own shipping labor cost. You save all shipping cost of merchandise coming *to* and from the supplier. You save *some* of the shipping cost to your customers by having your centrally located shipper ship UPS. You send him your labels, addressed to your customers. He puts the label on a carton and ships it.

For either UPS or the post office, shipping costs to most of the country will usually be lower from a midwest point than from either coast.

If you're making your product, can you manufacture it better and faster? Will making one or more molds or dies multiply production? If

336

you have temporary molds, will a permanent one speed things up? Is there a piece of equipment like an ultrasonic sealer or whatever that will do the job faster? Can you use home workers? Regulations by states vary. The law usually is that a piece worker can be given an incentive to work, but must be guaranteed a minimum wage. If a piece worker doesn't meet a quota, he or she usually isn't given work for the following week. Usually, he meets the quota. There is some spoilage of material given out and some is not returned and no product delivered. Such losses, if watched, are low. Overall labor cost is usually stable.

Sometimes, a small supplier who supplies a part does some processing or makes a complete product for you *cannot* do so at a practical price. He may lack facilities, have the wrong equipment or be inexperienced or even incompetent. Sometimes, we've found a substantially lower price, higher quality, and far more dependable delivery by switching to a more capable supplier.

In the testing phase, supplying the product is a speculation. It is hard to get cooperation. You, yourself, have little time to improve anything. The moment the test succeeds, the entire situation changes.

The order which you place for the demand caused by any projection of advertising is more interesting to the supplier. The prospect of getting still more volume becomes believable. You become more important to the seller. Competition begins its work. Some supplier is hungrier and needs business more at this time. His quotations are below your present supplier who suddenly discovers that he can quote lower prices too. One supplier discovers a shortcut that can make the item faster. Another comes up with a nice product improvement. You get a quote from another country with a landed price in the U.S. better than you can make it here. You find that you can often be loyal and fair to those that deserve it, switch in other cases where you can do better and get your costs lower as your volume goes higher.

You may improve costs by taking over some or all assembly and manufacturing functions yourself. It depends on whether you have room to work in or can get temporary month by month space. You must be suited to performing such functions. If not, it can cost more. Do what you're good at. Get others to do what you're weaker at. If you have partners, perhaps one has a feeling for and likes simple manufacturing. If so, you will probably improve your order margin with efficiencies and improve your product as well.

Analyze your returns. Are they too high? Overhigh returns sharply reduce an order margin. If the product is the cause and you can't correct the shortcoming, *drop it*. But is it the product? How about the directions

337

on how to use it? How about the way you pack it? Is there unnecessary breakage? Read the mail. See what those requesting refunds say. After you're sent refund checks, phone those who requested them and find out in more detail why they returned the item. Sometimes, just packing the product with more protection will almost eliminate breakage and cut returns.

Sometimes, rewriting instructions will make a big improvement. Your product may be good, but your advertising copy leads the customer to expect something better. If so, tone down your copy claims to avoid overselling. This may cut returns. Try to improve your copy to keep sales up. A test of revised, more believable copy may get more orders and less returns. Your product may be good, but the price too low. In some tests we've got as much or more orders at a higher price, while sharply improving the margin. How about an add-on of a deluxe model at a 20 percent or so, higher price. Usually, this does not cut total orders and does increase the average order, as well as the average order margin.

If you project a successful test, you can lower credit card costs to you by increasing volume. You may be able to get extra sales by inserting another offer in a package enclosure. Your customer names may be profitable for follow-up mailings and give you extra revenue from list rentals to other mail order firms.

Gradually, you develop a "feel" as to whether you can improve margins and particularly how much better a certain increased volume will make them. This in turn helps you make sounder decisions about buying increased advertising. Anyone new to business and to mail order has three quick shocks. The first is how high overhead actually is. The second is how high all direct costs of buying, making and shipping a mail order product are. The third is how high a percentage of sales the advertising cost is.

Some never realize these basic facts until the furniture is being sold at the bankruptcy sale. Facing these simple facts is a big step toward success.

Specialized catalogues that have survived over the last twenty years have had to change their ideas about the sales price versus the cost for items they handle. Years ago, a supplier could sell such catalogues at retail, less 50 percent. Then such catalogues began to push for 55 percent off then for 60 percent off, then for 66 $^2/_3$ off. Then they felt that they needed to import directly or buy from contract manufacturers at still better margins.

Their computer pinpointed more accurately what they needed in gross profit to break even for each square inch of catalogue space. A strong selling item with far bigger sales from the same square inches of space could still be safely bought at a lower margin. A weaker selling item had to be dropped or bought at a better margin. Some catalogues have some items imported, specially made up for them or manufactured by themselves with margins of four to one, even to ten to one. And still, their overall profits are tight.

These same catalogues sometimes make a better profit with a lower margin. If sales pour in for one item, advertising cost for it is often *lower* than average. Some of that saving of advertising cost can be put into paying more than average for your product and still leave a better than average profit.

Arbitrary definitions of the margin needed are unwise. I've seen one mail order man work on what I considered totally inadequate margins for a product and make $38,000 in a week. His margins were much lower than average. But his advertising cost percentage of sales was lower still than average.

When electronic hand held calculators came out, the problem was to get supply. Discounts were unbelievably low. Most mail order people assumed that the margins were too low for any reasonable hope of profit. But advertising cost to sell them was incredibly low. Those who rushed in where the mail order angels feared to tread made good money, while the Klondike lasted.

The pulling power of advertising for any product will always determine the margin required. A "hot" item pulling its head off can have a less than desired "spread" or margin. A run of the mill item can often only be modestly successful with lower product cost. Every mail order man dreams of a "hot item" with enormous margin, ten to one or better. And it sometimes happens. The real answer is to achieve the very best margins possible, create the best ad possible and pray. We test price and let the public decide at which price and with what margin we should sell them.

The tiny mail order operator will try to buy something at a jobber discount on an item which he feels can be sold for more than its usual retail price. By raising the price somewhat, he can achieve a three to one margin. Or he buys a discontinued remnant at a smaller fraction of retail price and achieves a four to one or better margin. Or he creates a product that requires only simple assembly and gets a margin of three to one to ten to one. We would not attempt to sell an item with less than a three and a half to one spread. We try for a four to one or better. Others are willing to try a three to one or better. Any generalization is a mistake.

You can determine fairly accurately the specific costs of an item "in the mail" before you advertise.

You know the cost of advertising before you buy it. But you only know the cost of advertising for each sale made from it *after* you run an ad. Then, it's pretty simple to judge an advertisement success or failure.

You count the mail, multiply the order margin by the orders received and compare this total order margin for all orders with the cost of the ad. The difference is profit or loss for sales keyed to the ad.

Look at the results objectively. Do not make excuses for them. Don't assume that you know a way to improve them. Just accept the results. Be neither overly optimistic nor pessimistic, but simply realistic.

If a test, do not include the production cost of the ad or commercial except as an extra percentage to add to the cost of the ad. Production costs are typography, art, layout, engraving, photostats, announcers, studio, film, recording or tape, director, producer or any other preparation cost.

Many firms (including ours) use a figure of 5 percent of advertising space, time or direct mail costs which they add to any advertising cost in judging results. It seem to average out that way. But the less you run any ad or commercial, the higher the percentage of production cost to advertising cost will be. It's another reason to watch production costs like a hawk when you're small and to project reasonably safe advertising expenditures as widely as possible when you have a successful ad, commercial or direct mail piece.

Don't pass on price increases automatically. Test first. In periods of sharp inflation, when price increases of material and components on completed articles come in frequently, simply passing on the increases may *destroy* your business. In some cases, split-run tests have *proved* to us that we are far better off in working with a smaller percentage gross profit. This is because at the higher price, the sales drop dead, while at the lower price the ad keeps pulling. The profit may be smaller, but better than nothing.

How can you test two different prices each in one half of a split run and still be fair to all customers sold at either price? Include an extra free giveaway (not mentioned in the ad) with each shipment of orders at the higher price. This eliminates complaints of customers, or of the publication used, because each customer is getting a fair value at either price.

We determine the gross profit per order before advertising cost at

340

the higher and for the lower price. We do not include any cost for the giveaway used with the lower price. We do not offer it in the advertising and will not give it in the future, if the ad is successful. We now calculate the total number of orders received from each half of the split. We multiply this number by the gross profit per order and compare the totals.

Judge the success or failure of any test by the costs reasonably achievable if you project the test. Will advertising cost be consistently lower if you project? Color advertising cost per thousand for a few thousand mailing can be three times the cost of a million mailing. Because color is often too expensive and complex, it is usually impractical for mail order moonlighters. In a test of color in a small run, assume that test costs are prohibitive to pay out. Judge results on the cost per thousand of a big run.

Look at all costs in a realistic fashion. A test may be unprofitable judged on higher costs per thousand of test advertising, combined with higher costs of product in test quantites. But when the per thousand cost of advertising and of manufacture in any reasonable volume is calculated, the test can be judged successful.

Reality must rule, not hoped for savings that are speculative, but known savings easily available in volume. The volume must be realistically achievable as well. Again, it is a chicken and egg situation. Only volume achieves savings that make volume possible. Volume is often achievable that can make an apparent test failure a signal to proceed. But do so *with caution*.

The ideal profit to make in mail order is a dollar of profit for each dollar of advertising spent. If you had a gross profit margin of 60 percent, this would mean that advertising cost would have to be 30 percent. If you had a gross profit margin of 70 percent, your advertising could cost you 35 percent. If you had a gross profit margin (order margin) of 80 percent, your advertising including production costs would have to cost you 40 percent.

The safest and most productive, lowest cost per thousand magazines and newspapers are bought first. The most responsive lists are, too. The most effective stations are as well. If successful enough, more borderline advertising is bought. This means that as an advertising schedule is cautiously extended, the advertising cost tends to rise in proportion to sales. It is good business to extend the schedule as long as reasonably profitable. Even in a successful projection, there are usually some losers. Therefore, there is a tendency for a higher percentage profit initially to average out at lower percentage profit overall. A dollar for dollar profit in an initial projection is often lucky to become sixty to seventy cents for a dollar profit in the overall projection. It can come down to less.

Most tests fail. Advertising cost for each failed test may be small, but it mounts up. So does advertising production cost for each test. And some test losses are larger. Profit at year end is after subtracting loss advertising results from profitable advertising results and then subtracting all overhead expense. Anything left is profit before taxes.

This means that you may be lucky if one dollar in profit for one dollar in advertising settles down to 5 percent of sales as profit after taxes. How do some mail order companies consistently make *20 percent* before taxes? They minimize test losses, project more safely, get extra business without high advertising cost, get list rental income and fight overhead at all times. And you can too, if you are extra frugal, extra careful and extra ingenious.

Chapter 6

Safest Growth

Putting off expenses ... tax benefits ... keeping your
biggest advantage ... buying equipment ... buying inventory

From the moment it is a gleam in your mail order eye, the product that you develop or find requires a race against time.

You race to test early enough in season to be able to project without waiting for another year. You race against possible competition. You race to get the test behind you and be ready to give the next high priority item your maximum attention. After you succeed in your test comes the most important race of all. You race to get the *fullest projection* of the original ad or commercial before the season is too late. You race to get production at necessary speed and an adequate supply stream of all component parts or of the entire product. You race to translate your success into each logical form of advertising not yet tested. You race into each of *these* tests and if successful, also projections.

Haste makes much mail order waste. What is required is *meticulous speed*.

When you *start* as a moonlighter, you are *free* from all fixed overhead and have almost no overhead. You don't have factory rent or mortgages or payroll to sweat out for next week. You don't have lease payments to make for lavish equipment. You're free. This is your advantage. Keep that freedom. Make some money and spend only part

343

of it for overhead. Only add *any* overhead if you're sure it can help make more money. Drop it if it doesn't. Get along without. Work a little longer and a little harder.

If your growth is quite limited with few orders coming in daily, you may be able to get along indefinitely entirely on your own and virtually without equipment purchases. You're doing some things you would prefer others to do. You're doing each more slowly than if you had even the simplest equipment to help. You're spending most of your time on less creative work than you like. But you're making money. Hopefully, you have enough income from your job for your family's needs. You're building first capital. This is more important than efficiency. I'm often impressed with how efficient the equipment is at bankruptcy sales. From your start as a moonlighter, cut the pattern to the cloth. Keep overhead expenses to part of your profit after advertising and preferably a small part.

It's easy to walk into a luxury restaurant and order an elaborate meal. In no time, it's all over. The bill and even the tip charged to a credit card doesn't seem quite real. But it doesn't take many times for us to spend more than we earn. In business, it is the same way. I have investigated many small ventures which needed more money. Next to the owner taking out money when it wasn't coming in, the most frequent cause of financial anemia was hiring people or buying equipment not yet needed or warranted.

As your business grows you may find certain tax advantages. If you use part of your home or apartment for business you can rent part of it to your business, whether a corporation, partnership or proprietorship. If you need a car for business (and it certainly helps), you can rent or buy a car for business charged to business and deduct the cost from your business income for tax purposes. You can do the same with gasoline, oil, tolls, parking, maintenance, and repairs to keep your business car operating.

You can be the orphan of any specialized service you use. Cultivating them can make the difference. If you're trying to convince a supplier to give a lower price, entertaining may help. The same goes for each specialized service you use. And if, as we do, you use mail order to launch products into store distribution, you soon have trade customers to entertain as well.

If your wife is in business with you, she might be occasionally forced to entertain out as a business expense instead of cooking at home at your expense. If you entertain anyone for your business at home, this too becomes a business expense deductible from taxes on your business.

This includes liquor or any reasonable expense. In some cases, a business trip with a customer is also deductible.

If it's necessary to travel all over the world to look for desirable items, this too is a business expense. Phone calls made for business are also a business expense as is a portion of your minimum charge monthly telephone bill. Other purchases might well be needed for business. If you sold garden products, you might need to test them in your own garden at business expense. If in the leisure field selling fishing tackle, your business might require a fishing boat from a $200 dinghy to a $10,000 bass boat. Your business might need a trailer or motor home to travel and test products from or later sell to retail stores and demonstrate from.

You might need to join a somewhat more elaborate club to entertain from or take a summer home as a business think tank. A ski house might help your business brain waves. Your business might need to subscribe to the Wall Street Journal, buy a TV set or radio to view or hear commercials. When your business accumulates capital, it might find it a good investment to take a second mortgage on a home you buy. Certain books, courses (like this one), magazines, recordings, a film may be needed for business and charged to it.

Before you get carried away by all this, consult your accountant. In the end, it will come down to common sense. If you do virtually no business and charge many expenses to your business, it will probably be considered a form of tax evasion. I know one man who charged his wedding expense to his small business. It seemed a bit far out. If you are actually doing business and expenses are reasonable and logical, your accountant will probably feel that they will be allowed. He will also want you to write down each such expense with the business justification for it. Our own frugality and business common sense keeps us from enjoying most of the goodies. Use yours.

There are other quite important tax advantages. If you lose money as a proprietorship or partnership or one kind or corporation, you may deduct it from personal income. If a corporation makes profits, any losses for three years up to these profits can entitle it to a proportionate tax refund. If your corporation loses money in any year, those losses can be deducted for five years against any profits. In other words, the government is your partner. This is so for federal taxes. State tax practice on this matter varies, but often follows the federal practice. Check with your accountant.

As an employee, your taxes are taken from you weekly. As a corporation, you pay on estimated profits quarterly. Mail order profits are hard to estimate and sometimes greater than estimates. The difference between the dollars taken weekly from you as an employee by the goverment and less frequently taken by the government from your corporation, are really a loan to your corporation by the government.

All this may seem like favoritism but there is a reason for it. When you start any venture, however small, you become a part of this country's motor that makes everything else go. When you grow, you're creating for others as well as yourself. You may have no direct overhead but be adding to employment in the services you use. And when you go beyond your home and set up a place of employment, you're giving direct employment. You become a respected force in your community. And the more you succeed for your family and yourself, the more you are succeeding for and contributing to your town, your state, your country and the world. To do all this, you need a little help and you get it.

If a woman owns a sewing machine and uses it very little, she would be better off if she had not bought it. If used more frequently, it becomes a good value. If used quite frequently, it's a bargain.

In any business, there is an ego satisfaction in owning equipment and seeing it used. But you may not use it enough or you may not have the expertise needed to use it properly. Often, a business proudly makes a part that is *worse* and *higher in cost* than if bought outside. Equipment used sufficiently, frequently and long enough will often pay off. Mail order is irregular and unpredictable. Equipment payments are quite regular and predictable. Avoid buying equipment unless the savings on it can pay for it *quickly*.

Equipment can sometimes help you *avoid* other expenses and once purchased can seem indispensable.

As your bank account begins to grow, getting credit from equipment suppliers will ease. You can obtain elaborate machinery or equipment on a lease purchase equipment paid for over a five to seven year period. You can start with a typewriter and end up with a computer. But whenever possible, get along without, with primitive or with used, first class equipment. Start with corrugated files. Steel ones can come later. Don't be afraid of the impression your office makes. Concentrate on the impression your financial statement makes.

Fight each step to more equipment, stationery, business cards, forms or whatever. But let us hope your success gradually makes each step necessary. As you succeed, you can begin to expand from your moonlighting base. You can get some temporary space convenient to you either for an office, warehouse, manufacturing plant or all three.

It's more important to avoid *lease* commitment and get space *month-to-month* than to find a perfect situation. With little equipment it's not a big chore to move out.

You can avoid overhead and operate from home indefinitely. Or you can vary your activities, briefly taking on month to month leases, hiring personnel week to week or month to month for the same periods. Often, a mail order venture starting on a moonlighting basis will grow quite rapidly to be part in the home and part out. You need only make specific runs of merchandise. You do not *have* to make anything in your home or have to rent, build or buy a factory building.

Mail order items practical to ship are often small in size with the minimum of manufacturing labor. Often, the product is shipped disassembled. Some molded plastic items, with no painted decoration needed come straight from mold to shipping box. Many mail order items are almost this simple. Labor is mainly assembly of proper parts, inserting them into a box and mailing. In art prints, records and many items the entire product is printed, pressed, molded or stamped in one operation.

When such little labor is required, you can do a surprising volume in your garage where zoning permits. Just keep the cars outside and invite the neighbors in to help assemble and pack, paid by the hour as needed. Often, you can go on to simple unorthodox quarters without a regular lease. In a barn, you can do as much volume as in a small factory. One couple I know took over month to month the upstairs of a firehouse and did very well. They used it for a few months, sold their business at a good cash profit plus a perpetual royalty with guaranteed minimum and gave up their quarters. Others have taken over empty stores month to month until rented regularly. With a few tables and chairs they were in business.

Usually, when your first big mail order profits come in you're excited and thrilled and overcome by the sheer number of orders, all those beautiful checks in the mail and the rush of activity needed to fulfill orders. It seems absolutely necessary to hire some help and get some labor saving equipment. It seems wise to rent space and get a car. It seems ridiculous to do tasks yourself you could get others to do for very little and free yourself to make even more money. Yet, this rationale can build a prison of overhead and tie up needed cash.

Often, when a big rush in business seemed to make it necessary to expand, my wife has quietly gone ahead and gotten the orders shipped...without increasing overhead at all. And moonlighters have prospered with stripped down simplicity.

347

As soon as you do any real business, you can use a temporary bookkeeper, first for several hours a month as needed. Some moonlighters use as a shipping or manufacturing staff (and warehouse) a disabled person school or organization. They pay so much a unit for simple functions. There is some spoilage from damage but often surprisingly little. And the cost per unit is usually quite reasonable. Often, excellent professional supervisors are on hand and sometimes a good deal of equipment. They are also quite practical to use for mailings too small for the big automated mailing houses. Caution! Check other users of the organization's service before going ahead. Be careful; indoctrinate thoroughly and check work carefully or you may be disappointed.

You can make a transition from your home quite gradually. A good first step is to warehouse goods elsewhere and work there only yourself after hours and weekends. You may hire one part time trusted worker to be there some hours when you are not. It's only a step to one good full time employee while you, yourself, are still moonlighting. And from then on you can add on personnel as needed.

Be cautious about hiring. Building a permanent organization is not your objective. Making temporary money with temporary overhead is. You may make money for months, lose some, make none for more months, make a little, lose some and so on. A regular payroll is not what you want. You need flexibility with people, similar to the irregularity of income.

And always remember this. Even if your business jumps to a far bigger size, you can still operate from home with more services.

I know one airline employee who built a moonlighting business up to $1,500,000 yearly and still kept his job. Many businesses are operated mail order from home after retirement, particularly from Florida, Arizona, California and other sun states. Advertising and merchandise decisions are sometimes made from the swimming pool. You can use a public warehouse with your inventory insured and bonded warehouse personnel. You can use a time sharing computer service (or install your own mini-computer at home) to computerize your running inventory, automatically subtracting all shipments from inventory totals and adding purchases to them. If you ever sell on credit in volume, you can computerize your accounts receivable. A mini computer or computer service can automatically type statements and even address them monthly, deduct receipts, add new sales and keep running totals of monies owed you. The computer can break down on a dated basis the amount of overdue money owed you at all times.

You can build a team of sophisticated experts, work with them entirely from your home, and pay them only when you use them. You pay more per hour or job but risk less at all times. However large you get, you can benefit more and more from part time specialists without risking overhead.

You can distribute a successful mail order product through stores in the same way. You can build a national sales force of salesmen, each on commission with no commitment from you. You can salesmanage them from home. With little time from you, they can send in orders daily. You can ship these orders from inventory at your mail order shipping house or a public warehouse.

You can build a creative team the same way. However big and successful you become, you can assemble an entire "house" advertising agency owned by you with part time top experts only used when needed. This can include art directors, photographers, artists, retouchers, and film studios, each hired by the job only if and as needed.

Sometimes, first success and growth can come in a surprising rush. Mail order can grow so fast that the transition from part of one room at home to fifteen or twenty people in a separate place of business can be in a few months time. In a year or two, you can be doing one to several million dollars yearly. If so, you will buy more equipment and hire more personnel. But be careful.

Cautious mail order can pyramid profits with amazing speed. Some in mail order do everything as they should until that big bonanza comes but depart from the mail order straight and narrow soon thereafter. Only after losing the money they so quickly made, do they realize what they have lost and then take years to regain it if at all. The need for disciplined spending is greatest when success comes. In disaster the disciplining is done for you. But when you have money, you can spend it and it's only a step to spending more than you have.

Most who make their first big profits in mail order have no idea how temporary those profits are. When first profits come, many new mail order people count on more future profits than will occur. They assume that the same offer will pull year after year and that it will be easy to come up with new offers in an ever increasing golden flow. Only in adversity is it finally realized how *irregular* mail order income can be.

Don't make this mistake. When you make that first mail order killing, keep the bulk of net profits in the bank as capital. Overnight, it will change your life. From here on in through life, simply by conserving this first block of capital and gradually, if irregularly, adding to it you are in a postion of strength. Immediately, your profits start earning more profits in the form of interest. Most people are forever in the weakest of financial positions and can never take advantage of any business opportunity where cash is required. But now you can.

If you grow, you may begin to import in volume. Fluctuating currency can make anything you import a speculation. To protect yourself, try to pay in U.S. money. But most foreign suppliers prefer to be paid in their own currency. If you agree to pay in their currency, the dollar may go up or down before you pay. To avoid becoming a currency speculator as well as a mail order moonlighter, make a currency contract through your bank on the day you place your order. It takes such risk out of the transaction. Buy the needed foreign currency for future delivery on the date you need it. You know what you are paying, regardless of currency fluctuations.

You need not pay for the currency until the day you use it. Caution! Delivery by a foreign supplier can be in part or not at all. If so, you have bought more of the foreign currency than needed. The same thing happens if you *cancel* part of the order. You will have gambled in currency the difference. The bank will execute the contract, convert the unneeded foreign currency back into dollars and credit you or charge you with the profit or loss. But in most cases, the order will be shipped in full and you will have had no risk. FURTHER CAUTION! If your supplier ships *very late,* you need the leeway in your currency contract. For a tiny extra cost in purchasing the currency you can have up to *one year* from contract date to take delivery. This should give your supplier time to ship.

I know one mail order man who gave his company to his staff after a big campaign. To him it was preferable to keeping the "people overhead". The more you keep the personnel to partners and those on commission, the better off you are. You may give away twice as much money, yet always sleep at night.

Those new to mail order often draw too much money for themselves, buy too much equipment, hire too many people and then put off letting them go. Mail order gave us our capital and launched us into store distribution. Today, store distribution sales carry our overhead. This has allowed us to have a regular staff. You can do the same if you're interested in and have the ability to go after store distribution on products you control. But when you're starting in mail order, buy inventory hand-to-mouth, buy equipment you can self liquidate in a few months and hire personnel as week-to-week as possible, preferably day-to-day for however few hours a day employed.

If you do so and acquire good items, create or have created

effective advertising and test and project carefully, you have an excellent chance of success.

Most frugal housewives can buy frugally for a business. In each case, it's a matter of *shopping* for *value* at a *price*. Every wife knows that sending hubby to the supermarket is often not the lowest cost way to shop. She knows what each item ordinarily sells for. He doesn't. She can spot a bargain to pick up and a jump in price to stay away from. He can't.

It's easier for her to adapt her shopping technique to buying anything for business than it is for him to buy anything if he doesn't have a buying background. She knows that some stores charge less than others. And that some stores charge less *sometimes* for products. She has a nose for sales and for value as well as price.

In business, anything bought can often vary in price depending on when bought and from whom. And in business, every salesman is itchy to know how his price compares with his competitor. "How does my price look?" he asks with a worried look. Some printers will meet or beat any competitive price and expect to pick up above average profit on smaller jobs hurriedly given out without getting competitive quotes. When something is important and is needed in a hurry, there's a tendency to order it without questioning price. Ordering in this way is handing out a blank check.

Simply getting competitive quotes from three sources almost always improves costs. We try to be loyal to suppliers and not run from one to the other for slight differences. We try to buy quality and not switch for lower price and still lower quality. We try to be appreciative of cooperation, prompt delivery, and good quality. We try not to leave any supplier without good reason.

But differences in costs are often not minor, but very major indeed. There is one very small component for one of our products that my wife got quotes for from all over the world. She only got a good quote from one company in one country, West Germany. For year after year, despite inflation, currency revaluation, freight and duty, my wife has saved *two thirds* of the cost of the component if otherwise purchased, saving thousands of dollars *each year* on this one transaction.

When a first test is made, it is sometimes too speculative to devote the time and expense necessary to locate the lowest cost sources. As soon as the *results* of a test justify, it *is* worth it. Sometimes, you can successfully sell a product in a very small way. You don't have volume and can't hope for volume savings. But even in small volume, savings are often possible. Often, key parts of a product are laboriously made by

351

hand when molds or dies for a useable equivalent already exist. This is because the part exists somewhere for another purpose. A key part for a music stand turned out to be quite practical to perform the same function for a dress form stand *for us*. It ingeniously replaced *several* parts we had previously needed. The same supplier made it for the music stands and for us.

You may see no opportunity to make savings in your item. But someone with plastics, chemical, die casting or other production background right for your product might instantly see a way to cut the cost *in half* and *improve* it as well. It pays to be loyal to suppliers. Any competitor can quote slightly lower, get the business and raise the price at which point your original supplier may not welcome you back at as favorable a price.

If you buy anything requiring plates, engravings, dies or molds determine who owns them. You may think you do—but don't. Or your supplier may dispute ownership and refuse to give them up. This means that to change suppliers you must duplicate your original investment and pay whatever increased cost inflation has created. The rationale for the supplier's opinion is that you could not have bought the plates, etc. at the price paid except through him or that he helped in their creation or selection; and his reward is perpetual continued business.

I have not had any supplier refuse a first order (where plates, etc., were needed) that specified in writing that *we* owned such plates, etc. And where specified in writing, we've never had difficulty removing such plates, etc. at will. Often, the fact that we periodically got competitive quotes made it unnecessary to switch.

However, it is also unfair to get periodic quotes from some firm only as a stalking horse, simply to get your supplier to come down in price.

It costs any supplier money to give quotes. If he doesn't get business, he will stop quoting. Therefore, it's fair and wise to alternate suppliers occasionally. Each knows that he has a real chance if competitive. For any supplier who consistently keeps his word, delivers when he says and consistently delivers quality as represented, we are willing to pay slightly more than competitors we know and more so than competitors we don't have experience with.

Last minute buying costs more and risks surprises in quality as well. You're in the hands of your supplier. Success in mail order selling simplifies mail order item buying. You can order in bigger amounts at one time. You save on product, shipping and handling at your end. But when you buy inventory, be *cautious*.

352

Conditions *change* rapidly in mail order. A competitor can knock you out of the box in a week with what appears to the public to be the equivalent of your product, but selling at one-third the price. There's nothing more totally depressing than to buy expensive advertising and find such devastating competition on the same page or if you have a full page, a page or so away. Or a product looking like yours at one-third the price can suddenly appear in every Woolworth display window, or so it seems, and mail order for the item collapses. The art of mail order is to be quick on your feet and pull back fast when trouble comes. You can be *caught* and badly! The answer is hand to mouth inventory purchase or manufacture to the maximum degree feasible.

Often, it is not feasible. But to the degree it is, it's usually a matter of mail order life or death. Many mail order men prefer to use drop shippers for all tests possible and then stock, *carefully*. One mail order friend of mine who sells millions of dollars a year is able to confine most of his buying to *once a week* purchases for the *following week* like buying groceries.

Inventory overstocking is the cause of most depressions, many bankruptcies and can be *particularly disastrous* in mail order.

In any mail order test of a new item, you may be amazed by the almost *total lack of response*. I have seen a full page ad in a major city newspaper *pull seven orders* for several dollars each. It's bad enough to lose money on the advertising. You compound the loss if you purchase or make inventory the ad didn't sell and that you haven't the slightest idea in the world how to move in any other way.

Caution in buying or making inventory is necessary in any business as any recession has proved. But in mail order, it's particularly important. The shrewdest mail order men I know have assumed that all sales of any item could stop instantly at any time and they have been determined not to be caught with excess inventory at that time.

This means having the ability to buy or make *more* inventory is all important. The *stability* of those whom you deal with is important, and their ability and honesty. There are plenty of reliable people, but it takes time to build up a trusted team. Meanwhile, dreamers, paupers or liars who say they can make or ship and cannot can harm you. Your ability to make, assemble, package by yourself or via suppliers to *fulfill* promptly and efficiently orders you receive must be constantly checked.

Mail order inventory problems can be insidious. You may be buying fairly conservatively but simply go into a variety of items. A little inventory here and a little inventory there adds up. Total inventory as it builds up ties up cash. Soon, you're not as liquid as you were. And once loss of liquidity comes, insolvency may not be far behind.

And the more inexperienced in mail order you are, the faster it can happen. On the other hand, properly used mail order can be the means of turning into cash inventory you might not otherwise be able to sell.

When you are left with inventory, it can sleep quietly for years. Some inventory you may have optimistically bought may never respond to mail order. But other inventory may be just what the doctor ordered for a new approach to a successful ad. Occasionally, I have written an ad that moved out inventory that was gathering dust for years and the ad had actually forced us to go back into production. And every mail order man has had this experience.

Often, the way to move out inventory in mail order is *indirectly*. Instead of straining to sell a hard to move "dead" item, sometimes the easiest way to move it is with a "related" hot item, using a mailing insert or as an "ad-on" item to a hot item in a mailing piece or ad. Even an unrelated insert can gradually move off inventory. Often, it pulls just as well at full retail price as at a mark down price. Sometimes, an item that hasn't sold can be an excellent giveaway item to add value and urgency to one that does.

Generally, if you can have a major mail order success, judicious package inserts and mailings to your customer list can gradually move off most "mistakes" at a profit. You may never have to sell off distress inventory. It may be possible to move off inventory gradually. It is far better to buy so cautiously that the problem never comes up.

The more gypsy the mail order operation, the more important it is to buy from others. The more *permanent* and bigger the volume and more interest you have in building a distribution business, the more important it can be to manufacture yourself. But only manufacture yourself to obtain better quality control and lower price. With high equipment costs and low volume, you won't satisfactorily amortize set-up costs. If you have no space to manufacture you may be better off to buy than to make. If manufacturing is technically complex, it may be beyond you. You can easily spend far *more* per unit, make the product far more imperfectly and tie up a lot of money in equipment and labor as well.

We manufacture where manufacturing is the simplest of assembly, painting and decorating. We do not attempt to make component parts unless it is extremely easy to do so. We make only products our personnel is comfortable with. And even then, we sometimes find it preferable to have an item made outside.

We have owned our own molding plant but found it didn't pay.

354

Our volume was too irregular. Sometimes, it's even more feasible to have a supplier assemble, paint and decorate rather than ourselves.

We stick to original products preferably patented and protected but extremely simple to assemble. The same staff can switch from making a fish lure to a dress form in our plant because of this simplicity.

A supplier can be your creative partner. We have three fishing lures, we formerly made ourselves, and now have made by one small manufacturer for us. We can still make these lures at lower cost ourselves. But our supplier has *improved* each one. He has become almost a co-inventor as far as his contributions go. An inventor needs the help of a creative,product development minded manufacturer, just as an author needs a publisher with a superb editor. We make less on each lure, but we are adding strengths and building a sound, long life business. On our imported lures, we import them in bulk and simply warehouse and blister pack.

My suggestion is again, to be guided by your natural talent, your experience, your present facilities and alternatives now open to you.

Chapter 7

Policy Decisions

Concentrating vs. diversifying...limited specialized niche vs. unlimited growth...timing...discretion.

Should you concentrate on one item at a time or sell a variety of items? Assuming that you're not in the catalogue business this is an important choice.

One friend and former partner has sold at considerable profit up to $5,000,000 a year, but rarely more than one or two basic items in any one year.

He has no interest in volume, only in the largest profit from each dollar of sales. He's a perfectionist. He says it's not enough for an ad or commercial to be good; it must be superb. His interest is to buy or make an item at *rock bottom* cost eliminating every unnecessary cost. He has little confidence in others and wants to control every aspect of his business himself. He even prefers to concentrate his selling in one form of advertising such as TV. He will not operate outside the U.S.A. His personal way of working is perfectly suited to concentrating on just one item. Another former partner has made far more millions of dollars, with far more concentration. For close to twenty years, he has concentrated on just *one* item all that time to his great profit.

But two other equally wealthy men, each of whom have made all their money in mail order (and with each of whom I've worked closely for many years) have made their money in just the opposite way. Each

356

has sold a myriad of items and has been associated with a myriad of mail order ventures, all at the same time. Each seems to thrive from the interaction of many simultaneous mail order activities and transactions. Each has combined a variety of functions. Each has owned an advertising agency, space representative firm and mass circulation magazines at the same time. And the overall operation of each is dependent on the intermeshing of the many ventures each is involved in.

I've seen many people make big money in mail order in quite different ways. I've observed that each mail order man or woman entrepreneur can best make mail order profits in the way best suited to his or her personality and personal way of thinking and working.

I'm stimulated by diversity; others are driven out of their mind by it. Most mail order creative people go stale trying constantly to come up with new and more effective approaches for the same product or services. Other people work best in a straight line...1-2-3-4 organized manner. So, work the way you feel most comfortable and effective in and concentrate or diversify, accordingly.

Where should you operate a mail order business? One highly successful mail order business owner told me, "Once I got into the mail order business, I decided I could run it from *anywhere*. I made an objective survey of where to live for the best development of my children and greatest happiness of my wife. I chose Tucson, Arizona for its year round climate, schools, cultural activities and nice people. We've been happy ever since and my business has prospered."

If you use experts, advertising agencies, consultants and specialists in specific media and advertising techniques who are usually located in large cities, this can in some ways permit you to live and work outside big cities.

Handling of incoming orders can be done anywhere. Shipment can too and (for heavier and bulkier products) at the lowest cost from a mid-American point. Most mail order items are light and compact enough to allow shipping from many different U.S.A. locations at a profit.

Only if you are out to become a really large mail order firm do you need to consider being near the big centers where the mail order advertising opportunities are most available and soundest. So if you graduate from moonlighting to full time mail order, live where you and your family are happiest.

Should you consider specialized niche mail order or broad common denominator products? Your reasons for being in mail order at all will usually determine the answer.

357

Are you out for a simple, secure living or to make a fortune? Some have done both with either method. A specialized niche can often sell by mail order a special kind of service, which is not sufficiently available in other forms of distribution. If so, it can be both safer for initial tests and more limited for projection. The more specialized the field, the more limited it usually is. Fewer broad common denominator products succeed, but when they do volume can be enormous.

A box company has a cardboard magazine case covered in leatherette which it advertises very profitably in a special way by mail order. The magazine case is for back issues of magazines with the name of the magazine printed on the front cover. Almost all magazines have a hard core of devotees who keep back copies and value a case for it as a neat way of keeping it on file. This one company seems to have the exclusive for most magazines. In some magazines the advertising is on a percentage of sales, no risk basis. The publications consider it a service to readers. Usually, the ads are in every issue. This is a specialized niche situation. It is an extremely simple business to operate. It has considerable continuity. There are 1001 different situations like this one. Your own background may come up with the need and solution. Sometimes, such a specialized niche business is suited to only a very small field using only several small circulation magazines.

Skin diving started as such a specialized field but became very big. Skydiving and hot air ballooning are two tiny specialized fields that may never grow or surprise us all. If you intimately know such a field and come up with a unique product or even an intriguing specialized catalogue for it, you've got a good chance of some limited success. It's ideal for someone in love with that activity. It's great for someone who wants a limited activity in time, work and money.

The mail order firm or man or woman who goes after broad common denominator product mail order success is usually out for the big money. Tests are riskier. It takes more test failures to come up with one success. It usually takes more work, more time and more risk before coming up with success. But if a test succeeds for any such item, even with cautious projection, it's hard not to sell in big volume. It takes more capital to project a successful test. But sales are apt to be in millions of dollars with profits in the hundreds of thousands of dollars.

Broad common denominator successes attract ''knock-offs'' faster. Competitors jump in. It's a race to get there first. I've never had a broad common denominator mail order success without having a number of competitors move in with attempted ''knock-offs''. It involves fighting commercially and often legally to protect your rights.

Conditions change faster in these big campaigns. Weather, economic collapse, currency devaluations, many factors can catch you in midstream. But it's the mail order "big tent". It's where the action is and where the mail order high rollers congregate. It's quite a thrill to spend $30,000 in one week on TV and make $20,000 or spend $70,000 on a weekend in national supplements and make $40,000. I once made $30,000 in a single newspaper in one day. But be careful. You can be wiped out just as fast.

But obey the "laws" of mail order, proceed with caution and pull back the instant the mail order wind changes. Once you've got your original test success, your projection in masss media is usually fairly safe. So, if you want to go for the big time in mail order, *do it* but *obey those traffic lights*.

Should you keep a product's original name?

Let's consider two points. First, do *you* own this name or do you just have limited rights to the product and name, perhaps just for mail order or just as long as you fulfill a contract, perhaps with a minimum quota of purchases or guaranteed royalty payments? Do you want to build up a name which under any set of circumstances you might in the future lose the rights to or only have limited rights to now? The time to decide is when you *can* decide, when you sign the first contract for the rights. Otherwise, you must later renegotiate this all important point.

Let us presume that you take over the sole import of a product known world wide, but under a name you can never own. You have good relations, but are not sure you can meet the ever growing minimum yearly quotas of purchases called for under the contract. But if you can just negotiate agreement with the exporting company, changing the name (vital to you) can easily be done.

Once it's done, all your advertising benefit is to *your* sole benefit. Because, if you ever part company from your exporter, you can now import from another supplier an equivalent product or make it in the U.S.A. under a name *you* built and *you* own. You can even *export* to other countries under that name.

If you do want to change the name, go about it with all possible speed. For a new struggling mail order product scarcely known under its old name, there's almost nothing lost in simply switching to the new name from the next mail order ad on.

With a well known name, the change can be gradual. First, use the new name as an adjective to precede the old name. The new name can be the minor element and the old name dominate. As time passes, the new name adjective can grow in size while the old name shrinks. the new name can now dominate. Finally, make the new name the only name. Make the adjective a noun. The old name will have completely shriveled away with no loss of goodwill at any point.

Selling for cash is the simplest mail order and most necessary for individuals starting out in mail order. Fortunately, more and more people are willing to pay cash for mail ordered merchandise. But credit cards have opened the door to mass selling of ever higher ticket items. Cost of the credit card service to a mail order operator varies by cards, but usually starts at 10 percent for test volume. After actually receiving major volume from a projection, the credit card company on its own formula reduces its percentage in stages. If you run advertising in page space in the credit card company's magazine or mail to its list, the volume quickly goes up high enough for a reduction down to 7 percent 6 percent or less. Bank Americard and Master Charge have no magazine but are so widely distributed that cost can come down even faster, in big volume to as low as 4 percent. Check current rates.

Merchandise sold through credit cards will usually start at $15 to $20 and go up to over $1,000. If you use the magazines, you will probably sell merchandise closer to the low end; if you use inserts somewhat higher, and for solo direct mail pieces to the list, you will probably range more from $100 to $1,000.

Credit card selling is particularly helpful for smaller mail order companies. It eliminates selling on a credit risk. The credit card company guarantees payment. It particularly eliminates lengthy time payments. You can even sell your product on time payments through the credit card company and be paid by them in one payment. Payment is quite fast, usually within three weeks after shipping and processing the order to the credit card company for their billing.

If you start selling your product to the trade, need you give up your own mail order sales? Years ago, we were quite concerned as to whether mail order would *harm* our relationship with the trade.

We were afraid that if we sold our product by mail order that buyers for stores would be offended, feel that we were unfairly competing with them and stop buying from us. At one time, this may have been so. Once I called a few buyers, said we were considering selling mail order and asked for their reaction. The reaction was *negative*. Some buyers said that if we sold mail order they would refuse to buy again. After weighing pros and cons we decided to go ahead anyway and did. Not one store stopped buying from us. Our sales to stores we already had went up. And for the first time, we really *broadened* our distribution from scattered to more intensive coverage.

We do take particular care to sell mail order at a retail price as high as or higher than our trade customers do. Our trade customers now complain when we *stop* mail order on a given item. They also complain if they are not told in advance when we run a mail order ad in their area for an item they stock. Because they know they'll benefit. Sometimes, when we are running a page ad in a national supplement, we'll run a cooperative ad in one city the same day. Results are usually far above average for our department store ad, although we know it hurts sales for our mail order ad. TV mail order can have a tremendous distribution forcing effect. A mail order ad runs once and, if successful usually repeats quite a long time later. On radio and TV, mail order commercials can often successfully run a number of times a week for a number of weeks. The result is longer continuity from an intense medium that drives a succession of customers into the store for the same item.

You can start with mail order ads or commercials, then adapt them to cooperative store ads or commercials for key retailers and then as key retailers are obtained, convert the ads and commercials to a more general go-to-your-dealer basis. You then can go after broad distribution selling wholesalers and retailers. You may then give up mail order and sell through the trade only.

Timing is all important in going into some mail order items. Consider inflatable furniture. Some of it was imported from Italy. It caught on with young people. The momentum of the success began to build. It was knocked off (copied) in Japan. Hong Kong went into it, then Taiwan, then Korea. Prices collapsed. The market for it fell apart. This is a risk of any form of retailing. In mail order, it can be far worse. When ads pull well, you're tempted to project your advertising nationally in a big way. Yet, your big projection can be at the point of collapse of the entire field. With every new field of items we consider, we ask, "Is it too late?" And you should too!

When mail order success is great, retailers ofen move in and mail order falls off! Mail order has been the launching pad for many successful store products.

Butcherboard furniture, water soluble fertilizer, inflatable swimming pools, the telephone style shower head, safari shirts, jackets and suits, creative stitchery, decorative switch plates, many do-it-yourself kits and endless other, entire fields of items have been originated and made known by mail order advertising.

A new item can be a big mail order success. But we've found that when department stores in every city run co-op ads promoting the product, suddenly the mail order ads stop pulling. And when the item

361

goes into more universal distribution, the department store ads stop pulling. That's why each product we have is a proprietary product, why so many are patented and why we use mail order to help launch the product into distribution. In this way, we get a benefit year after year from former mail order campaigns.

It's also why we like to originate items and stay out of items that already have been knocked off by others in wide store distribution.

Years ago, one of our now great alumni wrote a cosmetic ad that made a good deal of money for us in mail order. We wanted to convert it to a store distribution success. Unfortunately, the ad although profitable was *ugly*. Department stores simply did not want to run it as a cooperative ad. I called in one of the grand old copywriters of all time who had started as a very young man working for my father. The old master did a fine job of converting our ugly mail order ad into a beautiful cooperative department store ad retaining all the mail order power.

Within one year, we were a department store success. We did over $1,000,000 in sales to department stores and made over $200,00 profit. I was happy and grateful. Meanwhile, a top advertising publication wanted to do a major story on my old friend. He asked whether the story could be built around the department store success. I gave him the okay and full facts. The story broke.

Virtually every major cosmetic company in the country duplicated my product, packaging and advertising. My product was universally available in 30,000 outlets under various brand names with no profit to me. Within six months my cosmetic business shrivelled to virtually nothing. My co-op ads simply did not pull. I was swamped with returns.

I was not discreet. Don't let it happen to you!

Chapter 8

Mail Order Negotiation

Joint ventures ... manufacturing royalty ...
with or without patent or copyright...
sole rights import ... buy-out ... mold rental

Mail order is ideal for joint ventures splitting profits after actual costs. Such agreements can be simple. Mail order often leads to setting up different corporations in different fields, often with different partners. Each agreement can be most important. Mail order leads into trade distribution businesses which can later be sold for capital gains or turned into public corporations. All this requires agreements.

When in mail order is a detailed written understanding worth the time and effort to make it?

For a mail order catalogue house, it is not practical or feasible to make a contract for every item featured. Nor is it sensible to make a written agreement in detail for any item needed only for short term special purposes, as a related package insert, for a specialized publication where you have a good rate or for a one time mailing to your list. It usually is not necessary when you buy a generic product easily available from other suppliers.

But there are many times when you do need a precise agreement, particularly if it concerns a proprietary and perhaps patented product that you hope to build a business on for years to come and possibly expand in various areas beyond mail order. A contract always seems to be so simple you could best write a one paragraph letter on it...until you write a rough draft. Then, it almost always stretches out to several pages. For it is far better to have no contract than a contract that does not refer to points of possible differences most likely to come up. Some of the best relationships I've had and in biggest dollar volume have been in complete mutual trust without a word in writing.

We try to acquire sole rights to a product on a royalty basis or outright or to originate, the product ourselves. Everything we have is proprietary. If we import, it is on a sole rights basis for the U.S. and usually North America. We usually pay royalties, own molds or dies have them run outside by a molder or a machine shop and then assemble in our own plant. If so, we either have a worldwide rights, royalty contract to manufacture and sell or own the item outright. This takes time consuming negotiation and usually commitments, guarantees or cash. We feel we must do so to build a permanent business. We feel a royalty is expensive and try to have a buy-out option in each royalty contract. If we're successful later, it's a reasonable gamble to exercise the option and end up royalty free.

A rights contract is most important if you acquire original items. It is not needed if you copy. Many mail order men make no effort to obtain exclusives, just as they have no interest in store distribution. They save the time of negotiation and happily jump in and out of items with no commitments on either side.

So, it's your pleasure but I thought you'd like to know both viewpoints.

How much royalty can you afford to pay? Any royalty is profitable to pay if there's a good profit left over after you pay it.

Long ago, we found the range of royalties we consider practical for us. If we offered less than 3 percent royalty, most people were offended by our proposing it. If we offered more than 5 percent, we usually found later that it left us too borderline a profit. Therefore, we try to keep our range of royalties from 3 percent to 5 percent of sales. We usually provide for 5 percent dropping to 3 percent in volume. If the gross profit on the item is slim we may make it a flat 3 percent. If the gross profit is large, we may make it a flat 5 percent. Even with quite a large gross profit, we find it best for both parties to keep the royalty to 5 percent and simply spend a bigger percentage than usual, if necessary, in advertising.

Exceptions make the rule. Recently, we negotiated an agreement to pay a jewelry designer 5 percent and a Rock Group 10 percent on top of that on a piece of jewelry designed for the Rock Group to be worn and promoted by them with tremendous promotional tie-ins.

364

Any royalty leaves less profit than if there were no royalty and the same sales. On any business with royalty free items, it's still hard to make money. 10 percent to 12 percent before taxes, would be considered satisfactory. A 5 percent royalty would subtract 40 percent to 50 percent of profits .... *perpetually*.

From a business standpoint, paying outright in one lump sum for all future rights is preferable. But in mail order each untested item is a pig in a poke. Even the financially strongest mail order operators hesitate to pay for rights in a lump sum *before* testing. The buy out option is the answer.

Usually, an inventor or rights owner walking into your office will expect one sum of money if a flat payment, and a far larger one if on a when, if and as royalty basis. The sum of a buy out figure on an option basis would be in between.

The psychology of the inventor or rights owner changes rapidly *after your successful test*. Before the test, his morale is dubious and his hopes vague. After the test, his future income is to him a reality and all the grief and difficulty of creating his product seems worth infinitely more. Thereafter, the more you succeed with his product, the less interested he is in any buy out agreement and the higher the royalty, the bigger the guarantees and the more protection he wants. So make your agreement *before* your test, include a buy out option, and make it crystal clear.

Inventing is a business, but few inventors realize it. A successful inventor usually makes a series of inventions, some of which he sells to others. Income on one invention is often small. But the continuation of that small income when added to the income on the next invention and the next, gives him a living. The same is true of an author. Only a rare invention or publication hits such a jackpot that it alone can support an inventor or author for life, rather like winning a huge lottery prize.

The very compulsion that drives a creative mind to originate, develop and perfect a product or book or whatever without being underwritten seems to convince him of the huge potential it has. The inventor usually has a vague idea he can make a good deal of money from his work, more than maybe actually feasible for the businessman to ever hope to pay. Often, the inventor is quite unrealistic asking for a big *cash* payment, a big, yearly guarantee of income and then a too high perpetual royalty.

We try to avoid *cash* payments. We substitute for a guarantee cancellation privileges if we don't deliver an agreed royalty minimum. We keep royalties to our limitations. We try to be frank and if the

365

inventor seems unrealistic, to forget the transaction.

Once you have made a number of royalty contracts with inventors and owners of items, the next agreement seems like a minor variation.

The situation of the inventor or rights owner is often quite different. This one agreement may seem the most important in life. He may feel that never again will he have an opportunity to make so much money. A businessman by the very discipline he submits his daily operations to would rarely speculate over months and years to the degree the inventor has done. No wonder the inventor is nervous about the wording of any agreement.

Few inventors are financially strong. Most *need* money *quickly*. Few inventors understand the economics of business. They often believe the business man can afford a far higher royalty and still make plenty of money. Few are familiar with contracts. All have wives, husbands, fathers or friends to warn them they're probably being cheated. Often, their lawyer is a small town real estate or other specialist lawyer, not too familiar with your marketing problems.

Any contract seems threatening when read by anyone without careful explanation. Before submitting any written contract, I get verbal agreement of the business points in a contract, point by point, in business, not legal language. Before going over *any* points of an agreement, I try to explain my concept of an agreement.

A contract can be evaded, broken or cheated on by anyone really trying to be crooked. A contract cannot give perfect protection from crooks. Legal enforcement may be difficult. Most people are honest. But anyone interprets to his advantage situations not provided for in a contract. If a contract is detailed, covering almost any probable eventuality, most people will live up to it. A contract usually becomes obsolete in some ways, in years or even months. But the more carefully it is spelled out, the more likely is a long and happy mutual adherence to the spirit of the contract.

A contract should *remove fears*. The biggest reason to seriously question a contract is *fear* of some way of being taken advantage of. I do not want to take advantage of anyone. Therefore, if you have any fear, let's remove that fear with a protective clause in the agreement.

I point out that just "stealing" the item and copying it with no royalty would be easier and cheaper than any contract and that just submitting the contract is evidence of good faith. I try hard to get across my thinking regarding agreements in general. Any royalty contract is a form of partnership between the inventor and businessman. To be a good partner, the businessman must be both honest and competent.

The most favorable seeming contract may be the worst deal if the businessman does not intend to or cannot fulfill it. Royalties may be and sometimes are paid quite fraudulently. A businessman may go bankrupt. I ask that before signing any agreement they check carefully our reputation and our Dun & Bradstreet rating.

I try to explain worrisome points to wife, husband, friend and associates before the actual contract is submitted. I try to read each word of each clause of the contract to the other party and explain which are just standard legal clauses and the reasons behind each clause.

Lawyers like to mail each other contracts. A lawyer receiving a contract likes to suggest changes. Back and forth correspondence can stretch out interminably. I like to set up a joint meeting of clients and lawyers and then either agree to disagree or stay and modify and *sign*.

At this time, I try to concede any unimportant points, compromise in any reasonable way, but hold firm on anything important and make or break the deal in that one session.

Other types of agreements may be even more important for the mail order man. If you import on a sole rights basis, it's very hard to tie down exactly what you desire. But it is very important to do so. You may be importing from a small manufacturer to whom a lengthy contract is particularly frightening.

In dealing with someone in another country, there are really *four,* not two, languages to cope with: the two actual languages and the two quite different ways of thinking. Mailing a contract is particularly dangerous. Only a trip will do and *staying* on that trip until the agreement is signed. The foreign exporter must retain the right to increase prices, yet the very act of raising prices too high can in effect be a cancellation privilege. We try for a clause limiting price increases to provable percentage increases of his labor and material costs.

There must be hundreds of thousands of molds and dies in this country that are *not in use*. The original investment in each mold or die can go into a good many thousands of dollars. Often, it's possible to get a cash purchase or royalty sole rights option on a mold or die and buy enough merchandise for a mail order test. A skilled and creative mold or die maker can often *convert* a mold or die into something *quite different* from it's original product. You can create a mail order item together.

Harrison-Hoge Industries, Inc. and subsidiaries own hundreds of thousands of dollars of original value molds and dies now valued at zero on the books because nothing made with them is currently being sold. In toys and other volatile fields, once an item stops selling the molds and dies are considered worthless. But to us a mold or die can at any time

367

become again more valuable than ever.

All we have to do is come up with a new successful ad and the mold or die has a brand new life. It's often safer and easier to create a new ad for an old item than for a new one. And many items *are* cyclic. We've been selling dress forms for home sewers for twenty-two years. And three times, about each seven years, we've sold five or six times the average year. And circumstances cause the wheel of fortune to spin back to an item's success when you least expect it.

A mold or die can be worthless to the owner and unsaleable to anyone else. Your new ad can make it suddenly valuable. An option contract signed before you test can often be negotiated very favorably. Later , this may not be so.

Negotiate *first*. It can save you an immediate major cash outlay and perhaps avoid higher royalty payments if negotiated later.

Chapter 9

Keeping Customers Happy

*Prompt shipping ... answering correspondence ... guarantees
... handling complaints ... living with the government*

Your handling of customers must be responsible or you will live to
regret it. Orders must be shipped and promptly. Going into many items
multiplies the chances of customer disappointment because the more
suppliers you rely on, the bigger chance that one or more will let you
down. If you're manufacturing, just one component supplier failing to
deliver can make it impossible for you to deliver the entire product.

Realistic appraisal of your manufacturing and shipping capacity
before major purchases of mail order advertising are made is essential.
Nothing maddens a customer more than getting his or her cancelled
check back from the bank and no delivery of the product. The moment
you run out of merchandise, stop cashing checks of those ordering the
merchandise. It saves most correspondence on the product. Cashing the
check, if you have no merchandise, is illegal. Even keeping the check
more than thirty days after receipt and nondelivery is illegal without
taking certain legally required steps. Consult the FTC.

Set up a proper complaint department from the very start. Answer
complaints immediately and meticulously. Form replies will do for
most situations. Avoid cashing checks when out of merchandise,
promptly answer consumer complaints and above all, instantly mail out
refund checks when merchandise is returned. You'll build a good

369

reputation. Just treat customers as you like to be treated when you buy anything.

When small mail order companies grow fast, delivery problems can come, too. Small businessmen have an old saying that "if you can make it, you can't sell it ... and if you can sell it, you can't make it." In boom times, little manufacturers get shortage components last. In bad times the mail order ads often don't pay out. Usually, the small mail order firm's difficulties with delivery logistics are caused by poor planning, ordering, expediting, delayed hiring or other disorganization.

When my wife first came into our business, she had only one year's experience in a clerical job in this country. I explained that I would be *away* from the business every day but one or two, every four to six weeks. Our business involved simple manufacturing of various items which in total included hundreds of components. I told my wife that although she would have to do all buying, as well as hiring and firing personnel, not to worry. I said that buying supplies for manufacture was the same as buying at the supermarket. If she had an insufficient shopping list, we could have a chicken dinner without chicken. As that had never happened, I felt sure that she would make up a proper business shopping list and get each item in ample time.

My wife took over, made her list, did her shopping and followed through. From that day we have rarely had delivery problems. A housewife looks in her ice box before going to the supermarket. Any businessman has to look in his ice box too. He has to know his inventory before he buys. A housewife needs to know how many guests are coming to dinner and order accordingly. A mail order man has to keep track of advertising bought, guestimate orders coming in from the advertising and be ready. The problem is to buy hand to mouth *and* still ship on time. It is amazing how cautiously you can buy or make inventory and yet make plans for rapid expansion of production as needed.

Assume that your scheduled ad will break even. Order in advance what you will need if it does so. If it produces *more* orders than assumed, you will need to buy more and get immediate delivery. Before you run your ad, make sure that your supplier has ample inventory. For each one hundred units that you buy, ask him to hold one hundred units of back up-stock for you. Specify that you have the right to buy but are not obligated to take this inventory and that you require that reorders be shipped within twenty four hours notice.

Reach a clear understanding. Some suppliers will do exactly what they say. Others will be guarded, infer faster shipping without actually promising it and then ship slower. Others will promise but not ship or even lie that they have shipped. Assume the worst until you have a record of performance. Even then, *check* after you order. Ask if your order was received and exactly what day it will be shipped.

Logistical expediting becomes necessary when a "hot" item starts jumping. Careful follow through can speed delivery and save risk and cash layout of too big opening orders. It's work, but you want to buy carefully and ship promptly. You may get everything from one source. More likely, you will get directions printed, boxes made, labels purchased and products from different sources.

Anything may happen. Your mailed purchase order may never have arrived because of insufficient postage. Your supplier may be ignoring your order pending clearing of your credit. You may have ordered at the wrong price again holding up processing. Or your supplier may be closed down for vacation or by a strike. Take nothing for granted. If you manufacture, delay on any single component can hold up your production, increase your labor costs by slowing production and prevent you from shipping. Often, if one supplier falls down in delivery and you know, you can get almost immediate delivery from an alternate source. Try to keep a supplier file with a card for each of two *alternate* suppliers to be used.

When you're caught in a hold-up of one part, it can be quite costly. It's usually better to pay sharply more if necessary for immediate shipment of the needed component. The same goes for rush shipment. Air expediters like Emory Airfreight (find them in the yellow pages) offer to pick up at one end, rush to the airport, pick up at the airport at this end and rush to you. It's expensive and often slower than expected but usually improves delivery of a desperately needed part. If you import a component, it's good to have an alternate higher priced source nearby in the U.S. that you can use for emergency fill-in orders. Advance and contingency planning can go a long way to insure prompt shipping without over investment in inventory.

It is possible to make a fortune in mail order without ever owning one cent of inventory. It requires using a drop shipper. A drop-shipper stocks inventory, allows you to draw on his inventory and will actually ship individual mail orders for you. You simply receive the orders and have labels typed and forwarded to your drop shipper.

There are many trustworthy drop shippers. A good friend of mine has sold millions of dollars of indoor plants where he has actually put the drop shipper's address in the mail order coupon and directed all orders to the drop shipper. He has trusted the drop shipper to bank the

371

checks, type the orders, ship and send him his share of money without any verification. Year after year, the relationship has worked and prospered mutually. My friend has confined his activities to creating and speculating on advertising.

You may very well find someone you can trust too. Just be careful! We have used drop-shippers dozens of times to great advantage, but we have been badly hurt several times where our judgement of character was poor.

It's important to be vigilant. One time years ago, we successfully sold over $1,000,000 of nursery plants in several months time. One nursery supplied us with one nursery item and drop-shipped for us. Another did the same for a different item. We did about $500,000 on each. Our mail order tests were successful and so were our projections. The orders poured in. In several months, we made over $300,000 profit and we were most content.

We had worked extremely hard on the entire campaign. We particularly checked thoroughly the plants, the growers, and their reputations. To the lesser known of the two nurseries, we sent an employee who stayed for three months and personally checked each day that shipments were made and they were...perfectly.

The other grower was beyond dispute of high reputation, president of his regional growers association and the third generation of a long trusted family. We felt it an insult to send an employee to check on him daily. He assured us all would be fine. But he *did not ship*. We took in over $500,000 in cash, paid for all our advertising, sent an advance payment, made a success in every way and faced disaster because of a gentleman's failure to keep his word.

He shipped a fraction of our orders that spring. After that, it was too late. One of our greatest creative star alumni (then my partner) wrote a masterpiece of direct mail follow up. It got enough customers to accept shipment next fall to save us from being wiped out. We refunded the balance.

Lesson! Assume *nothing* is done unless you check and verify that the action is completed.

Unstable people under disastrous financial emergency conditions will do almost anything. One drop-shipper of a one dollar item swore he shipped every order he received from us but claimed the local post office had a series of thefts. We refunded over $15,000 to angry people who never received their merchandise. We had endless correspondence; we upset our relations with the media advertised in and we believe the drop-shipper was the thief. We never got our money back. On another

372

occasion, the drop-shipper swore he was shipping promptly. He finally confessed he hadn't and promptly went bankrupt. In this case, we retrieved the actual orders, secured merchandise elsewhere and shipped ourselves. But we lost advances for shipping sent him with the orders.

My advice is to work with a drop-shipper you know *well* and trust *entirely*. Then check up on him constantly. Get the post office or UPS receipts of shipment. If in big volume, keep someone on his premises. I recommend *against* selling a wide variety of items this way using a considerable number of drop-shippers. Control is almost impossible. It's too complex. You're almost sure to have some drop-shippers let you down and it *can close you down*.

If your strength is in mail order promotion, if you lack space and facilities, if you don't want the detail, drop-shipping can be very sound policy. But protect yourself as suggested.

A retail store or famous catalogue house has a known guarantee policy. If great emphasis is placed on the guarantee of any one item, the inference is that its *other* items are not equally guaranteed. Therefore, a store or catalogue prefers to make its return and refund policy crystal clear and known to apply to all products unless under special circumstances. For instance, the possible need of *servicing* requires a special guarantee commitment for a specific product. A mail order moonlighter needs to establish a guarantee policy, too. Being unknown, it is important to make that policy clear in advertising and more than live up to it. He needs to emphasize it for each item.

For lower priced items, we don't question a request for refund or refusal for *any* reason. The higher the price of the product, the more it becomes necessary to handle each request in conformance to the actual terms of your guarantee.

Guarantees can be written with intent to avoid replacement or refund, in practically all cases. Your desire is to be fair and reasonable. Your guarantee must be fair, specific and clear.

For more expensive items, guarantee limitations may be needed. Any product can be *misused*. Any product has a *use life*. Most products need reasonable care. To flagrantly misuse a product, get the majority of reasonable use life, or give *not the simplest reasonable* care contrary to product instruction and still demand replacement or refund, is not reasonable.

For higher ticket items, the trial period should be brief. An item that can be reasonably judged upon seeing it, needs a trial period of only five to ten days. An item that can only be judged after use might require a fifteen to thirty day trial period. Returns, for reason of the product being defective, need be allowed for replacement or refund after a longer period. For more expensive items, we usually keep the trial period ten to thirty days, but will accept a return of defective merchandise within six months to one year.

Before you determine the terms of your guarantee, write down all the possible situations that may come up. Establish specifically the kind of product damage caused by misuse of the product by the customer and by a defect of material or fault in construction. Then write a description of each of these two sets of circumstances, stating specifically what you will or will not guarantee clearly enough to be understood by the average person.

Look over the guarantees in the advertising of equivalent competitive products. Call the trade association of the field the product is in. Discuss the guarantee policy of members. Check if the FTC has an industry advertising code covering guarantees. Check the BBB. Does it have any recommendations regarding guarantees in this product field. In particular, consider the length of the free trial after which you do not consider the product returnable except for defects of material or product workmanship. Consider the length of time or amount of use you wish the defective guarantee to cover. Consider whether you wish to limit your guarantee to replacement or to extend it to refund if desired.

If a user has eight months of good use of your product, then finds a defect covered by your guarantee and applies for recourse, will you replace with a new product or an equivalently aged used product? Will you refund the full cash paid or will you refund pro rata, based on the percentage of reasonable use life not attained? Spell it all out, and revise your guarantee accordingly. Clear it with your lawyer. Have at least ten people read and tell you their understanding of the guarantee. You must live up to what the average person expects after reading your guarantee. You cannot take refuge in tiny type exceptions and qualifications or weasel worded limitations that most people simply don't understand.

If your product needs servicing your guarantee will specify it and you must be equipped to fullfill the repairs and replacement of component parts needed. Here's why moonlighters should avoid such products.

You will need competent, trained personnel, capable of making repairs. You must carry an adequate inventory of all component parts. If you sell mail order only, you can do all servicing from your factory or warehouse. If you sell through the trade as well, you will be expected to set up service stations in various areas. Each must have competent personnel and adequate stock of components. Some manufacturers turn over all servicing to independent service stations, to make their repairs self liquidating versus service charges to customers, and to sell component parts at a normal profit. If you do, you may create a nightmare of customer complaints to you and to your valued dealers, from whom they originally bought. If so, your service stations will quit in disgust.

If a product requires servicing because of occasional defective parts or construction and you guarantee it, be fair. Absorb such servicing costs. This will average out to a certain percentage of *all* unit sales. When your sales are small and scattered and you set up servicing, this percentage will be highest. When your sales are far larger and when your service is better organized, it will be lower. It is feasible for big volume, nationally distributed products to make money overall in servicing and replacement parts. The profit in parts replacements not guaranteed can be larger than the losses of no charge guarantee parts replacement. But that comes later.

You are responsible for every word and comma of your advertising. Ignorance of what your product can or cannot do is no excuse. You must know its limitations, dangers and specific benefits accurately enough to write or approve advertising claims safely.

The government reactions whether national, county or city are usually based on common sense. You must be able to vouch for the product's safety. Tiny type disclaimers or modifiers of too strong claims are no excuse if the general effect of the overall ad on the average reader is otherwise.

Government people (and BBB) are human. They're paid in the FTC, Post Office Fraud Department, District Attorney's office and other regulatory agencies to find trouble. Catching a malefactor can be a desired accomplishment. For some, it can be good politics. They can prejudge you, form a negative opinion and act accordingly. When any government regulatory authority starts investigating anything about your advertising, they investigate everything. Suddenly, their files seem to contain every advertisement you've ever run on any product you've ever sold even the most obscure test. The most minor infraction of rules you never heard of can affect their attitude in the case against you. Your delaying tactics can only make their investigation more thorough and more urgent. You become a higher priority

Occasionally, the government is wrong. More often, it's right. In any case, it's almost always far more practical to cooperate completely and instantly. Let's assume you want to cooperate, but are nervous as to what you can and cannot safely say in future advertising. If so, the best policy for some time to come is to submit future advertising to such authorities *before* you run it. They may not even want you to do so. But submit copy. If you're near Washington and you're submitting copy to a federal agency, go there personally. They may refuse to give a written answer, but informally give their reaction. They may say that they reserve the right to *change their mind* later and if so, your changing copy as they suggest will be no excuse. If you know the revised copy is truthful, run it. And for every verbal suggested change, send a *written* answer confirming that you have changed the copy as they have suggested. Build up such a file of correspondence with the government authorities showing a continuing and conscious desire to cooperate. If you keep your copy clean and cooperate in this way, it's very doubtful that you will ever again have governmental problems on your advertising.

But why have trouble in the first place? Check your products and advertising thoroughly. Tell the truth. Familiarize yourself with the law on advertising the kind of products you sell. The BBB and FTC will give you information, guidelines, industry codes and even the transcribed FTC legal cases of violators. All this takes very little time. A little common sense, caution and discretion should let you live with the government very well regarding mail order business.

The phony price reduction is the oldest sin in retailing and in mail order. If you do it, you run into two problems: credibility and the law. A price reduction offer must be believed to be effective. If your price reduction is false, you risk prosecution by government agencies.

The accepted requirement for a legitimate price reduction claim, is that sales should have taken place widely at the higher price. Advertising a price reduction of prepriced items almost never sold at the ticketed price is considered fraudulent. A set-up of the original price in one or two stores, one or two limited circulation publications, for a very brief period or in just part of the country, is not justification for a national price reduction campaign.

The Better Business Bureau and Federal Trade Commission have been through the wars in interpretation of legitimate vs. illegitimate price reduction ads. Since their attitudes change to some degree, for latest interpretations consult them.

If you sell on credit, and there is any interest charge, you are a lender under the "Truth in Lending Law". You must conform to the full disclosure provisions of the law or you are violating it. Your lawyer can interpret exactly what words and phrases of disclosure will in his opinion conform to the law. We usually avoid charging any interest for credit or time payments when we give credit directly, rather than get

376

into the wording required.

It is quite complex to offer time payments via a choice of credit cards. Not all credit card companies charge interest in the same manner and state laws differ.The detailed qualifications required for all time payment interest payments seriously slow up readership and pulling power of the advertising. It's more practical to work through a single credit card company in their magazine or in a mailing to their members. The required wording is simpler.

Chapter 10

Creating the Business You Desire

Building into it stability and security ...
pride and ethics ... avoiding all possible risk

We try to do a fairly even business each month throughout the year. We are able to do so even more by mixing our mail order business with traditional distribution businesses. We have accomplished our product mix over a period of time. It will probably take you effort and time to do the same. But you will find it well worth it.

Stretching the selling season can often be done for a seasonal product. A pre-season sale will often prove profitable. Often, so will a late season sale. A spring item can sometimes do a good winter business in the south. A seasonal item can often also be a good Christmas item. Even more stretching can be done when mail order is used as a spring board to get into a conventional business to the trade as well. The trade selling season starts long before the mail order season and ends earlier.

Consider this question: "Is mail order secure?"

In mail order, the insecurity is out there in each day's mail.

The fragility of other types of business is less apparent. A fine building, nice offices, continued paychecks and raises over several years give an air and illusion of permanence and to the employees a false feeling of security. Little do they realize how dubious that stability may be and how insecure their future income may be or even how close they may individually be to losing their jobs. Getting that dismissal slip is always a surprise.

But in mail order, it's all glaringly apparent. Mail order results are seen immediately. They force you to take actions which give the best chance of security later. They force you to resort to *new* items and methods and keep you from drifting to disaster.

In my lifetime, I've seen America become a nation of employees of ever larger, more anonymous corporations. Today's executives seem less secure, more susceptible to sweeping economic change than their fathers. Many of today's small businesses seem on the verge of disappearing into the maw of larger ones.

The art and science of mail order means *extra* security for individuals who go into it. And I've found individuals in mail order *more flexible*, less "frozen" by wildly changing conditions, more able to land on their feet at a profit and do so safely. Yes, mail order can be very "secure".

Can you make money in mail order in an honorable way? Mail order simply involves using the United States Government to ship your product or deliver your advertising literature.

Of course, some "mail order" today is really advertised in many ways, not by mail and delivered by United Parcel or some other Post Office method. But the Post Office usually still delivers the order, although more and more, even the "mail order" comes by telephone. But none of this makes mail order shady. Only the people in mail order and the way they operate can do so. Only you and your associates by choice of product, writing, authorizing or approval of copy, use of art, layout or TV presentation can make mail order sneaky fraud or the most authentic offer of top quality and presentation.

There have been and are shady people in mail order and many, many more highly honorable people in the same proportion as in any other field. Firm after firm sells by mail with taste and restraint products they are proud of, making good money and YOU can too.

Too often, a newcomer to mail order believes that the right mail order technique can sell anything. And often, an enthusiastic mail order advertising man believes this too. This approach does not give enough *respect* for the *product itself*.

A poor quality product can be sold profitably by mail order before the word gets out. But selling it is building on sand. A good product will *satisfy* the customer and create a *repeat* customer for other mail order items from you. Satisfied customers will build a list that will pull so well that list rentals become a really important part of your income. A good product can be sold to quality catalogues and syndicated with successful advertising for inserts and solo mailings of top mail order advertisers. A quality product can build a store distribution business launched with the aid of mail order. Such a business can grow year after year, long after your mail order has stopped.

A business or individual with a fine quality mail order product, but no mail order experience, can usually find an expert to help market it profitably. But a mail order expert whose product does not live up to claims can rarely find a way to convert the shoddy product into a quality one.

Work and expense is the same for a good or bad product. *Respect* your product; look for the best product you can live with for life. Anyone who believes that the mail order marketing technique is *all* important rarely attempts to *improve* the product. We concentrate on businesses where we have a reasonable expectation of constant product improvement. We never regret royalties if the inventor or author can constantly help improve his original work.

Each of our family has certain pet items in our business. My son lives our inflatable boats. He drives a volkswagon camper full of boats to different white water locations, up to Maine, down to Pennsylvania, west to Colorado, south to the Rio Grande. In between, he tests our different boats weekends in the ocean or Long Island Sound. Our French partner has been in the inflatable boat business continuously for fifteen years. Together, they know their product as few do and each year help design new changes. My son's wife goes to jewelry making school and lives our costume jewelry business.

Our inventors keep us up on fishing lures while my wife concentrates on lure quality control. I live our publishing business. And in our other products, we're trying to hire experts or equivalent enthusiasts who can become experts, to take in partners who can do this or to get out of the business. We'd rather match our mail order expertise with an advertising client who *is* a specialist in one of these fields and *can* constantly improve the product.

Would you like to sell your product to mail order people? Perhaps you're a salesman and would like to marry mail order to *your* skills and take no promotional risk at all. Or you may have never sold anything in your life. You may be intrigued by mail order but want to avoid the promotional risk. Perhaps you feel at home in investing a little money in inventory or even quite simple manufacturing if someone else will promote your product.

If you get a free write-up or several for your item and get orders, you want to go further but without promotional risk. Let's hope you have a ''protected'' item, preferably patented, and at least, not easy to duplicate. Seek out the catalogue houses particularly suited to your item.

By selling Sunset House, Creative Village (General Foods), Edmund Scientific or another catalogue, you are getting a mail order test *free*. You must be able to produce stock as needed but you're not gambling one cent for promotion. The copy you have prepared for the shopping column and the photo is ample to show them, plus a sample. The catalogue house may sharply *improve* your presentation in their version in their catalogue. Often, they will take entirely new photographs at their expense to better dramatize your product. You're not only benefitting from the test they're giving you, but also from their creative work. If it works for one catalogue, it will work for others. However, it may pay to give your first catalogue house an exclusive, allowing them to feature it in advertising elsewhere (if its test works).

And if it works in catalogues, submit it to department stores for featuring in *their* catalogues or in cooperative newspaper ads. Your success with the catalogue house may influence them favorably. Selling catalogues and department stores your own item, you should be able to get a gross profit of 25 percent or better of your sale price to them.

Next, approach the mail order divisions of various magazines. From Cosmopolitan to Playboy, many magazines have their own mail order departments. Each has specific ideas of the kind of items desired. And each can give you your mail order start at no risk to you and often surprising volume.

If a catalogue sells more of your product than its break even quota of sales for the space used, you may have something. If it sells a lot more, you've got a hit. Now, you have a chance to get far bigger sales without any promotional risk. The catalogue house will probably repeat your item in future catalogues and may wish to promote it in other ways. You may get your item in more catalogues appropriate to your item. Now, you can approach mail order firms who can promote your item in media beyond a catalogue.

Be realistic and objective. Be sure your item really *was* successful for the first catalogue. Why waste your time trying to persuade another mail order firm to do something it shouldn't do? Put yourself in the mail order man's shoes. Did your product really make a profit for the first catalogue after payment for it to you, carrying its share of catalogue printing and mailing costs and allowing for returns?

When you speak to other mail order firms, don't exaggerate—just tell the truth. You can make a one time sale with misleading information

381

about your product's sales but then you're through. Tell the truth and the results for the mail order firm with your product will bear you out. You'll be trusted. And your statement that a new product of yours made a profit for someone will get you a new order from a firm to whom you gave an earlier success.

Master mail order if you want to sell the maximum to mail order people. The more you know about mail order, the more that you can sell to mail order firms. Keep your eye out for old molds and dies that you can get rights for. Find out if, before being discontinued, one of these items was sold to mail order firms. If so, try to revive it by getting a free shopping column write-up with orders coming to you. Often, it *will* revive. Find out if your item has had any previous history, however old, of success in any way that would interest a mail order firm. If imported, it could have been a success in demonstration or mail order in another country. Or, if domestic, it might have been here. Check if any product directly competitive to yours has successfully sold via mail order.

As you develop trust and respect in your dealings with mail order customers, you can submit such suggestions and get a serious hearing. Offer to contribute an attractive extra discount to a mail order customer who tests a new item for you, but check with your lawyer that you can do it legally. Get your business by selling new money making mail order items to mail order people and *keeping them from buying mail order failures*. It's your responsibility if you want to be welcomed back.

Be discreet. Don't gossip to one mail order customer about another. Keep confidences. If a mail order customer gives you a mail order hit, cooperate to give him first chance to make money from it.

Should you give a mail order exclusive? It can be very simple and profitable to have one exclusive mail order marketer for your product or even for all of them. If you want to concentrate on acquiring and developing products and also creating advertising and promotion for them, it's nice to have a relationship with a mail order firm that will gamble its money to test them and their money to project them. But how do you find the right marketer to marry?

The pioneer who proved you had an item should get first consideration for an exclusive. But the only reason to give anyone an exclusive is if the mail order firm can give you far more volume and profit than selling a number of firms. Your original customer whose ad worked may have no interest in running it widely, no money to do so or lack of know-how and facilities. Your customer may be a small catalogue house running only a small amount of other advertising. Your original customer may advertise very heavily in one form of advertising and

382

scarcely at all in others.

Once his reorders have indicated to you that you have a hit, talk to him, size up the situation and decide what to do. Usually, a hit one place will work every equivalent place. Don't rush into an exclusive. Don't upset your original customer by offering your item to those of his competitors he seems most concerned about. Judiciously seek out other mail order firms, not too competitive to your first customer, give each a taste of your success, get to know them and consider which is best for an exclusive relationship.

You want a firm that's aggressive, fast moving to get the business while it's still around and perhaps before one of *your* competitors gets a smell of your success. You want someone who's honest, with integrity, who will not test your product and expand with his own. You want a firm that's strong financially, so you can sleep nights after getting your new and big (perhaps biggest) customer. You want a firm that you can live with and get along with, so a lot depends on how you *like* each other. Have lunch with the key men of the different firms. Get to know them. Find out who sells them. Phone their suppliers and ask how each is making out. Finally, listen to and compare the volume discount each mail order firm may ask for. And when you've found the right one, start the courtship.

The more you master mail order the more you can understand the kind of items your customer can best sell and the faster you can acquire or develop them.

An exclusive can be for a limited time, for a single or specific item or for a single form of advertising. We have always retained store distribution and foreign rights. You may have a detailed contract or do business on a handshake. I've often found the handshake the best. I recommend an informal exclusive without a commitment beyond several months—but extending as long as mutually desired. There will be a time when the exclusive arrangement will have maximum mutual advantages and a time when the advantage of an exclusive to either party will be less desirable.

You make less money per item but avoid advertising risk. It's far simpler with lower overhead than your normal trade sales. The heavy advertising of your mail order marketer for your products can often launch you into, or increase trade sales. It can often lead to highly profitable *export* business to other mail order marketers in those countries following the lead of your U.S. mail order marketer. And this can lead to more export trade to normal markets, stimulated by the local mail order promotion of your products.

383

So pick your firm, make your deal and be free to part in friendship at some future time.

Chapter 11

Mail Order Money Troubles

What can cause them ... how to avoid them ...
or if the need arises ... overcome them

In a full page New York Times advertisement of one of the world's largest advertising agencies, whose direct response division is headed by one of our alumni, I read the phrase, "Direct response is no panacea."

It certainly is not. The slaughter of the mail order innocents never ceases. Large companies have mail order disasters of enormous magnitude. Countless little entrepreneurs lose their shirts every week pursuing the evasive brass ring of mail order profit. Most of those tempted by mail order, even spending good money on mail order tests, are relying on special interest advisers trying to *sell them* something.

There are many who benefit from the constantly ever greater goldrush to these new mail order Klondikes. From trade publications, suppliers, advertising agencies, advisors, brokers, promoters, salesmen, the accent is a bit on the positive to a degree I sometimes fear for the bankroll of the newcomer. This is because in the real mail order world such dangerous misconceptions can quickly destroy you. So, at the risk of discouragement, let's discuss what you are really up against before you start.

Psychologists have described the setting and mood of a supermarket as those of a party for the housewife. The housewife is said to be

385

affected by the brightness ... background music ... rhythm ... and fun of moving through ... rolling the cart ... almost hypnotically reaching for the packages .. almost without will ... and without thought of the cash register to come.

For the would-be mail order entrepreneur, the equivalent can be the endless stories of success ... the tiny scale of the tests ... the explosive growth ... the sheer *speed* of success ... and the Fifty Billion Dollar *enormity* of today's estimated direct response market.

The truth is that mail order is almost as fast as betting on a horse and even riskier for many people. Yet, it need not be. Tiny tests cannot cause huge losses. Caution and dogged thoroughness can avoid much test risk before taking each.

You can be surprisingly safe if you treat mentally each advertising risk as a *total* loss before you take it. Regard it as a purchase of experience for a hobby. You should be able to keep making tests from time to time with losses no more than expenditure on another hobby. Yet, any of these tests, if profitable and projected, could make you money and perhaps rich.

As a moonlighter, you have a tremendous advantage. Hopefully, you can live on your *regular* job income and bank your irregular mail order profits. If you need to draw income from your mail order moon-lighting, draw only *part* of profits *after* you make them.

There's no reason for you to fall into any of the pitfalls I've described, now that I've pointed them out. I'm less concerned about failure to start than I am about success too soon with too great future hopes and too little experience.

It is surprising how consistently a proper business discipline can keep up sales and profits. But surprises can occur in business, particu-larly in early business years where experience has not yet prepared you for a variety of disasters that can occur and before the disaster cushion of a strong capital reserve is built up.

Few people or companies do not have ups and downs.

Simply *being* in business involves business risk. Anyone can sue you, for any reason in his head and only costly litigation can prove him wrong. A currency devaluation can that instant increase the money required to pay for a shipment on a boat by many thousands of dollars. Sudden inflation of product cost can catch anyone. And in these pages I describe many mail order mishaps that have happened to me and others and could happen to you. Let's hope you never get wiped out in mail order. And with prudence and a little luck, you never will. But if you dare to be in business it *could happen*.

Many losses in business are self-caused and often have very little to do with business. When the Good Lord does not give us our share of natural disasters, he gives us the ability to create our own.

Losing money usually comes from ineffective working, carelessness or poor judgement. Poor judgement usually comes from failure to dig up facts, face facts or *act* on facts. Mental laziness can cause any of these situations. Another reason for loss is using business for another purpose than the simple one of making money. Using business as a way to gain love and popularity by hiring people, buying things and paying too much for either is a misuse of your business and quickly gets you out of it. Many executives and business owners I have known have thought money was their main object, but ego really was. Using business to build ego can lose money. Any personal hang-ups usually cause loss. Getting over hang-ups often starts you winning again.

Let's discuss the symptoms of going broke in mail order. When trouble comes, it can be a *combination* of troubles. Divorce, sickness, business collapse can occur almost simultaneously, each helping cause the other. Your mail order ads don't seem to be working. Your overhead is continuing. You're drawing too much money. Yet you cannot seem to reduce overhead or personal expenses. Each expenditure seems impossible to cut. Your cash is drying up. Creditors are beginning to push. Your stomach tightens up. You're drifting to disaster and cannot seem to stop.

In mail order, there is an easy way to put off immediate disaster and make the final collapse infinitely worse. Here is what *not* to do.

Simply *buy advertising,* even when your advertisements don't pull quite enough orders to pay out. Let's assume you need one hundred orders to pay out but get only seventy orders. Cash is still coming in. You pay for your merchandise and your payroll with your cash and *double* your advertising schedule. More cash comes in. There is enough to pay another payroll, the rent, for some more merchandise and the first advertising. It's the mail order version of a Ponzi operation (the famous Boston Swindler) and can only hurt others badly and yourself. But it's *so easy* to keep increasing the advertising and *hope* that things will get better that many a mail order man going broke resorts to it. Don't be tempted.

In any business, avoid borrowing unnecessary money and avoid personal guarantees like the plague. This means either to the bank or a supplier. You owe it to your spouse and children *not* to do so. Don't put up your house, insurance or any possession as collatoral. If your business goes broke, you'll simply *lose* your house or whatever. Don't

387

fail to deposit unemployment and social security trust money. Never use such monies in *any* emergency. Doing so becomes a personal loan from the government. That plus interest will later be remorselessly collected, however desperate your circumstances may be.

Let's presume you're determined to pay off every creditor every cent. To do so, you must preserve from the wreckage every possible asset of your business. You must not mortgage yourself to individual creditors. You must keep free to pay the kindest creditor as well as the roughest. You must take to the lifeboat in time. You must fight to survive against creditors in order to pay creditors.

Few in disaster can fully realize the *strengths* of their situation.

Doing so is the first step back. However bad your situation, however tangled your affairs, you have lost the battle but not yet the war. However successful you may ever be, there is no security and you can be wiped out tomorrow. But only surrender to *perpetual failure* can keep you from rising again.

However discouraged and disheartened you may be, realize that disaster is *temporary*. Good things can and will happen again. Write down the good things about your situation and don't forget them. Do not in any way be concerned with what others may think of your temporary failure. I have been congratulated and envied for my success when I was in my most desperate hours and commiserated with and pitied when my next boom was already in full swing. Others rarely know about your affairs and even less frequently care. Even if your troubles are publicized, they have far less interest to others than you think. And to those who really know you, rebound from difficulty will gain all the more respect.

Every step in business success tends to increase business inefficiency. The faster the success, the more so. And many business disasters have the seeds of far greater future business success. Every drastic slash in expenses lays the groundwork for a tighter, tougher, more efficient operation in the future. I remember in my worst days walking to work in New York City past the newest building activity. I noticed that the *deepest* holes were dug to build the *tallest* buildings. And properly analyzed and acted upon, the greatest difficulty you may be in can lead to your far, greater future success.

Don't *drift!* Don't *freeze!* Don't *panic!* Don't *dream!* Tomorrow ... next week ... next month...the results of your next test, your newest projection, your greatest hopes, must be analyzed coldly ... suspiciously ... objectively. Make an estimate of the situation. Set deadlines for successive emergency actions if the hoped for next hit does not occur by then. Then, take the actions. Fire the personnel, cancel the lease, take your children out of private school, do what has to be done. Don't be concerned about status personally or for your business.

Changes in your personal and business life which you may have considered impossible will simply occur. You may cut down from a floor to a one room office and from a beautiful home to a furnished room, but when you do so you're already on the road back. You may lose inventory, equipment, furniture and personal possessions. You may lose your house or the business itself and still be taking your first steps to new success. Accept your situation. Start planning your come-back. You will find that in some way you will eat and feed your family, keep a roof over your family's head and have some effective working time.

If you preserve your business in simplified form, you'll *have* to fire "indispensable" employees. Business will still go on. Employees you felt responsible for and worried about will get a better job. You'll find that the standards you set as a minimum for your family can be cut and cut again. I've seen many fight to preserve a way of life they struggled hard to attain. But I've seen the fastest rebound for those who adjusted to their difficulty, dropped out of clubs, moved away from expensive suburbs and stripped down to their new situation.

Often, only business difficulties can make a man of you in business and lessons learned can be acquired in no other way. Water will seek its own level. You must first live within your reduced business and personal income and then make your new start rising from the mail order ashes. All that you have to remember is that you are starting over.

The degree of your disaster determines the number of rungs you must drop back. You may be able to keep a stripped down operation and live within its income. You may have to submerge your business with others and become a partner. You may have signed personal guarantees and be so pursued by creditors that you cannot personally own anything without it's being immediately seized. You may have to work on commission turning your business over to others with a verbal option to convert to an ownership partner for nothing paid. You may lose all and have to work for someone else in another field and make a new start as a mail order moonlighter.

But life will go on. Your main assets will be your know-how, experience and working habits. You will have to seek a money partner on some basis. But remember you will be able to make the biggest contribution. With your know-how you can come up with items, copy presentations, media negotiation, profit creation that perhaps your partner cannot. No matter how hard creditors press you, you will find a way to go on. First, monies earned will go for survival, personal and business. Only gradually will you be able to parcel out creditor payments. They will not be able to accept, nor will you, the fundamental fact of life that a business mess takes a long time to clean up. You may have to go personally bankrupt to get relief, but this is highly unlikely. Some creditors won't trouble you at all. Others will gradually give up their efforts. And the worst and toughest will have to accept very gradual and very slow payment. You'll have to accept the fact that unless you go personally bankrupt you must make such minimum payments regardless of the effect on your personal life. But time will pass and your situation will improve and can do so at any time with lightning speed.

Because the sum of all your previous experience sharpened and honed by adversity is there, ready at any time to apply itself to the new opportunity that will surely come.

Chapter 12

The Mail Order Revolution

*Getting in on it ... associating with the best ... keeping up
with change ... attaining lifelong benefits*

If it's so tough, how in the world do so many people get rich in it?
Because mail order is an art and a science that can be mastered. It's a
way to start out with virtually no money and end up with big money. It's
a way for the smallest venture to make it in a big time world.

There is risk in mail order as in your own business of any kind and
as in life. From the first breath out of the womb to the last expiring one,
there is risk in simply living. We try to warn and caution our children
and yet not overworry them. In this exploratory trip with you through
the mail order world, I've tried to do the same.

In mail order, with a little caution, there is little chance of real
disaster. There is great opportunity, a wonderful chance for a better life
and a great deal of fun. And in employed lives, there is *more* risk. There
is risk of being fired and risk of a slower lifetime failure of our hopes.

Reasons for failure are often all too simple. In youth, we want to
enjoy the moment and we rob our future. In middle life, we get bogged
down in getting through the week, catching up on bills and trying to
escape it all. In later life, terrified by the ticking of Life's clock, we
dream of a last minute coup to change our fortunes, but feel it's too late
to make a long term push in a new direction.

Yet, Youth need not wait twenty years to make a fortune.

391

The man or woman in middle life can escape his or her troubles with a mail order money making hobby just as effectively as with a tool shop, travel or big wardrobe and have an easier life, thereafter.

Those later in life can be late business bloomers, even in their sixties or thereafter. In tennis, the old players, by control and placement, can make the young and strong run. The young and strong have all the advantages, but don't use them. If you're older, take it easy. Use the hidden assets you've accumulated. Realize that regardless of needs and wants and the quick passing of remaining years, you can only correct your situation gradually. You may still make it in mail order.

Anyone successful in anything may well accelerate that success in mail order. Anyone who has failed in anything may get a new start. Right now is a wonderful time to do so.

It is growing.

As huge as mail order and direct response is today, everything points to its faster future growth. Computers, cable TV and microfiche, alone will cause mail order volume to soar even faster. And variations of credit cards and computerized no-cash ways of transferring cash from your bank to seller of product or service without checks can only make mail order grow still more.

Many consider mail order the last frontier for the tiny venture, a frontier open to anyone as was the frontier that made America. Anyone *could* make it on the old frontier. It was the safety valve for failure elsewhere. Yet many *did fail* to make it; just as many fail to make it on the new frontier of mail order.

Those who failed were generally, quite ill prepared for the real frontier or unwilling or unable to work at it. Those who tried to get rich quick with no knowledge of frontier conditions failed most quickly. Those who succeeded most often applied their past experience and know-how effectively to the new conditions.

Basque sheepherders headed for Boise, Idaho and did what they were good at - sheepherding. Swedes, Norwegians and Finns took off for the North Woods of Minnesota and did what *they* were good at - farming. Carpenters, brewery workers, doctors, lawyers, bakers or whoever, used past experience in new places and ways to make it. From the days of John Smith, those who failed to use past experience and skills or who had *nothing* to contribute to the frontier, no background or skills, and no willingness to acquire them and work, often did badly.

It's pretty much the same in mail order today. Success will come fastest to those who apply effective advantages they possess to mail order, develop a "feel" for it and work at it.

My mail order moonlighting method can jump income and create capital all your life. I have tried to give you the facts on the real mail order world, a "feel" and sense of strategy for it. With this "feel"and sense of strategy, you can take fuller advantage of the exciting mail order technology on the way. Because, while techniques never stop changing, the "feel" and sense of strategy to *use* the new techniques does not change.

Let's recap what my mail order moonlighting method is designed to do. First, to help you analyze your own suitability for, and real interest in mail order.

Second, to show you how to use any special background, knowledge or abilities which you now have to give *your* mail order moonlighting method the maximum chance of success.

Third, to aid you to determine whether you are better off on your own or with a partner, and if with a partner, to help you select the right one and make the right deal with him.

Fourth, to give you enough basic know-how in different aspects of mail order and small business to help you start and grow soundly.

Fifth, to help you avoid some dangers I've observed and mistakes I have made in mail order.

Ask yourself once again these questions.

Is mail order *your* cup of tea? Should you go into it at all? Consider the psychology needed for mail order success and the psychology *not* needed.

A salesman *needs* to be cheerful, to feel good, happy, optimistic, hopeful and to spread the good news. In mail order this psychology is often excellent for creating the selling message.

For other phases of mail order a different psychology is required. The happy soul rarely wants to and almost trains himself not to, hear or know any bad news. Often, he does not care to get into the drab nitty gritty of everyday. How about you? Do you have an average or better I.Q., consider yourself reasonably stable, work reasonably hard and not get discouraged too easily? Anyone with too low an I.Q., too unstable a personality, too much laziness or too little heart is not going to make it in mail order with or without my method.

Business operators must balance the optimistic with the pessimistic, cheerful hope with dour suspicion of what might be wrong or might be about to be wrong or even could conceivably become wrong. In this way, they can often prevent or correct disaster.

Do you have a money sense? If you pay too much for your items, either to buy or manufacture them, you will lose money. If your overhead is too high or your own draw too great, you will lose money. If you purchase inventory you later don't sell or buy advertising that doesn't produce sufficient money, you will lose money. If you don't have a feeling for money matterrs, have you a plan to compensate for this lack? Can you capitalize in mail order on your business or professional background or hobbies and interests? It can be a tremendous help.

This is so if you work in business, a profession, an institution or in government. It is so whether you are in white collar or blue collar work, whether you're starting out or retired, whether you're a housewife, in a service trade, in the retail business or whatever. A newcomer to mail order may be a teacher, a salesman, a bank executive or whatever and have some experience and background quite helpful for future mail order success. With no business experience a housewife, student or anyone may have a special hobby or interest suited to mail order.

A lady math teacher whom I know invented a dice game to help her students master math principles faster and more thoroughly. Her husband, an electronic sales executive, helped her set up and operate a mail order business to sell the game to other math teachers and to schools.

Operating frugally and in small volume on a moonlighting basis, the couple made over $20,000 in the next few months. They adapted the mail order ad first to a Brentano Book Store ad and then to an ad in an F.A.O. Schwarz Toy Catalogue. They never unduly gambled in overhead or inventory. They did not need to draw their living from the business. They didn't want to build an empire. They simply sold out to a major game company within a year or so of starting up. Now, they're off on their next project to *repeat* the pattern. I've seen this sort of thing happen again and again. They limited their objectives to the easily achievable. Can you?

What is your job or profession? Are you good at it? If so, in what ways are you better than others in it? How can your know-how apply to mail order in your present field? Is there any *trend* in your field which you see developing, but that is still quite new? Do you know of any product or service in your field which is *better* than competitive products or services?

If your job is boring and you've learned nothing to apply in it to mail order, let's consider your hobbies and interests. Are you good at any activity from cooking to working with tools, any sport or game? If you are, can you apply what you know? Do you have any ideas for better backpacking equipment, new recipes, different and original creative stitchery designs, or projects to keep children happy?

394

If you have no hobbies, interests, sports, do you have a natural curiosity? If so, do you notice new and different developments, new products and new ventures? Do you know of one that seems better than others, but is not yet off the ground?

Do you travel? Do you ever notice interesting products or services in one country, but not yet here, or in part of the U.S. but not nationally? Do you have any ideas of different and better ways of doing anything? Do you use anything that you find quite superior to any other way of doing the same thing, yet not widely known? Do you feel sure of yourself going into mail order on your own or will you be better off with partners? If so, whom can you get as a partner? Do you have friends or even casual acquaintances who have talent or ideas in any of these directions? Could you team up with them in a venture?

Some who have asked me about mail order in my lifetime were *not* by themselves, suited to it and were best persuaded *not* to go into it, except with the right partner. Do you have a friend with any advantage to contribute to a mail order business? A retail store owner sees which new items sell best. In a large city, a retail store may be able to buy newspaper advertising substantially below the cost to national advertisers, including mail order advertisers. A talented copywriter as a partner can make you rich. A shrewd buyer of advertising can do the same. A printer as a partner may gamble unused press time. A venture that failed may have molds or dies that you can obtain for no cash on a partnership with a strong partner.

A little analysis of your own experience, background and interests can best show you whether you're better off to be on your own or to match *your* expertise with others in any of the many forms of profitable association possible.

I've tried to get across to you the basic know-how you need. I've spelled out the potentials, limitations, dangers and requirements of the real mail order world. What I have described may be more effort than you care to make or seem too risky for your situation. If so, mail order may not be for you.

If you're willing to go ahead, knowing the odds against you and the effort and discipline required, don't worry *too much* about the mail order difficulties and losses which I have described.

In all probability, you will not encounter anything so difficult. But a little worry in time about a possibly dangerous disaster or trouble can be the first step to preventing it. Forewarned *is* forearmed. Let us hope that you may easily avoid any such mishap by recognizing what is coming. In any business, including mail order, each company must

395

have a reason for being: to survive and prosper.

Those who are tempted into the mail order business to make easy money fast, but have no real reason to be in it, will easily lose their money fast. Your background, your previous skills, your way of thinking and working, your common sense, your overall suitability to mail order or that of yourself and associates must justify your being in the business. You simply must have or develop a ''feel'' for it. You must have special advantages or be able to develop them to survive and succeed. This entire course is an attempt to help you find a place where you feel you ''fit in'' this fascinating business, your own personal mail order Raison d'Etre or reason for being. Mail order is growing fast. It can be an aid to your *career*.

To be in mail order, you should be good at *something* that can contribute to your mail order success. You should not associate with anyone who is not *equally* good or better in any area you feel weak in. I'm a bit of an egotist and like to feel I have acquired top mail order know-how and ability. If I team up with anyone, a sales manager, fashion expert, manufacturing supervisor, agency client, supplier, partner or royalty inventor or author, I like to feel I've got the best.

Dead wood can be a very heavy load. Mediocrity in associates is a constant brake on *your* potential. Patience with a poor supplier, less than competent inventor, goof-off employee, inadequate anybody is a tax on every competent associate and employee you have and on *your* family. Your family may stand for it. Others will not.

So be careful with any association. Keep an escape hatch open so that no proven poor association becomes a lifetime mortgage on you and your family. Make the best associations you can. Get out of proven bad ones and try again.

As soon as you run your first successful mail order item ''once around the track'', much of the confusion you may feel about mail order will disappear. Once you get that first mail order success, you'll find ways to repeat the success again and again. You'll be inclined to stick to what is working as much as possible. This will affect the items you select in the future and how you sell them. And now, the experience of others will help you apply your first success to your next. New techniques and methods, as fast as you learn them, will multiply your chances of success further.

Once you have confidence, doubts disappear. Your decisions become surer. You work faster. You've had a chance to see what you're good at and *not* good at, the activities you like and *dislike*. You have a much better idea as to whether you can compensate for weakness by acquiring certain specific know-how, by staying away from certain kinds of mail order businesses or items, by turning over certain activities to suppliers, by hiring employees strong where you are weak or by seeking a partner or partners to supply those extra strengths. You're getting a "feel" for what you should do and how you should operate in each aspect of mail order.

Mastering any hobby often yields benefits all your life. When you make a hobby of making money and master it, benefits can come lifelong, too *in cash*. You may find that you can apply your mail order know-how in some way in any business field. Success in mail order can make you more successful in any other business in retail, wholesale, manufacturing and other areas. It can make you a better executive, manager, partner or business owner.

You may choose as we did to *use* mail order to build distribution businesses or sell only by mail. You may choose to sell just by radio, only via credit cards, only for cash, just via direct mail (even to only highly responsive lists). You may be able to set up the kind of special niche operation that can be the safest form of mail order. It may keep you busy profitably for years to come such as a joint venture with just one big consumer publication, broadcaster or a group of trade publications.

Sometimes, you can get started in mail order *without* a penny's risk and then make money continuously. All that is required is willingness to *share* mail order profits with others, *patience* with a slower pace of profit for you and *understanding* that you are dependent on the cooperation of others.

Keep on the look-out for the right new item. It may be anywhere. My eyes and ears are drawn as by a magnet to any mail order advertising. Any article in any show or store flashes a mail order red or green light at me when I first see it. And it will for you too as you get a "feel" for it. Be jaundiced before you test. Don't be premature about projecting. Take full advantage of each test success.

Remember to be thorough in research and never stop improving your copy and layouts. Be painstaking in your media selection. Remember always to seek a special advantage to help you survive and succeed. Large mail order advertisers get their "edge" from maximum discount contracts for advertising, buying each advertisement for less. They also get protected back cover and other premium positions in publications or the equivalent in broadcasting. They often "lock-in" these "position franchises" year after year.

A special relationship with a publication, television station, radio station or printer may give lower cost or less risk advertising to a large (or small) mail order firm. For giant mailers, one million to ten million piece mailings slash costs for everything but postage. This gives the giants mail order profits not possible for others. Find yours.

Be a competitor. Don't expect to win the very first time. In any competition, more lose than win. Most winners must first lose before winning regularly. Most stars must start in the bush leagues. Anyone (with any aptitude for any activity) who concentrates on it gets better at it than those who don't. In mail order, as in anything else, you must train to become a winner.

Don't be afraid of the giants.

The very formula for success of giant companies now creates niches of success for small ones. The giants play it safe and concentrate on safe winners and big chances for success. They concentrate on shorter and shorter lines. They copy each other. Even the giant companies that go into mail order tend to go into the same items, run the same type of ads, mail to the same lists and leave vast areas untapped for you.

Beware of mail order quack "expert" advice. Any specific advice to select a certain article, sell it at a certain price, use certain "sure-thing" forms of advertising, create advertising in a certain "fool proof" way, almost any *simple and certain* advice to make money almost automatically disappoints a newcomer in mail order.

Avoid simplistic get-rich-quick mail order courses, books or schemes of any kind. Their trade mark is the absence of any difficulty. They take advantage of those least qualified. They give even those who would otherwise have a chance advice that can often be a recipe to lose money in mail order. Rather than being professionals in mail order, they are professionals in getting people into mail order the wrong way with the least chance.

But once you know that you are in the mail order business to stay, keep up with mail order change. The most successful mail order men and women never stop learning. Once you start making mail order money, the cost of keeping up with latest change is trifling in comparison. Professionals feel that taking time out to keep up to date is a requirement of being professional and can return the small costs involved many times over. They keep on learning from the leaders.

Don't expect mail order to *give* you a fortune on a silver platter with no thought, plan or work on your part. But give mail order a chance. Many, many others succeed in it and are happy in it with all its limitations.

I have written as I have spoken personally with those who have come to me with no knowledge of mail order. Many have later graduated into their own mail order enterprises. I have always been interested in the later success of each. It's been a pleasure writing this book to you and I am interested in your success as well. Please write me after you read my book. Tell me whether it has benefitted you or if you have found shortcomings and what you consider them to be.

Good luck to you. The mail order world for all its big opportunity is like a village. I welcome you as a neighbor in that village.

ADVICE FROM THE EXPERTS WHO HAVE SOLD BILLIONS IN MAIL ORDER:

Another great book for your mail-order bookshelf, with stories and advice from people who have sold billions of dollars for large corporations and those who have "kitchen table" businesses. Help, advice, and expertise from the very best people in the field.

". . . written by one of the business's great practitioners . . ."
                                        —*Adweek*

"*Mail Order Know-How,* suggests Hoge, can be gained by osmosis, by immersion in the world of direct marketing. With this volume he offers such immersion, through 125 short chapters that include experiences, advice, and strategies gleaned from his own knowledge and from interviews with other experts in the field. Like Hoge's *Mail Order Moonlighting* it is packed with information that is difficult to get at in an orderly fashion."

                                        —*Library Journal*

8½ × 11 inches   472 pages   Illustrated
Paper, $16.95   Cloth, $19.95

🏃 TEN SPEED PRESS   P O Box 7123   Berkeley, California 94707